For future generations and, in particular, Jack, Megan, and Mia (in alphabetical order)

Acknowledgments

My enduring gratitude to Judy Woodruff and her team at the PBS Newshour for asking me to provide expert commentary at not one, but two, Senate Impeachment Trials of Donald Trump. My efforts at public translation inspired this book: written about a great constitutional moment less for experts and more for students of law, politics, and democracy. Unlike the vast majority of official constitutionalists, I have worked in the Senate and the White House. My life attests to what this book teaches: The Constitution is a governing document, one which creates three branches, a Presidency and a Congress, not simply a Supreme Court, as is too often assumed in law schools.

I owe an enormous debt to those who have written wonderful books about impeachment from Professor Larry Tribe, and his coauthor Joshua Matz, to Professors Charles L. Black Jr., Philip Bobbitt, and Cass Sunstein. I owe an even greater debt to the important historical work of Professors Frank O. Bowman III and Michael Gerhardt. Special kudos go to Professor Frank O. Bowman III for providing comments on this manuscript. I am also grateful to scholars of the Presidency, Congress and the separation of powers, including Professors Josh Chafetz, Michael McConnell, Jide Nzelibe, Peter Shane, Kate Shaw, and Matthew Stephenson. In my view, there can be no theory of the Presidency or of Congress, or of impeachment for that matter, without understanding the ways in which these institutions interact and understand themselves.

This book is not simply about impeachment, however. It is about the nature of constitutional argument. I must ask scholars of constitutional interpretation for their forgiveness. I have mercilessly simplified constitutional modalities elegantly described by Professors Philip Bobbitt, Richard Fallon, Larry Tribe, and Akhil Amar. In my view, legal argument will continue, in the future, to consider not only the thoughts and words of the Founders but also the lessons of a continuing history. The modalities reflect how ordinary people reason: they think about the past, they consider what they have learned from those decisions, and they try to anticipate the future consequences of those decisions.

This book would not have been possible without the tireless work of excellent research assistants from Georgetown's Law Class of 2021: Kosta Karamanakis, Jasdeep Kaur, and Kaitlin Prior. Last but most definitely not least, my husband, Dr. Richard Cupitt, endured my complaints with patience and kindness, reminding me that the democracy he works to save from weapons of mass destruction requires all kinds of very, very hard work. Finally, my apologies to those of my gender: my citations to scholarly work remain almost exclusively male because, sadly, it remains the case in law schools that top constitutionalists studying constitutional structure remain almost exclusively male.

Summary of Contents

Table of Contents

THE IMPEACHMENTS OF DONALD TRUMP

AN INTRODUCTION TO CONSTITUTIONAL INTERPRETATION

Introduction

IMPEACHMENT AND CONSTITUTIONAL ARGUMENT

This book considers one of the greatest constitutional clashes of our time: the impeachment of President Donald J. Trump, not once but twice. My aim is two-fold. First, I hope to recount this dramatic experience for a wide variety of students both inside and outside law schools. Second, I want to teach something seemingly undramatic but perhaps more important—how lawyers reason about the Constitution.

To some, this dual aim may seem odd. As Professor Cass Sunstein has confessed, when he went to law school, "no class spent as much as a minute on impeachment."[1] Law professors, and most especially law students, tend to think legal argument belongs to courts, not Congress or the White House. In my opinion, this teaches a view of the Constitution—and law—that is a mistake. Courts are only one part of the Constitution and our constitutional government. Constitutional law courses spend far too little time on the operation of the Constitution and democracy as a whole.[2] Time is scarce in constitutional law courses, but it should not be scarce enough to leave the impression that our Constitution exists only for and about courts.

History tells us that many of our greatest constitutional clashes never end up in the Supreme Court. President Jefferson worried about whether he had the constitutional power to massively increase the size of America by the Louisiana Purchase.[3] No court ever decided whether he exceeded his constitutional powers. President Lincoln proposed the Emancipation Proclamation, freeing slaves in the South through his war powers because he denied that he had the power to do it under the general executive power.[4] No court ever decided whether this action violated the Constitution. Presidents are not alone in having the power and the duty to decide constitutional

1 Cass Sunstein, Impeachment: A Citizen's Guide 4 (2017).

2 When I use the term "democracy," I am using it in the colloquial sense that the average citizen uses to describe a form of government based on self-governance. Technically, we have a "republic" since a republic means rule through representation.

3 *See* Martin S. Flaherty, *Post-Originalism*, 68 U. Chi. L. Rev. 1089, 1094 (2001) (explaining that President Jefferson raised doubts about the constitutionality of his own actions).

4 *See* Michael Stokes Paulsen, *The Constitution of Necessity*, 79 Notre Dame L. Rev. 1257, 1278 (2004) (explaining that Lincoln disclaimed his authority to issue the proclamation as a matter of mere executive power, as opposed to military necessity).

questions that may never arrive in courts. Congress worried for decades about whether it had the constitutional power to pass laws against racial discrimination, including anti-lynching laws, but fought about them and sometimes passed them nevertheless.[5]

This book provides an important reminder to students that our Constitution is bigger than just courts: it is a framework for self-governance. Eliminate the Congress and the Presidency, and democracy is dead. Even the courts are gone. For without a Congress and a President, there is no one to nominate and confirm judges. The Founders began with the Congress, creating it in the *first* Article of the Constitution. They went on to create the Presidency, in the *second* Article, and only then turned to the Judiciary in the much smaller third Article. If we were to leave only the courts, we would eviscerate the Constitution, leaving out what we know as democracy.

Constitutional scholars have rarely taught impeachment precisely because law schools focus on courts. This book serves as an antidote to that tradition. It is particularly important for those who study the Constitution's structure, otherwise known as the "separation of powers." Impeachment reveals that the separation of powers is a not as much a state of affairs as a constitutional activity and an interbranch encounter that one cannot fully appreciate through traditional legal materials. The Supreme Court is situated *within* the separation of powers, it does not control it. Impeachment is thus a classic study in constitutional behavior outside of courts.

The only real judge in the case of impeachment is the "court of public opinion." The impeachment trials of President Trump were highly publicized events, watched by millions of Americans. Members of the House and the Senate and the President's lawyers spoke to the public. But in speaking to the public they deployed the language of law. Professor Charles L. Black Jr. once wrote that "impeachment is a matter of law, foursquare and all the way,"[6] and the lawyers for the President and the House acted accordingly. Because the impeachment was directed to the public, public actors had to explain their constitutional arguments—arguments about legal interpretation—in ways that the general public could grasp, which makes them easier to understand than they otherwise might be.

[5] Opponents argued that laws to end segregation in theaters and restaurants violated their freedom of association. The Supreme Court ultimately upheld the 1964 Civil Rights Act barring segregation not because racial prejudice was wrong, but because Congress had the power to regulate commercial matters. *Heart of Atlanta Motel, Inc. v. United States*, 379 U.S. 241 (1964). According to one source, over 200 anti-lynching bills have been introduced. Why was passage so difficult? Perhaps because the Fourteenth Amendment only applies to "state action," and lynching is done by private actors. *See United States v. Morrison*, 529 U.S. 598 (2000) (affirming the state action requirement).

[6] Charles L. Black Jr. & Philip Bobbitt, Impeachment: A Handbook 22 (2018).

Members engaged in what Professor Lawrence Lessig might call an act of "translation" by explaining a complex legal case in less than technical terms.[7] Academic materials on constitutional argument use terms largely unknown outside the faculty lounge: "originalism," or "modalities," or "canons" (not cannons) of interpretation, or the "interpretation/construction" distinction.[8] This book seeks to expand the audience for interpretive inquiry by providing explanations that may be more friendly to the legally untutored ear.

Consider the most obvious issue of interpretation. Under the Constitution, a President may only be impeached based on "Treason, Bribery, or other high Crimes and Misdemeanors." U.S. Const. art. II, § 4. During the Trump Impeachments, Members of Congress appealed to standard arguments about legal interpretation. They argued about the meaning of the text of the Constitution: What is a "high crime"? They looked to past precedent, meaning the past practice of the Congress: What had triggered prior impeachments of prior Presidents? They worried about creating precedents for the future: How would the legal standard they chose apply in future impeachments? Finally, they considered what impeachment might do to the structure of our democracy, whether a trial of a President would undermine basic constitutional structure. These are precisely the kinds of inquiries that lawyers make before courts in cases about the Constitution and statutes, the same kinds of argument I once made as an appellate lawyer for the Department of Justice.

There is a good deal of fine writing suggesting that the Supreme Court is the Constitution's final arbiter. There is far less writing about constitutional decision making outside courts.[9] Constitutional argument does in fact take place outside the courts—on the floor of Congress and inside the White House. Long ago, Professor Charles L. Black Jr. explained that, in discussing impeachment, constitutional lawyers needed to "divest ourselves of the common misconception that constitutionality is discussable or determinable only in the courts."[10] Because law schools have ignored this wisdom,

[7] Lawrence Lessig, Fidelity & Constraint: How the Supreme Court Has Read the American Constitution (2019).

[8] *See* Randy E. Barnett, Restoring the Lost Constitution: The Presumption of Liberty ch. 4 (2004) (originalism); Philip Bobbitt, Constitutional Interpretation (1991) (modalities); Antonin Scalia, Reading Law: The Interpretation of Texts (2012) (canons of interpretation); Larry Solum, *The Interpretation-Construction Distinction*, 27 Const. Comm. 95 (2010).

[9] I recognize that there is a lot of writing about how the Constitution should be taken from the courts or how courts are inadequate to make many constitutional decisions, sometimes called the "Constitution outside the courts" movement. *See generally* James E. Fleming, *The Constitution Outside the Courts*, 86 Cornell L. Rev. 215 (2000) (reviewing Mark Tushnet, Taking the Constitution Away from the Courts).

[10] Charles L. Black Jr. & Philip Bobbitt, Impeachment: A Handbook 22 (2018).

and taught constitutional law as something confined to the judicial branch, they have managed to miss some of the most dramatic constitutional clashes in history. More importantly, they have taught a partial Constitution, one denuded of the democratic branches. Inadvertently they have demeaned or at least obscured the ways in which the rule of law penetrates even the most political institutions in a healthy democracy.

Legal argument in Congress has similarities to conventional court-focused arguments in that it follows a regular pattern—the Constitution's **text**, **history** (meaning evidence from the Founding), **past precedent** (meaning past Congressional actions on the same constitutional question) and **future precedent** (meaning the example that any constitutional ruling will create for future cases). In addition, we will see that lawyers and legislators appeal to more difficult arguments about **shared ethics** and **constitutional structure**.[11] These are not the only forms of argument, but they are the most basic ones that lawyers encounter—whether they are dealing with statutes or the Constitution. This book is a deliberately simplified account of a highly complex topic—legal interpretation.

Importantly, these arguments should be considered as a whole because, like cables, they are stronger together than apart. (And lest you think this just a fine metaphor, take a walk over the Brooklyn Bridge, as I once did when I clerked for a Judge named Edward Weinfeld: upon cables we depended). For theorists, it is worthy to note that no single mode of interpretation was privileged as ending the impeachment's legal inquiry. Members did not stop at text. The President's lawyers did not confine their claims to history or "original meaning." Both sides wove the language of law into a story whose parts were more powerful together than apart.[12] I call this "strong interpretation," precisely because the claims reinforce each other as in a cable.[13]

Some modern scholars might dispute this approach, preferring to favor particular kinds of arguments.[14] In the past twenty years,

---

[11] In emphasizing these forms of argument, I stand on the shoulders of many. The classic work is Philip Bobbitt, Constitutional Fate: Theory of the Constitution (1984); *see also* Richard Fallon, Law & Legitimacy in the Supreme Court (2018).

[12] William N. Eskridge Jr. & Philip P. Frickey, *Statutory Interpretation as Practical Reasoning*, 42 Stan. L. Rev. 321, 351 (1990).

[13] Victoria Nourse, The Responsible Interpretation Project (draft on file with author).

[14] For example, originalists claim that the Constitution's meaning was fixed in 1787 and that meaning controls, without regard to precedent or consequences. Given the audience of this book, I leave it to others to introduce these concepts. For a good introduction in the impeachment context, *see* Cass Sunstein, Impeachment: A Citizen's Guide ch. 5 (2017). Some have recently argued that Members of Congress should be

some legal scholars have focused on the Founders claiming that "original" meaning should control. As the Dean of the constitutional legal academy, Larry Tribe, has argued, this "simple, superficially appealing" view of constitutional interpretation is wrong.[15] As this book shows, as a *descriptive matter*, lawyers and legislators in both impeachment trials did not stop at text or history. In this, they recall a practice that has endured for some time, reaching back to Blackstone's method of statutory interpretation.[16] To misquote Justice Holmes, tradition may mislead and even prove revolting[17]; after all, this country has endured quite horrific traditions, like slavery. In my opinion, the conventional modalities of argument (which look to text, history, precedent, structure, future consequences, and shared constitutional values) have endured as a "practice"—something lawyers do.[18] This does not mean that they achieve moral insight or virtue, they can go terribly wrong. The point is empirical and sociological: this *is* the practice of lawyers and in the case of the Trump Impeachments, even legislators.

No one should think the arguments are a grab-bag in which the interpreter picks and chooses. As Professors Eskridge and Frickey have explained, "[a] chain is no stronger than its weakest link, because if any of the singly connected links should break, so too will the chain. In contrast, a cable's strength relies not on that of individual threads, but upon their cumulative strength as they are woven together."[19] Legal arguments often appear chain-like, but they are stronger when they are cable-like, when they reinforce each other. To be sure, this does not necessarily result in any given "answer."[20] Like the game of chess or tennis, law is a practice, a way

---

faithful originalists, but the impeachment record does not, in my opinion, support that claim as a descriptive matter.

[15] Laurence H. Tribe, *Foreword,* It Is a Constitution We Are Expounding: Collected Writings on Interpreting Our Founding Document 7 (2009).

[16] 1 Blackstone, Commentaries on the Laws of England *59 (1765) ("The fairest and most rational method to interpret the will of the legislator, is by exploring his intentions at the time when the law was made, by signs the most natural and probable. And these signs are either the words, the context, the subject matter, the effects and consequences, or the spirit and reason of the law.")

[17] Holmes, The Path of the Law 22 (2012 reprint ed.)("It is revolting to have no better reason for a rule of law than so it was laid down in the time of Henry IV. It is still more revolting if the grounds upon which it was laid down have vanished long since, and the rule simply persists from blind imitation of the past.").

[18] Richard Fallon, Law and Legitimacy in the Supreme Court ch. 4 (2018).

[19] William N. Eskridge Jr. & Philip P. Frickey, *Statutory Interpretation as Practical Reasoning,* 42 Stan. L. Rev. 321, 351 (1990).

[20] As Professor Fallon has noted, most legal arguments muster multiple arguments that cohere to support a particular end. Fallon, *A Constructivist Coherence Theory of Constitutional Interpretation,* 100 Harv. L. Rev. 1189 (1987). In my opinion, that is not a bug, but a feature, of the system. As this is a work for students, I do not engage here with the debates about whether originalism "is our law," as some have put it. I note only that the evidence in this book, of what the lawyers and Members on

of speaking, a way of deploying language that exists not because it achieves uncontested answers in hard cases but because it invites us to ask the relevant questions—questions that help us "keep the peace."[21] In the vast majority of cases, the law aims to substitute reason for moral righteousness, intuition, feeling, pure partisanship, and violence.

This raises the final question addressed in the book: how does legal argument in the Congress or the Presidency differ from arguments made in court? My provisional answer here is that it is bent to institutional ends. My point is most definitely **not** to give the impression that legal argument dominates political institutions; arguments made in legislatures can appeal to emotion rather than reason, self-interest rather than the common good. That is precisely why law resists politics. Nor is my aim to normalize the impeachments of a President whose term was decidedly unnormal, by every conventional measure. But, as we will see, no matter how "political" (meaning either partisan or directed toward public audiences) the impeachment, when politicians see the matter as one "of law," the forms of argument track the kinds of argument lawyers use in legal cases.

At the same time, we will also see how elected officials' legal arguments can and should be understood as reflecting their *institutional* position as much as their personal politics. The point: institutions tend to "think" themselves,[22] to use a term popularized by the anthropologist Mary Douglas. They reproduce their values in the concepts they deploy. In the Trump Impeachments, legal argument by Members of Congress bends toward Congress's institutional interests, just as legal argument by the President's lawyers bends toward the Presidency's institutional interests, just as legal argument by the judiciary bends toward the judiciary's institutional interests and capacities.[23] Institutional interests are different from partisan interests because they may cross party lines, serving the institution's interests as a whole.

There were many who, during the course of the Trump Impeachments, decried President Trump's attacks on the media, lawyers, and judges, and his repetitive lies, as posing an unprecedented danger to democracy.[24] Candor compels me to reveal

both sides argued, runs contrary to that descriptive claim. Nor do I engage with scholarly attempts to provide a lexical ordering or hierarchy of arguments.

21 Lief H. Carter & Thomas F. Burke, Reason in Law 6 (2016).

22 Mary Douglas, How Institutions Think (1986).

23 Andrew Coan, Rationing the Constitution: How Judicial Capacity Shapes Supreme Court Decisionmaking (2019).

24 *See, e.g.*, Michael J. Klarman, *Foreward: The Degradation of American Democracy—and the Court*, 134 Harv. L. Rev. 1 (2020).

that I have worked, periodically, as a lawyer for his political rival and a man I much admire, President Joseph R. Biden Jr.[25] But for the vast majority of my working life, I have been a scholar of the separation of powers, constitutional structure, and legal interpretation. Prior to the Trump Administration, I regularly appeared at the *Federalist Society* to defend my scholarly views. I have bent over backwards to be fair to both sides of the arguments made in the Trump Impeachments. My aim is less to add to the scholarly literature on impeachment generally or the overflowing number of existing legal indictments of former President Trump,[26] than to provide a curated summary of the major legal arguments for use by students of the Courts, Congress, the Presidency and the Constitution entire.

The Trump Presidency was not "normal" on any number of dimensions. But that is not why I am writing this book. Precisely because I have worked as a lawyer in the political branches, I value the rule of law.[27] This book reveals law's power to infiltrate and structure debate even in the most partisan institutions and the most hyper-partisan political environments, which I believe is essential to maintaining a healthy democracy. Some lawyers will find this entirely strange, given the legal profession's tendency to view political institutions as law-free zones. To such critics, I ask that they strike out the word "politics" and replace it with the word "democracy." That semantic move allows one to see that politics constitutes law and law structures politics. Just as there is a law of the executive branch (*e.g.* the Administrative Procedure Act among other statutes), there is a law of Congress. If nothing else, recent

---

[25] In the early 1990s, as a very young lawyer, I served as a special counsel to the Senate Judiciary Committee, when then-Senator Biden was its Chairman. During 2015, I served as his chief Counsel in the White House, the year his son Beau was dying.

[26] *See* Roaul Berger, Impeachment: The Constitutional Problems (1974); Frank O. Bowman III, High Crimes and Misdemeanors: A History of Impeachment for the Age of Trump (2019); Michael J. Gerhardt, The Federal Impeachment Process: A Constitutional and Historical Analysis (2019.) For more user friendly, and shorter but also classic, treatments by law professors, *see* Charles L. Black Jr. & Philip Bobbitt, Impeachment: A Handbook (2018); Michael J. Gerhardt, Impeachment: What Everyone Needs to Know (2018); Cass Sunstein, Impeachment: A Citizen's Guide (2017). On the Trump Impeachment, *see* Laurence H. Tribe & Joshua Matz, To End a Presidency: The Power of Impeachment (2018) and Neal Katyal & Sam Koppelman, Impeach: The Case against Donald Trump (2019). For insiders' tales of proceedings in the House of Representatives, *see* Norman Eisen, A Case for the American People: The United States v. Donald J. Trump (2020) and Eric Swalwell, Endgame: Inside the Impeachment of Donald Trump (2020). For the opposite perspective, *see* Alan Dershowitz, The Case Against Impeaching Donald Trump (2019).

[27] Plenty of academics have worked in the executive, but few in the legislative branch. *See* Dakota Rudesill, *Closing the Legislative Experience Gap*, 87 Wash. U. L. Rev. 699 (2010) (providing data that 5 percent of all law professors in the top twenty schools have worked in a legislature).

debates about the filibuster show how important Congress's internal rules can be to shape not only Congress but also democracy as a whole.[28]

Other skeptics will worry that this book teaches formalism. Liberal legal academics are famous for snobbishly rejecting legal doctrine even as they teach it. They believe legal argument is no different than a political campaign. Democracy, not to mention empiricism, requires us to reject that simplistic view. Surely, even for skeptics and congressional critics, it should be curious that Members of the House, the Senate and the President's lawyers invoked what appear distinctively *legal* arguments in what was perhaps the most heated political drama of my lifetime. Nothing required them to do so. They might as well have all just thrown up their hands, and placed statements in the congressional record insulting each other and quoting political polls. But if that were all an impeachment required, no Member or lawyer would have felt compelled to provide any legal claims at all. If legal argument were only window-dressing, then why engage in the practice at all?

Finally, some may take the lesson from this book that legal argument failed to convict a dangerous President, not once but twice. Legal arguments are no panaceas and can paper over failure. Anyone who thinks that Presidents are likely to be removed by impeachment has failed to learn the power of constitutional structure: a 2/3 vote in the Senate is required, meaning conviction is *never* likely. That could have been predicted *before* both Trump Impeachments. Impeachment's virtue lies in its ability to communicate to the public dangers to democracy. In my lifetime, I never expected to watch the Nation's Capitol stormed. In such an environment, that rational arguments were made should remind us of the possibility of impeachment's great virtue: peace and public accountability. As my colleague Professor Josh Chafetz has reminded us, and Benjamin Franklin first warned, impeachment serves as democracy's humble resistance to the dangerous alternatives of drawn swords and assassination.[29]

I have relied in this book on a bevy of impeachment scholars who have spent years studying its history. To the extent this book adds anything to that scholarship, in its notes and questions, I offer three modest points. First, impeachment does not necessarily serve, in my opinion, only to remove a dangerous President. The 2/3 Senate vote

---

[28] *See, e.g.*, Jonathan S. Gould, *Law Within Congress*, 129 Yale L. J. 1946 (2020); Jonathan S. Gould, Kenneth A. Shepsle & Matthew C. Stephenson, Democratizing the Senate from Within (available on SSRN) (showing how filibuster reforms could change the Senate's malapportionment).

[29] Josh Chafetz, *Impeachment and Assassination*, 95 Minn. L. Rev. 347 (2010).

requirement means that an impeachment trial serves as a democratic fire drill: its most important purpose, when done correctly, is to *inform the people of dangers to democracy*. In this sense, it is a particularly dramatic instance of Congress's more banal and quite regular informing and oversight functions. Second, overheated claims about a new onslaught of impeachments will not be realized in the future because of what I call "the political safeguards of impeachment." Party differences are unlikely to yield an impeachment trial unless proponents can convince party moderates in the House—*and* the typically inattentive American people—of a danger to democracy more vital than the issues in people's day-to-day lives. Actual impeachment has political and collective action costs, which explains its rarity. Finally, those who rely upon Founding history, and particularly debates at the constitutional convention, to argue for particular impeachment standards (*i.e.* what constitutes a high crime or misdemeanor) have largely picked their favorite quotations. Students of the Founding need to attend to the sharp break in constitutional structure that occurred after the early debates on impeachment. Only at the very end of the constitutional convention, once the President was to be elected nationally, and not by Congress, when a true separation of powers was fixed, can we be confident that discussion of impeachment sheds light on the proper constitutional standard.

* * *

Note to Teachers: This book was originally written about the First Trump Impeachment. Who could have possibly predicted that there would be two impeachments, given the small number of presidential impeachments in our history? Part One is devoted to the First Trump Impeachment where legal argument is pronounced. Part Two is devoted to the Second Trump Impeachment which relied more heavily on the events of the January 6, 2021 assault on the U.S. Capitol in Washington.

For those most interested in the impeachments themselves, skip to Part One's Chapters 3 and 4 (the First Trump Impeachment) and Part Two's Chapters 1 and 2 (the Second Trump Impeachment).

For those seeking to teach legal argumentation to those not yet in law school or in courses on the Constitution outside law schools, Chapter 1, an introduction to legal argument, should be added. For those interested in larger themes, such as the battle between a populist President fighting democratic institutions, Part Two should be your focus.

For law students, Part One's Chapters 2 and 5 are focused on Supreme Court caselaw relevant to legal arguments on congressional and presidential power. These chapters allow law professors to supplement existing materials on the separation of powers, notoriously difficult to teach based on Supreme Court doctrine.

Part One

THE FIRST IMPEACHMENT TRIAL OF DONALD TRUMP

Chapter One

ARTICLES OF IMPEACHMENT

On December 18, 2019, the House of Representatives voted for Articles of Impeachment against President Donald J. Trump. This was only the third time in American history that a sitting President had been impeached—meaning that a charge had been made that the President should be removed by congressional vote. In 1868, President Andrew Johnson was impeached, tried, and acquitted. In 1974, President Nixon resigned from office before he could be impeached and tried. In 1998, President Bill Clinton was impeached and, in 1999, he was tried and acquitted. In 2019, the House of Representatives issued and approved two Articles of Impeachment against President Donald Trump. He was tried and acquitted in 2020. The fourth presidential impeachment in American history occurred the next year in 2021 when President Trump was impeached for inciting an insurrection against the Nation's Capitol during Congress's January 6, 2012 election certification proceedings. Part One of this book focuses on the First Trump Impeachment and introduces basic forms of constitutional argument. Part Two of this book focuses on the Second Trump Impeachment.

I. IMPEACHMENT BASICS

From the outset, it is important to recognize that the Constitution's rules are stacked against presidential removal. Once the House approves Articles of Impeachment, a President is forever "impeached." The Senate then tries the President and, if it returns a verdict of guilty on the conduct alleged by the House, the President will be removed from office. U.S. Const. art. II, § 4. However, acquittal is the most likely outcome in any impeachment because the Constitution requires a super-majority of Senators (2/3 of the body, or 67 Senators) to agree to the President's removal. U.S. Const. art. I, § 3, cl. 6. The Founders never wanted this to be an easy process. Moreover, impeachment takes two Houses: both the Senate and the House. A simple majority of the much larger House's 435 Members is required to approve impeachment charges. This means that the House is more likely to vote for Articles of Impeachment than the Senate is to convict. The Constitution provides no super-majority rule for approving Articles of Impeachment by the House—in fact, the Constitution says nothing about how many votes are necessary. U.S. Const. art. I, § 2, cl. 5. As has been the general practice, the House has defaulted to the position that, as in passing legislation, a majority of votes suffices to charge the President with Articles of Impeachment.

The standard criminal trial process helps us understand the different roles of the House and the Senate, even if impeachments depart in many ways from a criminal trial. In a criminal trial, charges are brought by a prosecutor or a grand jury. A prosecutor is an elected or appointed official responsible for applying the criminal law to individuals. A grand jury is a group of citizens who vote on charges after evidence is presented to them by the prosecutor. After charges are brought, there is a trial before a different jury (sometimes called a "petit" jury to distinguish it from the grand jury). The trial jury, not the prosecutor, determines whether to convict. The prosecutor has to believe that a jury could convict beyond a reasonable doubt before charging someone. In difficult cases, prosecutors can lose because it is often easy for a lawyer to establish "doubt" about a criminal charge or the facts in a case.

In an impeachment trial, the House is like a prosecutor or a grand jury in a criminal trial: it brings the charges. The Senate is like the trial jury: it determines whether to convict. The Constitution explains this clearly: "The House of Representatives shall * * * * have the sole Power of Impeachment." U.S. Const. art. I, § 2, cl. 5. And "The Senate shall have the sole Power to try all Impeachments." U.S. Const. art. I, § 3, cl. 6. This division of responsibility helps to explain why the House could issue Articles of Impeachment against the President, reasonably believing that the President had committed an offense against the Constitution, and the Senate could nevertheless acquit. A prosecutor's burden of proof in bringing a charge is lower and more speculative than a jury's. The prosecutor has to anticipate whether a reasonable jury would find the defendant guilty "beyond a reasonable doubt." Jurors often disagree about reasonable doubt. Senators at trial often disagree, too, in part because of the drastic nature of the remedy—unseating a President elected by the People.

The analogy between a criminal case and an impeachment should not be taken too far. First, an impeachment does not mean that anyone goes to jail. Impeachment is about governance and its remedy is about governance: namely, who will sit in the Oval Office as the Nation's chief executive officer. The President is not sent to jail if the Senate convicts; the President is removed from office and disqualified from holding office in the future. U.S. Const. art, I, § 3, cl. 7. Later, of course, if a President is removed from office, federal or state authorities may pursue criminal charges if applicable (for example, if the President were impeached for money laundering or tax fraud, then it would be possible for a prosecutor to charge him for money laundering and tax fraud after removal). Second, precisely because impeachment is about removal from office rather than prison time, there has been a persistent dispute about whether the House of Representatives has to prove its charges by the criminal standard, "beyond a reasonable doubt." In America, that standard governs all criminal trials. In an impeachment trial, however, the standard is left to each Senator, based on their oath of impartiality, to determine.[1] Some Senators insist that the charges be proven "beyond a reasonable doubt," others do not.[2] Finally, there are no formal rules of evidence as there would be in a federal court civil or criminal trial. Instead, as did occur in both Trump Impeachments, Senators rule on the admission of evidence.

II. HOUSE AND SENATE BACKGROUND

There is an old joke in Washington that it is not the Republicans and Democrats who hate each other, it is the House and the Senate. Why? Some of it is snobbery. Senators are fewer and serve longer terms, and some seem to think themselves higher and better—more "national"—than House Members, who serve smaller, more local constituencies. But the truth is that, even without that snobbery, the institutions have developed very different traditions because they operate using entirely different rules. This is not a bug, but a feature of the Constitution. Article I, Section 5 provides that the House and the Senate are to create their own rules. Think of baseball and cricket. They both involve players on a field with a ball and a bat, but the rules are entirely different—meaning that playing baseball and cricket are entirely different. So, too, the House and Senate are so entirely different in their operations that I have been told by one senior Senate official that he knows someone knows nothing about Congress if they use the word "Congress"; one can only make generalizations about the proceedings of either the House or the Senate, individually.

---

1 Thomas B. Ripy, Cong. Research Serv., Standard of Proof in Senate Impeachment Proceedings 3 (1999) (noting that the impeachment of U.S. District Judge Harry Claiborne established that "individual members [are] free to apply a standard of their choice, including, but not limited to the reasonable doubt standard").

2 During the Clinton Impeachment, for example, some Senators used a "clear and convincing evidence" standard while others used "beyond a reasonable doubt." *See, e.g.*, 145 Cong. Rec. 2558 (1999) (statement of Sen. DeWine) ("I have used the standard of proof of 'clear and convincing evidence' "); *id.* at 2447 (statement of Sen. Frist) ("I believed that I should apply a 'beyond a reasonable doubt' burden of proof."). *See, generally*, Russ Feingold & Chuck Hagel, Presidential Impeachment Trial: What a Senator Should Know 15–18 (2019).

If the Constitution tells the two Houses to create their own rules, those rules are also shaped by the constitutional provisions constituting the Members. What I mean by "constituting" is election. A large chunk of the Constitution's text provides how people are elected. U.S. Const. art. I, §§ 2, 3. How are the House and Senate created? By the election of their Members. Even if they had the very same procedural rules, these institutions would remain distinct because House and Senate Members are elected by different constituencies and for different periods of time. The Members of the Senate speak to and are elected by citizens within large bodies we call states. U.S. Const. art. I, § 3, cl. 1. The Members of the House speak to and are elected by much smaller numbers of citizens, typically within districts. U.S. Const. art. I, § 2, cl. 3. Members of the House have to think of reelection every 2 years as opposed to 6 years for Senators, meaning that the Members' incentives will differ in scope and urgency.

It is said that the Framers hoped that the Senate would be the saucer cooling the hot liquid poured into the political cup by the hotheads in the House of Representatives. They imagined that the House would be more urgent and more intense—election was always right around the corner and there were many, many more of them (435 or so Members now) than Senators, making them "closer" or more "dependent" upon the people, as Madison would say.[3] Meanwhile the now-100-Member Senate would proceed more cautiously.[4] Over the course of the twentieth century, this divide deepened. The House has become more majoritarian—party leaders will only consider majority-backed legislation, and Members grant significant power to their leadership to enforce party discipline. If you know how the majority is going to vote in the House, you know which bills will be considered and which will not. Meanwhile, the Senate is governed by far different, super-majoritarian rules. As a matter of practice, the near-constant filibuster—which permits unlimited debate about a bill unless 60 Senators vote for "cloture,"[5] or an end

3 The Federalist No. 52 (James Madison) ("As it is essential to liberty that the government in general should have a common interest with the people, so it is particularly essential that the [House of Representatives] should have an immediate dependence on, and an intimate sympathy with, the people").

4 Federalist No. 62 (Madison) ("[an] advantage accruing from * * * * the Senate is, the additional impediment it must prove against improper acts of legislation. * * * *The mutability in the [House] arising from a rapid succession of new members * * * *points out, in the strongest manner, the necessity of some stable institution in the government").

5 *See, e.g.*, Dakota Rudesill, *Hyperpartisanship and the Law: Framing the Debate*, 11 Geo. J.L. & Pol'y 343, 343 (2012) ("Majority Leader Harry Reid (D-NV), for example, has faced more than 300 filibusters from 2007 to 2012, compared with the one filibuster faced by then-Majority Leader Lyndon Johnson (D-TX) from 1953 to

to the debate—means that the Senate moves slowly and, typically, only when there is wide bipartisan support for measures. Even if you have 51 votes for a Senate bill, it is unlikely to pass, because the ever-present threat of a filibuster means that you must come up with the 60 votes required to end debate and call for an up-or-down vote. This aggravates the well-known fact that the Senate is malapportioned, meaning that because Senators are elected by states rather than populations, voters in small states have a disproportionately loud voice.

III. BEWARE THE MANY MEANINGS OF "POLITICAL"

To say that constituencies and elections matter is not to say how individual Members represent voters. Representation follows two basic ideas. One theory is called "trusteeship," meaning that elected officials do not necessarily do exactly what their constituents want. Trustees believe that they must act in the "best interests" of the client even if, in the short term, that may seem contrary to their wishes. Another is called the "delegate" theory. The idea here is that representatives simply "re-present" the views of the voters, meaning that there should be no difference of opinion between voters and representatives. The truth is that representatives do not always know what the voters want; they may confuse their own self-interest with that of the public, or the information may simply be unavailable. In fact, since House and Senate Members are not omniscient, their decisions depend upon *anticipating* the public's views, which is often a very difficult job.[6] All representation is, in this sense, anticipatory.

For our purposes, it is important to note that, during an impeachment, representatives are constitutionally enjoined to play distinct roles and take a special oath of impartiality. They remain,

---

1960."). Although the filibuster is associated with post-2008 hyper-partisanship, the near constant use has existed since the 1990s. One could predict, in 1990, that any controversial bill would provoke a threat of a filibuster, but it was a practice typically deployed by Senators on the ends of the political spectrum, liberal and conservative. What has changed since then is that more Senators have been elected on platforms that are essentially anti-government and anti-Senate, meaning that the filibuster is part of increasing procedural warfare.

6 *See* Hanna F. Pitkin, The Concept of Representation 8–9 (1972) (representation "means the making present in some sense of something which is nevertheless not present literally or in fact"); R. Douglas Arnold, The Logic of Congressional Action 5–6 (1990) ("I argue that legislators * * * *are partly constrained by anticipating the actions of citizens in future elections * * * * electoral calculations shape everything from legislators' roll-call decisions to the strategies and tactics of coalition leaders"); Jane Mansfield, *Rethinking Representation*, 97 Am. Pol. Sci. Rev. 515 (2003) ("Representatives focus on what they think their constituents will approve at the next election, not on what they promised to do at the last election").

however, in institutions that we typically define as "political" because the Members are elected—and therefore always anticipating how the voters will react to their participation in an impeachment. By contrast, federal judges are not elected; they have a more distant relationship to the public because they serve for life and never have to face the electorate to keep their jobs. Moreover, it is part of the judicial identity to maintain "impartiality" in the face of politics. No judge would think it sufficient to write an opinion that merely said, "the Republican party wins." Perhaps for this reason, few doubt the opinion that deciding impeachment by taking periodic public polls would be, as Professor Charles L. Black Jr. once put it an "unspeakable indecency."[7]

This raises an important point that needs clarification before we move further. *The term "political" has many meanings, and precisely because it has so many it is important to be clear*. Sometimes, lawyers use "political" as the equivalent of a swear word: they mean favoritism or blind loyalty rather than reason decides a question. Notice that can be easily turned around. Our Constitution's most important act was to create "political institutions." What "political" means in that sentence is not partisanship, but democracy. When we replace the term "political" with the term "democracy," it sounds pretty good. When we replace the term "political" with "partisanship," it sounds bad. In what follows, I will try to avoid the term "political" precisely because of its many and contradictory meanings. I will use "partisan" to mean allegiance to a party. And I will use "democratic" to mean elected as opposed to non-elected. Otherwise, I will try to make clear which meaning of political I am using. And so should students of the Constitution!

This leaves me with a final word on a related concept: *political parties*. In America, we have weak and few parties. Congress consists of the Republicans and the Democrats. In other countries, there are often many parties: recent Parliaments of the United Kingdom have included Members from the Labor (left), Liberal (center), and Conservative (right) parties, regional and religious parties like the Plaid Cymru (Welsh), and the Democratic Unionist Party (Presbyterian), and even single-issue parties like the United Kingdom Independence Party (pro-Brexit). American parties are "weak" in the sense that they do not have the structural power that parties do in a country like the United Kingdom or Brazil or France. (And this is true even in a day of hyper-partisanship). Voters vote for party slates in other democracies and, because of the structure of

7 Charles L. Black Jr. & Philip Bobbitt, Impeachment: A Handbook 19 (2018).

parliamentary government, when a party wins it takes over *both* the executive and legislative branches. Our parties are weakened by the separation of powers, which allows for parties to simultaneously win some branches but not others. As the famous political scientist David Mayhew once explained, "Divided we Govern,"[8] meaning that the House and Senate may belong to different parties just as the Presidency and Congress may be in different parties. That would not happen in a parliamentary system. For more on political parties and the separation of powers, *see* Chapter 2.

IV. THE ROLE OF THE HOUSE IN IMPEACHMENT

The House of Representatives begins the impeachment process. It often begins by conducting an investigation and then drafting Articles of Impeachment, although there is no rule that there be any kind of formal investigation. In 2019, the House voted for two Articles of Impeachment against President Trump. (*See* Appendix A). The First Article charged him with seeking foreign interference in an election and withholding funds from Ukraine for his personal electoral benefit, thus violating his oath of office to faithfully execute the law. The Second Article charged him with "obstruction of Congress," meaning that he willfully failed to disclose facts to congressional investigators concerning the withholding of aid and his personal electoral benefit.

The facts giving rise to these Articles were summarized by the Chairman of the House Judiciary Committee, Rep. Nadler (D-NY) in what is known as a committee "mark-up"—when the House considers the precise language of the Articles to be voted on by the entire House of Representatives. (Mark-up means what it says: Members take the draft and make (mark-up) changes.) Four law professors, for example, testified about the propriety of the Articles.[9] The Articles' factual basis was established by a report emerging from October 2019 hearings conducted by the House Intelligence Committee, Foreign Affairs Committee, and Oversight Committees.[10] This report built upon a much earlier set of hearings involving claims that President

---

[8] David R Mayhew, Divided We Govern: Party Control, Lawmaking, and Investigations, 1946–1990 (1991).

[9] Adam Liptak, *Key Excerpts from Legal Scholars' Arguments on Impeachment* (Dec. 4, 2019) https://www.nytimes.com/2019/12/04/us/politics/karlan-feldman-turley-gerhardt.html.

[10] *See* House Permanent Select Committee on Intelligence, The Trump-Ukraine Impeachment Inquiry Report Pursuant to H. Res. 660, 116th Cong. (2019) (in consultation with the House Committee on Oversight and Reform and the House Committee on Foreign Affairs).

Trump had interfered in the 2016 presidential election against his opponent Hillary Clinton by seeking help from Russia to smear her. The new charges claimed that President Trump was again interfering in the 2020 presidential election by seeking to gain dirt on one of the most prominent candidates for the Democratic 2020 presidential nomination, former Vice President Joseph R. Biden, Jr.

In the Judiciary Committee, Rep. Lee (D-TX) explained the charges succinctly:

> *First, President Trump violated his oath of office by placing his personal and political interests above the national interests by scheming to get Ukraine to investigate a potential election opponent. Second, President Trump betrayed the national interest by withholding vital, congressionally appropriated security to a beleaguered and besieged ally facing armed aggression from Russia, America's implacable foe. Third, the essential purpose of the scheme concocted by President Trump was to enlist a foreign country to help him fix the 2020 presidential election in his favor, the very type of interference our Framers most feared. And then he blocked witnesses and documents obstructing Congress.* Hearings, H.R. Doc. Serial No. 116-69, vol. 1, at 11 (2019).[11]

The Chairman of the committee Rep. Nadler (D-NY) described how the committee was to proceed to determine the charges:

> *Today, we begin consideration of two Articles of Impeachment against President Donald J. Trump. The first article charges that the President used the powers of his public office to demand that a foreign government attack his political rivals. The second article charges that the President obstructed the congressional investigation into his conduct. Other Presidents have resisted congressional oversight, but President Trump's stonewall was complete, absolute, and without precedent in American history. Taken together, the two articles charge President Trump with placing his private political interest above our national security, above our free and fair elections, and above our ability to hold public officials accountable.* Hearings, H.R. Doc. Serial No. 116-69, vol. 1, at 2 (2019).

---

[11] The full citation is to Hearings before the House Committee on the Judiciary, Markup of H. Res. 755, Articles of Impeachment against Donald J. Trump, Serial No. 116-69, 116th Congress, 1st Sess. (Dec. 11-13, 2019).

This committee now owes it to the American people to give these articles close attention and to describe their factual basis, meaning, and importance. I believe that three questions should frame our debate: First, does the evidence show clearly that the President committed these acts? Second, do they rise to the level of impeachable high crimes and misdemeanors? Third, what are the consequences for our national security, for the integrity of our elections, and for our country if we fail to act? Id.

The President's supporters did not challenge the fact that President Trump had made a call to Ukrainian President Zelensky on July 25, 2019, or that President Trump requested that the Ukrainians announce an investigation into his political rival, Joseph R. Biden Jr. Nor did they challenge the timing of the call. One day before the Ukrainian call, the Special Counsel Robert Mueller testified to Congress for seven hours about allegations that the President had interfered in the 2016 elections. In his report, Mueller refused to come to any conclusions about whether the President had committed a crime at least in part because Justice Department guidelines prevent the indictment of a sitting President.[12] The President claimed that he had been "exonerated" by the report when it was released and again when Mueller testified.[13] The House Articles did not mention the Mueller investigation specifically, focusing instead on the July 25 call (*see* Appendix A to this Chapter), referencing a pattern of prior misconduct. The White House released the Zelensky call transcript (*see* Appendix B) after a whistle-blower complaint was filed with the House Intelligence Committee.[14]

The President's supporters challenged whether the evidence was legally sufficient to impeach. They complained about the speed of the investigation and the process in the House. They questioned facts concerning the timing of money sent to Ukraine, whether the money

---

[12] Special Counsels are authorized by Department of Justice regulations to investigate sensitive matters. *See* 2 Robert S. Mueller, III, Report on The Investigation into Russian Interference in the 2016 Election 2 (2019) ("* * * *while this report does not conclude that the President committed a crime, it also does not exonerate him"); *see id.* at 2 ("[T]his Office accepted OLC's legal conclusion for the purpose of exercising prosecutorial jurisdiction").

[13] CNBC, *Trump Responds to Mueller findings: "No Collusion, No Obstruction, Complete and Total EXONERATION. KEEP AMERICA GREAT"* https://www.cnbc.com/2019/03/24/trump-responds-to-mueller-findings-no-collusion-no-obstruction-complete-and-total-exoneration-keep-america-great.html (caps in original).

[14] The anonymous whistleblower filed a complaint on Sept. 9, 2019. The White House released a transcript of the President's call with Ukraine on Sept. 25, 2019. Peter Baker, *Trump Pressed Ukraine's President to investigate Democrats as 'a Favor,'* N.Y. Times (Sept. 25, 2019).

was actually withheld, and whether the Ukrainian President felt pressured to start an investigation into former Vice President Biden. Some suggested that President Trump's call was justified because it aimed to uncover corruption, although media outlets deemed allegations of corruption by then-candidate Biden baseless.[15]

Most insistently, supporters questioned whether the Articles of Impeachment were legally sufficient under the Constitution—whether the House had alleged a "high crime" or "misdemeanor," as the Constitution requires.

One of the most senior Members of the House Judiciary Committee, Rep. Sensenbrenner (R-WI), spoke directly to the nature of the Articles. Much of the full speech appears below. We will go on to look at parts of it in greater depth. I have deliberately chosen an *opponent* of the Impeachment Articles to focus readers on the form of the arguments.

> *Mr. Chairman, I agree with everybody that tonight is a very solemn night. This is the third time in the last 40 years, 45 years that this committee has sat to* [consider]* * * * *Articles of Impeachment against the President of the United States.* * * * * Hearings, H.R. Doc. No. 116-69, vol. 1, at 9 (2019).
>
> *Now, let's look at these two articles. Unlike the Nixon and Clinton impeachment, there is no crime that is alleged to have been committed by the President of the United States. There are policy differences, but I would submit that given the definition of treason, bribery, and other high crimes and misdemeanors, that does not mean that policy differences should be enough to remove a President from office. There is no allegation of bribery in these articles. There is no allegation of extortion. They have defined for themselves what a high crime and misdemeanor will be. This bar is so low that what is happening is that a future President can be impeached for any disagreement when the presidency and the House of Representatives are controlled by different parties.* * * * * *Id.* at 10.
>
> *The Framers didn't want that. We had an independent presidency. The President was independently elected. He did not serve at the sufferance of Congress. He served for a fixed*

[15] *See* H.R. Doc. Serial No. 116-69, vol. 1 (2019) (statements defending President Trump); Nicholas Fandos, *Republican Inquiry Finds No Evidence of Wrongdoing by Biden*, N.Y. Times (Sept. 23, 2020). *See, e.g.*, Camille Caldera, *Fact-Check: Biden leveraged $1B in aid to Ukraine to oust corrupt prosecutor, not to help his son*, USA Today (Oct. 21, 2020).

*term, and it was only if he really obstructed the functions of government or was treasonous, he could be impeached. * * * * So, yes, the Constitution is at stake. The Framers of our Constitution's enlightened decisions are at stake. We are not to go on the road to becoming a parliamentary democracy, like England and Canada are. We need an independent President who does not have to suffer to anything a congressional majority might throw at him. * * * * And I would appeal to my chairman, the majority members of this committee to listen to what Madison and Hamilton had to say during the ratification of the Constitution, and during the debates at the convention. Put aside your partisan politics * * * * because the future of our country and the viability of our Constitution, as the Framers decided it, are at stake. Id.*

V. ANALYZING THE ARGUMENTS

Legal analysis is just that—it focuses in on the *way* that people argue and the kind of evidence that they invoke. To suggest a musical analogy, we are not looking at the particular notes used, but the general form, the key in which they are played. In this section, we will focus on the form of arguments in Rep. Sensenbrenner's (R-WI) statement. Note again that the point is not whether you agree or disagree with the statements, but what kind of evidence or argument is deployed. We will begin by focusing on particular pieces of the argument and try to put them into 4 buckets:

A. Constitutional Text

Textual argument is as basic as it is ancient in traditional legal argument. Lawyers make arguments typically by starting with the text. You know you are making a textual argument if you are quoting the text of the Constitution. Rep. Sensenbrenner (R-WI) is quoting the Constitution's text when he argues that the definition *of treason, bribery, and other high crimes and misdemeanors*, U.S. Const. art. II, § 3, does not cover what the President had done. Rep. Sensenbrenner's words:

Unlike the Nixon and Clinton impeachment, there is no crime that is alleged to have been committed by the President of the United States. There are policy differences, but I would submit that given *the definition of* ***treason, bribery, and other high crimes and misdemeanors****, that does not mean that policy differences should be enough to remove a President from office. There is no allegation of bribery in*

> *these articles. There is no allegation of extortion. They have defined for themselves what a high crime and misdemeanor will be.* H.R. Doc. No. 116-69, vol. 1, at 10 (2019).

The argument here is a **textual** argument because it depends upon the words of the Constitution, which defines an impeachable offense as one of treason, bribery, and other high crimes and misdemeanors. U.S. Const. art. II, § 3.

Notice that the form of the argument is separate from the legal truth or virtue of the argument. As we will see in the next Chapter, hundreds of law professors and many Members contended that no crime was needed to impeach a President—that the text of the Constitution reads "other high crimes and misdemeanors," which simply refers to conduct with grave consequences for the public trust.[16] We will hear a lot more about this argument in the next Chapter.

B. Textual Drafters and Ratifiers

In novel constitutional cases, modern lawyers want to know what the drafters meant by the words they used. Impeachments are, by definition, novel. Typically, when we have doubts about an expression, we want to know what its author meant. And, in normal conversation, we simply ask the speaker. Imagine that a general was to order a corporal to "attack." In the fog of war, the corporal did not hear whether there was any further instruction to "attack now" or "attack at dawn." The corporal will ask, what did the general "mean" by attack? But in this case, the Constitution's authors are long dead. We can, however, consult the writings that they left behind to provide more information. Courts do this increasingly frequently, and have always done this in cases of novel constitutional questions.

Rep. Sensenbrenner (R-WI), like many Democratic and Republican Members, invoked the Framers of our Constitution to try to resolve the question of whether the Constitution's words, its text, required the naming of a crime in the Articles of Impeachment. You will know a "Framer's" argument when you see reference to the Framers or the Founders or other men who lived in 1787. Rep. Sensenbrenner explained why he believed that the Framers did not want Presidents impeached for policy disputes—disputes between

---

16 Matt Zapotosky, *More than 500 law professors say Trump committed 'impeachable conduct'*, Wash. Post (Dec. 6, 2019), https://www.washingtonpost.com/national-security/more-than-500-law-professors-say-trump-committed-impeachable-conduct/2019/12/06/35259c16-183a-11ea-a659-7d69641c6ff7_story.html.

Congress and the President about the wisdom of a particular course of action, as opposed to a violation of a criminal law.

> *The Framers didn't want that. We had an independent presidency. The President was independently elected. He did not serve at the sufferance of Congress. He served for a fixed term, and it was only if he really obstructed the functions of government or was treasonous, he could be impeached.* H.R. Doc. No. 116-69, vol. 1, at 10 (2019).

> *And I would appeal to my chairman, the majority members of this committee to listen to what Madison and Hamilton had to say during the ratification of the Constitution, and during the debates at the convention. Put aside your partisan politics * * * * because the future of our country and the viability of our Constitution, as the Framers decided it, are at stake. Id.*

The distinctive part of this paragraph is its invocation of the "Framers," men like Madison and Hamilton who helped draft the Constitution. One could call this historical argument, but that would be vague because there are lots of kinds of history that might be invoked (history of the times, history of social classes, history of legal thought, or past presidential impeachments). Law professors sometimes call references to the Founders "originalist" argument. There is a raft of writing on that term, which means a lot of different things to different people. We will see more on that question in the next Chapter. For students, I will call this a "Founders" argument. When you see the term "Founders," that is a sign of an argument based either on the Constitution's drafters or ratifiers. It also applies when you see the names of Framers, such as James Madison or Alexander Hamilton (yes, that Hamilton).

C. Past Precedent

As a general rule, both people and institutions prefer consistency. Assessing one's actions against the past is a way of checking bias. I may not like the look of an apple at the store, but if I know I have bought the same kind of apple before and it was delicious, I will be tempted to overlook superficial differences. Courts are heavily invested in precedent. Congress, like the courts, uses its own prior precedents to judge its actions. This is, in fact, the first part of Rep. Sensenbrenner's (R-WI) comments: *This is the third time in the last 40 years, 45 years that this committee has sat to the Articles of Impeachment against the President of the United States. What we are debating here, in my opinion, is the weakest case in history.* H.R. Doc. No. 116-69, vol. 1, at 10 (2019).

Note that Rep. Sensenbrenner (R-WI) is talking about **past precedent:** the past practice of the Congress in prior impeachments of other Presidents. He is saying that Congress has impeached a President in only a few cases in 40–45 years. And he is comparing that precedent to the current case, urging that the case is weak as compared to prior impeachments. Again, you do not have to decide at this point whether you think the case is weak or strong. As we will see later, President Clinton was impeached because he lied about an extra-marital affair; President Trump would be impeached in 2021 for inciting a riot inside the U.S. Capitol. The important point to see is that constitutional lawyers look to a particular type of evidence: prior **precedent**. Precedent, whether in Court or Congress, requires comparing current circumstances to past ones of a similar type.

D. Future Precedent and Constitutional Structure

Members, like judges, are eager to determine how their legal rules will play out in future cases. In general, people look to the consequences of their actions to determine their rationality and morality. So, too, Members of Congress argue about the consequences of their actions. Often, this requires a good deal of speculation. Notice that this kind of speculation is not about the particular case—whether the President will win or lose. The speculation is about what will happen if the Members adopt a particular rule in future impeachments.

> *They have defined for themselves what a high crime and misdemeanor will be. This bar is so low that what is happening is that a future President can be impeached for any disagreement when the presidency and the House of Representatives are controlled by different parties.* * * * * H.R. Doc. No. 116-69, vol. 1, at 10 (2019).

Notice that Rep. Sensenbrenner (D-WI) is not quoting the **text** of the Constitution, nor the **Founders**, nor is he speaking to **precedent** (historical impeachments). He is talking about the future legal consequences of adopting a particular rule for impeachment. He is *not talking about the consequences of impeachment in the actual case*—whether President Trump will be removed. He is talking about the "rule consequences" in the future: what happens in future impeachment cases. For shorthand, we will call this kind of argument one about "**future precedent**."

This type of argument is a frequent feature of legal argument. When you appear before a court, the judge wants to know not only about the past, but also about the future. If she adopts Rule X, what will happen in similar future cases? Here, the question is how the standard for impeachment (should it require a crime?) will play out in the case of a future impeachment of a future President. Lawyers often call this "pragmatic" argument, but that term is vague. Many things are practical, but that does not mean that they involve future precedent for Congress. Philosophical pragmatism[17] is an important concept, telling us that arguments are stronger together than apart, but it too is different from **future precedent** as I have described it here.

Arguments about the future can extend very far. Rep. Sensenbrenner (R-WI) is not only making claims about what will happen in the next impeachment, he is also making even larger claims about what will happen to the very structure of the Constitution. His claim is that, if the power of impeachment goes too far, the President will not be an "independent" agent, but will simply serve at the whim of the Congress. He is imagining something of a "parade of horribles," that Presidents will be impeached for all sorts of policy disagreements about health care or taxes or pension policies.

This is a consequentialist argument: it speculates about future consequences. It focuses on future impeachment cases, including the future structural relationship between the President and the Congress. Constitutionalists sometimes call this "**structural**" argument because it refers to the relationship between institutions. One way in which you know you are making a structural argument is if you are talking about institutional relationships between the Congress and the President. We will see structural argument later, in greater depth, in Chapter 3, along with argument based on "**shared constitutional norms**."

Note, for now, that Rep. Sensenbrenner (R-WI) did not stop at the Constitution's **text**. Nor did he stop at **Founders'** statements. He used a series of arguments, including past **precedent** to make his point. As we will see, this invocation of different kinds of evidence is common to legal argument. Although some call this "pluralism," the better view is that the arguments are intended to present a coherent cable of claims that are more forceful together than apart.

---

[17] Philosophical pragmatism arises in the early twentieth century and is associated with the proposition that truth could only be assessed by reference to experience. William N. Eskridge Jr. & Philip P. Frickey, *Statutory Interpretation as Practical Reasoning*, 42 Stan. L. Rev. 321, 351 (1990).

PROBLEM 1-1: ARTICLES OF IMPEACHMENT

On December 18, 2019, the full House of Representatives passed its first Resolution of Impeachment against President Trump. That Resolution is repeated in full below. Read it slowly and carefully. As you read, see if you can annotate the Articles to identify the **textual** arguments (Appendix A to this book includes the Constitution's **text**). For students, I have italicized the textual arguments. Are there any arguments about **future precedents**? All judgments about the future are speculations at the time they are made. In this case, however, we know that President Trump was impeached again in 2021 for interfering in the 2020 election.

APPENDIX A

CONGRESS OF THE UNITED STATES OF AMERICA, IN THE HOUSE OF REPRESENTATIVES December 18, 2019.

RESOLUTION

Resolved, That Donald John Trump, President of the United States, is impeached for high crimes and misdemeanors and that the following articles of impeachment be exhibited to the United States Senate:

> Articles of impeachment exhibited by the House of Representatives of the United States of America in the name of itself and of the people of the United States of America, against Donald John Trump, President of the United States of America, in maintenance and support of its impeachment against him for high crimes and misdemeanors.

ARTICLE I: ABUSE OF POWER

The Constitution provides that the House of Representatives "*shall have the sole Power of Impeachment*" and that the President "*shall be removed from Office on Impeachment for, and Conviction of, Treason, Bribery, or other high Crimes and Misdemeanors*".

In his conduct of the office of President of the United States—and in violation of his *constitutional oath faithfully to execute the office of President of the United States and, to the best of his ability, preserve, protect, and defend the Constitution of the United States, and in violation of his constitutional duty to take care that the laws be faithfully executed*—Donald J. Trump has abused the powers of the Presidency, in that:

Using the powers of his high office, President Trump solicited the interference of a foreign government, Ukraine, in the 2020 United

States Presidential election. He did so through a scheme or course of conduct that included soliciting the Government of Ukraine to publicly announce investigations that would benefit his reelection, harm the election prospects of a political opponent, and influence the 2020 United States Presidential election to his advantage. President Trump also sought to pressure the Government of Ukraine to take these steps by conditioning official United States Government acts of significant value to Ukraine on its public announcement of the investigations. President Trump engaged in this scheme or course of conduct for corrupt purposes in pursuit of personal political benefit. In so doing, President Trump used the powers of the Presidency in a manner that compromised the national security of the United States and undermined the integrity of the United States democratic process. He thus ignored and injured the interests of the Nation.

President Trump engaged in this scheme or course of conduct through the following means:

(1) President Trump—acting both directly and through his agents within and outside the United States Government—corruptly solicited the Government of Ukraine to publicly announce investigations into—

(A) a political opponent, former Vice President Joseph R. Biden, Jr.; and

(B) a discredited theory promoted by Russia alleging that Ukraine—rather than Russia—interfered in the 2016 United States Presidential election.

(2) With the same corrupt motives, President Trump—acting both directly and through his agents within and outside the United States Government—conditioned two official acts on the public announcement that he had requested—

(A) the release of $391 million of United States taxpayer funds that Congress had appropriated on a bipartisan basis for the purpose of providing vital military and security assistance to Ukraine to oppose Russian aggression and which President Trump had ordered suspended; and

(B) a head of state meeting at the White House, which the President of Ukraine sought to demonstrate continued United States support for the Government of Ukraine in the face of Russian aggression.

(3) Faced with the public revelation of his actions, President Trump ultimately released the military and security assistance to the

Government of Ukraine, but has persisted in openly and corruptly urging and soliciting Ukraine to undertake investigations for his personal political benefit. These actions were consistent with President Trump's previous invitations of foreign interference in United States elections.

In all of this, President Trump abused the powers of the Presidency by ignoring and injuring national security and other vital national interests to obtain an improper personal political benefit. He has also betrayed the Nation by abusing his high office to enlist a foreign power in corrupting democratic elections.

Wherefore President Trump, by such conduct, has demonstrated that he will remain a threat to national security and the Constitution if allowed to remain in office, and has acted in a manner grossly incompatible with self-governance and the rule of law. President Trump thus warrants impeachment and trial, removal from office, and disqualification to hold and enjoy any office of honor, trust, or profit under the United States.

ARTICLE II: OBSTRUCTION OF CONGRESS

The Constitution provides that the House of Representatives *"shall have the sole Power of Impeachment" and that the President "shall be removed from Office on Impeachment for, and Conviction of, Treason, Bribery, or other high Crimes and Misdemeanors."* In his conduct of the office of President of the United States—and in violation of his *constitutional oath faithfully to execute the office of President of the United States and, to the best of his ability, preserve, protect, and defend the Constitution of the United States, and in violation of his constitutional duty to take care that the laws be faithfully executed*—Donald J. Trump has directed the unprecedented, categorical, and indiscriminate defiance of subpoenas issued by the House of Representatives pursuant to its *"sole Power of Impeachment."* President Trump has abused the powers of the Presidency in a manner offensive to, and subversive of, the Constitution, in that:

The House of Representatives has engaged in an impeachment inquiry focused on President Trump's corrupt solicitation of the Government of Ukraine to interfere in the 2020 United States Presidential election. As part of this impeachment inquiry, the Committees undertaking the investigation served subpoenas seeking documents and testimony deemed vital to the inquiry from various Executive Branch agencies and offices, and current and former officials.

In response, without lawful cause or excuse, President Trump directed Executive Branch agencies, offices, and officials not to comply with those subpoenas. President Trump thus interposed the powers of the Presidency against the lawful subpoenas of the House of Representatives, and assumed to himself functions and judgments necessary to the exercise of the *"sole Power of Impeachment"* vested by the Constitution in the House of Representatives.

President Trump abused the powers of his high office through the following means:

(1) Directing the White House to defy a lawful subpoena by withholding the production of documents sought therein by the Committees.

(2) Directing other Executive Branch agencies and offices to defy lawful subpoenas and withhold the production of documents and records from the Committees—in response to which the Department of State, Office of Management and Budget, Department of Energy, and Department of Defense refused to produce a single document or record.

(3) Directing current and former Executive Branch officials not to cooperate with the Committees—in response to which nine Administration officials defied subpoenas for testimony, namely John Michael "Mick" Mulvaney, Robert B. Blair, John A. Eisenberg, Michael Ellis, Preston Wells Griffith, Russell T. Vought, Michael Duffey, Brian McCormack, and T. Ulrich Brechbuhl.

These actions were consistent with President Trump's previous efforts to undermine United States Government investigations into foreign interference in United States elections.

Through these actions, President Trump sought to arrogate to himself the right to determine the propriety, scope, and nature of an impeachment inquiry into his own conduct, as well as the unilateral prerogative to deny any and all information to the House of Representatives in the exercise of its *"sole Power of Impeachment."* In the history of the Republic, no President has ever ordered the complete defiance of an impeachment inquiry or sought to obstruct and impede so comprehensively the ability of the House of Representatives to investigate *"high Crimes and Misdemeanors."* This abuse of office served to cover up the President's own repeated misconduct and to seize and control the power of impeachment—and thus to nullify a vital constitutional safeguard vested solely in the House of Representatives.

In all of this, President Trump has acted in a manner contrary to his trust as President and subversive of constitutional government, to the great prejudice of the cause of law and justice, and to the manifest injury of the people of the United States.

Wherefore, President Trump, by such conduct, has demonstrated that he will remain a threat to the Constitution if allowed to remain in office, and has acted in a manner grossly incompatible with self-governance and the rule of law. President Trump thus warrants impeachment and trial, removal from office, and disqualification to hold and enjoy any office of honor, trust, or profit under the United States.

APPENDIX B

MEMORANDUM OF TELEPHONE CONVERSATION

SUBJECT:	Telephone Conversation with President Zelenskyy of Ukraine
PARTICIPANTS:	President Zelenskyy of Ukraine Notetakers: The White House Situation Room
DATE, TIME AND PLACE:	July 25, 2019, 9:03–9:33 a.m. EDT Residence

The President: Congratulations on a great victory. We all watched from the United States and you did a terrific job. The way you came from behind, somebody who wasn't given much of a change, and you ended up winning easily. It's a fantastic achievement. Congratulations.

President Zelenskyy: You are absolutely right Mr. President. We did win big and we worked hard for this. We worked a lot but I would like to confess to you that I had an opportunity to learn from you. We used quite a few of your skills and knowledge and were able to use it as an example for our elections and yes it is true that these were unique elections. We were in a unique situation that we were able to achieve a unique success. I'm able to tell you the following; the first time, you called me to congratulate me when I won my presidential election, and the second time you are now calling me when my party won the parliamentary election. I think I should run more often so you can call me more often and we can talk over the phone more often.

The President: [laughter] That's a very good idea. I think your country is very happy about that.

President Zelenskyy: Well yes, to tell you the truth, we are trying to work hard because we wanted to drain the swamp here in our country. We brought in many many new people. Not the old politicians, not the typical politicians, because we want to have a new format and a new type of government. You are a great teacher for us and in that.

The President: Well it is very nice of you to say that. I will say that we do a lot for Ukraine. We spend a lot of effort and a lot of time. Much more than the European countries are doing and they should be helping you more than they are. Germany does almost nothing for you. All they do is talk and I think it's something that you should really ask them about. When I was speaking to Angela Merkel she talks Ukraine, but she doesn't do anything. A lot of the European countries are the same way so I think it's something you want to look at but the United States has been very very good to Ukraine. I wouldn't say that it's reciprocal necessarily because things are happening that are not good but the United States has been very very good to Ukraine.

President Zelenskyy: Yes you are absolutely right. Not only 100%, but actually 1000% and I can tell you the following; I did talk to Angela Merkel and I did meet with her. I also met and talked with Macron and I told them that they are not doing quite as much as they need to be doing on the issues with the sanctions. They are not enforcing the sanctions. They are not working as much as they should work for Ukraine. It turns out that even though logically, the European Union should be our biggest partner but technically the United States is a much bigger partner than the European Union and I'm very grateful to you for that because the United States is doing quite a lot for Ukraine. Much more than the European Union especially when we are talking about sanctions against the Russian Federation. I would also like to thank you for your great support in the area of defense. We are ready to continue to cooperate for the next steps specifically we are almost ready to buy more Javelins from the United States for defense purposes.

The President: I would like you to do us a favor though because our country has been through a lot and Ukraine knows a lot about it. I would like you to find out what happened with this whole situation with Ukraine, they say Crowdstrike* * * *I guess you have one of your wealthy people* * * *The server, they say Ukraine has it. There are a lot of things that went on, the whole situation. I think you're surrounding yourself with some of the same people. I would like to have the Attorney General call you or your people and I would like you to get to the bottom of it. As you saw yesterday, that whole nonsense ended with a very poor performance by a man named Robert Mueller, an incompetent performance, but they say a lot of it started with Ukraine. Whatever you can do, it's very important that you do it if that's possible.

President Zelenskyy: Yes it is very important for me and everything that you just mentioned earlier. For me as a President, it is very important and we are open for any future cooperation. We are ready to open a new page on cooperation in relations between the United States and Ukraine. For that purpose, I just recalled our ambassador from United States and he will be replaced by a very competent and very experienced ambassador who will work hard on making sure that our two nations are getting closer. I would also like and hope to see him having your trust and your confidence and have personal relations with you so we can cooperate even more so. I will personally tell you that one of my assistants spoke with Mr. Giuliani just recently and we are hoping very much that Mr. Giuliani will be able to travel to Ukraine and we will meet once he comes to Ukraine. I just wanted to assure you once again that you have nobody but friends around us. I will make sure that I surround myself with the best and most experienced people. I also wanted to tell you that we are friends. We are great friends and you Mr. President have friends in our country so we can continue our strategic partnership. I also plan to surround myself with great people and in addition to that investigation, I guarantee as the President of Ukraine that all the investigations will be done openly and candidly. That I can assure you.

The President: Good because I heard you had a prosecutor who was very good and he was shut down and that's really unfair. A lot of people are talking about that, the way they shut your very good prosecutor down and you had some very bad people involved. Mr. Giuliani is a highly respected man. He was the mayor of New York City, a great mayor, and I would like him to call you. I will ask him to call you along with the Attorney General. Rudy very much knows what's happening and he is a very capable guy. If you could speak to him that would be great. The former ambassador from the United States, the woman, was bad news and the people she was dealing with in the Ukraine were bad news so I just want to let you know that. The other thing, there's a lot of talk about Biden's son, that Biden stopped the prosecution and a lot of people want to find out about that so whatever you can do with the Attorney General would be great. Biden went around bragging that he stopped the prosecution so if you can look into it* * * *It sounds horrible to me.

President Zelenskyy: I wanted to tell you about the prosecutor. First of all I understand and I'm knowledgeable about the situation. Since we have won the absolute majority in our Parliament, the next prosecutor general will be 100% my person, my candidate, who will be approved, by the parliament and will start as a new prosecutor in September. He or she will look into the situation, specifically to the company that you mentioned in this issue. The issue of the investigation of the case is actually the issue of making sure to restore the honesty so we will take care of that and will work on the investigation of the case. On top of that, I would kindly ask you if you have any additional information that you can provide to us, it would be very helpful for the investigation to make sure that we administer justice in our country with regard to the Ambassador to the United States from Ukraine as far as I recall her name was Ivanovich. It was great that you were the first one who told me that she was a bad ambassador because I agree with you 100%. Her attitude towards me was far from the best as she admired the previous President and she was on his side. She would not accept me as a new President well enough.

The President: Well, she's going to go through some things. I will have Mr. Giuliani give you a call and I am also going to have Attorney General Barr call and we will get to the bottom of it. I'm sure you will figure it out. I heard the prosecutor was treated very badly and he was a very fair prosecutor so good luck with everything. Your economy is going to get better and better I predict. You have a lot of assets. It's a great country. I have many Ukrainian friends, they're incredible people.

President Zelenskyy: I would like to tell you that I also have quite a few Ukrainian friends that live in the United States. Actually last time I traveled to the United States, I stayed in New York near Central Park and I stayed at the Trump Tower. I will talk to them and I hope to see them again in the future. I also wanted to thank you for your invitation to visit the United States, specifically Washington DC. On the other hand, I also want to ensure you that we will be very serious about the case and will work on the investigation. As to the economy, there is much potential for our two countries and one of the issues that is very important for Ukraine is energy independence. I believe we can be very successful and cooperating on energy independence with United States. We are already working on cooperation. We are buying American oil but I am very hopeful for a future meeting. We will have more time and more opportunities to discuss these opportunities and get to know each other better. I would like to thank you very much for your support.

The President: Good. Well, thank you very much and I appreciate that. I will tell Rudy and Attorney General Barr to call. Thank you. Whenever you would like to come to the White House, feel free to call. Give us a date and we'll work that out. I look forward to seeing you.

President Zelenskyy: Thank you very much. I would be very happy to come and would be happy to meet with you personally and get to know you better. I am looking forward to our meeting and I also would like to invite you to visit Ukraine and come to the city of Kyiv which is a beautiful city. We have a beautiful country which would welcome you. On the other hand, I believe that on September 1 we will be in Poland and we can meet in Poland hopefully. After that, it might be a very good idea for you to travel to Ukraine. We can either take my plane and go to Ukraine or we can take your plane, which is probably much better than mine.

The President: Okay, we can work that out. I look forward to seeing you in Washington and maybe in Poland because I think we are going to be there at that time.

President Zelenskyy: Thank you very much Mr. President.

The President: Congratulations on a fantastic job you've done. The whole world was watching. I'm not sure it was so much of an upset but congratulations.

President Zelenskyy: Thank you Mr. President bye-bye.

Chapter Two

PRESIDENTIAL POWER AND IMPEACHMENT

To understand the great clash of institutions known as impeachment, let's start with the **structure** of American government. Three principal institutions govern the United States. Article I of the Constitution creates a Congress. Article II creates the Presidency. Article III creates the Courts. States, like California or New York, have their own independent governments and elections, which forms a base layer of government. In this book, we focus on the federal government, its structure, and how the federal branches clash during an impeachment.

I. THE ELECTORAL CONSTITUTION

Elections sit at the heart of our Constitution. The central principle of our federal government is representation, meaning that our elected officials are to represent "We the People." The First Article of the Constitution establishes a Congress—by election. U.S. Const. art. I, § 2. The Second Article constitutes the Executive—again by election. U.S. Const. art. II, § 1. Finally, the Third Article constitutes the judiciary, not by election: the elected President nominates and the elected Senate confirms judges. U.S. Const. art. II, § 2, cl 2. Without elections, none of these officials would exist. To oust a corrupt or tyrannical President by impeachment, before an election, the House and the Senate must agree. The President's ouster from office does not result in his imprisonment. The result: The Vice President takes office in the former President's place.

A. The Congress and Impeachment

The Congress is divided between two branches elected differently—the House of Representatives and the Senate. Every two years, people elect Members of the House of Representatives, known as Members. Members represent voters in parts of states or what are called "congressional districts" (although some states have such small populations that they are represented by a single Member). By contrast, Senators represent people aggregated in states.[1] Even the least populated states, like Delaware or Rhode Island, have two Senators. That means the Senate is malapportioned: voters in small

---

[1] Originally, state legislatures named Senators, but the Constitution has been amended to provide for Senators elected by popular vote within States.

states carry more weight.[2] At the Founding, the Senate was conceived as more temperate than the House, its Members being further removed from the people because elected by a much larger state-wide set of voters and for a longer term (6 years). As we will see, the House initiates the impeachment process under the Constitution, while the Senate tries impeachments under the Constitution.

B. The President and Impeachment

In 1787, when the Constitution was created, the Founders debated long and hard about how the President would be elected. For much of the constitutional convention, the constitutional plan provided that Congress elected the President.[3] That would have made a far different form of government than we now have. In that system, the President would have had a natural tendency to try to tailor his policies to favor Congress, just as anyone has an interest in satisfying their boss. The Founders would have said that the President was "dependent" upon the legislature. Dependency was a central concept to the Framers but has been lost to time;[4] today, we would not use the word "dependency," we would say that representatives have an incentive, due to reelection, to tie themselves to the interests of those who elect them. This would be particularly true if the President was to be reelected by Congress. As one Founder worried, under the original plan, the President would "be the mere creature" of the legislature.[5]

At the end of the Constitutional Convention, the Founders made a highly significant change: they created an independent Presidency. They agreed that the President was to be elected by the nation, not those inside Washington. A compromise position—the electoral college—gave state legislatures the power to name "Electors" for the Presidency, but crucially gave the President a national—rather than a congressional—electoral boss. A President elected by the Members of the national legislature would have had an incentive to cultivate House Members and Senators at dinner tables in Washington D.C., but a President elected by a nationally-distributed constituency, even

---

2 For example, the voting power of a citizen in Wyoming, a sparsely populated state, may be as much as 67 times that of a citizen in California, a highly populated state.

3 *See, e.g.*, II Farrand, The Records of the Federal Convention of 1787 80–81 (June 2, 1787); *but see* II Farrand at 500–501 (Sept. 4, 1787) (discussing proposal for the electoral college).

4 *See* Victoria Nourse, *Toward A "Due Foundation" for the Separation Of Powers: The Federalist Papers As Political Narrative*, 74 Tex. L. Rev. 447, 451–452 (1996).

5 Michael W. McConnell, The President Who Would Not Be King: Executive Power under the Constitution 54 (2020) (quoting Gouverneur Morris).

one mediated by state "Electors,"[6] would look outside Washington, to the states, for his reelection.

When the Convention envisioned Congress electing the President, they imagined a system in which the executive and legislative were aligned as in the British "parliamentary-ministerial" system.[7] In that system, since the putative King (the American President) was closely tethered to Congress, the constitutional convention agreed to a fairly liberal impeachment standard, meaning that Congress could impeach for a wide range of reasons, allowing for the Congress to oust a President who simply neglected his duties.[8] In that system, the Framers put the power to try impeachments in the Supreme Court, as an independent third party, as a check against both the Congress and the President.

At the end of the convention, after the President was made independent of Congress, the Founders redrafted the impeachment clauses.[9] A President independent from Congress needed to be checked from committing "high crimes and misdemeanors." Judging the impeachment was taken away from the Supreme Court and given back to Congress at least in part on the theory that the Congress was less likely to be corrupted than the fewer members of the Supreme Court. (It is easier to purchase the favor of smaller than a larger number of persons). Today, the President, like any other officer in government, is subject to impeachment by the House and trial by the Senate for "high crimes and misdemeanors." U.S. Const. art. II, § 4. The Chief Justice sits as the presiding officer in impeachments of sitting Presidents. The Chief Justice does not act as a judge in the normal sense; the Senate rules on its own trial procedures.[10]

---

[6] II Farrand 500 (Sept. 4, 1787) (statement of Gouverneur Morris) (Members approving of election "throughout the U.S. and at so great a distance from each other, the great evil of cabal was avoided.")

[7] The best and most recent account of this appears in Michael W. McConnell, The President Who Would Not Be King: Executive Power under the Constitution (2020).

[8] *See* Cass Sunstein, Impeachment: A Citizen's Guide 43 (2017) (discussing June 2 decision on "mal-practice or neglect of duty"); *id.* at 46 (discussing August 20 provision "neglect of duty, malversation, or corruption.").

[9] *See* II Farrand 550–551 (Sept. 8, 1787). As we will see, commentators tend to pay little attention to the different structural conditions existing when various impeachment language was added. In my view, the language that existed in June was consistent with a model (*i.e.* the Congress electing the President similar to a parliamentary system) that the ultimate Constitution rejected.

[10] The Senate's rules provide the Chief Justice with power to regulate the proceedings, but the full Senate may overrule any ruling by the Chief. Rule VII, Rules of Procedure and Practice in the Senate when Sitting on Impeachment Trials. As a general rule, Chief Justice Rehnquist and Chief Justice Roberts played very minor roles in the impeachments of Presidents Clinton and Trump. Typically, they take their cues from experts on Senate procedure, the Senate parliamentarian. For more on these rules, see Part Two, Chapter 2.

C. The Courts and Impeachment

Members of the Supreme Court are nominated by the President and confirmed by the Senate. They serve for as long as they exhibit "good behavior," meaning for life, unless impeached. Of all of our major governmental institutions, the judiciary is the smallest branch. U.S. Const. art. III. The Constitution does not fix the number of Justices, although in modern times the number has stood at 9. As we will see below, courts decide cases between disputing parties. Congress has seen fit to create a set of lower federal courts, including federal district courts which try cases, and federal appellate or Circuit courts which decide appeals. Final resort is to the Supreme Court, although most of the cases that the Supreme Court hears are not about constitutional matters; most are about statutes (laws passed by Congress) and most cases are taken at the discretion of the Court.

Unlike Members of Congress, federal judges are not elected by voters. They hold their jobs for life (unless impeached), and precisely because they are not elected, the Founders believed that they would be less swayed by partisan concerns. Judges pledge to honor the rule of law, to protect both majorities and minorities, evenhandedly and without favor to the high or low, rich or poor. This, of course, is an ideal. There is an indirect connection between the voters and Supreme Court Justices since Presidents nominate them and the Senate confirms them. There is a vast political science literature showing that the Supreme Court does not generally deviate from views held by the majority of voters. Judging cannot be reduced to partisanship however; studies show that legal reasoning plays a constraining force in the many cases the Court decides about which there is no large public controversy.[11]

From the early days of our republic, the Supreme Court, and the lower federal courts, have asserted the power to reject an action by the President or the Congress that violates the Constitution. This is known as the *power of judicial review*. It is typically (if somewhat misleadingly) associated with the Supreme Court case of *Marbury v. Madison* 5 U.S. 137 (1803)[12] and the slogan from that case: "It is emphatically the province and duty of the Judicial Department to say what the law is." 5 U.S. at 177. As we will see in the cases below,

---

11 *See* Michael Bailey & Forrest Maltzman, The Constrained Court: Law, Politics and the Decisions Justices Make (2011).

12 Judicial review pre-dated *Marbury*. William Michael Treanor, *Judicial Review Before* Marbury, 58 Stan. L. Rev. 455, 457 (2005) ("judicial review was dramatically better established in the years before *Marbury* than previously recognized"); Larry D. Kramer, The People Themselves: Popular Constitutionalism and Judicial Review 7 (2004) ("a practice of judicial review did emerge, and early on—well before *Marbury v. Madison*, which mostly repeated arguments already developed by others").

courts today assert that they are the supreme interpreters of law, which is a more modern view than one might think from the citation to *Marbury*. The truth is more complex. All of the departments—the President, the Congress, and the Courts—claim to "say" what the law is. Legislatures "say" law by enacting it; Presidents say "law" when they execute it. To those steeped in courts, however, the nostrum that courts "say what the law is" means something like "we have the last word," a theory of *judicial supremacy* on matters of legal interpretation. Impeachments challenge this notion: courts have generally refused to review matters related to impeachments. *Impeachments are an example of the ways in which central constitutional issues are remitted to departments other than the judiciary to solve.*

II. SEPARATION OF POWERS #101

Institutions clash in an impeachment: The Congress pits itself against the President in a trial to determine whether the President shall remain in office. Because institutions battle, we need to understand the basics of our constitutional structure. That structure goes by the name of the "separation of powers." As we will see later, in Chapters 3 and 4, House Managers and the President's lawyers in the First Trump Impeachment frequently used the phrase "separation of powers." What does it mean? The truth is that there are some popular slogans about the separation of powers, but these slogans are incomplete and confusing. Often, "separation of powers" is simply short-hand for what Justice Jackson famously called "cancelling" quotations, causing grief to many constitutional scholars. As he explained: "A century and a half of partisan debate and scholarly speculation yields no net result but only supplies more or less apt quotations from respected sources on each side * * * *. *Youngstown Sheet & Tube Co. v. Sawyer*, 343 U.S. 579, 634–35 (1952) (Jackson, J., concurring).

Despite Justice Jackson's despair, there are some things we can say about our constitutional system:

A. Separate Functions

The School House Rock version of the separation of powers tells us that the branches serve different functions, meaning that Congress, the President and the Courts perform distinct tasks. The Congress passes laws—it *legislates,* creating general rules for individual citizens. The President *executes* the laws—he or she executes the laws that Congress passes; he or she puts them into action. The Courts settles disputes about laws—they *adjudicate,* they decide cases between disputing citizens (the litigants in the lawsuit).

The problem with this simple division is that it is true in major outline, but appears false if one takes the "function" idea too far. Depending upon how generally you describe what the departments do, you may find yourself very confused. It is said for example that the Supreme Court makes law when it decides new cases (think of the infamous Dred Scott case[13] whose ruling embracing slavery helped to cause the civil war). Moreover, in modern government, much law, perhaps most law, is made by rules and regulations issued by executive branch agencies—albeit agencies bound to follow Congress's more general directions. (Regulations are issued by agencies in the executive branch; statutes are laws created by the Congress).

As scholars have known for some time, the idea of functional separation—taken at a high level of generality—does not describe the government we have.[14] One should not, however, take from this a cynicism about the departments' separate institutional existence. There are key differences. The Congress creates the rules but, once it passes legislation, it cannot reach down to send its Members to execute the law. The President (at least in domestic affairs) cannot create rules out of whole cloth. The Constitution says that he must execute "the law," so that there must be a congressional statute for him to execute. Finally, courts cannot create rules at all without a case or controversy (typically caused by an individual injury) and they typically cannot act unless there is a statute permitting them to act.

B. Shared Powers

Another reason that the "separate functions" theory is incomplete is that the departments share functions by constitutional decree. Take the most obvious shared power: legislation. The President has the veto power, meaning that he can reject Congress's legislation (subject to a 2/3 override). Note that the President's power is listed in Article I in the Constitution, the part of the Constitution that vests "all legislative powers" to the Congress. *See* U.S. Const. art. I, § 7. That means that in the very first part of the Constitution, Article I, the Constitution grants a "legislative" power to the executive. Put in other words, the legislative power is "shared" by the President and the Congress. There are plenty of other important powers that are, in effect, shared and were so understood at the Founding. For example, the President cannot create the executive

---

[13] Dred Scott v. Sandford, 60 U.S. 393 (1857).

[14] *See* Peter L. Straus, *Formal and Functional Approaches to Separation-of-Powers Questions—A Foolish Inconsistency?*, 72 Cornell L. Rev. 488, 492 (1987) ("our formal, three-branch theory of government—at least as traditionally expressed—cannot describe the government we long have had * * *").

branch: the Congress must create departments or agencies to assist the President. So, too, the President and the Senate share power to create treaties, the President negotiating and the Senate ratifying, and the appointing of Supreme Court Justices and Cabinet officials, the President nominating and the Senate confirming.

C. Checks and Balances

Another common concept associated with the separation of powers is the idea of "checks and balances." Like separated and shared powers, this is generally true, but incomplete. One of the ideas behind the separation of powers at our Founding was the notion that no man should be a judge in his own cause. Checking power is a way to hold another branch accountable. If the king is both a judge and an executor, he will be a judge in his own cause, and will likely prefer himself. Colonial citizens' experience with a distant king was fundamental to their idea of a new government. The idea of kingship, as tyranny, was fueled by a history of British monarchs who had arrogated to themselves the power to decree and execute the law, but also to judge themselves free of law. To check power was an important Founding constitutional concept.

Constitutional checks arise three different ways: *shared powers, distributed powers, and specifically checking powers*. Shared powers mean that two institutional actors have to work together to achieve an end, meaning that, if either fails to cooperate, they are "checked." For example, the President can veto legislation. If he did not share legislative power, he could not "check" the legislature. Similarly, the President and the Senate share the power of appointing Supreme Court Justices: the President nominates and the Senate confirms. If the Senate does not like a nominee, it can "check" the President's choice. Checks also arise because powers are distributed across institutions. So, for example, the Congress has the power of the purse, to spend money. The President may be the "Commander-in-Chief" but if she wants to fund her army, she needs to go to Congress for the money to support that Army. Finally, there are some powers that exist primarily to serve a "checking" function. Impeachment is such a power. It allows the Congress to control executive and judicial power by removing the persons exercising those powers.

D. Separate Institutions

If the Departments share powers, why don't they just collapse into each other? The answer is that they are separate institutions. Think of your college or law school. It teaches law. So does the law school at Georgetown and Yale. Just because these institutions perform the same task does not mean that they are not separate institutions. What makes the institutions separate is that they have separate people and separate institutional identities. Similarly, different people are required to run the departments under our Constitution. Perhaps more importantly, these different people have separate incentives to serve different constituencies. Just as the Georgetown Law School serves Georgetown students, not Harvard students, the departments serve different (albeit sometimes overlapping) sets of customers, namely groups of voters. Although this is entirely simplified, as a default assumption, it is fair to say that the President cares more about the nation as a whole than a single state like Delaware, the Senator from Alaska cares more about voters in Alaska than those in Delaware, and the House Member representing the 5th district of Texas cares more about voters in that district than those in the 10th district of New York. More importantly, these people all have an incentive to respond to some set of voters, otherwise, they will lose their jobs.[15] Just as Georgetown and Harvard compete for students and professors, so do separate institutions of government, who compete for votes.

III. JUDICIAL OPINIONS RELEVANT TO IMPEACHMENT

There are few more complex constitutional topics than the separation of powers.[16] There is no express textual statement in our Constitution to "separate powers" as exists in some state constitutions. But there are some basics that lawyers agree upon. They agree that each branch's powers are limited in some ways and that includes the President and the executive branch. The President has the power to "faithfully execute the laws" made by Congress. That, of course, means that there must be a *law* to execute. A law (or what we call a statute) is different from a constitutional provision. A law is passed by the House and the Senate and signed by the President. A Constitution is "higher law," in the sense that if the Congress passes an unconstitutional law, the Supreme Court may exercise the power of *judicial review* to strike down that law. Striking

---

15 David Mayhew, The Electoral Connection (1974); Matthew Stephenson & Jide O. Nzelibe, *Complementary Constraints: Separation of Powers, Rational Voting, and Constitutional Design*, 123 Harv. Law Rev. 617 (2010).

16 For further reading, *see* Peter M. Shane, Harold H. Bruff, & Neil J. Kinkopf, Separation of Powers Law: Cases and Materials (4th ed. 2018); Victoria Nourse, *Toward A "Due Foundation" For The Separation Of Powers: The Federalist Papers As Political Narrative*, 74 Tex. L. Rev. 447 (1996); Victoria Nourse, *The Vertical Separation of Powers*, 49 Duke L. J. 749 (1999); Victoria Nourse, *Toward A New Constitutional Anatomy*, 56 Stan. L. Rev. 835 (2004); Peter L. Strauss, *Formal and Functional Approaches to Separation-of-Powers Questions—A Foolish Inconsistency?*, 72 Cornell L. Rev. 488 (1987); Daryl J. Levinson & Richard H. Pildes, *Separation of Parties, Not Powers*, 119 Harv. L. Rev. 2331 (2006); Matthew Stephenson & Jide O. Nzelibe, *Complementary Constraints: Separation of Powers, Rational Voting, and Constitutional Design*, 123 Harv. L. Rev. 617 (2010).

down a law means to refuse to give it effect. But the Supreme Court does not always "review" all matters; they have refused to decide questions involving impeachment, for example.

Our mission in reading the following cases is two-fold. The first mission is to understand something about impeachment and constitutional limits on presidential actions. Our second mission is at least as important: to learn how lawyers argue about these questions.

A. Analyzing Constitutional Arguments

Legal analysis is just that—it focuses in on the *way* lawyers argue and the kind of evidence they invoke. I introduced you to the form of arguments briefly in Chapter 1. Here, we consider them in more depth. Repetition is often a sign of bad writing, but in teaching, it is essential to understanding.

To suggest a musical analogy, we are not looking at the particular notes used, but the general form, the key in which they are played. *Note that there is nothing sacrosanct about the order of arguments.* A court or a Member of Congress might start with precedent or text. Generally, in novel cases, constitutional text is treated first. Note as well that arguments often overlap; discussions of the text will involve those who drafted the text and the consequences of a particular textual interpretation. Do not be overly concerned about overlap. For scholars, I recognize that these terms vary from those asserted by other theorists[17] but have tried to use terms suitable for an audience of students who may be just beginning their careers studying law.

1. ***Constitutional Text:*** Textual argument is as basic as it is ancient. Typically, lawyers make arguments by starting with the text. You know you are making a textual argument if you are quoting the text of the Constitution. For example, if I say that the President has the duty to "faithfully execute" the law, I am quoting the text of Article II, § 3 of the Constitution, which provides that "he shall take care that the laws be faithfully executed."

[17] *See, e.g.,* Fallon, *A Constructivist Coherence Theory of Constitutional Interpretation*, 100 Harv. L. Rev. 1189, 1189–90 (1987) ("With only a few dissenters, most judges, lawyers, and commentators recognize the relevance of at least five kinds of constitutional argument: arguments from the plain, necessary, or historical meaning of the constitutional text; arguments about the intent of the framers; arguments of constitutional theory that reason from the hypothesized purposes that best explain either particular constitutional provisions or the constitutional text as a whole; arguments based on judicial precedent; and value arguments that assert claims about justice or social policy.").

2. ***Textual Drafters—the Founders:*** When we have doubts about the meaning of an expression, we want to know what its author meant. And, in normal conversation, we simply ask the speaker. But, in this case, the Constitution's authors are long dead. We can, however, consult the writings that they have left. Courts do this frequently, and have always done this in cases of novel constitutional questions. Not only do they look at what Founders—like James Madison or Alexander Hamilton said—but they also look at historical interpretations—what other figures in the past have said about a particular issue over time. Some emphasize the ratifiers (the people who, in state conventions, ratified the Constitution) rather than the drafters, as the drafters' comments were secret at the time, and the Constitution would never have gone into effect without the approval of ratification conventions in the states—namely, "we the People."[18]

3. ***Past Precedent:*** As a general rule, people and institutions aim for consistency. Assessing one's actions against another similar past instance is a way of checking bias. If the precedent is highly similar in its facts and law, it is said by lawyers to be "controlling." Of course, precedents can fail that test. When the facts are different, lawyers say that the prior case is not "on point" or can be "distinguished." Courts depend on precedent for their legitimacy; precedent allows them to argue that their results are not the results of will or political preference. As we will see, however, precedent operates in other institutions. In the impeachment, Congress and the President will look to their own prior precedents for guidance.

4. ***Future Precedent:*** Like most people, judges like to predict the consequences of their actions, if they can, so that they can avoid obvious errors. We reason about consequences every time we get out of bed and expect that there is a floor under our feet. Judges, in particular, want to know the *rule consequences* of their

---

[18] Some call this an argument from Framer's intent. I avoid the term "intent" for pragmatic reasons: it assumes that we are trying to gain a mental image inside another person's head, which is not what lawyers do. They look at actual evidence—the words left by the Framers, for example, exist on a page. *See, e.g.*, Victoria Nourse, Misreading Law, Misunderstanding Democracy 11 (2016) (explaining that one can replace the term "intent" with "meaning" and little is lost other than the tendency of lawyers to indict "intent" as subjective and therefore improper).

actions: if they adopt Rule X, what will happen in the future to a similar case? Lawyers often call this "pragmatic" argument, but that term is vague and has some unfortunate implications (i.e. that anything that "works, goes"). I will call it "future precedent," because it focuses on the future consequences of the rule. Note that it is focused *not* on the consequences in the particular case, but future consequences in a different set of similar cases likely to arise in the future.

5. ***Structural & Shared Constitutional Norms Argument:*** *These arguments are more difficult to identify, and we will see more of them in later Chapters.* For our purposes, structural arguments refer to arguments based on the structure of the Constitution—what lawyers call the "separation of powers." You can tell a "structural" argument when you see the word "structure" or "checks" or "separation of powers." Since lawyers disagree about structure, however, these arguments may be difficult to spot. An argument from "shared constitutional norms" is also more difficult because norms vary. The term "shared" indicates important limits on these kinds of arguments that we will explore as we move forward.

Notice that these arguments are woven together in these cases. They are not discrete boxes sealed off from each other. If they are persuasive, they tend to form a cable, woven together, rather than a logical chain.

B. Walter Nixon v. United States

The following case arose during a **judicial** impeachment. One might think courts would have a particular interest in their own members, judges. However, in this case, the Supreme Court came to the conclusion that **they should refuse to decide**—they invoked a doctrine called the "political question" doctrine to hold that the case was non-justiciable, which is law-speak for "cannot be adjudicated" by a court, leaving the final decision to Congress. Because the opinion is about **impeachment procedure**, you will learn some things about how the Congress goes about its job of impeachment, a topic to which we turn in more depth in Chapter 3.

This case sets the stage for discussion. Do not worry too much about the "political question doctrine" as you read the case. You know the result: the Court will not second-guess how Congress runs an impeachment trial, at least an impeachment trial of a judge. The important question is how the Court comes to that decision. The "how" question depends upon looking at **the kind of evidence** the Court uses. And that question depends upon the forms of argument noted above: **text, Founders' evidence, past precedent and future precedent. The bolded material guides you through the forms of argument.**

Vocabulary: Justiciability—ability for a court to decide a question; **Non-justiciability**—court's inability to decide.

WALTER L. NIXON V. UNITED STATES ET AL.

United States Supreme Court
506 U.S. 224 (1993)

CHIEF JUSTICE REHNQUIST delivered the opinion of the Court.

[Walter] Nixon, a former Chief Judge of the United States District Court for the Southern District of Mississippi, was convicted by a jury of two counts of making false statements before a federal grand jury and sentenced to prison [based on an illegal bribe]. * * * * On May 10, 1989, the House of Representatives adopted three articles of impeachment for high crimes and misdemeanors. The first two articles charged Nixon with giving false testimony before the grand jury and the third article charged him with bringing disrepute on the Federal Judiciary.

[Judge Nixon argued that the taking of evidence in his trial was done by a **committee of Senators** pursuant to the Senate's rules of impeachment, and that the Senate's "committee" procedure was unconstitutional.]

[The opinion begins by focusing on the constitutional text]

In this case, we must examine Art. I, § 3, cl. 6, to determine the scope of authority conferred upon the Senate by the Framers regarding impeachment. It provides:

> "The Senate shall have the sole Power to try all Impeachments When sitting for that Purpose, they shall be on Oath or Affirmation. When the President of the United States is tried, the Chief Justice shall preside: And no Person shall be convicted without the Concurrence of two thirds of the Members present."

The language and structure of this Clause are revealing. The first sentence is a grant of authority to the Senate, and the word "sole" indicates that this authority is reposed in the Senate and nowhere else. The next two sentences specify requirements to which the Senate proceedings shall conform: The Senate shall be on oath or affirmation, a two-thirds vote is required to convict, and when the President is tried the Chief Justice shall preside.

Petitioner argues that the word "try" in the first sentence imposes by implication an additional requirement on the Senate in that the proceedings must be in the nature of a judicial trial. From there petitioner goes on to argue that this limitation precludes the Senate from delegating to a select committee the task of hearing the testimony of witnesses, as was done pursuant to Senate Rule XI. " '[T]ry' means more than simply 'vote on' or 'review' or 'judge.' In 1787 and today, trying a case means hearing the evidence, not scanning a cold record." Petitioner concludes from this that courts may review whether or not the Senate "tried" him before convicting him.

There are several difficulties with this position which lead us ultimately to reject it. The word "try," both in 1787 and later, has considerably broader meanings than those to which petitioner would limit it. Older dictionaries define try as "[t]o examine" or "[t]o examine as a judge." *See* 2 S. Johnson, A Dictionary of the English Language (1785). In more modern usage the term has various meanings. For example, try can mean "to examine or investigate judicially," "to conduct the trial of," or "to put to the test by experiment, investigation, or trial." Webster's Third New International Dictionary 2457 (1971). Petitioner submits that "try," as contained in T. Sheridan, Dictionary of the English Language (1796), means "to examine as a judge; to bring before a judicial tribunal." Based on the variety of definitions, however, we cannot say that the Framers used the word "try" as an implied limitation on the method by which the Senate might proceed in trying impeachments. "As a rule the Constitution speaks in general terms, leaving Congress to deal with subsidiary matters of detail as the public interests and changing conditions may require * * * *" Dillon v. Gloss, 256 U.S. 368, 376, 41 S.Ct. 510, 512–513, 65 L.Ed. 994 (1921).

The conclusion that the use of the word "try" in the first sentence of the Impeachment Trial Clause lacks sufficient precision to afford any judicially manageable standard of review of the Senate's actions is fortified by the existence of the three very specific requirements that the Constitution does impose on the Senate when trying impeachments: The Members must be under oath, a two-thirds vote is required to convict, and the Chief Justice presides when the President is tried. These limitations are quite precise, and their nature suggests that the Framers did not intend to impose additional limitations on the form of the Senate proceedings by the use of the word "try" in the first sentence. * * * *

The commonsense meaning of the word "sole" is that the Senate alone shall have authority to determine whether an individual should be acquitted or convicted. The dictionary definition bears this out.

"Sole" is defined as "having no companion," "solitary," "being the only one," and "functioning * * * * independently and without assistance or interference." Webster's Third New International Dictionary 2168 (1971). If the courts may review the actions of the Senate in order to determine whether that body "tried" an impeached official, it is difficult to see how the Senate would be "functioning * * * *independently and without assistance or interference."

[The opinion turns to the drafting history of the clause and the Founders' understanding of the clause]

Nixon asserts that the word "sole" has no substantive meaning. To support this contention, he argues that the word is nothing more than a mere "cosmetic edit" added by the Committee of Style after the delegates had approved the substance of the Impeachment Trial Clause. There are two difficulties with this argument. First, accepting as we must the proposition that the Committee of Style had no authority from the Convention to alter the meaning of the Clause, we must presume that the Committee's reorganization or rephrasing accurately captured what the Framers meant in their unadorned language. That is, we must presume that the Committee did its job. This presumption is buttressed by the fact that the Constitutional Convention voted on, and accepted, the Committee of Style's linguistic version. * * * *

The history and contemporary understanding of the impeachment provisions support our reading of the constitutional language. The parties do not offer evidence of a single word in the history of the Constitutional Convention or in contemporary commentary that even alludes to the possibility of judicial review in the context of the impeachment powers. This silence is quite meaningful in light of the several explicit references to the availability of judicial review as a check on the Legislature's power with respect to bills of attainder, ex post facto laws, and statutes. *See* The Federalist No. 78, p. 524 (J. Cooke ed. * *738 1961) ("Limitations * * * * can be preserved in practice no other way than through the medium of the courts of justice").

The Framers labored over the question of where the impeachment power should lie. Significantly, in at least two considered scenarios the power was placed with the Federal Judiciary. Indeed, James Madison and the Committee of Detail proposed that the Supreme Court should have the power to determine impeachments. Despite these proposals, the Convention ultimately decided that the Senate would have "the sole Power to try all Impeachments." Art. I, § 3, cl. 6. According to Alexander Hamilton, the Senate was the "most fit depositary of this important trust" because its Members are representatives of the people. *See* The

Federalist No. 65, p. 440 (J. Cooke ed. 1961). The Supreme Court was not the proper body because the Framers "doubted whether the members of that tribunal would, at all times, be endowed with so eminent a portion of fortitude as would be called for in the execution of so difficult a task" or whether the Court "would possess the degree of credit and authority" to carry out its judgment if it conflicted with the accusation brought by the Legislature—the people's representative. In addition, the Framers believed the Court was too small in number: "The awful discretion, which a court of impeachments must necessarily have, to doom to honor or to infamy the most confidential and the most distinguished characters of the community, forbids the commitment of the trust to a small number of persons."

[The court invokes the Founders to discuss a structural argument: the relations of the branches to each other]

There are two additional reasons why the Judiciary, and the Supreme Court in particular, were not chosen to have any role in impeachments. First, the Framers recognized that most likely there would be two sets of proceedings for individuals who commit impeachable offenses—the impeachment trial and a separate criminal trial. In fact, the Constitution explicitly provides for two separate proceedings. *See* Art. I, § 3, cl. 7. The Framers deliberately separated the two forums to avoid raising the specter of bias and to ensure independent judgments:

> "Would it be proper that the persons, who had disposed of his fame and his most valuable rights as a citizen in one trial, should in another trial, for the same offence, be also the disposers of his life and his fortune? Would there not be the greatest reason to apprehend, that error in the first sentence would be the parent of error in the second sentence? That the strong bias of one decision would be apt to overrule the influence of any new lights, which might be brought to vary the complexion of another decision?" The Federalist No. 65, p. 442 (J. Cooke ed. 1961).

Certainly, judicial review of the Senate's "trial" would introduce the same risk of bias as would participation in the trial itself.

Second, judicial review would be inconsistent with the Framers' insistence that our system be one of checks and balances. In our constitutional system, impeachment was designed to be the only check on the Judicial Branch by the Legislature. On the topic of judicial accountability, Hamilton wrote:

> "The precautions for their responsibility are comprised in the article respecting impeachments. They are liable to be

> impeached for mal-conduct by the house of representatives, and tried by the senate, and if convicted, may be dismissed from office and disqualified for holding any other. This is the only provision on the point, which is consistent with the necessary independence of the judicial character, and is the only one which we find in our own constitution in respect to our own judges." *Id.* No. 79, at 532–533.

Judicial involvement in impeachment proceedings, even if only for purposes of judicial review, is counterintuitive because it would eviscerate the "important constitutional check" placed on the Judiciary by the Framers. Nixon's argument would place final reviewing authority with respect to impeachments in the hands of the same body that the impeachment process is meant to regulate.

Nevertheless, Nixon argues that judicial review is necessary in order to place a check on the Legislature. Nixon fears that if the Senate is given unreviewable authority to interpret the Impeachment Trial Clause, there is a grave risk that the Senate will usurp judicial power. The Framers anticipated this objection and created two constitutional safeguards to keep the Senate in check. The first safeguard is that the whole of the impeachment power is divided between the two legislative bodies, with the House given the right to accuse and the Senate given the right to judge. This split of authority "avoids the inconvenience of making the same persons both accusers and judges; and guards against the danger of persecution from the prevalency of a factious spirit in either of those branches." The second safeguard is the two-thirds supermajority vote requirement. Hamilton explained that "[a]s the concurrence of two-thirds of the senate will be requisite to a condemnation, the security to innocence, from this additional circumstance, will be as complete as itself can desire." Ibid.

[The opinion turns to the effect on future precedents—other impeachments—if they are subject to judicial review]

* * * * We agree with the Court of Appeals that opening the door of judicial review to the procedures used by the Senate in trying impeachments would "expose the political life of the country to months, or perhaps years, of chaos." This lack of finality would manifest itself most dramatically if the President were impeached. The legitimacy of any successor, and hence his effectiveness, would be impaired severely, not merely while the judicial process was running its course, but during any retrial that a differently constituted Senate might conduct if its first judgment of conviction were invalidated. * * * *

[The opinion rejects seemingly contrary past precedent in which the Supreme Court did exercise judicial review on a question about congressional procedures]

Petitioner finally contends that a holding of nonjusticiability cannot be reconciled with our opinion in Powell v. McCormack, 395 U.S. 486, 89 S.Ct. 1944, 23 L.Ed.2d 491 (1969). The relevant issue in Powell was whether courts could review the House of Representatives' conclusion that Powell was "unqualified" to sit as a Member because he had been accused of misappropriating public funds and abusing the process of the New York courts. We stated that the question of justiciability turned on whether the Constitution committed authority to the House to judge its Members' qualifications, and if so, the extent of that commitment. Article I, § 5, provides that "Each House shall be the Judge of the Elections, Returns and Qualifications of its own Members." In turn, Art. I, § 2, specifies three requirements for membership in the House: The candidate must be at least 25 years of age, a citizen of the United States for no less than seven years, and an inhabitant of the State he is chosen to represent. * * * * Our conclusion in *Powell* was based on the fixed meaning of "[q]ualifications" set forth in Art. I, § 2. The claim by the House that its power to "be the Judge of the Elections, Returns and Qualifications of its own Members" was a textual commitment of unreviewable authority was defeated by the existence of this separate provision specifying the only qualifications which might be imposed for House membership. The decision as to whether a Member satisfied these qualifications was placed with the House, but the decision as to what these qualifications consisted of was not.

In the case before us, there is no separate provision of the Constitution that could be defeated by allowing the Senate final authority to determine the meaning of the word "try" in the Impeachment Trial Clause. * * * * [W]e conclude * * * * that the word "try" in the Impeachment Trial Clause does not provide an identifiable textual limit on the authority which is committed to the Senate.

NOTES ON THE WALTER NIXON CASE

Bad Conduct and Impeachment: Judge Nixon was convicted of a crime before his impeachment. He continued to receive his federal salary (which cannot be "diminished" under the Constitution), so he had to be impeached if the government was to save itself the cost of continued salary. The Articles of Impeachment were not limited to alleging a crime, they included "bringing disrepute on the Federal Judiciary." The Court's opinion quotes Alexander Hamilton for the proposition that judges are "liable to be impeached for mal-conduct." In Chapter 3, we will ask about what conduct is impeachable and whether it is different for impeaching a President as opposed to a judge. Must a crime be alleged?

Impeachment Process v. Judicial Trials: An impeachment is not a trial like one conducted in a court. Federal courts have complex rules for trials, limiting the nature of the evidence and regulating the nature of testimony and the verdict, not to mention lots of rules for how to pick juries and when the law requires a jury trial. The Constitution itself governs impeachments and its directions are spare, but as far as the *Walter Nixon* case suggests, there are only three very specific requirements that the Constitution imposes on Senate impeachments: "The Members must be under oath, a two-thirds vote is required to convict, and the Chief Justice presides when the President is tried." *Nixon (Walter) v. United States*, 506 U.S. 224, 231 (1993). The *Walter Nixon*[19] case leaves all the particulars beyond this to the Senate, which has passed its own Senate rules for trying impeachments. Those rules are different from the rules that apply when the Senate is legislating.

Judicial Review and Impeachments: Judge Nixon invited the Supreme Court to review his case, arguing that the courts would be a necessary "check" on the legislature. But the Supreme Court declined the invitation. The *Walter Nixon* case stands as a precedent that courts do not want to get involved in impeachments. To be sure, the *Walter Nixon* case was about a judge, and that factual difference could be a basis to distinguish it as a precedent in a presidential impeachment by emphasizing its different facts. But there are even more reasons why a court would want to stay away from a presidential than a judicial impeachment. At issue is the fate of the highest elected official in the land. Courts have developed the "political question" doctrine to stay their own hand in cases that they feel undermine their reputation as being "above" partisanship. Even though there are plenty of examples where the court has engaged in what the average person would think a political question, such as *Bush v. Gore*, 531 U.S. 98 (2000), most legal scholars believe that it would be highly unlikely for a court to review a presidential impeachment.

Limits on the Power of Judicial Review: In setting forth its reasons, the Supreme Court relied upon the Founders who, in turn, asserted the following reasons for courts not to involve themselves in impeachments: (1) members of the Supreme Court are unelected and would be judging an elected official for suitability in office and would be unlikely to have the "fortitude" (the guts) to go against the will of the majority of voters; (2) the Supreme Court, with fewer members, could be more easily "corrupted" than a more numerous body like the Senate; and (3) the Supreme Court has no army, it has no power to enforce its judgment. What if the Court ruled against the President and the President ignored the Court? There have been times in the past, where there were questions whether the President or state leaders would in fact follow the Court's decisions. What after all is to prevent a President from simply ignoring the Court? The power of the Court lies in its ability to convince the public that it wields its power with restraint and pursuant to the rule of law.

---

19 Typically, a case is known by the last names of the parties to the case. Because we will see a case later in the book involving a different Nixon, meaning former President Richard Nixon, we deploy a more specific name here.

This explains, in part, why the Court has developed a set of rules of passivity, like the political question doctrine, which allow it to decline ruling on certain kinds of cases.

C. Clinton v. Jones

Presidents may be impeached for official or unofficial conduct. President Clinton was impeached for conduct having *nothing to do with official behavior and then lying about it*: he had an affair with an intern, and then lied about it in an official court proceeding. As we will see, the Supreme Court did not issue any rulings in the impeachment case because impeachment is left "solely" to the power of Congress to decide. However, the Supreme Court did decide a case involving whether President Clinton was "above the law," to put it colloquially, in a civil case seeking money damages. Paula Jones claimed President Clinton sexually harassed her. This conduct occurred before he was President. President Clinton argued that he was "immune" from suit while in office. The Supreme Court rejected that claim.

As you look for arguments based on **text, Founders' meaning, past judicial precedent, and future precedent**, note that there is no precise constitutional text on whether the President can be sued. There are constitutional provisions saying that Members of Congress cannot be sued for statements made in Congress,[20] but no similar provision for the President.

Vocabulary: Stay—pausing a legal action; **Damages**—money a court orders to be paid; **Petitioner**—the party petitioning (asking) the Supreme Court for review; **Respondent**—the party responding to the petition; **Action**—a legal proceeding; **Complaint**—the document that starts a civil legal proceeding; **Immunity**—legal protection from suit; **Discovery**—the process in a civil case in which the parties exchange information before trial; **Sanctions**—monetary and other penalties imposed on lawyers who bring frivolous suits; **Pleading stage or summary judgment**—early parts of the civil lawsuit process before a trial.

---

[20] U.S. Const. art. I, § 6, cl. 1 ("The Senators and Representatives shall * * * *be privileged from Arrest * * * * during Attendance at the Session of their respective Houses * * * *and for any Speech or Debate in either House, they shall not be questioned in any other Place").

WILLIAM JEFFERSON CLINTON V. PAULA CORBIN JONES

United States Supreme Court
520 U.S. 681 (1997)

JUSTICE STEVENS delivered the opinion of the Court.

I

Petitioner, William Jefferson Clinton, was elected to the Presidency in 1992, and re-elected in 1996. His term of office expires on January 20, 2001. In 1991 he was the Governor of the State of Arkansas. Respondent, Paula Corbin Jones, is a resident of California. In 1991 she lived in Arkansas, and was an employee of the Arkansas Industrial Development Commission.

On May 6, 1994, she commenced this action in the United States District Court for the Eastern District of Arkansas by filing a complaint naming [Clinton] and Danny Ferguson, a former Arkansas State Police officer, as defendants. * * * * Those allegations principally describe events that are said to have occurred on the afternoon of May 8, 1991, during an official conference held at the Excelsior Hotel in Little Rock, Arkansas. The Governor delivered a speech at the conference; respondent—working as a state employee—staffed the registration desk. She alleges that Ferguson persuaded her to leave her desk and to visit the Governor in a business suite at the hotel, where he made "abhorrent" sexual advances that she vehemently rejected. She further claims that her superiors at work subsequently dealt with her in a hostile and rude manner, and changed her duties to punish her for rejecting those advances. Finally, she alleges that after petitioner was elected President, Ferguson defamed her by making a statement to a reporter that implied she had accepted petitioner's alleged overtures, and that various persons authorized to speak for the President publicly branded her a liar by denying that the incident had occurred.

Respondent seeks actual damages of $75,000 and punitive damages of $100,000. Her complaint contains four counts.

II

In response to the complaint, petitioner promptly advised the District Court that he intended to file a motion to dismiss on grounds of Presidential immunity, and requested the court to defer all other pleadings and motions until after the immunity issue was resolved. * * * *

III

[The opinion opens with discussions of precedent—the past decisions of the court in civil suits against a President]

Petitioner's principal submission—that "in all but the most exceptional cases," the Constitution affords the President temporary immunity from civil damages litigation arising out of events that occurred before he took office—cannot be sustained on the basis of **precedent**.

Only three sitting Presidents have been defendants in civil litigation involving their actions prior to taking office. Complaints against Theodore Roosevelt and Harry Truman had been dismissed before they took office; the dismissals were affirmed after their respective inaugurations. Two companion cases arising out of an automobile accident were filed against John F. Kennedy in 1960 during the Presidential campaign. After taking office, he unsuccessfully argued that his status as Commander in Chief gave him a right to a stay under the Soldiers' and Sailors' Civil Relief Act of 1940. The motion for a stay was denied by the District Court, and the matter was settled out of court. Thus, none of those cases sheds any light on the constitutional issue before us.

The principal rationale for affording certain public servants immunity from suits for money damages arising out of their official acts is inapplicable to unofficial conduct. In cases involving prosecutors, legislators, and judges we have repeatedly explained that the immunity serves the public interest in enabling such officials to perform their designated functions effectively without fear that a particular decision may give rise to personal liability. * * * *

That rationale provided the principal basis for our holding that a former President of the United States was "entitled to absolute immunity from damages liability predicated on his official acts," Harlow v. Fitzgerald, 457 U.S. at 749. Our central concern was to avoid rendering the President "unduly cautious in the discharge of his official duties." This reasoning provides no support for an immunity for *unofficial* conduct. As we explained in *Fitzgerald*, "the sphere of protected action must be related closely to the immunity's justifying purposes." Because of the President's broad responsibilities, we recognized in that case an immunity from damages claims arising out of official acts extending to the "outer perimeter of his authority." But we have never suggested that the President, or any other official, has an immunity that extends beyond the scope of any action taken in an official capacity. * * * *

Moreover, when defining the scope of an immunity for acts clearly taken *within* an official capacity, we have applied a functional approach. "Frequently our decisions have held that an official's absolute immunity should extend only to acts in performance of particular functions of his office." Hence, for example, a judge's absolute immunity does not extend to actions performed in a purely administrative capacity. As our opinions have made clear, immunities are grounded in "the nature of the function performed, not the identity of the actor who performed it."

Petitioner's effort to construct an immunity from suit for unofficial acts grounded purely in the identity of his office is unsupported by **precedent.**

V

[The opinion moves to historical practice and the Founders]

We are also unpersuaded by the evidence from the **historical record** to which petitioner has called our attention. He points to a comment by Thomas Jefferson protesting the subpoena *duces tecum* Chief Justice Marshall directed to him in the Burr trial, a statement in the diaries kept by Senator William Maclay of the first Senate debates, in which then-Vice President John Adams and Senator Oliver Ellsworth are recorded as having said that "the President personally [is] not * * * *subject to any process whatever," lest it be "put * * * *in the power of a common Justice to exercise any Authority over him and Stop the Whole Machine of Government," and to a quotation from Justice Story's Commentaries on the Constitution. None of these sources sheds much light on the question at hand.

Respondent, in turn, has called our attention to conflicting historical evidence. Speaking in favor of the Constitution's adoption at the Pennsylvania Convention, James Wilson—who had participated in the Philadelphia Convention at which the document was drafted—explained that, although the President "is placed [on] high," "not a single privilege is annexed to his character; far from being above the laws, he is amenable to them in his private character as a citizen, and in his public character by impeachment." 2 J. Elliot, Debates on the Federal Constitution 480 (2d ed. 1863) (emphasis deleted). This description is consistent with both the doctrine of Presidential immunity as set forth in *Fitzgerald* and rejection of the immunity claim in this case. With respect to acts taken in his "public character"—that is, official acts—the President may be disciplined principally by impeachment, not by private lawsuits for damages. But he is otherwise subject to the laws for his purely private acts.

VI

[The opinion turns to textual and structural argument]

Petitioner's strongest argument supporting his immunity claim is based on the **text and structure of the Constitution**. He does not contend that the occupant of the Office of the President is "above the law," in the sense that his conduct is entirely immune from judicial scrutiny. The President argues merely for a postponement of the judicial proceedings that will determine whether he violated any law. His argument is grounded in the character of the office that was created by **Article II of the Constitution**, and relies on separation-of-powers principles that have structured our constitutional arrangement since the founding.

As a starting premise, petitioner contends that he occupies a unique office with powers and responsibilities so vast and important that the public interest demands that he devote his undivided time and attention to his public duties. He submits that—given the nature of the office—the doctrine of **separation of powers** places limits on the authority of the Federal Judiciary to interfere with the Executive Branch that would be transgressed by allowing this action to proceed.

We have no dispute with the initial premise of the argument. Former Presidents, from George Washington to George Bush, have consistently endorsed petitioner's characterization of the office. After serving his term, Lyndon Johnson observed: "Of all the 1,886 nights I was President, there were not many when I got to sleep before 1 or 2 a.m., and there were few mornings when I didn't wake up by 6 or 6:30." * * * * As Justice Jackson has pointed out, the Presidency concentrates executive authority "in a single head in whose choice the whole Nation has a part, making him the focus of public hopes and expectations. In drama, magnitude and finality his decisions so far overshadow any others that almost alone he fills the public eye and ear." We have, in short, long recognized the "unique position in the constitutional scheme" that this office occupies. Thus, while we suspect that even in our modern era there remains some truth to Chief Justice Marshall's suggestion that the duties of the Presidency are not entirely "unremitting," United States v. Burr, 25 F. Cas. 30, 34 (No. 14, 692d) (C.C. Va. 1807), we accept the initial premise of the Executive's argument.

It does not follow, however, that separation-of-powers principles would be violated by allowing this action to proceed. The doctrine of separation of powers is concerned with the allocation of official power among the three coequal branches of our Government. The Framers "built into the tripartite Federal Government * * * * a self-executing safeguard against the encroachment or aggrandizement of one branch at the expense of the other." Thus, for example, the Congress may not exercise the judicial power to revise final judgments, or the executive power to manage an airport. Similarly, the President may not exercise the legislative power to authorize the seizure of private property for public use. Youngstown, 343 U.S. at 588, 72 S. Ct. at 867. And, the judicial power to decide cases and controversies does not include the provision of purely advisory opinions to the Executive, or permit the federal courts to resolve nonjusticiable questions.

Of course the lines between the powers of the three branches are not always neatly defined. But in this case there is no suggestion that the Federal Judiciary is being asked to perform any function that might in some way be described as "executive." Respondent is merely asking the courts to exercise their core Article III jurisdiction to decide cases and controversies. Whatever the outcome of this case, there is no possibility that the decision will curtail the scope of the official powers of the Executive Branch. The litigation of questions that relate entirely to the unofficial conduct of the individual who happens to be the President poses no perceptible risk of misallocation of either judicial power or executive power.

[The court considers future precedent: burdens on future Presidents]

Rather than arguing that the decision of the case will produce either an aggrandizement of judicial power or a narrowing of executive power, petitioner contends that—as a byproduct of an otherwise traditional exercise of judicial power—burdens will be placed on the President that will hamper the performance of his official duties. We have recognized that "[e]ven when a branch does not arrogate power to itself * * * * the separation-of-powers doctrine requires that a branch not impair another in the performance of its constitutional duties." As a factual matter, petitioner contends that this particular case—as well as the potential additional litigation that an affirmance of the Court of Appeals judgment might spawn—may impose an unacceptable burden on the President's time and energy, and thereby impair the effective performance of his office.

Petitioner's predictive judgment finds little support in either history or the relatively narrow compass of the issues raised in this particular case. As we have already noted, in the more than 200-year history of the Republic, only three sitting Presidents have been subjected to suits for their private actions. If the past is any indicator, it seems unlikely that a deluge of such litigation will ever engulf the Presidency. As for the case at hand, if properly managed by the District Court, it appears to us highly unlikely to occupy any substantial amount of petitioner's time.

Of greater significance, petitioner errs by presuming that interactions between the Judicial Branch and the Executive, even quite burdensome interactions, necessarily rise to the level of constitutionally forbidden impairment of the Executive's ability to perform its constitutionally mandated functions. "[O]ur * * * *system imposes upon the Branches a degree of overlapping responsibility, a duty of interdependence as well as independence the absence of which 'would preclude the establishment of a Nation capable of governing itself effectively.' " As Madison explained, separation of powers does not mean that the branches "ought to have no *partial agency* in, or no *controul* over the acts of each other." The fact that a federal court's exercise of its traditional Article III jurisdiction may significantly burden the time and attention of the Chief Executive is not sufficient to establish a violation of the Constitution. Two long-settled propositions, first announced by Chief Justice Marshall, support that conclusion.

[Note that in rejecting the burden argument—the President is too busy—the court reasons that Presidents are already burdened by the exercise of judicial review, meaning the exercise of the power of courts to strike down a President's official actions as unconstitutional]

First, we have long held that when the President takes official action, the Court has the authority to determine whether he has acted within the law. Perhaps the most dramatic example of such a case is our holding that President Truman exceeded his constitutional authority when he issued an order directing the Secretary of Commerce to take possession of and operate most of the Nation's steel mills in order to avert a national catastrophe. Despite the serious impact of that decision on the ability of the Executive Branch to accomplish its assigned mission, and the substantial time that the President must necessarily have devoted to the matter as a result of judicial involvement, we exercised our Article III jurisdiction to decide whether his official conduct conformed to the law. Our holding was an application of the principle established in Marbury v. Madison, 1 Cranch 137, 2 L.Ed. 60 (1803), that "[i]t is emphatically the province and duty of the judicial department to say what the law is."

Second, it is also settled that the President is subject to judicial process in appropriate circumstances. Although Thomas Jefferson apparently thought otherwise, Chief Justice Marshall, when presiding in the treason trial of Aaron Burr, ruled that a subpoena *duces tecum* could be directed to the President. We unequivocally and emphatically endorsed Marshall's position when we held that President Nixon was obligated to comply with a subpoena commanding him to produce certain tape recordings of his conversations with his aides. United States v. Nixon, 418 U.S. 683, 94 S. Ct. 3090, 41 L.Ed.2d 1039 (1974). As we explained, "neither the doctrine of separation of powers, nor the need for confidentiality of high-level communications, without more, can sustain an absolute, unqualified Presidential privilege of immunity from judicial process under all circumstances."

Sitting Presidents have responded to court orders to provide testimony and other information with sufficient frequency that such interactions between the Judicial and Executive Branches can scarcely be thought a novelty. President Monroe responded to written interrogatories, President Nixon—as noted above—produced tapes in response to a subpoena *duces tecum,* see *United States v. Nixon,* President Ford complied with an order to give a deposition in a criminal trial, and President Clinton has twice given videotaped testimony in criminal proceedings. Moreover, sitting Presidents have also voluntarily complied with judicial requests for testimony. President Grant gave a lengthy deposition in a criminal case under such circumstances, and President Carter similarly gave videotaped testimony for use at a criminal trial, *id.,* § 7.1(b) (Supp. 1997).

In sum, "[i]t is settled law that the separation-of-powers doctrine does not bar every exercise of jurisdiction over the President of the United States." If the Judiciary may severely burden the Executive Branch by reviewing the legality of the President's official conduct, and if it may direct appropriate process to the President himself, it must follow that the federal courts have power to determine the legality of his unofficial conduct. The burden on the President's time and energy that is a mere byproduct of such review surely cannot be considered as onerous as the direct burden imposed by judicial review and the occasional invalidation of his official actions. We therefore hold that the doctrine of separation of powers does not require federal courts to stay all private actions against the President until he leaves office. * * * *

VIII

[Here again the opinion refers to future precedent and whether future Presidents will be harassed by civil litigation]

We add a final comment on two matters that are discussed at length in the briefs: the risk that our decision will generate a large volume of politically motivated harassing and frivolous litigation, and the danger that national security concerns might prevent the President from explaining a legitimate need for a continuance.

We are not persuaded that either of these risks is serious. Most frivolous and vexatious litigation is terminated at the pleading stage or on summary judgment, with little if any personal involvement by the defendant. Moreover, the availability of sanctions provides a significant deterrent to litigation directed at the President in his unofficial capacity for purposes of political gain or harassment. History indicates that the likelihood that a significant number of such cases will be filed is remote. * * * * Several Presidents, including petitioner, have given testimony without jeopardizing the Nation's security. In short, we have confidence in the ability of our federal judges to deal with both of these concerns. * * * *

JUSTICE BREYER, concurring in the judgment.

The majority points to the fact that private plaintiffs have brought civil damages lawsuits against a sitting President only three times in our Nation's history; and it relies upon the threat of sanctions to discourage, and "the court's discretion" to manage, such actions so that "interference with the President's duties would not occur." I am less sanguine. * * * * An increasingly complex economy has led to increasingly complex sets of statutes, rules, and regulations that often create potential liability, with, or without fault. And this Court has now made clear that such lawsuits may proceed against a sitting President. The consequence, as the Court warned in *Fitzgerald,* is that a sitting President, given "the visibility of his office," could well become "an easily identifiable target for suits for civil damages." * * * *

A Constitution that separates powers in order to prevent one branch of Government from significantly threatening the workings of another could not grant a single judge more than a very limited power to second-guess a President's reasonable determination (announced in open court) of his scheduling needs, nor could it permit the issuance of a trial scheduling order that would significantly interfere with the President's discharge of his duties—in a private civil damages action the trial of which might be postponed without the plaintiff suffering enormous harm. As Madison pointed out in The Federalist No. 51: "The great security against a gradual concentration of the several powers in the same department consists in giving to those who administer each department the necessary constitutional means and personal motives to resist encroachments of the others. *The provision for defense must in this, as in all other cases, be made commensurate to the danger of attack.*" *Id.*, at 321–322 (emphasis added). I agree with the majority's determination that a constitutional defense must await a more specific showing of need; I do not agree with what I believe to be an understatement of the "danger."

NOTES ON THE CLINTON CASE

The Clinton case's holding (the term "holding" is lawyer-speak for the principle embraced by the majority opinion) is that a President does not have absolute immunity from civil cases while he sits in office. He may be sued for damages for his personal behavior before taking office, even though he is immune from suits for his official actions as President, *Harlow v. Fitzgerald*, 457 U.S. 800, 818 (1982). For example, in theory, if a woman alleged that President Obama or Trump harassed them, then she could sue. Put more colloquially, the President is not above the civil law, he is like an ordinary citizen, when it comes to his *personal* behavior.

Judicial Review: This case is an example of judicial review. In this case, President Clinton believed that he had a constitutional immunity from trial, on the theory that it would divert him from his duties to the nation. The court reviewed and rejected that presidential immunity argument. As we will see in Chapter 4, President Trump too asserted forms of immunity in resisting his impeachment. House Managers argued that the *Clinton* case stood for the proposition that the President is not above the law.

Criminal v. Civil Immunity: A criminal action may yield imprisonment. For some time, the Justice Department has claimed that no sitting President can be indicted (we will see more of this in Chapter 3 and 4), on the same grounds asserted in *Clinton*: that the indictment will divert the President from his job. This all leads to the importance of impeachment: if a criminal prosecution is unavailable, then impeachment may be the only remedy for a President who has committed criminal behavior. Few disagree that a President may, however, be indicted, *after he leaves office*, either by the federal government for a federal crime or by a state government for a state crime. The Constitution explicitly contemplates this when it says:

> Judgement in Cases of Impeachment shall not extend further than to removal from Office, and disqualification to hold and enjoy any Office * * * *but the Party convicted shall nevertheless be liable and subject to Indictment, Trial, Judgement and Punishment, according to law. U.S. Const. art. I, § 3, cl. 7.

Judicial Power v. the President: The separation of powers issue in this case pits the courts against the President. And the courts chose themselves! They asserted their own power. Does this make the courts more powerful than the President? Thomas Jefferson was worried about that, as Justice Breyer notes:

> But would the executive be independent of the judiciary, if he were subject to the *commands* of the latter, & to imprisonment for disobedience; if the several courts could bandy him from pillar to post, keep him constantly trudging from north to south & east to west, and withdraw him entirely from his constitutional duties? (Breyer, J., concurring).

Jefferson was making an argument about process, meaning whether he, as President, had to comply with a legal order from a court. We will see this argument again, however, in slightly different form during the First Trump Impeachment. President Trump's lawyers argued that his advisors had an absolute immunity from testifying before Congress in the impeachment inquiry because it would interfere with the functioning of executive branch. The Court in *Clinton* seemed not to accept that argument in a civil suit.

Should an impeachment be different? We will return to these questions in Chapter 4.

NOTE ON PRESIDENTIAL POWER THEORIES

There are many legal theories of the President's constitutional powers. Who decides questions about presidential power? Can the President decide whether his own actions are constitutional? He has a duty to consider whether they are constitutional, but is he the final decisionmaker? Here, we first consider two theories that provide the President with enormous power: *departmentalism* and the *unitary executive*. We also consider a theory—the *democratic trustee*—that is far more limited. When you read the lawyers' impeachment arguments in the next Chapters, you might want to ask yourself which constitutional theory they are deploying.

Departmentalism: Each of the Departments, Congress and the President, has a duty to determine the constitutionality of their own actions. The theory that each department is the *final* determiner of their constitutional power is known as departmentalism. This theory is controversial for some who believe that the courts have the final power to say what is constitutional. Nevertheless, as we will see in an impeachment, because courts have generally refused to intervene (*see Walter Nixon* above), departmentalist approaches abound. In an impeachment, the President and the Congress battle it out as to whether Congress or the President is the ultimate decisionmaker. Not surprisingly, we will see Congress argue that it is the "sole" and final decisionmaker on impeachment and the President argue that he is the final decisionmaker on presidential privileges.

Unitary Executive: The President is one person; the Founders originally believed that the executive branch should be headed by more than one person. Because they settled on a single individual, lawyers say that we have a "unitary executive." In the late twentieth century, that term became controversial when deployed by President George W. Bush to justify the use of torture in the war against terror prompted by the bombing of New York's Twin Towers.[21] In a series of cases, the Supreme Court ruled against President Bush, appearing to reject the notion of a "unitary executive"[22] meaning that "anything the President says goes." President Trump, however, revived the argument in various legal filings during his tenure in office.

The "anything goes" claim relies on a textual argument made by Justice Scalia and others,[23] based on the "vesting clause" of Article II of the Constitution which says that "The executive power shall be vested in a President of the United States." U.S. Const. art. II. Justice Scalia wrote: "this does not mean some of the executive power, but *all* of the executive power * * * *It is not for us to determine, and we have never presumed to

---

[21] *See, e.g.*, Detainee Treatment Act, 42 U.S.C. §§ 2000dd–2000dd–2 (2005); Military Commissions Act, 10 U.S.C. 948–949 (2006).

[22] *Rasul v. Bush*, 542 U.S. 466 (2004); *Hamdi v. Rumsfeld*, 542 U.S. 507 (2004); *Hamdan v. Rumsfeld*, 548 U.S. 557 (2006); *Boumediene v. Bush*, 553 U.S. 723 (2008).

[23] *See* Steven G. Calabresi and Kevin H. Rhodes, *The Structural Constitution: Unitary Executive, Plural Judiciary*, 105 Harv. L. Rev. 1153 (1992).

determine, how much of the purely executive powers of government must be within the full control of the President. The Constitution prescribes that they *all* are." *Morrison v. Olson*, 487 U.S. 654, 709 (1988) (Scalia, J. dissenting). The argument presumes that there is something called constitutional "executive" power and all of it resides with the President. Notice that both liberals and conservatives make similar pronouncements: see Justice Breyer, who asserts in *Clinton v. Jones,* that the "entire executive power" is given to the executive. 520 U.S. 681, 710 (1997).

There is one big problem with this form of the "unitary executive" argument: the Constitution does not say that the President has "all" executive power or the "entire" executive power.[24] And it does not tell us what the term "executive power" means. In the *Steel Seizure* case, one of the most important presidential power cases ever decided, Justice Jackson rejected the government's argument that the President had all executive power: "I cannot accept the view that this clause is a grant in bulk of all conceivable executive power but regard it as an allocation to the presidential office of the generic powers thereafter stated." *Youngstown Sheet & Tube Co. v. Sawyer,* 343 U.S. 579, 641 (1952). (Jackson, J. concurring). Justice Jackson compared this unitary executive argument to an assertion of dictators: "And if we seek instruction from our own times, we can match it only from the executive powers in those governments we disparagingly described as *totalitarian.*" *Id.*

The President as Democratic Trustee: As Justice Jackson explained, the Constitution's grant of "executive" power at the beginning of Article II is fleshed out by "the generic powers thereafter stated." *Id.* For example, Article II goes on to say that the President is the Commander and Chief and may "make treaties," and appoint executive officers with the consent of the Senate. U.S. Const. art. II, § 2. It also says that the President must "take care" to faithfully execute the laws, *id.* art. II, § 3, and provides an oath of office: "I do solemnly swear (or affirm) that I will faithfully execute the Office of President of the United States, and will to the best of my Ability, preserve, protect and defend the Constitution of the United States." *Id.* art. II, § 1. Recently, law professors have argued that the President serves as a trustee of the people, what lawyers call a democratic "fiduciary,"[25] meaning that the trustee must prefer the interests of the people, rather than his own personal interest. In the impeachment, the Congress relied upon this notion to suggest that the President had failed to "faithfully" protect the people.

NOTE ON THE SEPARATION OF POWERS AND PARTIES

The President is not alone in the Constitution. His office does not appear first in the Constitution. The First Article creates the Congress. We have three main constitutional Departments, often described by the term

---

[24] Victoria Nourse, *Reclaiming the Constitutional Text from Originalism: The Case of Executive Power,* 106 Calif. L. Rev. 1 (2018).

[25] *See* Gary Lawson & Guy Seidman, A Great Power of Attorney: Understanding the Fidelity of the Constitution (2017); Andrew Kent, Ethan J. Leib & Jed Handelsman Shugerman, *Faithful Execution and Article II,* 132 Harv. L. Rev. 2111 (2019). For a new critique of the originalist approach, *see* Peter Shane, Democracy's Chief Executive: What the Constitutional Presidency Means Today (forthcoming).

"separation of powers." You will read a lot about the separation of powers in the next Chapters because the impeachment lawyers used the concept a lot. Above, we gave you some basic vocabulary—functions, checks, etc. Here, we dive a bit deeper.

Separate Institutions and Separate Electoral Incentives: We saw above that the School House Rock separation of functions idea has some problems. It looks like all the institutions can be described as doing tasks assigned to other institutions. For example, the courts appear to make law, just as does the President, even though we conventionally describe law-making to the Congress. The important point to remember is not to get too bogged down in the functional descriptions—the terms "lawmaking" or "executing" or "judging." *Institutions can remain separate even if they perform the same functions.* This is particularly true if the institutions are structured with incentives to keep them separate. Functions do not offer a clean line to separate the branches, but their internal structures provide a good deal more of an explanation for why overlapping functions does not lead to institutional collapse.

Consider the following example. When Joseph R. Biden Jr. was a Senator, he cared a lot about the state of Delaware and its constituents, because he was elected from Delaware. When he became Vice-President and later President, however, he switched institutions; he moved to the Executive branch. As such, he was much more likely to calibrate the wisdom of policies based on the nation's interests than solely those of Delaware. It is organizational sociology #101 that individuals tend to identify with their institutions. Just as Yale professors tend to identify more with Yale than Georgetown, they identify with Yale students more than Georgetown students. Two hundred years earlier, James Madison assumed this principle when he explained that for the constitutional structure to work, "ambition must be made to counteract ambition."[26] Political science #101—namely the idea that representatives respond to what they anticipate their constituents want—tells us that these differing incentives will tend to keep the departments from collapsing into each other, even if the institutions perform overlapping functions. This definitely does not mean that it is a good idea to start reallocating functions willy nilly. It does mean that function-talk can be deceiving.

Separate Parties: Some legal scholars are skeptical that we have a system of separated powers. Professors Rick Pildes and Daryl Levinson have argued that we have a separation of political *parties* not a separation of powers.[27] The idea is simple (and one we will see in the Trump impeachments): there will be no checking or institutional clash when the departments are held by the same party. If ultimately Yale and Georgetown are allegiant to the same overarching organization, that allegiance will trump their separate identities and likely determine a joint course of action. So, for an example, President Harry Truman, despite calls for his

---

26 Federalist No. 51.

27 Daryl J. Levinson & Richard H. Pildes, *Separation of Parties, Not Powers*, 119 Harv. L. Rev. 2331 (2006); *see also* Samuel Issacharoff & Richard H. Pildes, *Politics As Markets: Partisan Lockups of the Democratic Process*, 50 Stan. L. Rev. 643 (1998).

impeachment, prior to the *Steel Seizure* case noted above, was never impeached because the Members of the House were Democrats, members of his party. The opposite was the case with President Trump: the House was held by the Democrats and Trump was the leader of the Republican Party. So too President Clinton: when he was impeached, the House was held by Republicans and Clinton was a Democrat.

This thesis has obvious truth but is incomplete. For example, the Founders thought that they were building a structure long before there were political parties. What did they think they were doing? Once parties developed, they did have an impact on the design, but they are not a complete explanation for constitutional behavior. Proposed impeachments are legion, but actual numbers tiny (4 over the course of American history). If party division dominated the decision to impeach, then we would see actual impeachments all the time. The House is frequently held by the party opposite to the President. Conversely, party unity across the branches does not predict behavior any better. President Trump had a unified government when first elected, meaning a Republican led House and Senate, and yet he could not end the Obamacare law, as his party had promised. Finally, party division does not explain why the institutions of Congress and the Presidency have separate identities and norms even when held by the same parties. If parties were key, why wouldn't some scheming powerful party consolidate the executive and the legislature, for example? This has not happened.[28]

Why is party division insufficient? Our Constitution provides electoral mechanisms that resist party discipline.[29] Even if the same party holds the House, Senate and Presidency, the Members of those institutions still speak to different constituencies, which may give Members an incentive to reject party loyalty (the Republican Senator from Alaska might not like the Republican President's plan for the nation, for example). Moreover, loyalty to institutions and institutional power can give reasons for Members to defect from party loyalty. Even in the Trump era, where party solidity of the Republican party was extremely high, the branches have not collapsed and do not operate in lockstep. As we can see from this book, once the House was held by a different party, impeachment calls mounted. But there was only an *actual vote to impeach* when moderate members of the Democratic party[30] (the ones with the weakest party ties) believed it was in their interest, and when House leaders saw impeachment as necessary to preserve their institutional powers (oversight), to attempt to "check" a President they believed a threat to the next election.

Parliamentary Systems and Separation of Personnel: You will also read a fair bit in the impeachment trial about the differences between a system of separated powers (ours) and parliamentary systems (many other countries).

---

28 *See* Josh Chafetz, Congress's Constitution: Legislative Authority and the Separation of Powers 28–35 (2017) (critiquing the Levinson/Pildes thesis).

29 Victoria Nourse, *The Vertical Separation of Powers*, 49 Duke L. J. 749 (1999).

30 *See* Norm Eisen, A Case for the American People: The United States v. Donald J. Trump 171 (2020) (describing the fact that Speaker Pelosi was highly influenced by the moderate Members called "majority makers"—those Members seeking reelection from vulnerable purple or red districts").

President Trump's lawyers argued, for example, that the House's action would lead to something that would do grave harm to the republic, and create a constitutional structure much more like a parliamentary system. What was he arguing about? In a parliamentary system, the Prime Minister sits as head of government and is elected out of the parliament, and retains his seat in Parliament, even as he sits simultaneously as Prime Minister. So, too, the executive ministers are members of Parliament. This is impossible in our government because of the least known but most powerful structural clause known as the "incompatibility" clause. U.S. Const. art. I, § 6, cl. 2 ("no Person holding any Office under the United States, shall be a Member of either House during his Continuance in Office"). Nancy Pelosi (D-CA), who is now the Speaker of the House in the Congress, cannot sit simultaneously as head of the State Department in the Executive.

In a parliamentary system like Britain's, structural unity works hand in hand with strong political parties. When the Conservative Party wins in England, the party takes over both the executive and legislative branches, unifying them under a party platform. In the American separation of powers system, the House may be held by one party and the Senate by another. As the famous political scientist David Mayhew once explained, "Divided we Govern,"[31] meaning that the House and Senate may belong to different parties just as the President and Congress may be in different parties. This may be a bad system for getting things done because it makes legislation so difficult. The system tilts libertarian precisely *because* it is difficult to get things done. On the other hand, as Professors Jide Nzelibe and Matthew C. Stephenson have shown, this may the best system for voters, which is to say it gives voters flexibility: if one part of the government disfavors them, they have far more avenues of redress than in a parliamentary system.[32] It may also resist dictators who must control three independent institutions.

Partisanship v. Politics: Finally, we will see that there is much talk about the Trump impeachments as "partisan" in nature. It is certainly true that impeachment is highly unlikely if the President is in the same party as the House of Representatives, which must bring charges. Getting 435 Members to do anything, including legislation, is a difficult thing to do; given the stakes of presidential ouster, the incentives are all against Members uniting to impeach. (In this case, House Speaker Nancy Pelosi argued for a very long time against the First Trump Impeachment). But the term partisanship carries a negative connotation as biased. Structurally, all impeachments are driven by the representative relationship. If Members did not believe that voters would support impeachment, it would not happen. If partisanship simply means that Members have to make the calculation that impeachment is in the best interests of the people, then all impeachments are partisan, whether supported by Members of different parties or not. As

---

[31] David Mayhew, Divided We Govern: Party Control, Lawmaking, and Investigations, 1946–2002 (2005).

[32] For example, if the public is finding no redress in the Congress, they may seek relief from the executive or judicial branches. *See* Matthew Stephenson & Jide O. Nzelibe, *Complementary Constraints: Separation of Powers, Rational Voting, and Constitutional Design*, 123 Harv. L. Rev. 617 (2010).

Hamilton would say—it is a "political" remedy.[33] If this is right, is it pointless to call impeachment partisan? Or does it simply mean to call attention to the fact, as was the case in the First Trump Impeachment, that no members of the opposition party supported the Articles of Impeachment?

PROBLEM 2-1

Imagine you are working as a lawyer for a future President X. She is impeached by the House of Representatives and wants to know if she can go to court to stop the impeachment. You learn that President Trump told the press, before the First Trump Impeachment, that the Articles were a "hoax," and should be stopped in court. What do the materials in this Chapter tell you to tell future President X about what a court will do in an impeachment?

[33] Federalist No. 65.

Chapter Three

HIGH CRIMES AND MISDEMEANORS I: ABUSE OF POWER

Imagine you are drafting Articles of Impeachment in the House of Representatives. The drastic nature of the remedy should give anyone pause. With grave consequences should come the desire to "be very careful to draw [the] Articles so as to charge offenses that can be proved, and that are likely to be held impeachable by the Senate."[1] Article II, § 4, of the Constitution provides:

> The President, Vice President and all civil Officers of the United States, shall be removed from Office on Impeachment for, and Conviction of, Treason, Bribery, or other high Crimes and Misdemeanors.

What do these words mean? Law students often think that there must be answers to constitutional questions and that courts provide those answers. But many very serious constitutional questions never get to the courts, or the courts refuse to decide them. This holds particularly true in an impeachment.[2] Why? Because the Constitution's text gives the power to decide impeachments "solely" to the Congress, not the courts. U.S. Const. art. I, § 2, cl. 5 ("The House of Representatives * * * * shall have the sole Power of Impeachment"), *id.* § 3, cl. 6 ("The Senate shall have the sole power to try all impeachments"). As a result, courts have never directly intervened in an impeachment trial.[3]

What follows examines how lawyers argue about the Constitution *outside the courts.* It reflects the basic idea that constitutional argument is "a practice open to and engaged in by not

---

1 Charles L. Black Jr. & Philip Bobbitt, Impeachment: A Handbook 14 (2018).

2 This Chapter and the one that follows relies on the classic books cited in the Introduction as well as a variety of scholarly articles from diverse perspectives, including the following: Akhil Amar, *On Impeaching Presidents*, 28 Hofstra L. Rev. 291 (1999); Nikolas Bowie, *High Crimes Without Law*, 132 Harv. L. Rev. F. 59 (2018); Josh Chafetz, *Impeachment and Assassination*, 95 Minn. L. Rev. 347 (2010); Neil Kumar Katyal, *Impeachment as Congressional Constitutional Interpretation*, 63 Law & Cont. Probs. 169 (2000); Michael Stokes Paulsen, *To End A (Republican) Presidency*, 132 Harv. L. Rev. 689 (2018); Jack N. Rakove, *Statement on the Background and the History of Impeachment*, 67 Geo. Wash. L. Rev. 67 (1999).

3 *See Nixon (Walter) v. United States,* 506 U.S. 224 (1993) (in a congressional proceeding impeaching a judge, holding that the Court had no power to review the decisions of Congress as "political questions" reserved to the Congress for decision).

only judges and lawyers but politicians and citizens alike."[4] This is a feature of the Constitution's plan, which places the impeaching power in the House and the Senate, bodies elected by the public.[5]

So, imagine that you are a conscientious Member of Congress trying to draft Articles of Impeachment. You know that the Constitution allows for impeachment for treason, bribery or other high crimes or misdemeanors. U.S. Const. art. II, § 4. But what does "treason, bribery or other high crimes or misdemeanors" mean? What **evidence** will a conscientious legislator consider? As we will see, during the First Trump Impeachment, legislators marshalled arguments **similar in kind** to lawyers arguing before a court. This may seem surprising, but persuasion builds upon common meaning. As we saw in the Chapter 1, Members of Congress used the following kinds of arguments:

(1) the **text** of the Constitution;

(2) evidence from the constitutional **drafters or ratifiers**;

(3) Congress's own **past precedents** in impeachment (**prior impeachments**);

(4) the effect of the Articles on future impeachments (**future precedent**);

(5) **structural** argument (future effect on **constitutional structure**).

In this Chapter, we will add another argument to be considered:

(6) **shared constitutional norms.**

You will better understand them by seeing them applied.

I. SUMMARY OF CHARGES

In the First Trump Impeachment, the House approved two Articles of Impeachment: the first charged the President with "abuse of power." The President has a constitutional duty to faithfully execute Congress's laws. U.S. Const. art. II, § 3. The House Managers claimed that he violated that duty by engaging in a pattern of offenses which culminated in using his office to dig up political dirt on his opponent in the 2020 election, former Vice President Joseph R. Biden Jr. Congress had voted to send money to Ukraine to defend against Russian aggression. The House Managers alleged that the

---

[4] Jack M. Balkin & Sanford Levinson, *Constitutional Grammar*, 72 Tex. L. Rev. 1771, 1786 (1994).

[5] Michael J. Gerhardt, The Federal Impeachment Process: A Constitutional and Historical Analysis 5–6 (2nd ed. 2000).

President had withheld taxpayer money to force Ukraine to do him a personal political favor—investigate then-Vice President Biden. The second Article charged the President with "obstructing" Congress by covering up the corrupt bargain with Ukraine. The **legal question:** did these actions amount to an impeachable offense? The House Managers claimed that both Articles alleged "high" crimes. In this Chapter, we focus on the allegations made in the first Article of Impeachment. In the next Chapter, we consider the "obstruction of Congress" charge. The Second Trump Impeachment appears in Part Two.

Rep. Adam Schiff (D-CA) led the House Managers. He described the factual basis of the first Article in layman's terms. "President Trump's betrayal began in 2016, when he first solicited Russian interference in our election." He directly quoted then-candidate Trump at a campaign rally: *"Russia,* if you're listening, I hope you're able to find the 30,000 emails that are missing,"[6] made in reference to Trump's 2016 opponent, former Secretary of State Hillary Clinton, who was alleged to have lost thousands of sensitive emails held on a private server. Manager Schiff then set forth the "pattern" of abuse:

> *That betrayal continued in Helsinki [when Trump stood next to Russian President Putin at a press conference] in 2018, when, as we saw, he rejected the intelligence community's assessment about Russian interference in the [2016] election. * * * * The betrayal continued in 2019 when he carried out a scheme to cheat in the 2020 election by demanding that the leader of Ukraine—a U.S. partner under military attack by Russia—announce[ ] an investigation into the same baseless conspiracy theory about a DNC server and the bogus allegations about Vice President Biden. The abuse of power continues. He is still trying to cheat in the next election.*[7] 166 Cong. Rec. S543 (daily ed. Jan. 24, 2020).

---

[6] This refers to the claim, during the 2016 presidential campaign, that Secretary of State Hillary Clinton sent thousands of emails to her private server, contrary to law and national security. A State Department review of the recovered emails showed no major national security breach. Jason Krause, *But Their Emails! Some of the Most Contentious Political Issues Are, at Their Root, E-Discovery Disputes*, 104 A.B.A. J. 46, 48 (Dec. 2018). The Trump lawyers referred to an estimated 30,000 emails that could not initially be found, although FBI specialists recovered approximately 15,000 of them. *Id.*

[7] "Still trying to cheat" refers to allegations that the former Mayor of New York and President Trump's personal lawyer, Rudolph Giuliani, had continued to push for an investigation into presidential candidate Joseph R. Biden, Jr. and his son, Hunter Biden, related to Ukraine after Congress voted for Articles of Impeachment. Ben Protess, Andrew E. Kramer, Michael Rothfield, & William K. Rashbaum, Giuliani Associate Says He Gave Demand for Biden Inquiry to Ukrainians, N.Y. Times (Nov.

President Trump's lawyers rejected these contentions and argued that the President engaged in normal diplomacy, not an impeachable offense.

Every President tried before the Senate, prior to the First Trump Impeachment, has argued that his offense *did not amount to a* "high-crime." In 1868, President Andrew Johnson argued that he could not be impeached for violating a law barring him from firing the Secretary of War, a dispute that arose because Johnson aimed to reverse Lincoln's policies, fire Lincoln's cabinet secretaries, and reject Congress's program for reconstructing the post-Civil War South. In 1998, President Clinton contended that he could not be impeached based on lying about an extra-marital affair while under oath.[8] Similarly, in 2019, President Trump's lawyers argued that his actions seeking foreign assistance for his personal re-election campaign did not rise to the level of a crime and therefore fell outside Congress's impeachment powers. Despite this constant trend, conservative and liberal constitutional scholars have for decades, if not a century, claimed that impeachment can cover "[A] wide range of misconduct as judged, ultimately, by legislators themselves."[9]

II. CONSTITUTIONAL TEXT

Like a poem, the Constitution is made of few words—a mere 4400 in the original version without its amendments. Lawyers pay close attention to those words. Focusing on the words is what is meant by "textual" argument. Sometimes, textual arguments can be conclusive. For example, the President must be at least 35 years of age. U.S. Const. art. II, § 1, cl. 5. No one doubts what "attained to the Age of thirty-five Years" means. *Id.* However, in many of the most urgent cases, text does not resolve matters. If it did, there would be no arguments about the Constitution, and no need for lawyers to study constitutional law.

10, 2019), https://www.nytimes.com/2019/11/10/nyregion/trump-ukraine-parnas-fruman.html.

[8] *See* Frank O. Bowman III, High Crimes and Misdemeanors: A History of Impeachment for the Age of Trump, chs. 7, 9 (2019); Richard A. Posner, An Affair of State: The Investigation, Impeachment, and Trial of President Clinton (1999); David O. Stewart, Impeached: The Trial of President Andrew Johnson and the Fight for Lincoln's Legacy (2010).

[9] Michael Stokes Paulsen, *To End a (Republican) Presidency*, 132 Harv. L. Rev. 689, 701 (2018); *see id.* at 691 ("The academic consensus on this point is strikingly universal," Paulsen writes, "uniting the best serious scholarly books on impeachment over the last fifty years and scholars across the ideological spectrum."). *See* Nikolas Bowie, *High Crimes Without Law*, 132 Harv. L. Rev. F. 59 (2018) (explaining that when Justice Curtis sought to defend President Andrew Johnson, the Justice acknowledged that he was adopting a position *rejected* by most of the "learned dissertations" on the question of what should constitute an impeachable offense.") (emphasis added).

As we will see below, President Trump argued that the **constitutional text** required that he could be impeached only for committing an ordinary crime. The House Managers disagreed. On many separate occasions, and over several days, the House Managers and the President's lawyers argued about the **text** of 8—a mere 8—words: "Treason, Bribery, or other high Crimes and Misdemeanors." U.S. Const. art. II, § 4.

A. The House Managers' Arguments

Rep. Schiff (D-CA) explained the House Managers' position that inviting foreign interference in a presidential election constituted a "high crime," by violating the public's trust, based on the **constitutional text**:

> *The [**Constitution** provides for] impeachment for treason, bribery, or other high crimes and misdemeanors to underscore the requirement of an offense against society. In this phrase, "**high**" modifies both the crimes and the misdemeanors in that both relate to a high injustice, a transgression committed against the people and to the public trust.* 166 Cong. Rec. S446 (daily ed. Jan. 22, 2020) (emphasis added).

1. The "High Crimes" Clause: Treason, Bribery, or Other High Crimes and Misdemeanors

Rep. Nadler (D-NY) explained that a "high crime" differed from an ordinary crime. If an ordinary crime were enough, a President could be impeached for failing to pay speeding tickets. Ordinary crime presented too low a bar.[10] He argued:

> *[T]he President's position is contradicted by the **Constitution's text**.*
>
> *The phrase "high Crimes" refers to offenses against the State rather than to workaday crimes, and it matters because the phrase "high crimes and misdemeanors" had a rich history in England, where it had been applied in many, many cases that did not involve crimes under British law. When the Framers added "high Crimes" here but nowhere else in the Constitution, they made a deliberate choice.* 166 Cong. Rec. S492 (daily ed. Jan. 23, 2020) (emphasis added).

[10] At least one House Manager argued that the President had committed something akin to bribery, by conditioning aid to Ukraine on a personal favor, but we will see difficulties with that claim later in this Chapter. As we will also see, the House Managers argued that the President violated an existing civil law, the Impoundments Act.

Rep. Jeffries (D-NY) contended that the President had committed a "crime" against the Constitution. The President, under Article II, had a duty to "faithfully" execute the law, and he had in fact done the opposite: he had executed the law for his personal benefit, thus violating the Constitution. *See* U.S. Const. art. II, § 3 (The President "shall take care that the laws be faithfully executed.").

> *Counsel to the President indicated that we have not charged President Trump with a crime. We have charged him with crimes against the U.S. Constitution—high crimes and misdemeanors and abuse of power. It strikes at the very heart of what the Framers of the Constitution were concerned about—betrayal of one's oath of office for personal gain and the corruption of our democracy. High crimes and misdemeanors are what this trial is all about.* 166 Cong. Rec. S411 (daily ed. Jan. 21, 2020).

Rep. Nadler (D-NY) echoed this theme, calling what the President had done a "constitutional crime." Technically, lawyers do not speak of "crimes" against the Constitution. Why? First, because lawyers associate crimes with imprisonment, and no President goes to jail based on impeachment. Second, a crime is typically understood to be something defined by the legislature, not the Constitution. On the other hand, treason is defined in the Constitution, and the word "crime" is often associated with a very serious legal violation.

> *A President who abuses his power in order to knee-cap political opponents and spread Russian conspiracy theories—a President who uses his office to ask for or, even worse, to compel foreign nations to meddle in our elections—is a President who attacks the very foundations of our liberty. That is a grave abuse of power. It is an unprecedented betrayal of the national interest. It is a shocking corruption of the election process, and it is without a doubt a crime against the Constitution, warranting, demanding his removal from office.* 166 Cong. Rec. S492 (daily ed. Jan. 23, 2020) (statement of Rep. Nadler).

2. Other Constitutional Text

The House Managers emphasized that the very idea of impeachment means something different from an ordinary crime because impeachment removes a President from office; the President does not go to jail. The **text** of Article II, § 4 provides in full that "*The President, Vice President and all civil officers of the United States, shall be **removed from office** on impeachment for, and conviction of, treason, bribery, or other high crimes and misdemeanors.*" (emphasis added). Removal from office differs from criminal punishment. The

text distinguishes the two, stating that the President may be indicted for criminal offenses after he has left office. U.S. Const. Article I, § 3 provides:

> Judgment in Cases of Impeachment shall not extend further than to removal from Office, and disqualification to hold and enjoy any Office of honor, Trust or Profit under the United States: but the Party convicted shall nevertheless be liable and subject to Indictment, Trial, Judgment and Punishment, according to Law.

3. Canons of Construction[11]

Lawyers use **canons of construction** to interpret **text**. A "canon" means an informal rule, something that can help in interpretation but is not required. Canons do not constitute *law* because law is created by the Congress and signed by the President. U.S. Const. art. I, § 7. Instead, judges create canons and have since the beginning of American history. The House Managers did not specifically invoke the term "canon," but applied one known as the absurdity canon. The House Managers argued that requiring an ordinary "crime" for impeachment would lead to absurd consequences.

Judges disfavor "absurd" interpretations: they presume Members of Congress and Constitution-makers are rational. Rational people choose rational ends. If an interpretation leads to absurd results, then interpreters pause to reconsider whether something about their approach is mistaken, whether they have missed something, or whether another interpretation would be better. The absurdity canon goes back to ancient English law and the famous commentator William Blackstone, who argued that courts should never read a law to reach absurd consequences.[12] In their brief, the House Managers wrote:

> *President Trump's theory would mean that the President could not be impeached even if he allowed an enemy power to invade and conquer American territory. The* ***absurdity*** *of*

---

[11] Canons of construction include much more than language rules. They are often substantive principles of law created by courts. William N. Eskridge, Jr., Interpreting Law: A Primer on how to Read Statutes and the Constitution (2016).

[12] In the principal "rules to be observed with regard to the construction of statutes," 1 William Blackstone, Commentaries on the Laws of England *87, Blackstone wrote: "[I]f there arise out of [acts of Parliament] * * * *any absurd consequences, manifestly contradictory to common reason, they are, with regard to those collateral consequences, void." *Id.* at *91. Some disfavor the canon of absurdity because it helps to focus the interpretation on interpretative consequences—what will happen if a court rules in a particular way. *See* John Manning, *The Absurdity Doctrine*, 116 Harv. L. Rev. 2387 (2003). Others worry that absurdity lies in the eyes of the beholder.

that argument demonstrates why every serious constitutional scholar to consider it—including the House Republicans' own legal expert—has rejected it. The Framers intentionally did not tie "high Crimes and Misdemeanors" to the federal criminal code—which did not exist at the time of the Founding—but instead created impeachment to cover severe abuses of the public trust like those of President Trump. House Managers Reply Brief, 166 Cong. Rec. S371 (daily ed. Jan. 21, 2020) (citations omitted) (emphasis added).

Readers should not confuse the absurdity canon with an off-hand use of the term "absurd." People use that term all the time to denigrate an argument. For example, House Managers chided one of the President's lawyers, Professor Alan Dershowitz, for "switching sides," taking one position on the "crime" question in the Clinton impeachment and another during President Trump's impeachment. *Id.* at S372.[13] House Managers called this switch "absurd." This use of absurdity differs from the canon. The canon is an instruction to judges to "think twice" before attributing to an author irrationality. By contrast, in the First Trump Impeachment, both sides used the term "absurd" as a general rhetorical criticism of each other's arguments.

B. The President's Lawyers' Arguments

The President's lawyers argued that **the text of the Constitution** barred an impeachment without an **ordinary crime**.

1. The Text

Professor Dershowitz stated: "I will begin, as all constitutional analysis begins, with the text of the Constitution governing impeachment." 166 Cong. Rec. S609 (daily ed. Jan. 27, 2020).

The structure and language of the clause—the use of the adjective "other" to describe "high Crimes and Misdemeanors" in a list immediately following the specific offenses "Treason" and "Bribery"— * * * *[means that] "other high* Crimes *and Misdemeanors" must be understood to have the same qualities—in terms of seriousness and their effect on the functioning of government—as the crimes of*

[13] Professor Alan Dershowitz argued during President Clinton's impeachment: "It certainly doesn't have to be a crime, if you have somebody who completely corrupts the office of president, and who abuses trust and who poses great danger to our liberty." 166 Cong. Rec. at S372 (quoting Professor Dershowitz) (daily ed. Jan. 21, 2020).

> *"Treason" and "Bribery."* President's Brief, 166 Cong. Rec. S316 (daily ed. Jan. 21, 2020).

The President's lawyers reinforced that idea by referring to the term "**high**." They argued that "[t]he use of the term 'high' in the Impeachment Clause is * * * * significant, and was clearly deliberate. Under English * * * * law, 'high' indicated crimes against the state; * * * * offenses against 'the supreme executive power, or the king and his government,' * * * * the highest civil crime."[14] *Id.*

2. Canons of Interpretation

The President's lawyers relied heavily on canons of interpretation. Typically, canons are used quite frequently in cases where courts interpret laws (statutes created by the Congress and signed by the President) but not as frequently in constitutional cases. The Trump lawyers relied upon the interpretive canon called "**ejusdem generis**." That Latin phrase simply means that general words are to be interpreted as similar to the examples that precede them.

> *The use of the adjective "other" to describe "high Crimes and Misdemeanors" in a list calls for applying the ejusdem generis canon of interpretation. This canon instructs that "[w]here general words follow specific words in a statutory enumeration, the general words are construed to embrace only objects similar in nature to those objects enumerated by the preceding specific words."* President's Brief, 166 Cong. Rec. S316 (daily ed. Jan. 21, 2020).

Different lawyers for the President called the canon by another name: **the canon of "noscitur a sociis."** That simply means that *words are known by their associates.* Professor Dershowitz contended:

> *[T]he Latin phrase "Noscitur a sociis,"—I am sorry for my pronunciation—referring to a classic rule of interpretation that when the meaning of a word that is part of a group of words is uncertain, you should look to the other words in that group that provide interpretive context.*
>
> *The late Justice Antonin Scalia gave the following current example. If one speaks of Mickey Mantle, Rocky Marciano, Michael Jordan, and other great competitors, the last noun does not reasonably refer to Sam Walton, who is a great*

---

[14] To a modern lawyer, the term "civil crime," taken from British history, appears self-contradicting. Today, the term "civil" means something different from "criminal," and no lawyer regularly uses the term "civil crimes." In a world where impeachment constituted an offense against the British King, the term "civil crime" makes more sense, the "crime" referring to the act or offense and the "civil" referring to a civil punishment—removal from office.

> *competitor, but in business, or Napoleon, a great competitor on the battlefield.* [Ed.: Mantle, Marciano and Jordan are athletes.]
>
> *Applying that rule to the groups of words "treason, bribery, or other high crimes and misdemeanors," the last five words should be interpreted to include only serious criminal behavior akin to treason and bribery.* 166 Cong. Rec. S610 (daily ed. Jan. 27, 2020).

3. Whole Text

The President's lawyers looked at **other text in the Constitution** considering impeachment, explaining that there were 7 other constitutional references to impeachment and arguing that each supported their reading.

> *Each of the seven other references in the Constitution to impeachment also supports the conclusion that impeachments must be evaluated in terms of offenses against settled law: The Constitution refers to "Conviction" for impeachable offenses twice and "Judgment in Cases of Impeachment." * * * * And it implies impeachable offenses are "Crimes" and "Offenses" in the Jury Trial Clause and the Pardon Clause, respectively. These are all words that indicate violations of established law.* 166 Cong. Rec. S316 (daily ed. Jan. 21, 2020).

In doing so, the President's lawyers invoked a **canon** known as the **"whole text" rule**, which is that interpreters should make sense of an ambiguous text in the context of the whole text. For example, the Impeachment Clause refers to "conviction," a term associated with crime: "The President, Vice President and all civil officers of the United States, shall be removed from office on impeachment for, and **conviction** of, treason, bribery, or other high crimes and misdemeanors." U.S. Const. art. II, § 4. The Pardon Clause provides that the President shall "have power to grant reprieves and pardons for **offenses** against the United States, except in cases of impeachment." U.S. Const. art. II, § 2. The term "offense" is often associated by lawyers to a criminal offense. Finally, the Jury Trial Clause provides that "[t]he Trial of all **Crimes**, except in Cases of Impeachment, shall be by Jury," the implication again is that impeachment is a subset of a larger group of "crimes," U.S. Const. art. III, § 2. In sum, the House Managers responded that impeachment required more than an ordinary crime—a high crime—because "conviction" only resulted in removal from office, not prison time, thus making it different from an ordinary crime. U.S. Const. art. II, § 4.

QUESTIONS: THE TEXT

You should keep in mind that textual argument tends not to yield answers in hard cases. As you think about these arguments, consider these points:

Zombie Theory?: As conservative scholar Michael Paulsen has pointed out about the "impeachment-requires-an-ordinary-crime" theory: "The academic consensus on this point is strikingly universal * * * * uniting the best serious scholarly books on impeachment over the last fifty years and scholars across the ideological spectrum."[15] Professor Charles L. Black Jr. called the crime-required position not only "unwarranted" but "absurd."[16] Professor Laurence H. Tribe and Joshua Matz punctuated the point: "[E]ven having died a thousand deaths, this theory staggers on like a vengeful zombie."[17]

Given this consensus, five hundred law professors (including the author of this book) signed a letter urging that the High Crimes Clause encompassed more than everyday crime or what Professor Alan Dershowitz called "crime-like" offenses. The law professors argued that the "standard is *constitutional;* it does not depend on what Congress has chosen to criminalize."[18] By that, they distinguished the Constitution as higher law. Surely, a President could be impeached because he violated the Constitution, even if Congress had not passed a criminal law barring the same unconstitutional behavior.

Professor Frank O. Bowman III summarized his view of the scholarly consensus before the Trump Impeachment:

> If there is one point established by eight centuries of Anglo-American impeachment practice, it is that the phrase "high Crimes and Misdemeanors" is not limited to indictable crime. Those tasked with defending officials facing impeachment invariably argue the contrary, but they are, and always have been wrong.
>
> British impeachments were chock full of allegations of and convictions for non-criminal behavior. American colonies before the Revolution, and American states after the Revolution but before 1787, all impeached officials for non-criminal conduct. The framers in Philadelphia had a high degree of familiarity with British impeachment practice and adopted a parliamentary phrase they knew reached beyond the narrowly criminal to political misconduct in a broad sense. The ratifiers in the states repeatedly spoke of impeachment in ways that affirmed their understanding that the constitutional impeachment power

---

[15] Michael Stokes Paulsen, *To End a (Republican) Presidency*, 132 Harv. L. Rev. 689, 691 (2018).

[16] Charles L. Black, Jr. & Philip Bobbitt, Impeachment: A Handbook 32 (1974).

[17] Laurence H. Tribe & Joshua Matz, To End a Presidency: The Power of Impeachment 45 (2018).

[18] Matt Zapotosky, *More than 500 law professors say Trump committed 'impeachable conduct'*, Wash. Post (Dec. 6, 2019).

extended beyond behavior cognizable in a criminal court. Since 1787, Congress has repeatedly impeached federal officials for non-criminal behavior. All serious modern scholars and commentators are unanimous that "high Crimes and Misdemeanors" need not be crimes.[19]

The Ordinary Crime Position—Does It Include Too Much?: Neither the President nor the House Managers disputed that impeachment required serious presidential misconduct. The House Managers argued that that the "crime" category was overly broad because it could reach large amounts of minor behavior. Put in other words, it was too low a bar for impeachment. For example, speeding or failing to pay parking tickets may constitute a crime. Should that be sufficient to impeach? Impeachment involves serious matters: as the President's lawyers argued, it would unseat a popularly elected President. President Clinton's lawyers during his impeachment made a similar argument that Congress could not impeach him because lying to a court about an extra-marital affair amounted to a minor offense, even if criminal.

The Ordinary Crime Position—Does It Include Too Little?: The House Managers argued that the "ordinary crime" position was both "overinclusive" (it *included* minor offenses) and "underinclusive" (it *excluded* very serious offenses). Ordinary criminal law does not cover many egregious presidential actions because ordinary criminal law is focused on the citizenry, not the President. It focuses on violence—shootings, bar fights, and drunk driving—the kind of individual wrongs citizens do to each other. By contrast, Presidents have enormous power to commit offenses against the people as a whole, ones every citizen would find disturbing. For example, a President could invite a foreign power to invade America. A President could, as Professor Charles L. Black Jr. once hypothesized, move to Saudi Arabia to marry 4 wives.[20] Let us assume that a President accepted a foreign offer to interfere with voting machines[21] during a presidential election so that he could win the election. Would not that be a sufficient basis for impeachment even if it was not a crime? Typically, the Constitution trumps ordinary law.

---

19 Frank O. Bowman III, High Crimes and Misdemeanors: A History of Impeachment for the Age of Trump 244 (2019). For other academics supporting this view, *see, e.g.*, Raoul Berger, Impeachment: The Constitutional Problems 56–57 (1973); Michael J. Gerhardt, Federal Impeachment Process 103 (2000); H. Lowell Brown, High Crimes and Misdemeanors in Presidential Impeachment 118–19 (2010); Cass R. Sunstein, Impeachment: A Citizen's Guide 62–63 (2017); Charles L. Black Jr. & Philip Bobbitt, Impeachment: A Handbook 32 (2018); Laurence H. Tribe & Joshua Matz, To End a Presidency: The Power of Impeachment 45 (2018). During the First Trump Impeachment, partially dissenting voices emerged. *See, e.g.*, Robert G. Natelson, *Impeachment: The Constitution's Fiduciary Meaning of "High * * * * Misdemeanors,"* 19 Fed. Soc. R. 68 (2018); Nikolas Bowie, *High Crimes Without Law*, 132 Harv. L. Rev. F. 59 (2018).

20 Charles L. Black Jr. & Philip Bobbitt, Impeachment: A Handbook 31 (2018).

21 Some states classify interference with voting machinery as a misdemeanor. There are federal computer crimes that might apply but unless Congress states specifically that a law applies outside the United States to foreign behavior, it does not.

If that is true, then how can anyone argue that a statutory crime—a law passed by Congress—is needed to impeach?

Should the House Managers Have Emphasized Constitutional Violations?: Before the First Trump Impeachment, some urged that the President had violated the Constitution's Emoluments Clause.[22] There is little question that the Founders feared a President in debt to foreign powers. As Gouverneur Morris, an important Founder, explained: "No one * * * * would say that we ought to expose ourselves to the danger of seeing the first Magistrate in foreign pay."[23] The Emoluments Clause bars a President from taking bribes or accepting any gifts from a foreign power without the consent of Congress. U.S. Const. art. I, § 9, cl. 8.[24] History may ask why the Managers did not include an article focusing on Emoluments Clause violations. Prior to the impeachment, the State of Maryland had attempted to sue President Trump for violating the Emoluments Clause (because he was receiving various benefits from foreign visitors staying at his hotels or resorts, among other claims).[25] So, too, did a group of Senators, but their suit was dismissed based on legal arguments that they had no authority to sue.[26] If that was right, that means that the only way Congress has the power to enforce the Emoluments Clause is through Impeachment. Why did the Articles not include Emoluments? The answer to this question lies in the politics of impeachment. Members had to anticipate that, if they included such a charge, it would have avoided the "crime only" argument, but it would have raised complicated constitutional and factual questions that would have diverted the public's focus from the President's threat to elections to his business enterprises. The public audience of an impeachment has a strong influence on how Articles of Impeachment are drafted.[27]

Should the House Lawyers Have Analogized to an Ordinary Crime?: No one disputes that the Constitution permits an impeachment based on "Bribery," as that term is explicitly stated in the Constitution. As Professor Akhil Amar has written: "bribery—secretly bending laws to favor the rich and powerful—involves official corruption of a highly malignant sort, threatening the very soul of a democracy committed to equality under the

---

[22] Frank O. Bowman III, High Crimes and Misdemeanors: A History of Impeachment for the Age of Trump 280–83 (2019) (considering the virtues and vices of these claims in the Trump case).

[23] Lawrence H. Tribe & Joshua Matz, To End a Presidency: The Power of Impeachment 32 (2018) (quoting Morris).

[24] U.S. Const. art. I, § 9 "[N]o person holding any office of profit or trust under them, shall, without the consent of the Congress, accept of any present, emolument, office, or title, of any kind whatever, from any king, prince, or foreign state.")

[25] Before the impeachment, Members of Congress and others sued President Trump for violations of the Emoluments Clause. *See, e.g., In Re Trump*, 958 F.3d 274 (4th Cir. 2020), *judgment vacated, Trump v. District of Columbia*, 141 S.Ct. 1262 (2021).

[26] *See, e.g., Blumenthal v. Trump*, 949 F.3d 14 (D.C. Cir. 2020), *cert denied* 2020 WL 6037222 (2020).

[27] Norm Eisen, A Case for the American People: The United States v. Donald Trump 172–79 (2020).

law."[28] And that is true whether the President actually receives a benefit, or whether he simply asks for a personal benefit. Imagine, for example, that the President were to offer $100,000 to state governors to rig voting machines in favor of the President. The mere "ask" constitutes bribery. And it poses a risk to democracy, meaning the integrity of our elections. As we will see at the end of this Chapter, when we address the criminal law, some House Managers argued that the President's conduct amounted to something like bribery. Would it have been better if the House Managers pushed the criminal analogy to bribery or other crimes? Or is bribery the wrong crime? Should House Members have analogized to laws in the corporate world barring self-dealing: for example, if the head of a corporation takes profits for himself when the money is owed to the shareholders, he breaches a duty of trust. The Constitution establishes that the President has a duty to prefer the people to his personal fate. U.S. Const. art. II (requiring that the President "faithfully" execute the law). We will look at the bribery question more specifically later in the Chapter.

Canons and False Precision: Canons of construction look precise, but they often lead to stalemate. The President's lawyers used the canons to read the "High Crimes" Clause to mean "only statutory crimes" or "only ordinary crimes." Of course, the Constitution does not say "only" or "ordinary" crimes. The President's lawyers also used canons to deploy a *generalization* that "other high crimes and misdemeanors" had to include ordinary crimes. The House Managers came up with a *different generalization*. They argued that the common generalization "high crime" included a grave breach of public trust, something more serious than an ordinary crime. The *ejusdem generis* and *noscitur a sociis* canons apply to **word lists**. It is common sense that words in a list are likely to express a common similarity, but what that similarity is can be disputed. Not only do these canons require interpreters to make generalizations (finding what is similar in the list), it is also inevitable that the generalizations will be over-generalized. For example, the "crime" generalization leaves out the possibility that the word misdemeanor means bad behavior (*see* below on the meaning of misdemeanor). The President's lawyers argued that the House Managers' interpretation effectively eliminated the word "crime" from the Impeachment Clause. But the opposite is true as well: the President's generalization of "crime" effectively strikes out the word "high" in "high crimes," not to mention other "high" misdemeanors.

What Is a "High Misdemeanor"?: No Member spent too much time arguing about the word "misdemeanor." Generally, in contemporary parlance, a misdemeanor is a lesser crime or minor offense. In criminal law, misdemeanors are contrasted with felonies, with a felony carrying a punishment of at least one year in jail or prison and a misdemeanor less than one year. On the other hand, "misdemeanor," as conceived in 1787, comes from the ancient term "demeanor" (meaning outward behavior or deportment) and we know that impeachments in the British system and the early American system included the failure to act appropriately given the

[28] Akhil Amar, The Constitution Today: Timeless Lessons for the Issues of Our Era 302 (2016).

nature of the office.[29] A judge who appeared drunk in court would not have proper demeanor. That does not explain what is meant by a "high" misdemeanor, which sounds something like an oxymoron in modern terms: for modern criminal lawyers, misdemeanor means a low or minor crime, so how can a low or minor crime become a "high" one? Since the First Trump Impeachment, however, one scholar has focused on the precise textual meaning of the term "high misdemeanor" and concluded it meant a "crime-like" offense in 1787. *See* Robert G. Natelson, *Impeachment: The Constitution's Fiduciary Meaning of "High * * * * Misdemeanors,"* 19 Fed. Soc. R. 68 (2018).

Unbearable but Necessary Vagueness: Students may well be frustrated with the fact that the Constitution does not spell out its terms more precisely. Lest this seem like a peculiar failure of our national Constitution, it is well to remember that the standard could be even vaguer. For example, the state of Georgia's Constitution provides that the "House wields 'the sole power to vote impeachment charges,' but does not say when impeachment is proper."[30] If one looks abroad, one sees some Constitutions that focus on specific offenses like treason or bribery, but there are also many Constitutions, such as in Argentina, Germany, India, South Africa, and Poland that simply "declare that all criminal violations or unconstitutional acts" are grounds for impeachment.[31] In short, language a student might find vague has recommended itself to many Constitution writers. Why? The nature of a Constitution is to set a blueprint for governing, not a behavioral code. As Chief Justice John Marshall explained, a well-written Constitution speaks in broad strokes and cannot "partake of the prolixity of a legal code."[32] Drafters cannot anticipate all possible events and thus are forced to speak in general terms. In short, vagueness is not a bug, but a feature, of a constitutional system, as it allows the people to be the ultimate arbiters of impeachment.

III. THE FOUNDERS

When constitutional text is unclear, lawyers refer to other sources and authorities: they often look to statements by the delegates to the Constitutional Convention of 1787 who drafted, debated, and approved the Constitution, and to those who debated and voted on ratification of the Constitution by the states in 1788. I will use the term "Founders" to cover both groups. As we discussed in Chapter 1, seeking clarification, if one can, from the authors of a document, or those knowledgeable about its meaning, is common sense. When an Army general gives a command, he may be misunderstood in the heat of battle; before one goes on the attack, it

---

[29] *See, e.g.*, Frank O. Bowman III: High Crimes and Misdemeanors: A History of Impeachment for the Age of Trump (2019).

[30] Lawrence H. Tribe & Joshua Matz, To End a Presidency 26 (2018) (quoting the Georgia constitution).

[31] *Id.* at 26–27.

[32] *McCulloch v. Maryland*, 17 U.S. (4 Wheat.) 316, 407 (1819).

would be best to check whether he urged attack or retreat if the words are unclear. But in the case of a 200-year-old Constitution, the past often seems like a "foreign country."[33] Translation difficulties abound, as we will see.

A. The House Managers' Arguments

During the First Trump Impeachment, both the House Managers and the President's lawyers referenced the Founders. **Rep. Schiff** (D-CA) explained the history of American democracy, in which the colonies broke from an unelected British King and replaced that King with an executive elected by the people:

> *Having broken free from a King with unbridled authority who often placed his own interests above that of the people, **the Framers** established a structure that would guarantee that the Chief Executive's power flowed only from his obligation to the people rather than from a sovereign whose power was confirmed on him by divine right.*
>
> *In this new architecture, no branch of government or individual would predominate over another. In this way, the Founders ensured that their elected leaders and their President would use the powers of office only to undertake that which the people desired and not for their personal aggrandizement or enrichment.* 166 Cong. Rec. S446 (daily ed. Jan. 22, 2020).

Rep. Schiff (D-CA) went on to explain what everyone agreed upon: impeachment required a grave breach of public trust—again invoking the **Founders** by quoting **Alexander Hamilton**. Hamilton, along with James Madison and John Jay, are the authors of a document relied upon by courts as evidence of the Constitution's meaning in 1787: The Federalist Papers. These essays were written to convince the people to support the Constitution, and to respond to public criticisms.

> *Impeachment and removal of a duly elected President was not intended for policy disputes or poor administration of the State. Instead, the Framers had in mind the most serious of offenses: those against the public itself. **[Alexander] Hamilton** explained that impeachment was not designed to cover only statutory common law crimes but instead crimes against the body politic. **Hamilton** wrote: 'The subjects of its jurisdiction are those offenses which proceed from the misconduct of public men, or, in other words, from the abuse or violation of some public trust. They are of a nature which*

[33] David Lowenthal, The Past is a Foreign Country (1999).

> *may, with peculiar propriety, be denominated political, as they relate chiefly to injuries done immediately to the society itself.'* 166 Cong. Rec. S446 (daily ed. Jan. 22, 2020) (emphasis added).

Notice that **Rep. Schiff** (D-CA) has not cited the **text** of the Constitution (our first form or argument); he channels the past, 1787. Although a return to the past is generally associated with conservative legal thought, Rep. Schiff, a liberal Member of Congress, mentioned the "Framers" dozens of times in his opening speech. Borrowing from the Framers, Rep. Schiff underscored the nature of impeachment as a "political" rather than a criminal remedy:

> *As **James Wilson**—a delegate of the Constitutional Convention and a future Associate Justice of the Supreme Court—reasoned that impeachment "was confined to political characters, to political crimes and misdemeanors, and to political punishments." The Framers determined that punishment would be neither prison nor fines but, instead, limited to removal from office and disqualification from holding future office.* 166 Cong. Rec. S446 (daily ed. Jan. 22, 2020) (emphasis added).

Rep. Schiff (D-CA) invoked the Framers to explain the House Managers' theory of the text as focused on "high" crimes against the State:

> *The **Framers** chose to undertake impeachment for treason, bribery, or other high crimes and misdemeanors to underscore the requirement of an offense against society. In this phrase, "high" modifies both the crimes and the misdemeanors in that both relate to a high injustice, a transgression committed against the people and to the public trust. The Framers had two broad categories in mind: those actions that are facially permissible under the President's authority but are based on corrupt motives, such as seeking to obtain a personal benefit through public office, and those that far exceed the President's constitutional authority or violate the legal limits on that authority.* 166 Cong. Rec. S446 (daily ed. Jan.22, 2020) (emphasis added).

Rep. Schiff (D-CA) explained that impeachment and removal would protect the 2020 election. For the House Managers, the President had subverted the electoral process itself by asking for dirt on his political opponents. Again, using the Founders, Rep. Schiff explained:

> ***George Mason** noted at the Constitutional Convention that impeachment was a necessary tool because 'the man who has*

> *practiced corruption and by that means procured his appointment in the first instance' could seek to repeat his guilt.* 166 Cong. Rec. S454 (daily ed. Jan. 22, 2020).

In other words, if a President had obtained the Presidency by trickery or corrupt aid, he could perpetuate himself in office, unless impeachment allowed the people to remove him.

The House Managers recognized that the Founders debated impeachment at the Constitutional Convention of 1787. **Rep. Nadler** (D-NY) explained the debate:

> *The* ***Framers*** *were not naive. They knew that power corrupts * * * * [A] minority feared vesting any branch of government with the power to remove a President from office. They would have relied on elections alone to address rogue Presidents. But that view was decisively rejected at the Constitutional Convention. Convening in the shadow of rebellion and revolution, the* ***Framers*** *would not deny the Nation an escape from Presidents who deemed themselves above the law. Instead, they adopted the power of impeachment. In so doing, they offered a clear answer to* ***George Mason's*** *question: "Shall any man be above justice?" As* ***Mason*** *himself explained, "some mode of displacing an unfit magistrate is rendered indispensable by the fallibility of those who choose, as well as by the corrupt ability of the man chosen."* * * * *
>
> *But this decision raised a question: What conduct would justify impeachment and removal? * * * * Given the many threats they had to anticipate, the* ***Framers*** *considered extremely broad grounds for removing Presidents. For example, they debated setting the bar at maladministration, to allow removal for run-of-the-mill policy disagreements between Congress and the President. They also considered very narrow grounds, strictly limiting impeachment to treason and bribery. Ultimately, they struck a balance. They did not want Presidents removed for ordinary political or policy disagreements, but they intended impeachments to reach the full spectrum of Presidential misconduct that might threaten the Constitution, and they intended our Constitution to endure for the* ages. *They adopted a standard that meant, as* ***Mason*** *put it, to capture all manner of "great and dangerous offenses" incompatible with the Constitution.* 166 Cong. Rec. S489 (daily ed. Jan. 23, 2020) (emphasis added).

Finally, the House Managers emphasized in their Brief the Founders' concern with **foreign influence** in our elections:

> *The Framers particularly feared that* ***foreign influence*** *could undermine our new system of self-government. In his farewell address to the Nation, President George Washington warned Americans 'to be constantly awake, since history and experience prove that foreign influence is one of the most baneful foes of republican government.' Alexander Hamilton cautioned that the 'most deadly adversaries of republican government' may come 'chiefly from the desire in foreign powers to gain an improper ascendant in our councils.'* ***James Madison*** *worried that a future President could "betray his trust to foreign powers," which "might be fatal to the Republic." And, of particular relevance now, in their personal correspondence about 'foreign Interference,' Thomas Jefferson and John Adams discussed their apprehension that 'as often as Elections happen, the danger of foreign Influence recurs.'* 166 Cong. Rec. S292 (Jan. 21, 2020) (emphasis added).

B. The President's Lawyers' Arguments

President Trump invoked the Founders to argue that there should be a limited scope to the "High Crimes" Clause. The "abuse of power" charges leveled by the House encouraged a broad reading, rather than a narrow reading, of the constitutional language. The lawyers urged:

> *The* ***Framers*** *foresaw that the House might at times fall prey to tempestuous partisan tempers.* ***Alexander Hamilton*** *recognized that 'the persecution of an intemperate or designing majority in the House of Representatives' was a real danger in impeachments, and* ***Jefferson*** *acknowledged that impeachment provided 'the most formidable weapon for the purposes of dominant faction that ever was contrived.' That is why the* ***Framers*** *entrusted the trial of impeachments to the Senate. As Justice Story explained, the Framers saw the Senate as a tribunal 'removed from popular power and passions * * * * and from the more dangerous influence of mere party spirit,' and guided by 'a deep responsibility to future times.' Now, perhaps as never before, it is essential for the Senate to fulfill the role* ***Hamilton*** *envisioned for it as a 'guard[ ] against the danger of persecution, from the prevalency of a factious spirit' in the House.* President's Brief, 166 Cong. Rec. S316

(daily ed. Jan. 21, 2020) (citations omitted) (emphasis added).

The President's lawyers also drew lessons from the **drafting history** of the "High Crimes" Clause, which they argued limited impeachment to existing crimes. Specifically, the Founders rejected a standard that included **maladministration**, crossing out that term and inserting "other high crimes and misdemeanors."

> *[T]he **Records of the Constitutional Convention** also make clear that, in important respects, the **Framers** intended the scope of impeachable offenses under the Constitution to be much narrower than under English practice. When the **draft Constitution** had limited the grounds for impeachment to 'Treason, or bribery,' **George Mason** argued that the provision was too narrow because '[a]ttempts to subvert the Constitution may not be Treason' and that the clause 'will not reach many great and dangerous offenses.' He proposed the addition of 'maladministration,' which had been a ground for impeachment in English practice. **Madison** opposed that change on the ground that '[s]o vague a term" would make the President subject to 'a tenure during [the] pleasure of the Senate,'[34] and the Convention agreed on adding 'other high crimes & misdemeanors' instead. By rejecting "maladministration," the **Framers** significantly narrowed impeachment under the Constitution and made clear that mere differences of opinion, unpopular policy decisions, or perceived misjudgments cannot constitutionally be used as the basis for impeachment.* President's Brief, 166 Cong. Rec. S316 (daily ed. Jan. 21, 2020) (citations omitted) (emphasis added).
>
> *Indeed, at various earlier points during the **Convention**, drafts of the Constitution had included as grounds for impeachment "malpractice or neglect of duty" and "neglect of duty [and] malversation," but the **Framers** rejected all of these formulations. The ratification debates confirmed the point that differences of opinion or differences over policy could not justify impeachment. **James Iredell** warned delegates to North Carolina's **ratifying convention** that "[a] mere difference of opinion might be interpreted, by the malignity of party, into a deliberate, wicked action," and*

---

[34] Madison is saying that the President's term in office will depend upon whether the Senate votes to impeach, and implying that giving the Senate this power was not appropriate since the whole people choose the President. Framers, like Madison, who came from large states feared the power of small states in the Senate.

> *thus should not provide the basis for impeachment. And* ***Edmund Randolph*** *pointed out in the Virginia* ***ratifying convention*** *that "[n]o man ever thought of impeaching a man for an opinion."* Presidents' Brief, 166 Cong. Rec. S316–17 (daily ed. Jan. 21, 2020) (citations omitted) (emphasis added).

The President's lawyers also invoked a British legal scholar: William Blackstone. In the President's Brief, the lawyers wrote that the Founders limited the "High Crimes" Clause to violations of **existing law based on Blackstone's view**.

> *[H]igh Crimes and Misdemeanors" had a technical meaning in English law, and there is evidence that the Framers were aware of this "limited," "technical meaning." In England, "high Crimes and Misdemeanors" referred to offenses that could be the subject of impeachment in parliament. No less an authority than Blackstone, however, made clear that "an impeachment before the lords by the commons of Great Britain, in parliament, is* ***a prosecution of the already known and established law****. As a result, nothing in the Constitution's use of the term "other high Crimes and Misdemeanors" suggests that impeachment under the Constitution could reach anything other than a known offense defined in existing law*. President's Brief, 166 Cong. Rec. S316 (Jan. 21, 2020) (citations omitted).

Finally, the President's lawyers urged that the House Managers' "abuse" theory was vague and rested upon the "subjective state of mind" of the President. We will return to the "subjectivity" question below.

> *House Democrats' novel conception of "abuse of power" as a supposedly impeachable offense is constitutionally defective. It supplants the* ***Framers' standard*** *of "high Crimes and Misdemeanors" with a made-up theory that the President can be impeached and removed from office under an amorphous and undefined standard of "abuse of power." The Framers adopted a standard that requires a violation of established law to state an impeachable offense. By contrast, in their Articles of Impeachment, House Democrats have not even attempted to identify any law that was violated.*
>
> *House Democrats cannot salvage their unprecedented "abuse of power" standard with fuzzy claims that* ***the Framers*** *particularly intended impeachment to address "foreign entanglements" and "corruption of elections." Those assertions are makeweights that* ***distort history*** *and add*

no legitimacy to the radical theory of impeachment based on subjective motive alone. Under the Constitution, impeachable offenses must be defined under established law. And they must be based on objective wrongdoing, not supposed subjective motives dreamt up by a hostile faction in the House and superimposed onto a President's entirely lawful conduct. President's Brief, 166 Cong. Rec. S318 (daily ed. Jan. 21, 2020) (citations omitted) (emphasis added).

QUESTIONS: THE FOUNDERS

Projection of the Present onto the Past: Pat Cipollone, the President's Chief Counsel, urged the Senate not to disrupt an upcoming election and to "let the people decide for themselves. That is what the **Founders** wanted." 166 Cong. Rec. S. 578 (daily ed. Jan. 25, 2020). The House Managers made similar comments that the Founders would have wanted Donald Trump impeached. Of course, the Founders, living in 1787, could hardly have imagined the modern presidency of Donald Trump. Historical argument creates risks that the interpreter will confuse the present with the past. Because we want a particular result, we project that result on the Founders: we impose on the Founders what we view today as correct. When invoking the Founders, best practice quotes *their* words in full historical context. Best practice also does not pick and choose Founders' quotes. For example, Professor Dershowitz quoted one Founder, Gouverneur Morris, for the proposition that there had to be a precise offense, but Morris ultimately changed his view.[35] Finally, some have rightly questioned whether the Founders themselves would have wanted future generations to be bound by their views, particularly since they chose to make their deliberations secret and anticipated that much would change if America survived.[36]

Ratifiers v. Framers: Constitutional scholars debate whether the proper perspective is that of the Framers or the Ratifiers. (I have used the word "Founders" to cover both). The Framers were a small group of prominent men who drafted the Constitution over the steamy summer of 1787. After that, the Ratifiers assembled in state conventions in every colony to debate and vote on whether to adopt the Constitution. Who should count more: the Framers or the Ratifiers? Since the Framers wanted their debate secret, the Ratifiers, whose deliberations were public, may be a sounder source of meaning. Of course, like the Framers, the Ratifiers expressed many different views. For example, the President's lawyers cited James Iredell's statements, but Iredell also stated that a President who provided false information to the Senate could be impeachable.[37] How is one to resolve such matters? One way

---

[35] William M. Treanor, *Trump's Attorneys Have Butchered A Crucial Founder's Take on Impeachment*, Washington Post (Jan. 20, 2020) https://www.washingtonpost.com/outlook/2020/01/31/trumps-attorneys-have-butchered-crucial-founders-take-impeachment/.

[36] H. Jefferson Powell, *The Original Understanding of Original Intent*, 98 Harv. L. Rev. 885, 887–88 (1985).

[37] Michael J. Gerhardt, The Federal Impeachment Process 19 (1996) (quoting Iredell).

may be to settle, at the least, what views were widely held across sectional or other interest. That would become the baseline: here, that impeachment required a very serious charge, and that maladministration was not enough.

Drafting History v. Individual Commentary: The House Managers and the President invoked the drafting history of the "High Crimes" Clause. By "drafting history," I mean the changes in words that led to the precise language: the words "other high crimes and misdemeanors." Both sides agreed that the history showed that the Constitutional Convention had rejected impeachments driven by policy disputes. Originally, the Clause had included impeachment for acts like maladministration.[38] At the end of the Convention, the Founders replaced previous formulations with the term "high crimes and misdemeanors." Scholars believe that this was a term of art taken from British practice.[39] Query whether drafting history provides sounder evidence than statements by drafters or ratifiers about their particular interpretation of the text. In related fields, it is often said that changes in actual language prove more reliable indicators of meaning than relying upon a curated or selective choice of quotations from drafters. But, in this case, does this resolve much?

The Dead Hand Problem: One of the sturdiest arguments against invoking the Founders is the so-called "dead hand" problem. Why should a 21st Century American be bound by an entirely alien society with entirely alien values (they condoned slavery and imagined women's legal existence dissolved into their husbands', for example). References to the Founders have gone in and out of fashion in American law. In the 1970s and 1980s, for example, the Founders' views were considered outmoded. Today, however, it is doubtful that a Supreme Court opinion on a novel question, even by the so-called "liberal" Justices, would not invoke the Founders.[40] For those who wonder why we should turn back the clock, consider that we as a nation of immigrants are always looking for standards upon which we can agree. Although "cultish" devotion to 1787 surely seems wrong,[41] particularly since the Founders' America looked so very different from America's contemporary visage, remember that even the abolitionists—including Black theorists of the Constitution—have sought to understand our Founding, as part of a collective American tradition, linking American identity across generations.[42] Perhaps this explains why modern legal scholars have attempted to advance views that marry liberal and conservative traditions.[43]

Subjective Theory of Impeachment: The President's lawyers argued that the Founders would not countenance an impeachment based on the "subjective motives" of a President. That was misleading in some respects.

---

[38] Charles Doyle, Cong. Research Serv., 98-894A, Impeachment Grounds: Part 2: Selected Constitutional Convention Materials 4 (1998).

[39] Frank O. Bowman III, High Crimes and Misdemeanors: A History of Impeachment for the Age of Trump (2019).

[40] *See, e.g.*, *NLRB v. Noel Canning*, 573 U.S. 513, 533–34 (2014).

[41] Mary Anne Franks, The Cult of the Constitution (2019).

[42] For a modern version of this, *see* Danielle S. Allen, Our Declaration: A Reading of the Declaration of Independence in Defense of Equality (2015).

[43] *See, e.g.*, Jack Balkin, Living Originalism (2014).

As a general principle of criminal law, one cannot be convicted for a "mental state" alone. Imagine, for example, that you want to rob Tiffany's. You think that you will rob Tiffany's. That's not a crime. You have to *actually* rob (or at least try to rob) Tiffany's, not just think about it, to be prosecuted. Ask yourself whether the House Managers were relying on something subjective, meaning inside the President's head. The House Managers relied upon actual transcripts of a phone call between President Trump and Ukrainian President Zelensky, among other evidence, and no one disputed that the President had asked for a favor involving his political rival. Is the transcript of the call "in someone's head," or is it recorded on a piece of paper?

IV. PAST PRECEDENT

Precedent means prior examples. Lawyers aim for consistency and one of the surest ways to maintain consistency is by following past behavior in similar circumstances. If I want to cook a great meal, I look at my latest culinary successes to find a proper recipe. Courts refer to their past decisions—what lawyers call precedents—for guidance in future cases. Most law students learn to reason from prior precedents in their first year in law school, typically by reading court decisions. But courts are not the only institutions that rely upon precedent. *All of our major government institutions employ this kind of reasoning.* Presidents look to prior presidential precedents. So, too, Congress looks to prior legislative precedents. In most constitutional cases, the courts rely upon precedent to maintain consistency in law and check their tendency to engage in motivated, or biased, reasoning—reasoning that justifies, after the fact, a mind that was already made up, before looking to the evidence.

In the First Trump Impeachment case, Congress could look to three prior presidential impeachment inquiries. The House impeached and the Senate tried President **Andrew Johnson** in 1868 and President **William Clinton** in 1999. In 1974, the House opened a formal impeachment inquiry into Richard Nixon and drafted Articles of Impeachment, but he resigned before the House could approve the Articles and the Senate could conduct a trial. Other precedents included the Senate's history of impeaching judges and prior British impeachment practice.

A. The House Managers' Arguments

Rep. Nadler (D-NY) argued that the past precedents of the Nixon and Clinton cases did not depend upon a "statutory" violation or common crime. At the end of the Chapter, we will look at the Nixon Articles of Impeachment and you can judge for yourself.

> *The House Judiciary Committee approved three Articles of Impeachment against President Nixon. Each of them encompassed many acts that did not violate Federal law.*

One of the articles—obstruction of Congress—involved no allegations of any legal violation. It is worth reflecting on why President Nixon was forced to resign. Most Americans are familiar with the story. The House Judiciary Committee approved Articles of Impeachment in July 1974. Those articles passed with bipartisan support, although most Republicans stood by President Nixon.

Then the smoking gun tape came out. Within a week, almost everyone who supported the President the week before changed his position, and the President was forced to resign because of what was revealed on the smoking gun tape. Within a week, Senator Goldwater and others from the Senate went to the President and said: You won't have a single vote in the Senate. You must resign, or you will be removed from office because of the evidence on the smoking gun tape.

But what was on the smoking gun tape? The smoking gun tape had recordings of President Nixon's instructing White House officials to pressure the CIA and the FBI to end the Watergate investigation. No law explicitly prohibited that conversation—it was not, in that sense, a crime—but President Nixon had abused his power. He had tried to use two government agencies—the FBI and the CIA—for his personal benefit. His impeachment and removal were certain, and he announced his resignation within days.

Decades later, in President Clinton's case, the Judiciary Committee's report on the Articles of Impeachment stated: "The actions of President Clinton do not have to rise to the level of violating the federal statute regarding obstruction of justice in order to justify impeachment." There is, thus, overwhelming authority against restricting impeachments to violations of established or statutory law. 166 Cong. Rec. S493 (daily ed. Jan. 23, 2020).

Rep. Nadler (D-NY) went on to defend the claim that "abuse of power" had been charged in prior impeachments:

But the Nixon case also exemplifies the second way a President can abuse his power. President Nixon faced two more Articles of Impeachment. Both of these articles charged him with abusing the powers of his office with corrupt intent. One focused on his abuse of power to obstruct law enforcement. The other targeted his abuse of power to target political opponents. Each article enumerated specific abuses by President Nixon, many of which involved the wrongful, corrupt exercise of Presidential power and many of which were likely not statutory crimes.

In explaining its second article, the House Judiciary Committee stated that President Nixon's conduct was "undertaken for his personal political advantage and not in furtherance of any valid national policy objective." That should sound familiar to everyone here. It reflects the standard I have already articulated: the exercise of official power to corruptly obtain a personal benefit while ignoring or injuring the national interest. 166 Cong. Rec. S490 (daily ed. Jan. 23, 2020).

Similarly, the House Managers' brief explains:

American ***precedent*** *confirms that the Impeachment Clause is not confined to a statutory code. The articles of impeachment against* ***President Nixon*** *turned on his abuse of power, rather than on his commission of a statutory offense. Many of the specific allegations set forth in those three articles did not involve any crimes. Instead, the House Judiciary Committee emphasized that President Nixon's conduct was "undertaken for his own personal political advantage and not in furtherance of any valid national policy objective"—and expressly stated that his abuses of power warranted removal regardless whether they violated a specific statute.* House Managers Brief, 166 Cong. Rec. S372 (daily ed. Jan. 21, 2020).

Previous impeachments *were in accord. In* ***1912****, for example, Judge Archbald was impeached and convicted for using his position to generate business deals with potential litigants in his court, even though this behavior had not been shown to violate any then-existing statute or laws regulating judges. The House Manager in the Archbald impeachment asserted that "[t]he decisions of the Senate of the United States, of the various State tribunals which have jurisdiction over impeachment cases, and of the Parliament of England all agree that an offense, in order to be impeachable, need not be indictable either at common law or under* any statute." *As early as* ***1803****, Judge Pickering was impeached and then removed from office by the Senate for refusing to allow an appeal, declining to hear witnesses, and appearing on the bench while intoxicated and thereby "degrading the honor and dignity of the United States."* House Managers Brief, 166 Cong. Rec. S372 (daily ed. Jan. 21, 2020) (emphasis added).

The House Managers referred to a long history of scholarly and judicial writings to support their arguments about these precedents. Judges do not consider scholarly writings as precedential, but such writings are evidence of experts' understanding of then existing precedents.

> *President Trump's argument conflicts with a long history of scholarly consensus, including among "some of the most distinguished members of the [Constitutional] convention." As a leading early treatise on the Constitution explained, impeachable offenses "are not necessarily offences against the general laws * * * * [for] [i]t is often found that offences of a very serious nature by high officers are not offences against the criminal code, but consist in abuses or betrayals of trust, or inexcusable neglects of duty." In his influential 1833 treatise, Supreme Court Justice Joseph Story similarly explained that impeachment encompasses "misdeeds * * * * as peculiarly injure the commonwealth by the abuse of high offices of trust," whether or not those misdeeds violate existing statutes intended for other circumstances. Story observed that the focus was not "crimes of a strictly legal character," but instead "what are aptly termed, political offences, growing out of personal mis-conduct, or gross neglect, or usurpation, or habitual disregard of the public interests, in the discharge of the duties of political office."* House Managers Brief, 166 Cong. Rec. S372 (daily ed. Jan. 21, 2020) (citations omitted).

The House Managers also invoked prior **British precedent**, practice that informed their view of "high crimes and misdemeanors."

> *This standard, borrowed from the British Parliament, was "high Crimes and Misdemeanors." In England, the standard was understood to capture offenses against the constitutional system itself. That is confirmed by the use of the word "high," as well as by parliamentary practice. From 1376 to 1787, the House of Commons impeached officials on a few general grounds—mainly consisting of abuse of power, betrayal of national security and foreign policy, corruption, treason, bribery, and disregarding the powers of Parliament. The phrase "high Crimes and Misdemeanors" thus covered offenses against the Nation itself—in other words, crimes against the British Constitution.* 166 Cong. Rec. S489 (Jan. 23, 2020) (statement of Rep. Nadler).

B. The President's Lawyers' Arguments

The President's lawyers emphasized that President Clinton's impeachment, for committing perjury related to an extra-marital affair, did allege an ordinary crime. **Mr. Robert Ray**, attorney for the President, invoked this **past precedent**, along with the **precedent** of Andrew Johnson's impeachment, to emphasize a high standard for impeachment:

> *Professor Akhil Amar of Yale Law School made largely the same point during the Clinton impeachment about the danger presented through Presidential impeachment of transforming an entire branch of government: "When they remove a duly elected President, they undo the votes of millions of ordinary Americans on Election Day. This is not something that Senators should do lightly, lest we slide toward a kind of parliamentary government that our entire structure of government was designed to repudiate."* 166 Cong. Rec. S605 (daily ed. Jan. 27, 2020).
>
> *In hammering home the constitutional uniqueness of Presidential impeachments, he emphasized the case of Richard Nixon and distinguished it from Andrew Johnson; that is to say, only when extremely high crimes and gross abuses of official power indeed pose a threat to our basic constitutional system, a threat as high and truly as malignant to democratic government as treason and bribery, he reasoned, would the Senate ever be justified in nullifying the votes of millions of Americans and removing a President from office. Id.*
>
> *My point is this: History—our American history—matters. To listen to how the House managers would have it, Articles of Impeachment are merely—as Chuck Ruff*[44] *warned a generation ago—empty vessels into which can be poured any number of charges, even those considered and abandoned. Id.*
>
> *At least in the case of President Clinton's impeachment, the articles actually charged crimes. The Senate thereafter determined, by its vote in that case, in effect, that while those crimes—perjury and obstruction of justice—may have been committed, those crimes were not high enough crimes damaging to the body politic to warrant the President's removal from office. Id.*

---

[44] Chuck Ruff was President Clinton's impeachment lawyer.

The President's lawyers further argued that the "*House Democrats' theory also has no grounding in the history of presidential impeachments.*" President's Brief, 166 Cong. Rec. S319 (daily ed. Jan. 21, 2020).

> *Until now, the House of Representatives has never impeached a President of the United States without alleging a violation of law—indeed, a crime. The articles of impeachment against President Clinton specified charges of perjury and obstruction of justice, both felonies under federal law. In the Nixon impeachment inquiry, the articles approved by the House Judiciary Committee accused the President of obstructing justice, among multiple other violations of the law. And as explained above, the impeachment of President Johnson provides the clearest evidence that a presidential impeachment requires alleged violations of existing law. When the House Judiciary Committee recommended impeaching Johnson in 1867 based on allegations that included no violations of law, the House rejected the recommendation. A majority in the House was persuaded by the arguments of the minority on the Judiciary Committee, who argued that "[t]he House of Representatives may impeach a civil officer, but it must be done according to law. It must be for some offence known to the law, and not created by the fancy of the members of the House." Congress did not impeach President Johnson until the following year, when he was impeached for violating the Tenure of Office Act. The history of presidential impeachments provides no support for House Democrats' vague "abuse of power" charge.* President's Brief, 166 Cong. Rec. S319 (daily ed. Jan. 21, 2020).

> *In the Nixon impeachment inquiry, none of the articles recommended by the House Judiciary Committee was labeled "abuse of power" or framed the charge in those terms. And it is simply wrong to say that the theory underlying the proposed articles was that President Nixon had taken permissible actions with the wrong subjective motives. Article I alleged President Nixon obstructed justice, a clear violation of law. And Article II asserted numerous breaches of the law. It claimed that President Nixon "violat[ed] the constitutional rights of citizens," "contraven[ed] the laws governing agencies of the executive branch," and "authorized and permitted to be maintained a secret investigative unit within the office of the President * * * * which unlawfully utilized the resources of the Central Intelligence Agency, [and] engaged in covert and unlawful activities." Those*

allegations did not turn on describing permissible conduct that had simply been done with the wrong subjective motives. Instead, they charged unlawful conduct. Id. at S320.

House Democrats' reliance on the Johnson impeachment fares no better. According to House Democrats, the Johnson impeachment supports their concocted impeachment-based-on-subjective-motives theory under the following tortured logic: The articles of impeachment actually adopted by the House charged the violation of the Tenure of Office Act. But that was not the "real" reason the House sought to remove President Johnson. The real reason was that he had undermined Reconstruction. Id.

Finally, and with some force, the President's lawyers argued that relying upon the impeachment of judges was an improper precedent because the Presidency differs:

The President's unique role in the constitutional structure sets him apart and warrants more rigorous standards for impeachment. "When Senators remove one of a thousand federal judges (or even one of nine justices), they are not transforming an entire branch of government. But that is exactly what happens when they oust America's one and only President, in whom all executive power is vested by the first sentence of Article II." President's Brief, 166 Cong. Rec. S317 (daily ed. Jan. 21, 2020).

QUESTIONS: PAST PRECEDENT

Conflicting Claims About Precedent: Notice that the House Managers and the President's lawyers invoked the same precedents but interpreted them differently. The House Managers argued that "The articles of impeachment against President Nixon turned on his abuse of power, rather than on his commission of a statutory offense." House Managers Brief, 166 Cong. Rec. S372 (daily ed. January 21, 2020). The President's lawyers argued that the Nixon impeachment involved a crime, obstructing justice. President's Brief, 166 Cong. Rec. S319 (daily ed. Jan. 21, 2020). (Obstruction of justice is a crime). One set of lawyers seems to be saying the Nixon impeachment failed the criminal law test; the other that it satisfied the criminal law test (assuming for argument's sake, and contrary to a good deal of opinion, that the crime test applies). To check on these claims, consider Appendix A and B to this Chapter, which reprint the Nixon and Clinton Impeachment Articles.

Judges v. Presidents as Precedents: Past impeachments of judges outnumber presidential impeachments. Since the impeachment of U.S. District Judge John Pickering in 1803, fifteen federal judges have been impeached and eight have been removed.[45] The House Managers invoked these impeachments to suggest that judges had been impeached for misconduct not amounting to a crime. The President's lawyers argued that the analogy failed: impeaching one judge did not bring down an entire branch of government. But is that accurate? Does impeaching the President bring down the executive branch, filled with as many as 2 million civilian employees? If Congress impeaches the President, then the Vice President (also elected by the American people) takes office. Is it really clear that an impeachment is undoing an election? Should precedent about judges count for or against impeaching a President?

British Experience v. American Precedents: Both the President's lawyers and the House Managers invoked the British impeachment experience. Historians agree that the British practice permitted impeachments that were not based on indictable crimes and that the Constitutional Convention chose the term "high crimes and misdemeanors," as a legal term of art borrowed from British practice.[46] History tells us, as well, that during the Constitutional Convention, the British Parliament was impeaching a well-known figure, Warren Hastings. Parliament impeached Hastings for something other than a crime, and the Framers knew of the impeachment.[47] Notice that the House Managers and the President wanted to reject some British precedent and accept other British precedent: the President's lawyers wanted to assert Blackstone's view that an existing law was necessary, but distance themselves from British impeachments that did not involve crimes. By contrast, the House Managers wanted to reject Blackstone's view (an existing law is necessary) but rely upon British practice (a crime is not necessary).

Should the British experience determine the meaning of the American Constitution? In many ways, the British Constitution is quite the opposite of the American Constitution. The British had a parliamentary system in which elected officials preserved the independence of parliament through a variety of means including impeachment. (On the parliamentary system's differences, *see* Chapter 2). In America, the Founders began with the idea of having the President elected by the Congress, but rejected a system that would have looked a good deal more like a parliamentary democracy. They also rejected the idea of a King. If this is true, how relevant is the British practice and how relevant are the opinions of a British commentator like Blackstone, who had to have been writing about British practice, not the new American Constitution?[48] As former Judge and now Professor Michael McConnell has recently shown, the American presidency differs in

---

[45] *Impeachment of Federal Judges*, Federal Judicial Center (Sept. 16, 2020), https://www.fjc.gov/history/judges/impeachments-federal-judges.

[46] Frank O. Bowman III, High Crimes and Misdemeanors: A History of Impeachment for the Age of Trump 45–49 (2019).

[47] Raoul Berger, Impeachment: The Constitutional Problems 351 (1973) ("Hastings was charged with governing 'arbitrarily,' the classic impeachable offense").

[48] *See generally* John Manning, *Textualism and the Equity of the Statute*, 101 Colum. L. Rev. 1 (2001) (arguing that the shift from the British system to a separation of powers system was a fundamental shift away from British legal practice).

substantial respect from the prerogative powers of a British King.[49] Moreover, some practices of the British system, namely the "Bill of Attainder" were expressly rejected in the American system. U.S. Const. Article I § 9, cl. 3. That the words "high crime" and "misdemeanor" were quite clearly borrowed from British practice, does not necessarily tell us how impeachment was to operate in America's *novus ordo seclorum* (new secular order).

Colonial Precedents: Although neither the House Managers nor the President's lawyers made much of the colonial experience, it is pretty clear that those who went to the Constitutional Convention or the ratifying conventions did know of such practices. The colonies did use impeachment, and states had constitutional provisions allowing officers to be impeached. Precise state constitutional terms varied, but the practice supports the view that an impeached official did not have to commit a crime. Professor Frank O. Bowman III has exhaustively researched colonial impeachments, and cataloged all of the early state constitutional provisions on impeachment.[50] He provides examples of what he calls early impeachments that were "in the purest sense political," meaning that impeachment was based on allegations that carried "no tincture of ordinary criminality or even technical violation of law."[51] His catalog of state constitutional provisions shows that the states varied in their language in interesting ways. For example, a number of states allowed for impeachment based on misconduct or maladministration or "misbehaviour," a very broad standard. Many also referred to "corrupt" conduct. The only states that referred to anything like crime referred to "state criminals" or "offending against the State" which Bowman reads as "official conduct presenting a danger to the fundamental interests of the state."[52] On the other hand, since the Founders believed that the states' constitutional structures should not be repeated in the federal government, how relevant are the state impeachment standards?

The Andrew Johnson Impeachment as Precedent: President Trump's lawyers invoked arguments made by President Andrew Johnson's lawyers. President Johnson ascended to the Presidency after the Civil War and the assassination of Abraham Lincoln. Today, many believe that the real reason for his impeachment was that Johnson refused to "reconstruct" the post-Civil War South to achieve equality between whites and formerly enslaved persons, contrary to the desires of the Congress. For example, Johnson made many rather pointed public statements to the effect that he was not bound by the Congress's policies. To quote Professor Nikolas Bowie's pungent description of Johnson:

---

49 Michael W. McConnell, The President Who Would Not Be King: Executive Power under the Constitution 54 (2020). McConnell argues that the standard kingly prerogative powers were divided between the President and Congress.

50 Frank O. Bowman III, High Crimes and Misdemeanors: A History of Impeachment for the Age of Trump ch. 3 (2019); *see id.* 68–72 (comparing language in the state constitutions).

51 *Id.* at 64.

52 *Id.* at 71.

> A white supremacist from Tennessee, President Johnson frequently clashed with members of Congress over what he termed "nigger equality." President Johnson vetoed civil rights laws. He accused senators of plotting with members of his Administration to undermine his policies. And at campaign rallies across the Midwest, President Johnson drew jeers and laughter by issuing "loud threats and bitter menaces" against a Congress whose commitment to helping black people he regarded as "Radical."[53]

The actual charges against Johnson involved some claims that involved a statute, but others that did not. For example, the Articles claimed that he had engaged in "harangues" against the Congress. Johnson's lawyers argued these charges were not an impeachable offense because there was no law against presidential speeches.[54] The Trump lawyers argued that some "law" was required. (For more on this, *see* the note at the end of this Chapter on the Bill of Attainder and Ex Post Facto clauses). These arguments help to explain why the Congress, in the First Trump Impeachment, argued that withholding aid to Ukraine violated a law known as the Impoundment Control Act.[55] As did Johnson before him, President Trump claimed the alleged statutory violation was irrelevant because the underlying statute was unconstitutional.[56]

Unfair Surprise and Self-Dealing: Was President Trump unfairly surprised by the first impeachment? Typically, ignorance of the law is no defense to a crime or civil sanction; just because you don't know the specifics of a law does not mean that you cannot go to jail or be required to pay a fine. But there are limits to which the Congress can sanction what everyone considers innocent behavior. Was the President simply caught unaware? In Trump's case, consider the fact that he took an oath to "take care" of the laws. Constitutional scholars from right and left have maintained that the President is a "fiduciary," or a trustee, representing all citizens, not just those who voted for him.[57] Fiduciary concepts are ubiquitous in business law. What if you knew that the average businessman knew that he could not divert his company's money for his personal benefit? Would that influence

---

[53] Nikolas Bowie, *High Crimes Without Law*, 132 Harv. L. Rev. F. 59, 59 (2018).

[54] Johnson was also charged with violating the Tenure of Office Act when he tried to fire the Secretary of War. Nikolas Bowie, *High Crimes Without Law*, 132 Harv. L. Rev. F. 59, 60 (2018) (stating that the Tenure of Office act was a "criminal" prohibition). The Act did provide criminal penalties, calling its violation a "high misdemeanor," suggesting that it was passed precisely to prepare for an impeachment. Johnson argued that the statute was unconstitutional because it granted too much power to the Senate and history has proven him correct. *Myers v. United States*, 272 U.S. 52 (1926).

[55] Government Accountability Office, Decision No. B-331564 (Jan. 16, 2020).

[56] Alan M. Dershowitz, *Trump Had Right to Withhold Ukraine Funds: GAO is Wrong*, Gatestone Inst. (Jan. 17, 2020), https://www.gatestoneinstitute.org/15462/trump-had-right-to-withhold-ukraine-funds-gao-is ("to the extent that [the Impoundment Control Act] constrains the power of the president to conduct foreign policy, it is unconstitutional").

[57] Gary Lawson & Guy Seidman, A Great Power of Attorney: Understanding the Fiduciary Constitution (2017).

your thoughts about the unfair surprise argument given Mr. Trump's past history in business?

V. FUTURE PRECEDENT

Judges worry about their rulings' future—how will their decision affect similar cases? So, too, in the First Trump Impeachment, Members of Congress worried about how the legal standard for impeachment they adopted would affect future impeachments. As the President's lawyers explained: "Whatever **precedent** is set, whatever this body accepts now as a permissible way to bring an impeachment proceeding and to bring it to this Chamber becomes the new normal." 166 Cong. Rec. S591 (daily ed. Jan. 27, 2020) (statement of Mr. Philbin) (emphasis added). On the other side of the coin, the House Managers argued that failure to impeach would authorize future Presidents to abuse their power and render the Congress helpless to bring them to account. They also predicted that the President, if unimpeached, would cheat in the 2020 election. As we now know, of course, President Trump did attack the 2020 election as a fraud leading to the Second Trump Impeachment based on the January 6, 2021 assault on the Nation's Capitol.

A. The House Managers' Arguments

The House Managers spoke openly about the **precedent** they were creating for future presidential action and future impeachments. They emphasized harm to the Congress—and its power to check and balance the President—if there was no impeachment.

> *A vote against the Articles of Impeachment will set a* ***dangerous precedent****. It will be used by future Presidents to act with impunity. Given what we know—that the President abused his power in office by attempting to extort a foreign government to interfere with an American election; that he willfully obstructed justice at every turn; and that his actions run counter to our Nation's most cherished and fundamental values—it is clear the President betrayed the trust the American public placed in him to fully execute his constitutional responsibilities.* 166 Cong. Rec. S931 (daily ed. Feb. 5, 2020) (statement of Rep. Schiff) (emphasis added).

Rep. Schiff (D-CA) made a similar point in his opening remarks that failure to convict would embolden future Presidents and make it harder for Congress to check a President bent on election interference.

> ***What message*** *will we send if we choose not to hold this President accountable for his abuse of power to solicit reelection interference in our upcoming election? The misconduct undertaken by this President may lead future Presidents to believe that they, too, can use the substantial power conferred on them by the Constitution in order to undermine it. Nothing could weaken the integrity of our elections more* * * * * 166 Cong. Rec. S455 (daily ed. Jan. 22, 2020) (emphasis added).

Rep. Garcia (D-TX) continued in the same vein:

> *If we allow this gross abuse of power to continue, this President will have free rein to abuse his control of U.S. foreign policy for personal interests and so would any other future President. Then this President and all Presidents become above the law. A President could take the powers of the greatest office in this land and use those powers not for the country, not for the American people but for him or herself. I ask you to make sure this does not happen because, in this country, no one—no one—is above the law.* 166 Cong. Rec. S519 (daily ed. Jan. 23, 2020).

B. The President's Lawyers' Arguments

The President's lawyers urged that "abuse of power" was too vague and would allow, in future cases, impeachment for policy disputes or maladministration.

> *One of the greatest issues—and perhaps the greatest issue—for your consideration in this case is how the* ***precedent*** *set in this case will affect the future. The Framers recognized that there would be partisan and illegitimate impeachments. In Federalist No. 65, Hamilton expressly warned about impeachments that reflected what he called "the persecution of an intemperate or designing majority in the House of Representatives." That is exactly what this case presents.* * * * * *One of the essential questions here is, Will the [Senate] adopt a standard for impeachment—a diluted standard—that fundamentally disrupts, damages, and alters the separation of powers in our constitutional structure of government?* * * * *
>
> *I will close with a quotation from one of the Republican Senators who crossed the aisle and voted against convicting President Andrew Johnson during his impeachment trial. It was Lyman Trumbull who I think explained the great principle that applies here. He said: "Once [we] set the example of impeaching a President for what, when the*

> *excitement of the hour shall have subsided will be regarded as insufficient causes, no future President will be safe* * * * * *and what then becomes of the checks and balances of the constitution, so carefully devised and so vital to its perpetuity? They are all gone.* 166 Cong. Rec. S595 (daily ed. Jan. 27, 2020) (statement of Mr. Philbin).

> *Danger, danger, danger. To lower the bar of impeachment based on these articles of impeachment would impact the functioning of our constitutional Republic and the framework of that Constitution for generations.* 116 Cong. Rec. S621 (daily ed. Jan. 28, 2020) (statement of Mr. Sekulow).

Professor Dershowitz, on behalf of **the President's lawyers**, emphasized the improper precedent this would set:

> *For the Senate to remove a duly-elected President on vague, nonconstitutional grounds, such as abuse of power or obstruction of Congress, would create a dangerous* ***precedent*** *and "be construed," in the words of Senator James N. Grimes, "into approval of impeachment as part of future political machinery." This is a realistic threat to all future Presidents who serve with opposing legislative majorities that could easily concoct vague charges of abuse or obstruction. The fact that a long list of Presidents who were accused of abuse of power were not impeached demonstrates how selectively this term has and can be used in the context of impeachment.*

> *I am sorry, House managers, you just picked the wrong criteria. You picked the most dangerous possible criteria to serve as a* ***precedent*** *for how we supervise and oversee* ***future Presidents****. The idea of abuse of power and obstruction of Congress are so far from what the Framers had in mind that they so clearly violate the Constitution and would place Congress above the law.* 166 Cong. Rec. S616 (daily ed. Jan. 27, 2020) (emphasis added).

> *[H]ow you vote on this case will serve as a* ***precedent*** *for how other Senators of different parties, different backgrounds, and different perspectives vote in future cases.* * * * * *As Justice Curtis said during the trial of Andrew Johnson, a greater principle is at stake than the fate of any particular President. The* ***fate of future Presidents*** *of different parties and policies is also at stake, as is the fate of our constitutional system. The passions and fears of the*

moment must not blind us to our past and to our future. Id. at S617.

QUESTIONS: FUTURE PRECEDENT

Precedents, Hypotheticals, and Predicting the Future: Lawyers ask hypothetical questions to test a principle's limits: What if the President invited a foreign enemy to invade the United States? Surely that would be impeachable, but no ordinary criminal law bars that, urged the House Managers.[58] Hypotheticals imagine a possible universe, one which may or may not happen. Remember as you consider these claims that the First Trump Impeachment will be a precedent for all future impeachments. But imagining its future effect at the time seemed something akin to guess-work. No one, at the time, is likely to have predicted a Second Trump Impeachment.

Implicit, and Questionable, Causal Claims: Is it really true that a vague impeachment standard would lead to more impeachments? The President's lawyers argued it would. Actual presidential impeachments have been extremely rare in American history—a mere 4 trials in two centuries. Does the rarity have much to do with the legal standard? Consider a different explanation: the difficulty of the process. Remember, a President can only be impeached if a majority of the House of Representatives (218 men and women) agree that he should be removed from office. Many a time, Members have called for Presidents to be impeached. They called for President Franklin Roosevelt's impeachment and President Eisenhower's; President Carter's and President Reagan's; President George W. Bush's and President Obama's.[59] As Professor Tribe and Joshua Matz explain:

> In the pre-Civil War period alone, federal legislators called for impeachment over a dizzying array of offenses. A nonexhaustive list from that period includes (1) John Adams's extradition of a mutinous British Navy sailor to England, amid rumors that the sailor was a captured American; (2) Thomas Jefferson's supposed 'deliberate neglect' in failing to appoint a Collector of the Port of Boston; (3) Andrew Jackson's contested decision to withdraw federal deposits from the Bank of the United States; (4) John Tyler's alleged misuse of the veto power; (5) Franklin Pierce's refusal to intervene militarily against pro-slavery forces in "Bleeding Kansas"; and (6) James Buchanan's suspected involvement in corrupt deals with members of Congress.[60]

---

58 Such an action could be treasonous, but treason has a deliberately narrow definition under the Constitution. U.S. Const. art. III, § 3 ("Treason against the United States, shall consist only in levying War against them, or in adhering to their Enemies, giving them Aid and Comfort").

59 Frank James, *Impeach Obama! (And FDR, Eisenhower, Carter, Reagan, Etc.)*, N.P.R. (Aug. 27, 2013), https://www.npr.org/sections/itsallpolitics/2013/08/27/216156619/impeach-obama-and-fdr-eisenhower-carter-reagan-etc.

60 Lawrence H. Tribe & Joshua Matz, To End a Presidency: The Power of Impeachment 34–35 (2018).

But no impeachment occurred in these cases. Why? The difficulty of collective action—the cost of getting many people to agree accounts at least as much as any legal standard for the difficulty of impeachment. A President has to make a lot of people very, very angry and commit an act serious enough to obtain a large and inattentive public's attention. His bad acts must inspire 218 Representatives to vote to unseat him; they must calculate whether the impeachment will hurt their own electoral chances.[61] And this is a problem whether or not the House, the impeaching body, is held by the same party as the President. One can predict that if the House is in the President's party that the Members will not impeach; but one cannot predict the opposite—that if the House is held by the opposite party, the President *will be impeached*. In fact, the data shows that, in most cases, the President has *not* been impeached by a House held by the opposite party.

Precedents and Consequentialism: To make an argument about a future precedent is to engage in what is called "consequentialist" reasoning. What lawyers mean by consequentialism is that one considers the consequences of one's actions. Some lawyers, however, worry about looking at consequences. They believe that this could bias the interpreter for one of the parties to the case. Both positions have merit, but they refer to different forms of consequentialism. When one decides to favor one side of a debate because they simply like that side, that is bias. When a judge says, 'I like the President so I will rule for him,' that is the essence of a lawless decision. The kind of consequentialism that lawyers and judges regularly engage in focuses on the consequences *of the rule* for a future case. Philosophers call this "rule-consequentialism," meaning that one is thinking about principles for future cases, not the parties in the case.[62]

VI. CONSTITUTIONAL STRUCTURE

Impeachments pit one branch of the government—the Congress—against another—the President. In such cases, it is natural to imagine consequences that will affect the **structure of government if the Congress applies the wrong rules**. Will the President have more power? Will Congress have more power? Constitutional lawyers call these structural arguments.

A. The House Managers' Arguments

The House Managers argued that, if President Trump remained in office, then he could cheat in another election, making him more powerful than the people. As we now know, President Trump was impeached again because of his refusal to recognize the results of the

---

61 It is widely believed, for example, that impeaching President Clinton lost the Republicans' leadership of the House of Representatives in the next election.

62 Stanford Encyclopedia of Philosophy, *Rule-Consequentialism*: "Earlier we saw that all consequentialists now accept that assessing each act individually by its expected value is in general a terrible procedure for making moral decisions. There is widespread acknowledgement that agents should decide how to act by appeal to certain rules." https://plato.stanford.edu/entries/consequentialism-rule/#TwoWayArgForRulCon.

2020 election inspired a mob to attack the Nation's Capitol. (*See* Part Two of this book).

The House Managers stressed that President Trump's conduct shifted the **balance of power** between the Congress and the President, resulting in a President who was far too powerful. Congress, they argued, existed to check the President.

> *If not remedied by his conviction in the Senate and removal from office, President Trump's abuse of his office and obstruction of Congress will permanently alter the* ***balance of power*** *among the branches of government, inviting future Presidents to operate as if they are also beyond the reach of accountability, congressional oversight, and the law.* 166 Cong. Rec. S445. (daily ed. Jan. 22, 2020) (statement of Rep. Schiff) (emphasis added).

> *The Framers fashioned a powerful Chief Executive but not one beyond accountability of law. When a President wields power in ways that are inappropriate and seek[s] to extinguish the rights of Congress, he exceeds the power of constitutional authority and violates the limits placed on his conduct. Obstruction of a separate and coequal branch of government for the purposes of covering up an abuse of power not only implies a corrupt intent but also demonstrates a remarkable antipathy toward the* ***balance of power*** *contemplated and enshrined in our Constitution.* 166 Cong. Rec. S446 (daily ed. Jan. 22, 2020) (statement of Rep. Schiff) (emphasis added).

> *[I]f Congress is unable to investigate and impeach a President for abuse of their office,* ***our democracy's essential check on a rogue President*** *would fail. It would no longer protect the American people from a corrupt President who presents an ongoing threat. This is the outcome every American should be concerned about* * * * *. 166 Cong. Rec. S456 (daily ed. Jan. 22, 2020) (statement of Rep. Schiff) (emphasis added).

B. The President's Lawyers' Arguments

Some structural arguments focus on terms like the "balance of power" or the "separation" of powers. Other structural arguments, particularly the kind once championed by Professor Charles L. Black, Jr. think of institutions as representing people.[63] For example, rather than seeing the House of Representatives as an empty box, these

[63] Charles L. Black Jr., Structure and Relationship in Constitutional Law (1969); *see also* Charles L. Black Jr. & Philip Bobbitt, Impeachment: A Handbook 31 (2018).

arguments focus on the fact that the House represents particular groups of people—its Members are elected from districts across the nation. Similarly, the President represents a larger set of people, aggregated not by small districts but by individuals who vote across the nation.[64] The President's lawyers made both kinds of structural arguments.

> *If this Chamber accepts that premise, that what has been asserted here constitutes an impeachable offense, it will forever damage the separation of powers. It will undermine the independence of the executive and destroy the bounds between the legislative and executive branches that the Framers crafted in the Constitution.* 166 Cong. Rec. S591 (daily ed. Jan. 27, 2020) (statement of Mr. Philbin) (emphasis added).

> *Conviction of a President raises particularly profound issues under our constitutional structure because it means overturning the democratically expressed will of the people in the only national election in which all eligible citizens participate. The impeachment power permits the possibility that "the legislative branch [will] essentially cancel[ ] the results of the most solemn collective act of which we as a constitutional democracy are capable:* ***the national election*** *of a President."* President's Brief, 166 Cong. Rec. S317 (Jan. 21, 2020) (emphasis added).

QUESTIONS: CONSTITUTIONAL STRUCTURE

Structural Tit for Tat: Understanding structural arguments can be difficult because there are widely different views about the Constitution's structure. For example, some people emphasize a "separation" model, which highlights the degrees to which the departments operate separately; others emphasize a "checks and balances" model which emphasizes the degree to which the departments check each other. Still others emphasize that the departments actually "share" powers (the Congress and the President must agree, for example, on legislation). Structural arguments too often depend upon vague metaphors: for example, many talk about the "balance of power," but never identify what "balance" or "power" means. Notice that when institutions make structural arguments, they can end up playing tit for tat. One institution says that the departments must be independent and cannot be controlled by the other department, invoking the phrase the "separation of powers." The other institution says that the departments "check" each

---

[64] This reality is complicated by the Electoral College, but irrelevant for this point, except perhaps to note that it is possible to win the Presidency, as did President Trump, having obtained less than a majority of individual voters, but a majority of electoral votes, as counted by states.

other and checks depend upon shared powers. For more on these slogans and their meaning, *see* Chapter 2.

Representation and Structure: Every lawyer learns some classic arguments of constitutional structure. The key to these arguments follows less from a particular understanding of structure than an understanding of the power of the people in that structure. Most lawyers learn this in the context of the famous case of *McCulloch v. Maryland*, 17 U.S. 316 (1819), where the Supreme Court held that a state could not tax the federal government because, if it could, in the future, the states could tax the federal government out of existence. That, in turn, would *make the people of the states more powerful than the people of the nation, upending the constitutional supremacy of the federal government*. Structural arguments of this kind consider the relative power of institutions in terms of their constituencies: why should the people of Maryland control the people of the entire country? In the impeachment context, the key institutions to consider are the Presidency versus the Congress, the key constituencies are those who elect the House and Senate versus those who elect the President.

Consider in this light the President's argument that "the legislative branch [will] essentially cancel[ ] the results of the most solemn collective act of which we as a constitutional democracy are capable: the national election of a President." President's Brief, 116 Cong. Rec. S317 (daily ed. Jan. 21, 2020). Is that a good argument? After all, the Constitution does provide the impeachment power. U.S. Const. art. II, § 4 ("The President * * * * shall be removed from Office on Impeachment for, and Conviction of, Treason, Bribery, or other high Crimes and Misdemeanors"). That power is given explicitly to the House and the Senate. U.S. Const. art. I, § 2, cl. 5 ("the House of Representatives * * * * shall have the sole Power of Impeachment"); *id.* art. I, § 3, cl. 6 ("the Senate shall have the sole Power to try all Impeachments").

Why shouldn't those elected to the House and the Senate, who are closer to the people, overturn the result of a national election? After all, those who elect the House and the Senate do represent the nation collectively; it is simply that individual Members are electorally responsible to smaller geographic constituencies (states and districts). The Founders believed that the President would be more distant from the people and this would pose what we today call "agency costs," that the President might not be a good agent for the people. When the President's lawyers said that the House Members were trying to overturn an election, what were they saying? That there should be no impeachment power? And, remember, removal of a President simply means replacement by his Vice-President until the next election.

Predictions and Baseline Problems: Structural arguments are hard to evaluate for two reasons. First, judges and lawyers disagree about constitutional structure (should powers be shared or separate? Should the departments check or cooperate with each other?). If you go back and look at the President's lawyers' arguments, for example, you will see that they assume that the President has a right to be entirely separate from the Congress, but that leaves out Congress's checking function. By contrast, you will see that the House Managers argue that they are a constitutionally-provided check against the President, ignoring the ways in which the President may be separate and independent. Second, to measure future structural change, one needs a settled baseline and yet the parties disagree here about the proper baseline. Structural argument involves predictions about the future relationship of Congress to the Presidency. If there is no agreed upon baseline, then predictions about the future are likely to diverge as well. If you believe that the default is departmental separation, then you are likely to predict dire consequences if Congress operates as a check. If you believe that the default is checking, then you are likely to predict dire consequences if Congress does not operate as a check. One thing that everyone does agree upon is that if Congress were to impeach a President every session, that would have an effect on presidential action: it would cause the President to cleave closer to Congress's policies. But, as we noted above, this has not happened, suggesting that there are political incentives against impeachment.

VII. SHARED CONSTITUTIONAL NORMS

Of all arguments, constitutionalists argue the most about ethical claims. As originally formulated by Professor Philip Bobbitt, the idea is that there are principles that can be found in the Constitution that Americans share and that these values come into play in hard cases.[65] This is not a claim that an extra-constitutional super-morality should guide constitutional arguments. Indeed, if ethical argument were all there is, then, as Bobbitt himself argues, the "conventions" of legal argument and their ability to achieve consensus among lawyers could easily be overtaken by pure partisan or ideological warfare.[66]

One simple constraint on ethical argument is that it must be traced to the Constitution. Another, in my opinion, is that these ethical principles are widely shared and widely shared across generations. One way of looking at ethical argument is that it is a check against the fact that legal formality—the conventions of traditional legal argument based on text and precedent—should not lead to results that violate long-held constitutional norms. The point is not to reduce law to morality, but to use morality as a check against formalism's limits. This idea is ancient and reaches back to Blackstone who used the following example of how law's formality could lead to results quite inconsistent with law's own aims. He posited a law that barred the "letting" of blood in the streets. He then considered that, if taken literally, the law would imprison a doctor who used an incision to cure a patient. This is an example of how legal language, and formality, can run contrary to law's own aims.

---

65 Philip Bobbitt, Constitutional Fate ch. 10 (1982).

66 *Id.* at 139.

"Ethical" argument is a general term: it has a tendency to encompass other forms of argument. One might characterize a number of arguments made above as ethical, but those arguments are keyed to particular text (high crimes), precedent (prior impeachments), or future consequences (future impeachments). For example, if one believes that the separation of powers is a "good," then one can dress up structural arguments using ethical garb. For our purposes, you should know that lawyers typically do not start with constitutional ethos, but often conclude their arguments by appealing to a common sense of constitutional morality.

In what follows, you will see that the lawyers appeal to the basic normative idea that, in a constitutional democracy, elected officials serve the people. Nowhere in the Constitution does it say that precisely. There is no text saying "officials serve the people." There is text enjoining the President to faithfully execute the law, but no specific statement that the President is "not above the law." This type of claim overlaps with claims about constitutional structure, but as we have said before, overlapping arguments are a feature of a cable-like system. Strong arguments are persuasive precisely because they reinforce each other.

A. The House Managers' Arguments

The House Managers argued that impeachment allowed the people to check a misbehaving President and this was consistent with basic democratic values, that a President must serve the people.

> *The Senate should convict and remove President Trump to avoid serious and long-term damage to our **democratic values** and the Nation's security. If the Senate permits President Trump to remain in office, he and future leaders would be emboldened to welcome, and even enlist, foreign interference in elections for years to come. When the American people's faith in their **electoral process** is shaken and its results called into question, the essence of democratic self-government is called into doubt.* House Managers Brief, 166 Cong. Rec. S298 (daily ed. Jan. 21, 2020) (emphasis added).

> *President Trump has betrayed the **American people and the ideals** on which the Nation was founded. Unless he is removed from office, he will continue to endanger our national security, jeopardize the integrity of our elections, and undermine our core constitutional principles. Id.* (emphasis added).

B. The President's Lawyers' Arguments

The President's lawyers argued that impeachment threatened the right of the people to elect their President. They invoked the basic ethical principle of self-governance: that the people have the right to choose their President. They began their brief as follows:

> *The Articles of Impeachment submitted by House Democrats are a dangerous attack on the right of the* ***American people*** *to freely choose their President. This is a brazen and unlawful attempt to overturn the results of the* ***2016*** *election and interfere with the* ***2020*** *election—now just months away. The highly partisan and reckless obsession with impeaching the President began the day he was inaugurated and continues to this day. * * * * Nothing in these Articles could permit even beginning to consider removing a duly elected President or warrant nullifying an election and subverting* ***the will of the American people.*** President's Brief, 166 Cong. Rec. S290 (daily ed. Jan. 21, 2020) (emphasis added).

They ended their brief in a similar way:

> *In order to preserve our constitutional structure of government, to reject the poisonous partisanship that the Framers warned against, to ensure one-party political impeachment vendettas do not become the "new normal," and to vindicate the will of the American people, the Senate must reject both Articles of Impeachment. In the end, this entire process is nothing more than a dangerous attack on the American people themselves and their fundamental right to vote.* President's Brief 166 Cong. Rec. S291 (daily ed. Jan. 21, 2020).

NOTE ON ABUSE OF POWER AS CONSTITUTIONAL CHARGE

How Do We Define "Abuse of Power"?: Although scholars seem to agree that an "abuse of power" is sufficient to impeach, there are reasons to worry about the term's vagueness. One might argue that almost anything could be an "abuse" of power. And, indeed, this is precisely what the President's lawyers argued. Is there any way to narrow this standard or at least specify it more clearly? Obviously, advocates did not mean any abuse of power, but one which gravely imperiled the nation. But that still leaves a rather capacious standard. What is "grave" to some may not appear so to others (after all, over 70 million people voted to continue President Trump in office in the 2020 election). Here are some possibilities suggested by myself and other scholars:

Reasonable Non-Partisan Citizen Standard: Professor Charles L. Black Jr. argued that the ultimate standard must be looked at from the eyes of the voters: "[w]hat a reasonable man might anticipate would be thought abusive and wrong, without reference to partisan politics or differences of opinion on policy."[67] In effect, this provides some clarity by looking at the proper decisionmaker—the people. But it refers again to what is "abusive and wrong," which may be in the eyes of the beholder, and difficult to distinguish from partisan differences, particularly in a hyperpolarized age.

Offense Against Democracy: One of the unifying aspects of both Trump Impeachments was that the House Managers claimed that the President was trying to rig the election in favor of himself. One limitation on the kind of abuse of power that should rise to an impeachable offense would be one that we know is dangerous to democracy. We know, for example, that despots and demagogues try to rig voting in their favor and refuse to peacefully transfer power. In short, the presumption should be that structural attacks on the election system are different than ordinary crimes. This standard would eliminate an impeachment like that of President Clinton which was based on a lie, but posed no direct threat to our electoral machinery, but would embrace President Trump's First Impeachment as well as his attack on the electoral certification process in 2020, which prompted the Second Trump Impeachment.

Switching Presidents to Limit Bias: One way to try to limit one's bias is the idea of "switching," borrowed from scholarship in the criminal law and elsewhere. One "switches" out an unpreferred group for a preferred group to analyze the problem: what would the reasonable nonpartisan voter think if the acts were committed by a President they admired? What if President Obama [or pick your President] had done the same deeds? Would President Obama have been impeached if he aimed to dig up (or manufacture) dirt on his campaign opponent? Would President Obama have been impeached if, during the certification of his opponent's election, he inspired a crowd of his supporters to attack the Capitol?

Urgency—an Operational Definition: The offense must be so grave that it could not wait until the next election. As Charles L. Black Jr. put it, "we remove him principally because we fear he will do it again."[68] House Members argued that President Trump had a pattern of cheating in elections, starting in 2016, when he sought help from Russia to falsely indict his opponent Hillary Clinton through stolen emails, and then, again in 2019, to falsely indict his principal opponent, Joseph R. Biden, Jr., during the presidential nomination contest. Surely, one should think an attack on our electoral system, if accepted, would make it urgent to impeach, if for no other reason than to raise the issues for the American public regarding the next election. Impeachment, after all, may serve a purpose other than removal; it may serve as a kind of "fire alarm system" of dangers posed by the President to the republic. Now that we know that President Trump was impeached again for claimed interference in the 2020 election, on the theory that he inspired an attack on the Capitol by denying the truth of the 2020 election

[67] Charles L. Black Jr. & Philip Bobbitt, Impeachment: A Handbook 30 (2018).

[68] *Id.* at 35.

results, should future impeachments focus on this "urgent warning sign" theory?

Alternative Remedy Definition: Professor Keith Whittington has argued that one should define abuse of power as an offense for which there is no alternative constitutional remedy.[69] For example, if the President's actions could be remedied by a constitutional decision by the courts—for example by exercising judicial review—then that conduct should not be impeachable. So, for example, if the courts were to review challenges to President Trump's receipt of funds from foreigners at his hotels under the Emoluments Clause, that would argue against impeachment based on an Emoluments Clause violation. But that raises questions because of the timing of judicial review. When are other alternatives *available*? As we will see in Chapter 4, there are many questions related to the Trump impeachments that the courts have not decided, such as whether close advisors to the President are immune from testimony before Congress. Although such a case was in the courts around the time of First Trump Impeachment, that case had not been decided even after the Second Impeachment. Moreover, as we know, the Courts have held that impeachments constitute nonjusticiable "political questions." (*See* Chapter 2 and the *Walter Nixon* case as well as the cases in Chapter 5). Should the Congress have to wait for the courts to impeach? Does that change the relationship between the courts and Congress?

PROBLEM 3-1

Imagine that you are a lawyer working for the House Judiciary Committee. The Chairman asks you to draft Articles of Impeachment. Any legal drafter looks at templates or examples, whether they are examples of statutes or contracts or Constitutions. Take a look at the **Nixon Articles of Impeachment** and the **Clinton Articles of Impeachment** in Appendix A and B. Then compare those Articles to the First Trump Impeachment Articles reprinted in Chapter 1.

In reviewing the First Trump Impeachment Articles, consider the following:

Do they charge the President's failure to abide by the Constitution?

Do they use the phrase "abuse of power"?

Do they say that the President has used public power for personal benefit—what is often called "self-dealing" in the corporate context?

Do they emphasize "corruption"?

Do they charge that the President violated his constitutional duty to faithfully execute the laws, U.S. Const. Art. II, § 3?

Do the Articles use the word "crime"?

---

69 Keith Whittington, When Does Abuse of Power Justify Impeachment? (forthcoming, on file with author).

Do the Articles describe actions (e.g. "breaking and entering") that sound like crimes?

Do they allege violations of specific statutes (criminal statutes are typically cited by reference to a title and section such as 18 U.S.C. § 924)?

Now that you have looked at the First Trump Impeachment Articles, do you think that the Clinton and Nixon impeachment Articles served as appropriate templates? If you were to give advice to the House Managers on drafting Articles of Impeachment, what would that advice be? Would you have been more specific about crimes alleged, even if a crime was unnecessary to impeach? Would you have emphasized the importance of elections to the Constitution? Would you consider an analogy to corporate law that prevents self-dealing?

NOTE ON THE CRIMINAL LAW AND THE ARTICLES

Historians will ask why the House did not allege an actual criminal violation thus anticipating and defeating the "zombie" argument that an ordinary crime was required. There are many reasons that could explain the House Managers' choice. First, impeachment is a trial before the public. History suggests that the more particular the charges, the more the trial is likely to descend into legalistic detail that does not translate well for public consumption. Generality is a virtue for the public. Second, and perhaps more importantly, there are serious questions about whether the President could have been charged with a crime while he sat in office. Note that nothing in this Note should undercut the claim, accepted by most scholars, that impeachment does not require a crime. In this Note, I explain why a more specific set of charges was likely to be disfavored by House drafters.

From the House Managers' View: One of the problems with specificity in Articles of Impeachment is that they tend to breed backlash. (In the President Andrew Johnson impeachment trial, for example, there was much argument about whether he had or could violate the Tenure of Office Act.) In the First Trump Impeachment, Norm Eisen, who worked as a lawyer for the House Judiciary Committee, has explained that the Speaker of the House Nancy Pelosi (D-CA) specifically argued for, and won, a spare set of charges, rather than a lengthy indictment (at one point Judiciary Chairman Jerrold Nadler (D-NY) wanted nine counts).[70] The Speaker of the House specifically rejected, for example, any attempt to relitigate the Mueller investigation, even if it seemed entirely doubtful that a President in the normal course would be impeached for a single phone call. In response, drafters attempted

[70] Norm Eisen, A Case for the American People: The United States v. Donald Trump 167–79 (2020). The book also explains that, before the Ukraine affair, committee staff members had drafted ten Articles of Impeachment. These would have covered everything from collusion with Russia, obstruction of the Mueller investigation, giving hush money to deceive the public about an extramarital affair, dangling pardons to encourage people not to testify against him, violating the Emoluments Clause, and spending money in ways unauthorized by Congress. The Tenth Article was blank, entitled "The Next High Crime." *See* Peter Baker, *House Democrats Considered 10 Impeachment Articles Before Narrowing Their Case Against Trump*, New York Times (July 22, 2020).

to emphasize a pattern of election interference that was evident to Americans at the time, given the widespread publicity about the Mueller investigation. (Query whether that pattern will be evident in the future, just from the face of the Articles.) This is an example of how and why congressional arguments may differ from those in other institutions, for example, arguments before the Supreme Court. If you were arguing a case in the Supreme Court, you would marshal all of the arguments in your favor in far more precise legal detail. For more on this institutional difference, consult Chapter 5.

From the President's View: Had the Articles been extremely specific, the President's defense would have focused on the legal details; the more general the Articles, however, there was the opposite risk. The President's lawyers argued that "abuse of power" was so vague that it was in the eye of the beholder, and thus his opponents were trying to impeach him for something "subjective." (Saying something is "subjective" has a negative ring for most lawyers who prefer to be "objective" (in the sense of non-biased)). The generality of the term "abuse of power" invited the predictable defense that no crime had been charged. Given that there was a long history of legal opposition to that claim, this argument would have been much harder to make in the Supreme Court. At the very least, lawyers in a courtroom would have had to acknowledge that conservatives and liberals had rejected the "ordinary-crime-is-required position. Most legal academics would have branded the President's "there must be a crime" argument as a loser in a court of law which helps to explain an outpouring of scholarly contempt for the "zombie" claim that an ordinary crime was required to impeach.

Bribery: The Constitution enumerates bribery as an impeachable offense. If in fact the President had committed bribery, it would have been very bad lawyering not to allege it in the Articles in the First Trump Impeachment. Bribery does not require that an official actually receive money; the official may simply ask for money. However, there were legal problems with a bribery offense in this case. No money was exchanged. What the President sought was "dirt"—information—on his opponent. As Professor Neal Katyal has argued, in likening Trump's actions to bribery, surely the President would not have sought such material if it was not of some value.[71] Candidates pay millions of dollars for sophisticated opposition research (think: polling). Claims that Trump's opponent appeared corrupt—even if it was not true—were of enormous value given that similar claims of apparent corruption appeared to work in the 2016 election to defeat candidate Hillary Clinton. Courts have held that asking for non-monetary benefits can constitute bribery. On the other hand, in the Trump case, the bribery allegation is complicated by the fact that the "benefit" was a "political" one. That opened up the claim that Trump was just engaging in opposition research and, if opposition research were an impeachable offense, almost every President would qualify for impeachment.

Had the House alleged bribery, President Trump had some easy defenses, that would be raised by any defendant charged with bribery in a court of law. First, he could claim that he had no "intent" to commit bribery,

---

71 Neal Katyal & Sam Koppelman, Impeach: The Case Against Donald Trump (2019).

it was a mistake. In an actual criminal trial, a prosecutor would have had to prove that the defendant had a "bad intent" beyond a reasonable doubt, a very high bar to meet. The President could have easily said that the House did not prove beyond a reasonable doubt that he did not have "good reasons" to inquire about corruption, even if those reasons turned out to be false.[72] Second, bribery makes the "intent" calculus even harder. It requires a "corrupt" or "willful" intent." A prosecutor who offers a plea bargain gives "something of value" to a criminal defendant, but he is not guilty of bribery because he has a good reason. As a general rule, one who commits a crime and has a "good motive" is not freed from punishment. (Imagine if you were a doctor who killed a dying patient; you may have had a good reason to prevent their suffering but you would still be guilty of murder.) But in cases of bribery, the jury must be convinced that the action was not simply a mistake, but also something that the President actively sought, "willfully" or "corruptly," posing an even higher burden.[73]

In the end, the "public audience" of an impeachment may have made House Managers and the Speaker chary of pursuing the bribery line. Why? Not only was it easily mired in detail, it would focus the trial on "why" the President called the Ukrainian President and that, in turn, would focus the trial on the alleged events involving a prominent rival, Joe Biden, and more particularly his son, Hunter Biden. As was said more than once in the Trump Presidency, repeating false claims can in fact make more people believe the claims are truthful. Query whether focusing on bribery would have undermined the very reason for the impeachment? If you believed, as press media revealed, that the corruption charge against former Vice President Biden was a lie, why would you want to engage in long debates about the detail of the conversation. Wouldn't the President's lawyers just repeat the President's claims that his opponent was corrupt?

Foreign Interference and Election Law Offenses: Inviting foreign interference in a campaign for the Presidency sounds like a campaign finance violation. Very few people believe that Russia or England or Moldova or France should determine American elections. This offense had obvious public resonance. As then-Judge Kavanaugh wrote, for the D.C. Circuit: "[T]he United States has a compelling interest * * * * in limiting the participation of foreign citizens in activities of democratic self-government, and in thereby preventing foreign influence over the U.S. political process." *Bluman v. FEC*, 800 F. Supp. 2d 281, 288 (D.D.C. 2011) (Kavanaugh, J., for three-judge court), *aff'd*, 565 U.S. 1104 (2012).

Why did the House Managers not allege a specific violation of the campaign finance law in the Articles? The Mueller investigation specifically addressed whether the President had violated the campaign finance law in

[72] In the criminal law, intent is different from motive. Motive is about one's ultimate reasons. Did he intentionally (as opposed to accidentally) point the gun, for example, is a question of intent. Motive would be something like: he pointed the gun to make his enemy pay for his rent. However, a "corrupt" intent requires a bad purpose.

[73] It is said that a person acts "willfully" if they act deliberately with a bad "purpose" to disobey or disregard the law. The person need not know the specific law he is violating, however.

2016, when President Trump publicly invited Russia to interfere in the election.[74] The Report reveals some of the legal difficulties. First, we return to the question of "anything of value" which bedevils the bribery charge because the value obtained is political. Special Prosecutor Mueller explained that many courts had found that valuable information could support a violation of the campaign finance laws.

> The phrases "thing of value" and "anything of value" are broad and inclusive enough to encompass at least some forms of valuable information. Throughout the United States Code, these phrases serve as "term[s] of art" that are construed "broad[ly]." United States v. Nilsen, 967 F.2d 539, 542 (11th Cir. 1992) (per curiam) ("thing of value" includes "both tangibles and intangibles"); see also, e.g., 18 U.S.C. §§ 201(b)(1), 666(a)(2) (bribery statutes); id. § 641 (theft of government property). For example, the term "thing of value" encompasses law enforcement reports that would reveal the identity of informants, United States v. Girard, 601 F.2d 69, 71 (2d Cir. 1979); classified materials, United States v. Fowler, 932 F.2d 306, 310 (4th Cir. 1991); confidential information about a competitive bid, United States v. Matzkin, 14 F.3d 1014, 1020 (4th Cir. 1994); secret grand jury information, United States v. Jeter, 775 F.2d 670, 680 (6th Cir. 1985); and information about a witness's whereabouts, United States v. Sheker, 618 F.2d 607, 609 (9th Cir. 1980) (per curiam). And in the public corruption context, " 'thing of value' is defined broadly to include the value which the defendant subjectively attaches to the items received." United States v. Renzi, 769 F.3d 731, 744 (9th Cir. 2014) (internal quotation marks omitted). Robert S. Mueller, III, *Report On The Investigation Into Russian Interference in the 2016 Presidential Election* 186 (2019).

So, too, in the election context, the Federal Election Commission, the agency that oversees federal election matters, has set forth regulations that the term "anything of value" includes "the provision of any goods or services without charge," such as "membership lists" and "mailing lists." 11 C.F.R. § 100.52(d)(1). Likewise, polling data provided to a campaign constitutes a "contribution." FEC Advisory Opinion 1990–12 (Strub), 1990 WL 153454 (citing 11 C.F.R. § 106.4(b)).

Despite this, the Mueller investigation ultimately chose *not* to charge President Trump or his campaign officials with a crime related to the 2016 election for two reasons: (1) no court had held that opposition research was a "thing of value" under the statute; and (2) constitutional considerations, including the First Amendment. That Amendment protects political speech.

---

[74] Robert S. Mueller, III, Report on The Investigation Into Russian Interference in the 2016 Presidential Election (2019) ("Several areas of the Office's investigation involved efforts or offers by foreign nationals to provide negative information about candidate Clinton to the Trump Campaign or to distribute that information to the public, to the anticipated benefit of the Campaign. As explained below, the Office considered whether two of those efforts in particular—the June 9, 2016 meeting at Trump Tower—constituted prosecutable violations of the campaign-finance laws.")

Asking for a bribe is speech that can be an indictable offense. Speech that encourages a foreign government to contribute to an electoral campaign can be indictable. But there are limits. Because of concerns about political speech and normal political activity, among other things, the Supreme Court has narrowly construed how far a prosecutor can go to charge public corruption under laws similar to the campaign finance laws. Under *McDonnell v. United States*, 136 S. Ct. 2355 (2016), the court emphasized the need for some "official act" as opposed to mere speech. Given these concerns, it is was not particularly surprising that, prior to the First Trump Impeachment, the Trump Justice Department concluded that the President had not committed a campaign finance violation in the call to Ukrainian President Zelensky.[75]

Obstruction of Justice in the Mueller Investigation: Historians may also ask why the Articles in the First Trump Impeachment did not allege obstruction of justice: the Mueller investigation report alleged several instances of claimed obstruction of justice. (This is a different claim than obstruction of Congress, it focuses on the President's attempts to fire Mueller and otherwise interfere with the Mueller investigation). The President and his Attorney General both claimed that the President could not obstruct justice by engaging in discretionary acts, such as firing a subordinate, such as the director of the FBI.[76] The Mueller investigation did not follow that line, finding instead that they could not rule out criminal conduct based on an obstruction of justice theory.[77] The answer here has less to do with the complexities of obstruction law (and it is complex) than that House Members wanted to avoid the appearance that it was "relitigating" the Mueller probe. The President had publicly, albeit falsely, claimed he was exonerated. The probe had lasted two years. As a strategic matter, the House chose to focus on *new* evidence, emphasizing a repeated pattern of election interference, without embroiling the impeachment in a re-do of the Mueller investigation.

Perpetual Lying: History may also ask why President Trump was not impeached for perpetual lying. Lying itself is not a crime. To be a crime, lying must be in an official proceeding. President Clinton, for example, was not impeached because he announced something on television but because of what he said during a legal proceeding. So, too, judges have been impeached for lying under oath.[78] On the other hand, those living through the Trump

---

[75] The Department's criminal division, including career officials, determined that the call did not violate campaign finance law since nothing "of value" was promised or exchanged during the call. https://abcnews.go.com/Politics/trumps-doj-clears-president-violating-campaign-finance-law/story?id=65849857. For a critique of the Department's actions on questions of campaign finance, *see* Katyal & Koppelman, *supra*.

[76] Bill Barr to Rod Rosenstein, Mueller's Obstruction Theory (June 8, 2018).

[77] Mueller Report at 2 ("If we had confidence after a thorough investigation of the facts that the President clearly did not commit obstruction of justice, we would so state. Based on the facts and the applicable legal standards, however, we are unable to reach that judgment. The evidence we obtained about the President's actions and intent presents difficult issues that prevent us from conclusively determining that no criminal conduct occurred. Accordingly, while this report does not conclude that the President committed a crime, it also does not exonerate him.").

[78] Frank O. Bowman III, High Crimes and Misdemeanors: A History of Impeachment for the Age of Trump 267 (2019).

Presidency, including impeachment scholars, noted that in many ways this formed an important context for the need for impeachment. Shortly after the release of the Mueller report, the Washington Post's factchecker database found that he had made 10,000 false statements or twelve a day. Six months later, after the impeachment failed, it had reached 20,000 factual misstatements or 23 a day, in light of the COVID-19 pandemic. The trend increased in the 2020 election.[79]

The President's defenders claimed that politicians "spin" the truth all the time. Note, however, that there is a difference between a spin on ambiguous facts and straight factual misstatements. As one commentator explained: "the undeniable fact is that [President Trump] lies all the time. Ceaselessly. Unrepentantly. About pretty much everything. Big things. Little things. Public matters and private ones."[80] Republican journalists did not disagree, calling his lying "reckless," dubbing it "rhetorical mustard."[81] One might argue that a perpetual liar's lies are more obvious and less damaging precisely for that reason. As Professor Frank O. Bowman III has argued, in theory, a course of lying which imperiled the nation (let us say lying about an invading military force) would be impeachable. Writing before the Second Trump Impeachment, he argued that indictment for such lies would be politically unpalatable, however, to the President's Republican allies. In the next Part, dealing with the Second Trump Impeachment, we will address the question of speech and lying more fully. Query whether the Articles in the First Trump Impeachment should have mentioned a pattern of deception more explicitly?

NOTE ON THE NEED FOR AN EXISTING LAW

The President's lawyers argued that the Constitution placed additional limits on impeachment. Following arguments made in President Andrew Johnson's impeachment, President's Trump's lawyers argued that the President had to violate an existing law, whether criminal or not, to comply with other parts of the Constitution, namely the Ex Post Facto and Bill of Attainder Clauses. U.S. Const. art. I § 9, clause 3.

The Founders placed explicit limits on congressional punishment of individuals to avoid abuses associated with the British parliamentary system. Here is the kind of thing that the Founders would not have wanted Congress to do: in 1641, Parliament tried to impeach the Earl of Strafford for explaining to the King how to collect revenue without the Parliament's

---

[79] On the Fact Checker database, *see* https://www.washingtonpost.com/graphics/politics/trump-claims-database/?utm_term=.27babcd5e58c&itid=lk_inline_manual_2&itid=lk_inline_manual_2. On the 20,000 mark, *see* https://www.washingtonpost.com/politics/2020/07/13/president-trump-has-made-more-than-20000-false-or-misleading-claims/. During the election campaign, the Factchecker concluded that the President was making 50 false claims a day. https://www.washingtonpost.com/politics/2020/10/22/president-trump-is-averaging-more-than-50-false-or-misleading-claims-day/.

[80] Frank O. Bowman III, High Crimes and Misdemeanors: A History of Impeachment for the Age of Trump 270 (2019).

[81] George Will, *The Nation is in a Downward Spiral. Worse is Yet to Come.* https://www.washingtonpost.com/opinions/this-is-what-national-decline-looks-like/2020/07/14/ef499fd4-c5f0-11ea-b037-f9711f89ee46_story.html.

consent. When it appeared that the impeachment might fail because no law barred such advice, Parliament passed a law decreeing that that the Earl was a traitor; he was promptly executed.[82] The law declaring the Earl a traitor was a "Bill of Attainder" which, in modern times, means trial by legislature that singles out an individual for punishment, tailoring the crime to fit the accused. The American Constitution expressly bars such Bills of Attainder as well as ex post facto laws. The ex post facto bar prevents punishments for any citizen violating a criminal law that did not exist at the time the offense was committed.

Relying on these provisions of the Constitution, some have argued that President Trump could not be impeached without an existing law (civil or criminal) otherwise, like any other citizen, he would be tried by a legislature without knowing that he had committed an offense.[83] For example, this was the principle upon which President Andrew Johnson defended himself. Some of the Johnson Impeachment Articles depended upon Johnson's "harangues" in speeches made across the nation in which Johnson denied the power of Congress's laws to bind him. But there was no law against "haranguing" speeches. The principle is *nullum crimen sine lege*: "There can be no crime, there can be no misdemeanor without a law."[84] (These concerns may explain why the House Managers in the First Trump Impeachment included reference to the President's violation of the Impoundment Control Act, as an existing law, even if it was not a criminal law).

The legal question comes down to whether the Constitution applies these principles in an impeachment. U.S. Const. art. I § 9, clause 3 provides: "No Bill of Attainder or ex post facto Law shall be passed." *Id.* art. I, § 9, cl. 3. Some have argued that these provisions do not apply in an impeachment because removal from office is a civil sanction, not a criminal one.[85] There are other reasons to worry whether they apply. "Bills" and "Laws" are governed by entirely different constitutional rules. Passing a "law" to impeach a President would be ludicrous since a law only exists with the President's approval. *See* U.S. Const. art. I, § 7. When Congress impeaches, the Constitution is specific about the process. The House acts in one way, and the Senate another; they do not pass a "bill" of impeachment. One worried about whether Presidents will somehow be caught unaware by post hoc punishment should remember that impeachment's ultimate arbiter is the people. If the average citizen would not see the offense as a serious breach of trust, knowable to millions of people, it will be difficult if not impossible to convince politicians in the House to impeach or a 2/3 Senate majority to convict. On the "political safeguards of impeachment," *see* Part Two.

---

[82] Nikolas Bowie, *High Crimes Without Law*, 132 Harv. L. Rev. F. 59, 69 (2018) (discussing the Strafford case).

[83] *Id.* at 61.

[84] *Id.*

[85] "The Supreme Court long ago concluded that the Ex Post Facto Clause and the Bill of Attainder Clause apply only to punishments, not to civil sanctions." Nikolas Bowie, *High Crimes Without Law*, 132 Harv. L. Rev. F. 59, 72 (attributing this argument to Laurence H. Tribe & Joshua Matz, To End a Presidency: The Power of Impeachment (2018)).

APPENDIX A

Articles of Impeachment Against Richard M. Nixon

RESOLVED, That Richard M. Nixon, President of the United States, is impeached for high crimes and misdemeanors, and that the following articles of impeachment to be exhibited to the Senate:

> Articles Of Impeachment Exhibited By The House Of Representatives Of The United States Of America In The Name Of Itself And Of All Of The People Of The United States Of America, Against Richard M. Nixon, President Of The United States Of America, In Maintenance And Support Of Its Impeachment Against Him For High Crimes And Misdemeanors.

Article 1

In his conduct of the office of President of the United States, Richard M. Nixon, in violation of his constitutional oath faithfully to execute the office of President of the United States and, to the best of his ability, preserve, protect, and defend the Constitution of the United States, and in violation of his constitutional duty to take care that the laws be faithfully executed, has prevented, obstructed, and impeded the administration of justice, in that:

On June 17, 1972, and prior thereto, agents of the Committee for the Re-election of the President committed unlawful entry of the headquarters of the Democratic National Committee in Washington, District of Columbia, for the purpose of securing political intelligence. Subsequent thereto, Richard M. Nixon, using the powers of his high office, engaged personally and through his close subordinates and agents, in a course of conduct or plan designed to delay, impede, and obstruct the investigation of such illegal entry; to cover up, conceal and protect those responsible; and to conceal the existence and scope of other unlawful covert activities.

The means used to implement this course of conduct or plan included one or more of the following:

1. making false or misleading statements to lawfully authorized investigative officers and employees of the United States;
2. withholding relevant and material evidence or information from lawfully authorized investigative officers and employees of the United States;
3. approving, condoning, acquiescing in, and counselling witnesses with respect to the giving of false or misleading statements to lawfully authorized investigative officers and employees of the

United States and false or misleading testimony in duly instituted judicial and congressional proceedings;

4. interfering or endeavoring to interfere with the conduct of investigations by the Department of Justice of the United States, the Federal Bureau of Investigation, the office of Watergate Special Prosecution Force, and Congressional Committees;

5. approving, condoning, and acquiescing in, the surreptitious payment of substantial sums of money for the purpose of obtaining the silence or influencing the testimony of witnesses, potential witnesses or individuals who participated in such unlawful entry and other illegal activities;

6. endeavoring to misuse the Central Intelligence Agency, an agency of the United States;

7. disseminating information received from officers of the Department of Justice of the United States to subjects of investigations conducted by lawfully authorized investigative officers and employees of the United States, for the purpose of aiding and assisting such subjects in their attempts to avoid criminal liability;

8. making or causing to be made false or misleading public statements for the purpose of deceiving the people of the United States into believing that a thorough and complete investigation had been conducted with respect to allegations of misconduct on the part of personnel of the executive branch of the United States and personnel of the Committee for the Re-election of the President, and that there was no involvement of such personnel in such misconduct: or

9. endeavoring to cause prospective defendants, and individuals duly tried and convicted, to expect favored treatment and consideration in return for their silence or false testimony, or rewarding individuals for their silence or false testimony.

In all of this, Richard M. Nixon has acted in a manner contrary to his trust as President and subversive of constitutional government, to the great prejudice of the cause of law and justice and to the manifest injury of the people of the United States.

Wherefore Richard M. Nixon, by such conduct, warrants impeachment and trial, and removal from office.

Article 2

Using the powers of the office of President of the United States, Richard M. Nixon, in violation of his constitutional oath faithfully to execute the office of President of the United States and, to the best of his ability, preserve, protect, and defend the Constitution of the United States, and in disregard of his constitutional duty to take care that the laws be faithfully executed, has repeatedly engaged in conduct violating the constitutional rights of citizens, impairing the due and proper administration of justice and the conduct of lawful inquiries, or contravening the laws governing agencies of the executive branch and the purposed of these agencies.

This conduct has included one or more of the following:

1. He has, acting personally and through his subordinates and agents, endeavored to obtain from the Internal Revenue Service, in violation of the constitutional rights of citizens, confidential information contained in income tax returns for purposes not authorized by law, and to cause, in violation of the constitutional rights of citizens, income tax audits or other income tax investigations to be initiated or conducted in a discriminatory manner.

2. He misused the Federal Bureau of Investigation, the Secret Service, and other executive personnel, in violation or disregard of the constitutional rights of citizens, by directing or authorizing such agencies or personnel to conduct or continue electronic surveillance or other investigations for purposes unrelated to national security, the enforcement of laws, or any other lawful function of his office; he did direct, authorize, or permit the use of information obtained thereby for purposes unrelated to national security, the enforcement of laws, or any other lawful function of his office; and he did direct the concealment of certain records made by the Federal Bureau of Investigation of electronic surveillance.

3. He has, acting personally and through his subordinates and agents, in violation or disregard of the constitutional rights of citizens, authorized and permitted to be maintained a secret investigative unit within the office of the President, financed in part with money derived from campaign contributions, which unlawfully utilized the resources of the Central Intelligence Agency, engaged in covert and unlawful activities, and attempted to prejudice the constitutional right of an accused to a fair trial.

4. He has failed to take care that the laws were faithfully executed by failing to act when he knew or had reason to know that his close subordinates endeavored to impede and frustrate lawful inquiries by duly constituted executive, judicial and legislative entities concerning the unlawful entry into the headquarters of

the Democratic National Committee, and the cover-up thereof, and concerning other unlawful activities including those relating to the confirmation of Richard Kleindienst as Attorney General of the United States, the electronic surveillance of private citizens, the break-in into the offices of Dr. Lewis Fielding, and the campaign financing practices of the Committee to Re-elect the President.

5. In disregard of the rule of law, he knowingly misused the executive power by interfering with agencies of the executive branch, including the Federal Bureau of Investigation, the Criminal Division, and the Office of Watergate Special Prosecution Force, of the Department of Justice, and the Central Intelligence Agency, in violation of his duty to take care that the laws be faithfully executed.

In all of this, Richard M. Nixon has acted in a manner contrary to his trust as President and subversive of constitutional government, to the great prejudice of the cause of law and justice and to the manifest injury of the people of the United States.

Wherefore Richard M. Nixon, by such conduct, warrants impeachment and trial, and removal from office.

Article 3

In his conduct of the office of President of the United States, Richard M. Nixon, contrary to his oath faithfully to execute the office of President of the United States and, to the best of his ability, preserve, protect, and defend the Constitution of the United States, and in violation of his constitutional duty to take care that the laws be faithfully executed, has failed without lawful cause or excuse to produce papers and things as directed by duly authorized subpoenas issued by the Committee on the Judiciary of the House of Representatives on April 11, 1974, May 15, 1974, May 30, 1974, and June 24, 1974, and willfully disobeyed such subpoenas. The subpoenaed papers and things were deemed necessary by the Committee in order to resolve by direct evidence fundamental, factual questions relating to Presidential direction, knowledge or approval of actions demonstrated by other evidence to be substantial grounds for impeachment of the President. In refusing to produce these papers and things Richard M. Nixon, substituting his judgment as to what materials were necessary for the inquiry, interposed the powers of the Presidency against the lawful subpoenas of the House of Representatives, thereby assuming to himself functions and judgments necessary to the exercise of the sole power of impeachment vested by the Constitution in the House of Representatives.

In all of this, Richard M. Nixon has acted in a manner contrary to his trust as President and subversive of constitutional government, to the great prejudice of the cause of law and justice, and to the manifest injury of the people of the United States.

Wherefore, Richard M. Nixon, by such conduct, warrants impeachment and trial, and removal from office.

APPENDIX B

Articles of Impeachment Against William Jefferson Clinton

House Resolution 611, One Hundred Fifth Congress, Second Session

CONGRESS OF THE UNITED STATES OF AMERICA, IN THE HOUSE OF REPRESENTATIVES,

December 19, 1998.

RESOLUTION

Resolved, That William Jefferson Clinton, President of the United States, is impeached for high crimes and misdemeanors, and that the following articles of impeachment be exhibited to the United States Senate:

Articles of impeachment exhibited by the House of Representatives of the United States of America in the name of itself and of the people of the United States of America, against William Jefferson Clinton, President of the United States of America, in maintenance and support of its impeachment against him for high crimes and misdemeanors.

ARTICLE I

In his conduct while President of the United States, William Jefferson Clinton, in violation of his constitutional oath faithfully to execute the office of President of the United States and, to the best of his ability, preserve, protect, and defend the Constitution of the United States, and in violation of his constitutional duty to take care that the laws be faithfully executed, has willfully corrupted and manipulated the judicial process of the United States for his personal gain and exoneration, impeding the administration of justice, in that:

On August 17, 1998, William Jefferson Clinton swore to tell the truth, the whole truth, and nothing but the truth before a Federal grand jury of the United States. Contrary to that oath, William Jefferson Clinton willfully provided perjurious, false and misleading testimony to the grand jury concerning one or more of the following: (1) the nature and details of his relationship with a subordinate

Government employee; (2) prior perjurious, false and misleading testimony he gave in a Federal civil rights action brought against him; (3) prior false and misleading statements he allowed his attorney to make to a Federal judge in that civil rights action; and (4) his corrupt efforts to influence the testimony of witnesses and to impede the discovery of evidence in that civil rights action.

In doing this, William Jefferson Clinton has undermined the integrity of his office, has brought disrepute on the Presidency, has betrayed his trust as President, and has acted in a manner subversive of the rule of law and justice, to the manifest injury of the people of the United States.

Wherefore, William Jefferson Clinton, by such conduct, warrants impeachment and trial, and removal from office and disqualification to hold and enjoy any office of honor, trust, or profit under the United States.

ARTICLE II

In his conduct while President of the United States, William Jefferson Clinton, in violation of his constitutional oath faithfully to execute the office of President of the United States and, to the best of his ability, preserve, protect, and defend the Constitution of the United States, and in violation of his constitutional duty to take care that the laws be faithfully executed, has prevented, obstructed, and impeded the administration of justice, and has to that end engaged personally, and through his subordinates and agents, in a course of conduct or scheme designed to delay, impede, cover up, and conceal the existence of evidence and testimony related to a Federal civil rights action brought against him in a duly instituted judicial proceeding.

The means used to implement this course of conduct or scheme included one or more of the following acts:

> (1) On or about December 17, 1997, William Jefferson Clinton corruptly encouraged a witness in a Federal civil rights action brought against him to execute a sworn affidavit in that proceeding that he knew to be perjurious, false and misleading.
>
> (2) On or about December 17, 1997, William Jefferson Clinton corruptly encouraged a witness in a Federal civil rights action brought against him to give perjurious, false and misleading testimony if and when called to testify personally in that proceeding.
>
> (3) On or about December 28, 1997, William Jefferson Clinton corruptly engaged in, encouraged, or supported a

scheme to conceal evidence that had been subpoenaed in a Federal civil rights action brought against him.

(4) Beginning on or about December 7, 1997, and continuing through and including January 14, 1998, William Jefferson Clinton intensified and succeeded in an effort to secure job assistance to a witness in a Federal civil rights action brought against him in order to corruptly prevent the truthful testimony of that witness in that proceeding at a time when the truthful testimony of that witness would have been harmful to him.

(5) On January 17, 1998, at his deposition in a Federal civil rights action brought against him, William Jefferson Clinton corruptly allowed his attorney to make false and misleading statements to a Federal judge characterizing an affidavit, in order to prevent questioning deemed relevant by the judge. Such false and misleading statements were subsequently acknowledged by his attorney in a communication to that judge.

(6) On or about January 18 and January 20, 21, 1998, William Jefferson Clinton related a false and misleading account of events relevant to a Federal civil rights action brought against him to a potential witness in that proceeding, in order to corruptly influence the testimony of that witness.

(7) On or about January 21, 23, and 26, 1998, William Jefferson Clinton made false and misleading statements to potential witnesses in a Federal grand jury proceeding in order to corruptly influence the testimony of those witnesses. The false and misleading statements made by William Jefferson Clinton were repeated by the witnesses to the grand jury, causing the grand jury to receive false and misleading information.

In all of this, William Jefferson Clinton has undermined the integrity of his office, has brought disrepute on the Presidency, has betrayed his trust as President, and has acted in a manner subversive of the rule of law and justice, to the manifest injury of the people of the United States.

Wherefore, William Jefferson Clinton, by such conduct, warrants impeachment and trial, and removal from office and disqualification to hold and enjoy any office of honor, trust, or profit under the United States.

Speaker of the House of Representatives.

Chapter Four

HIGH CRIMES AND MISDEMEANORS II: OBSTRUCTION OF CONGRESS

In this Chapter, we take a closer look at the Second Article of the First Trump Impeachment: Obstruction of Congress. The House Managers alleged that President Trump had illegally obstructed the impeachment inquiry. The President responded that he did not need to disclose any information to the Congress. As in the last Chapter, we consider how the parties argued about their positions. But we add an additional factor: with respect to the Second Article, the parties argued in the shadow of the law, invoking doctrines that depend upon claims about judicial decisions. Those court decisions appear in Chapter 5.

I. SUMMARY OF CHARGES

In the First Trump Impeachment, the Second Article asserted that the President obstructed Congress's impeachment inquiry unlawfully. Obstruction of Congress was asserted in the Nixon impeachment articles (*see* Appendix A to Chapter 3). There, the claim was that President Nixon was refusing to provide the audio tapes confirming his role in the Watergate burglary, as well as his interference with the FBI and other federal agencies. The President was ultimately ordered to release the tapes. *See United States v. Nixon*, 418 U.S. 683, 714 (1974) (reprinted in Chapter 5). However, the Court did not order them released because of Congress's demands, but because of an ongoing criminal case charging the Watergate burglars.

In the First Trump Impeachment, **the House Managers** argued that the President's obstruction was an assault on Congress's power of impeachment similar to that in the *Nixon* case. President Trump, like President Nixon, engaged in a cover-up. If the President could refuse to cooperate with the impeachment, then the power of impeachment was useless, they contended. The President had the information and was not releasing it. Moreover, since the whole point of impeachment is to check an errant President, allowing a cover-up would undermine that power. **Rep. Garcia** (D-TX) summarized the claim as follows:

> *At the heart of article II, obstruction of Congress, is a simple, troubling reality. President Trump tried to cheat, he got*

caught, and then he worked hard to cover it up. 166 Cong. Rec. S533 (daily ed. Jan. 24, 2020).

Following new, deeply troubling revelations about the President's July 25 call, on September 24, the Speaker of the House announced that the House investigations into the President's scheme to pressure Ukraine for personal gain would be folded into the ongoing impeachment inquiry. Just days later, the President began to attack the legitimacy of the House impeachment inquiry. Id. at S546.

*While standing on the tarmac at Andrews Air Force Base, President Trump argued that the House impeachment inquiry "shouldn't be allowed." He claimed "There should be a way of stopping it—maybe legally, through the courts." * * * *. Id.*

The President spent time at rallies, at press conferences, and on Twitter trying to persuade the American people that the House's inquiry was invalid and fraudulent. Here are just a few of President Trump's comments about the impeachment inquiry. He called it "a witch hunt," "a COUP," "an unconstitutional power grab," and "a fraud against the American people." He said it is "the phony Impeachment Scam," "the phony Impeachment Hoax," the "Ukraine Hoax," and "a continuation of the greatest Scam and Witch Hunt in the history of our Country." Id. (caps in original)

On October 8, the White House sent a letter to Speaker Nancy Pelosi informing her that President Trump would seek to completely obstruct the impeachment inquiry. They sent this letter. White House stationery. I shouldn't say this—I am a lawyer—but it is very lawyerly. It is an eight-page letter. You know, lawyers can't do one thing in one page; we have to do it in seven or eight. This was eight pages, and it is long. No worries, I am not going to read it all. I just want to get to the bottom line. It says: "President Trump cannot permit his Administration to participate in this partisan inquiry under these circumstances." The House investigating committees sought a total of 71 specific categories of documents from 6 different agencies and offices. President Trump blocked every single one of these requests—all of them. Id.

A. Vocabulary

A subpoena is a document ordering the presence of a person or the presentation of papers to a court or Congress. A **subpoena duces tecum** is an order for documents (Congress, like the courts, has **subpoena power** to support its legislative purposes); **Executive**

privilege is a claim that the President need not provide information to the Congress or a court. Privilege means a legal permission. There are many legal privileges, such as the privilege of an attorney not to testify against his client, or a priest against a parishioner.[1] These privileges aim to protect confidential relationships. **Obstruction of Congress** is a claim that a person has wrongfully refused to provide information to Congress. There is a statute that makes it a crime to wrongfully refuse to testify before Congress. 18 U.S.C. § 1505 (2018). It is similar to a claim that one has obstructed other kinds of investigations. So, for example, if one refuses to respond to a subpoena from a court, or a lawful request from a federal agency, that may constitute **obstruction of justice**, a very common legal concept. *See, e.g.,* 18 U.S.C. § 1512 (2018).

B. Background on Congressional Information Requests

There is a long history of congressional oversight of the executive branch. The very first congressional investigation occurred in 1792, during George Washington's tenure. *See McGrain v. Daugherty*, 273 U.S. 135, 161 (1927):

> [P]ower to secure needed information by such means has long been treated as an attribute of the power to legislate. It was so regarded in the British Parliament and in the colonial Legislatures before the American Revolution, and a like view has prevailed and been carried into effect in both houses of Congress and in most of the state Legislatures.

There are good reasons for this power, and they have to do with what we call the "separation of powers." For example, when Congress spends money, it wants to know (and Americans want to know) that the President, who is charged with "executing" the law, is spending the money properly. Congressional oversight is a natural response to separated institutions. Congress makes law; the President executes the laws passed by Congress. Congress wants to know if the President is following its orders.

As a general rule, you should assume that individuals and corporations must comply with congressional requests, and routinely do so, based on Congress's need for information in exercising its power to legislate. In fact, such sharing is an everyday occurrence in

---

1 *See Upjohn Co. v. United States,* 449 U.S. 383, 389 (1981) ("the attorney-client privilege is the oldest of the privileges for confidential communications known to the common law"); *Morales v. Portuondo,* 154 F. Supp. 2d 706 (S.D.N.Y. 2001) ("a minister, priest, or other member of the clergy may not disclose, at trial, a confession or confidence made to him in his professional character as spiritual advisor absent a waiver of the privilege by the confessing person").

Washington. *See* Elise J. Bean, Financial Exposure: Carl Levin's Senate Investigations into Finance and Tax Abuse (2018). No one in the impeachment trial disputed that the Congress has subpoena power, just as courts have subpoena power. Nor did anyone dispute that, as a normal course of business, if a person fails to show up under a valid congressional subpoena, they may be convicted of a crime. Wait: a crime? I thought Chapter 3 was all about whether there was a crime and most scholars believe a crime is not necessary to impeach. Yes, it is a crime to refuse to submit to a congressional subpoena. But, as we noted there, the President's political appointees in the Justice Department would have to prosecute and, as a general rule, both Democratic and Republican Presidents have refused to prosecute their own appointees. (Does that make sense? Perhaps not, but reform would require a legislative solution requiring that both the President and the Congress agree on the proper legislative approach.)

C. Summary of House Managers' Arguments

The House Managers argued that the power to compel documents in an **impeachment** was greater than in ordinary matters involving **legislation**. The House Managers argued that the President had violated the Constitution by failing to provide documents, that the cover-up was evidence of guilt, and that if a President could cover-up information related to impeachment, the impeachment power was useless.

Rep. Demings (D-FL) argued that obstruction was a violation of the Constitution:

> *President Trump's obstruction of the impeachment inquiry was categorical, indiscriminate, and historically unprecedented. And its purpose was clear: to impede Congress's ability to carry out its duties under the Constitution to hold the President accountable for high crimes and misdemeanors.* 166 Cong. Rec. S544 (daily ed. Jan. 24, 2020).

Rep. Schiff (D-CA) argued that Article II was essential because, without obtaining information from the President, Congress would have no impeachment power—in other words, the President was setting the rules for his own impeachment.

> *Article II is every bit as important as article I. Without article II, there is no article I ever again, no matter how egregious this President's conduct or any other's. It is fundamental to the separation of powers. If you can't have the ability to enforce an impeachment power, you might as*

well not put it in the Constitution. 166 Cong. Rec. S561 (daily ed. Jan. 24, 2020).

Rep. Lofgren (D-CA) contended that the failure to respond to the Congress's subpoenas showed that the President knew he was guilty of trying to interfere in the election improperly, and therefore had to cover it up. **Rep. Nadler** (D-NY) punctuated the point by saying that "Trump's obstruction reveals consciousness of guilt. Innocent people do not act this way. They do not hide all the evidence." 166 Cong. Rec. S551 (daily ed. Jan. 24, 2020). He further stated:

> *You may assume the documents that are being withheld would probably incriminate the President; otherwise, why wouldn't he have provided them? If he had a legitimate executive privilege claim, he could follow the rules and make each claim. Instead, he just said no—no to everything.* 166 Cong. Rec. S521 (daily ed. Jan. 23, 2020).

D. Summary of the President's Response

The President's lawyers responded with two major arguments which depend upon knowledge about executive privilege and the immunity of close presidential advisors.

First, they argued that the President could not be impeached for refusing to allow his **close advisors** to testify, since they were **absolutely immune** from appearance and testimony before Congress.

Second, they argued that the President could not be impeached for obstructing materials subject to **executive privilege**.

II. THE HOUSE MANAGERS' ARGUMENTS

The House Managers used traditional forms of constitutional argument to support the Second Article of Impeachment. In the following summary of the House case, **Rep. Schiff** (D-CA) spoke of **text, history** and **precedent**, and finally to the future **consequences** if Congress were to fail to convict.

> *The House's presentation of the second article will therefore focus on three core areas that confirm the President's obstruction and require his removal from office: first, the singular importance and role of* ***the impeachment clause*** *for our democracy and why an effort by a President to obstruct an impeachment inquiry is, in and of itself, an impeachable offense; second, why the President's extensive effort to cover up evidence of his misconduct is* ***unprecedented in American history*** *and without lawful*

cause or justification; and, finally, why the President's obstruction poses a direct threat to our system of self-governance, with consequences for all Americans—today and ***in the future****—and for both Chambers of Congress.* 166. Cong. Rec. S456 (daily ed. Jan. 22, 2022) (emphasis added).

A. Textual Argument and Founders' Meaning

As we saw earlier, the House Managers contended that the obstruction article did not need to be a common crime to be impeachable, but could be a violation of the Constitution. House Managers argued that a constitutional violation was sufficient to impeach. They further argued that the Impeachment Clause—the text—would be useless if it were to allow the President to retain control over all information in an impeachment inquiry. They asserted that the President was claiming the power of impeachment for himself, contravening the Constitution. U.S. Const. art. I, §§ 2–3.

> *The Constitution entrusts the House with the* ***"sole Power of Impeachment."*** *The* ***Framers*** *thus ensured what common sense requires—that the House, and not the President, determines the existence, scope, and procedures of an impeachment investigation into the President's conduct.* House Managers Brief, 166 Cong. Rec. S292 (daily ed. Jan. 21, 2020) (emphasis added).

> *By categorically obstructing the House's impeachment inquiry, President Trump claimed* ***the House's sole impeachment power*** *for himself and sought to shield his misconduct from Congress and the American people. Id.* (emphasis added).

> *Through the* **impeachment clause,** ***the Framers*** *of the Constitution empowered Congress to thoroughly investigate Presidential malfeasance—and to respond, if necessary, by removing the President from office. This entire framework depends on Congress's ability to discover, and then to thoroughly and effectively investigate, Presidential misconduct. Without the ability of Congress to do that, the impeachment power is a nullity. If you can't investigate it, you can't enforce it and can't apply it.* 166 Cong. Rec. S456 (daily ed. Jan. 22, 2020) (statement of Rep. Schiff) (emphasis added).

> ***The Framers of the Constitution*** *purposefully entrusted the power of impeachment to the legislative branch so that it may protect the American people from a corrupt President. Well, the times, Senators, have found us. If Congress allows*

President Trump's obstruction to stand, it essentially nullifies the impeachment power. Senators, we are the keepers, the protectors, the defenders of what the Framers intended. We must hold any unprincipled and undisciplined Executive accountable. 166 Cong. Rec. S545 (daily ed. Jan. 24, 2020) (statement of Rep. Demings) (emphasis added).

B. Past Precedent

The House Managers relied heavily on the Nixon impeachment articles which depended upon the President Nixon's "cover-up" of the burglary of his political opponents' offices, which led to his resignation. It was widely believed at the time that the "cover-up" (revealed by the Watergate Tapes) was far more damaging than the underlying offense. In the Nixon impeachment, there was an Article charging "obstruction of Congress." **Rep. Nadler** (D-NY) argued that President Trump's refusal to provide information was far worse than Nixon's behavior:

This Presidential stonewalling of Congress is unprecedented in the 238-year history of our constitutional Republic. It puts even President Nixon to shame. 166 Cong. Rec. S488 (daily ed. Jan. 23, 2020).

Rep. Garcia (D-TX), a former judge, explained the precedent, beginning with a comparison to President Trump's record. She makes particular reference to permission of White House aides to testify in the Nixon impeachment hearings. President Trump did not permit his close aides or lawyers to testify (even if a number of officials voluntarily stepped forward to testify in the House Intelligence committee).

*So let's recap. No documents—zero, goose egg, nada—in response to over **70** requests—**70** requests and 5 subpoenas. There was no attempt to negotiate, no genuine attempt to accommodate. There was categorical, indiscriminate, and unprecedented stonewalling. Again, never in my time as a lawyer or as a judge have I seen this kind of total disrespect in defiance of a lawfully issued subpoena—and all on President Trump's orders. And it could continue because this obstruction of Congress is real, and it is beyond—**beyond—comparison**.* 166 Cong. Rec. S458 (daily ed. Jan. 24, 2020) (emphasis added).

Rep. Lofgren (D-CA) elaborated:

*Even **President Nixon**, who famously attempted to defy a subpoena for tape recordings of his conversations, let his* *most senior staff testify before Congress.* 166 Cong. Rec. S548 (daily ed. Jan. 24, 2020) (emphasis added).

I remember listening on TV as John Dean testified before the Senate Watergate Committee. He was the President's lawyer. President Nixon didn't block him. Not only did President Nixon allow his staff to testify before Congress; he publicly directed them to testify and without demanding a subpoena. Actually, with the Senate Watergate investigation, President Nixon said:

> All members of the White House staff will appear voluntarily when requested by the committee. They will testify under oath, and they will answer fully all proper questions.

Now compare that to President Trump. He publicly attacked the House's impeachment inquiry, calling it "constitutionally invalid," and he ordered every single person working in the executive branch to defy the House impeachment inquiry. Id.

C. Future Precedent

Constitutional interpreters worry about their rulings' effect on future precedent—here, what a future precedent will mean for future impeachments. **Rep. Nadler** (D-NY) and **Rep. Crow** (D-CO) explained:

At bottom, the [President's] arguments amount to a claim that the President can dictate the terms of his own impeachment inquiry. President Trump's lawyers may insist his grounds for defying Congress are unique and limited; that they only apply here, just this one time; that it was the House, not the President, that broke from precedent; that he would gladly comply with subpoenas if only the House would do as he insists. That is pure fantasy. The President's arguments are not a one-ride ticket. They are not unique to these facts. Unless they are firmly and finally rejected here, these bogus excuses will reappear every time Congress investigates any President for serious abuses of power—every single time. They will constitute a playbook for ignoring oversight, available to ***all future Presidents****—Democratic and Republican.* 166 Cong. Rec. S551 (daily ed. Jan. 24, 2020) (statement of Rep. Nadler) (emphasis added).

Remember, the ***precedent*** *that you set in this trial will shape American democracy for the* ***future****. It will govern this President, and it will govern those who follow. If you let* *the President get away with his obstruction, you risk grave and irreparable harm to the* ***separation of powers itself****. Representative Lawrence Hogan, a Republican from Maryland, made this point during the Nixon impeachment hearing.*

(Text of Videotape presentation.)

Mr. HOGAN (Republican). The historical precedent we are setting here is so great because in every future impeachment of a President, it is inconceivable that the evidence relating to that impeachment will not be in the hands of the executive branch which is under his controls. So I agree with the gentleman from Ohio, Mr. Seiberling, if we do not pass this article today, the whole impeachment power becomes meaningless.

166 Cong. Rec. S559 (daily ed. Jan. 24, 2020) (statement of Rep. Crow) (emphasis added) (quoting Mr. Hogan).

If President Trump is allowed to remain in office after this conduct, historians will mark the date that this Senate allowed this President to break one of our mightiest defenses against tyranny. They will wonder why Congress so readily surrendered one of its core constitutional powers. They will wonder why Congress admitted that a President can get away with anything, can violate any constitutional rule, any liberty, any request for information, and get away with it simply by saying: I don't have to answer your questions. Congress has no power to make me answer questions about my conduct. 166 Cong. Rec. S552 (Jan. 24, 2020) (statement of Rep. Nadler).

D. Structure

Given that obstruction of Congress asserts a congressional prerogative to obtain information from the Executive branch, it is not surprising that the House Managers asserted structural arguments.

If we allow President Trump to escape accountability, we will inflict lasting damage on the ***separation of powers*** *among our branches of government—our fundamental system of* ***checks and balances****. It would inflict irreversible damage by allowing this Commander in Chief and establishing precedence[sic] for future Presidents to act corruptly or abusively and then use the vast powers of their office—the Office of the Presidency—to conceal their own misconduct from Congress and the American people. In other words, we would create a system that allows this*

> *President and any future President to really do whatever he or she wants.* 166 Cong. Rec. S545 (daily ed. Jan. 24, 2020) (statement of Rep. Demings) (emphasis added).

E. Shared Constitutional Norms

The House Managers stressed the ancient principle that '**no man is above the law**.' This is an ethical principle because it is broader than any statute or crime and it applies in many situations. For example, when the Supreme Court rejected the idea that President Clinton did not have to respond to a private lawsuit, in *Clinton v. Jones* (Chapter 2), it said that no President is "above the laws." 520 U.S. 681, 697 (1997). Similarly, this ethical adage applies to any person who seeks to serve the country in an elected position, whether in Congress or the Executive. The idea is that, in a democracy, all elected persons serve the people.

> *A system in which the President cannot be charged with a crime, as the Department of Justice believes, and in which he can nullify the impeachment power through blanket obstruction, as President Trump has done here, is a system in which the President is* ***above the law***. House Managers Brief, 166 Cong. Rec. S297 (daily ed. Jan. 21, 2020) (emphasis added).

> *The President should not be treated as immune from criminal liability because he is subject to impeachment but then be allowed to sabotage the impeachment process itself. That is what this President did. That places him dangerously* ***above the law*** *and beyond the separation of powers. Presidents can't be above the law. Presidents, like everyone else, must obey subpoenas served in an impeachment inquiry.* 166 Cong. Rec. S553 (daily ed. Jan. 24, 2020) (statement of Rep. Lofgren) (emphasis added).

> *[N]o other American could seek to obstruct an investigation into his or her wrongdoing in this way. * * * * We would not allow—I am convinced that we would not allow any member of our State or local governments to use the official powers of their office to cover up crimes and misdeeds. As this body is well aware, mayors and Governors have gone to jail for doing so. Sheriffs and police chiefs are certainly not immune.* 166 Cong. Rec. S545 (daily ed. Jan. 24, 2020) (statement of Rep. Demings).

QUESTIONS ON THE HOUSE ARGUMENTS

Impeachment Article II—Strong or Weak?: As we saw earlier, the House Managers insisted that an "abuse of power" was sufficient for impeachment.

The President argued that there needed to be an existing crime or statute that he violated. It is worthwhile knowing, however, that contempt of Congress is a crime. 2 U.S.C. § 192 (2018):

> Every person who having been summoned as a witness by the authority of either House of Congress to give testimony or to produce papers upon any matter under inquiry before either House, * * * * or any committee of either House of Congress, willfully makes default, or who, having appeared, refuses to answer any question pertinent to the question under inquiry, shall be deemed guilty of a misdemeanor, punishable by a fine of not more than $1,000 nor less than $100 and imprisonment in a common jail for not less than one month nor more than twelve months.

Does knowing that obstruction of justice is a crime put the Second Article on stronger constitutional ground? (Review the debate in Chapter 3 about why the consensus is that crimes alone are *not* the measure of an impeachable offense). More importantly, what is the relationship of Article I to Article II of the First Trump Impeachment? Could Article II have stood alone? Presidents often resist congressional requests for information, but few scholars believe that resistance alone is an impeachable offense.[2]

The Court of Public Opinion: As we have noted throughout the book, Members of Congress are elected and as such pay attention to public opinion. This is not a bug, but an essential feature of, our constitutional system. Members have a constitutional duty to represent their constituents. *See* Chapter 1 (discussing the concept of representation). In an impeachment, the House Managers were trying not only to convince the Senators but also the public—so that the public would convince the Senators. From the public's perspective, the second Article of Impeachment was likely quite a bit weaker than the first. Obstruction of justice may sound like a terrible wrong to lawyers or judges or Members of Congress, but it is an abstract idea to the average layman. Compare it to "taking bribes from America's enemies" or "cheating on an election" or "burglarizing your political enemy's headquarters." The constitutional audience for impeachments—the average voter—is likely to find these far more concrete charges of wrongdoing. Moreover, the Second Article hinged on the First Article. If one believed that President Trump had done nothing wrong in the telephone call to Ukrainian President Zelensky, then what was wrong with failing to respond to Congress's requests? From the layman's vantage point, if there was no substantive offense, no abuse of power, then what did it matter that the President failed to comply with Congress's demands? Even if Americans do

---

[2] Consider Cass Sunstein's analysis of the "obstruction" count in the Nixon impeachment: "On the one hand, failure to comply with a subpoena that stems from (mere) suspicion of independently impeachable actions is hardly as grave as those actions * * * * On the other hand, the Constitution certainly gives the House the authority to investigate whether impeachable wrongdoing has occurred. If the President declines to cooperate with a lawful investigation, and if he has no good-faith argument that he is legally entitled to do so, there is a strong argument that he has committed a misdemeanor within the meaning of the impeachment clause." Cass Sunstein, Impeachment: A Citizen's Guide 93–94 (2017).

not like liars, many at the time had seemed accustomed to President Trump's lies.

Why Bother with an "Obstruction of Congress" Article?: First, Congress is used to compelling the average citizen or corporation to comply with its orders (this is an everyday affair in Washington), so why not the President? Why should there be a different rule for him as opposed to the average individual? Second, wholesale refusal to cooperate had not happened in either the Nixon or Clinton impeachments. President Trump was prepared to defy those precedents. As Rep. Garcia (a former Judge) explained: President Nixon (whose misdeeds are now widely condemned) allowed his top advisors to testify before Congress. Third, if the law is fairly clear that individuals must comply with congressional requests for information in ordinary legislative matters, why should the President—or his aides—be able to refuse in the far more constitutionally important arena of impeachment? If the President must comply with Congress when it has an average need, why not when Congress has a more pressing need? Finally, the precedent of wholesale denial was troubling. Will future miscreant Presidents use the same strategy? By adding an "obstruction" count to the Articles, Congress furthered its institutional interest in claiming the "sole" power to impeach and to set the rules of impeachment.

Institutional Arbitrage—Inconsistencies in the President's Case?: In the 2017 Mueller investigation, the President's lawyers argued that President Trump could not be indicted in a criminal trial at least in part because the proper remedy was impeachment. Oversimplified, the argument was: You can't take me to criminal court, because Congress is the proper place to judge me. In the impeachment, however, the President took a different position. He claimed that the impeachment was illegal, unconstitutional, even a "hoax." 166 Cong. Rec. S533 (daily ed. Jan. 24, 2020) (statement of Rep. Garcia (D-TX), repeating the President's public statements). As Rep. Crow (D-CO) notes above, why should someone be able, on the one hand, to embrace impeachment to avoid a criminal trial, but then hamstring the impeachment? I have used the term "institutional arbitrage" here to suggest that in a system where there are multiple institutions, lawyers may try to take advantage of institutional differences by making arguments in one branch that are inconsistent with arguments made elsewhere, so that they win in both branches. (Arbitrage generally means that one benefits from taking advantage of different financial markets, but it also applies to institutions more generally). We will see this move again when we consider the President's arguments about executive privilege.

Criminal Contempt Power as Weak?: Presidents are unusually positioned to protect themselves and their aides against contempt of Congress charges. Criminal contempt proceedings are rarely used against members of the executive branch.[3] Why? Presidents are in charge of the Justice Department which must bring the criminal contempt charges. And

---

[3] *See, e.g.*, Todd D. Peterson, *Prosecuting Executive Branch Officials for Contempt of Congress*, 66 N.Y.U. L. Rev. 563, 576 (1991); Timothy T. Mastrogiacomo, *Showdown in the Rose Garden: Congressional Contempt, Executive Privilege, and the Role of the Courts*, 99 Geo. L. J. 163, 177–78 (2010).

this applies to both Democratic and Republican Presidents: when the House held President Obama's Attorney General Eric Holder in contempt[4] for failing to comply with its demands, he did not prosecute himself. If executive officials have committed criminal contempt, should not their cases be referred to an institution with no political conflict of interest—an independent body? That idea, which sounds perfectly plausible, led to a law authorizing "independent counsels" appointed to investigate presidential misconduct. That law lapsed, however, after the Clinton impeachment. Today, Attorneys General may name what are known as "Special Counsels," like Robert Mueller, to investigate the President and his aides, but there is nothing to require such inquiries. Given the lack of alternate means to investigate, is it not surprising that Congress would choose to use the impeachment power to enforce its power of inquiry? If that's true, why don't they use the impeachment power more often with respect to lower-level officials? (Hint: see the Note in Part Two on the political safeguards of impeachment).

Judging in One's Own Cause: The Congress argued that the President, by refusing to comply, was judging his own cause—acting above the law. No citizen or state official charged with an offense can refuse to comply with demands of a legally constituted court. But is that disingenuous? What is Congress doing? The House was saying that Congress was the judge to determine whether the President had to comply with its requests. Does the Constitution's text help here? What would you say if you were a Member of the House Managers' team and you were charged with being "above the law"? What constitutional text would you cite? Hint: think of the word "sole."

From Congress's perspective, the sole power of impeachment means that it has a duty to check an errant President. This textual commitment supports Congress's claim that the separation of powers does not exist only to separate our political institutions but also to check them. At least from a textual basis, Congress has a stronger constitutional claim that it is authorized to proceed, even if they are making rules for their own investigation. Presidents are likely to argue that they are head of their branch, but there is no text that actually grants Presidents the "sole" power of execution; some commentators and even judges have written that the President has "all" executive power, but it is worthwhile noting that the word "all" is not in fact in the Constitution's grant of executive power. (For more on the latter controversy, *see* Chapter 2 on the unitary executive.)

III. PRESIDENT'S ARGUMENTS

The President made two principal legal arguments against the Second Article. First, the President's lawyers argued that his close advisors were immune from testifying. Second, the subpoenas asked for materials covered by executive privilege and a President could not

---

[4] *See* Gbemende Johnson, *Adjudicating Executive Privilege: Federal Administrative Agencies and Deliberative Process Privilege Claims in U.S. Courts*, 53 Law & Soc. Rev. 823 (2019) (discussing the controversy about General Holder).

be impeached for asserting a lawful privilege.[5] The House responded to each of these arguments as explained below.

A. Presidential Advisors Absolute Immunity?

The President's lawyers argued that some of the persons subpoenaed were close advisors to the President and absolutely immune from testifying. The President's Brief explained:

> *The [House] sought testimony from a number of the President's closest advisors despite the fact that, under longstanding, bipartisan practice of prior administrations of both political parties and similarly long-standing guidance from the Department of Justice, those advisors are absolutely immune from compelled testimony before Congress related to their official duties.* President's Brief, 166 Cong. Rec. S290 (daily ed. Jan. 21, 2020).

As I write, this question remains unanswered by the courts, which we discuss in the notes below, although it is clear that the United States Supreme Court has held that the President himself has no absolute immunity in the case of criminal proceedings. *United States v. Nixon*, 418 U.S. 683, 714 (1974).

1. *Text and Founders' Meaning*

There is no constitutional text on the question whether close advisors to the President are immune from testifying before Congress. This is not unusual as the text is spare, and there are many, many constitutional questions that the Constitution does not specifically address. In this case, however, it is interesting that there is text on congressional immunity. The Speech or Debate Clause says that Members of Congress cannot be questioned about their statements made in the House or Senate. U.S. Const. art. I, § 6, cl. 1. In short, House Members are immune from prosecution for their political statements. There is no similar textual provision providing immunity for the President or the President's staff. Similarly, Congress has a textual basis on which to claim its investigative power based on the "necessary and proper" clause, which affords it all powers "necessary and proper" to perform its express powers and all other government powers. U.S. Const. art. I, § 8. There is no "necessary and "proper" clause for presidential power. If one were to apply a rule to the Constitution that everything unexpressed in the text was barred, then the President would have had no basis for

---

5 The President also argued that the subpoenas were not properly authorized under House rules and the House committee had not permitted "agency counsel" to appear with individuals to assert executive privilege. 166 Cong. Rec. S592 (Jan. 27, 2020) (Mr. Philbin). This book does not treat those claims.

refusing Congress's requests. Traditionally, however, Presidents as far back as George Washington have acted to the contrary, asserting that they have a duty to protect the nation that may supersede Congress's need for information. In short, they have allied themselves with the claims of their institution.

Rather than an express power, the President asserted powers "implied" from the nature of his power under Article II to faithfully execute the laws. U.S. Const. art. II, § 3. His claim: the President cannot "faithfully execute" the laws without confidential advice. Close presidential advisors must not be worried every time that they give advice to the President that the advice will be broadcast to the world. Why? Because this can retard an adviser from giving candid advice. A simple example reflects the advisor's dilemma. What if the advisor believes that a presidential course of action is both dangerous and unlawful. Should she fear to tell the President because then she may have to testify to Congress about her advice? Assume the President takes the advice, could Congress then call the advisor to testify that the President was thinking of doing something illegal? Throughout the law, special relationships are granted privileges of confidentiality: for example, at common law, lawyers could not be forced to testify against their clients and married persons could not be forced to testify against their spouses. Presidents have urged that a similar privilege should apply to their close advisors.

2. *Past Precedent*

The President's lawyers relied upon **executive branch precedent**, namely opinions of the Office of Legal Counsel (OLC), an office inside the Department of Justice that advises the President on constitutional questions. As part of their duties, the Office of Legal Counsel issues published opinions. Note that these are opinions, not law. OLC opinions may be deployed by courts, but are not dispositive of legal issues.[6] In this case, the President's lawyers relied heavily on the OLC opinions holding that close personal advisors are immune.[7]

---

6 *See, e.g. Campaign for Accountability v. U.S. Dept. of Justice*, No. 1068 (KBJ), 486 F.Supp.3d 424, 436 (D.C.D.C. 2020) ("OLC's ubiquitous function does not establish whether, or to what extent, an OLC opinion can ever speak with authority on [the law]"); *Brennan Center for Justice v. U.S. Dep't of Justice*, 697 F.3d 184, 203 (2d Cir. 2012) ("OLC's legal advice and analysis informs the decisionmaking of Executive Branch officials on matters of policy, but OLC's legal advice is not itself dispositive as to any policy adopted").

7 Testimonial Immunity Before Congress of the Former Counsel to the President, 43 Op. O.L.C. 1, 1 (2019); Immunity of the Assistant to the President and Director of the Office of Political Strategy and Outreach from Congressional Subpoena, 38 Op. O.L.C. (2014); Immunity of the Former Counsel to the President from Compelled Congressional Testimony, 31 Op. O.L.C. 191, 192 (2007); Assertion of Executive Privilege with Respect to Clemency Decision, 23 Op. O.L.C. 1, 5 (1999); Immunity of the Counsel to the President from Compelled Congressional Testimony, 20 Op. O.L.C. 308, 308 (1996).

Note the appeal to both Democratic and Republican officials who have asserted this immunity.

> *Following at least 50 years of* ***precedent****, the Department of Justice's Office of Legal Counsel advised that three senior advisers to the President—the Acting White House Chief of Staff, the Legal Advisor to the National Security Council, and the Deputy National Security Advisor—were absolutely immune from compelled congressional testimony. And based on that advice from the Office of Legal Counsel, the President directed those advisers not to testify*. 166 Cong. Rec. S591 (daily ed. Jan. 27, 2020) (statement of Mr. Philbin) (emphasis added).
>
> *Administrations of both political parties have asserted this immunity since the 1970s. President Obama asserted it as to the Director of the Office of Political Strategy and Outreach. President George W. Bush asserted it as to his former counsel and to his White House Chief of Staff. President Clinton asserted it as to two of his counsel. President Reagan asserted it as to his counsel, Fred Fielding, and President Nixon asserted it. This is not something that was just made up recently. There is a decades-long history of the Department of Justice providing the opinion that senior advisers to the President are immune from compelled congressional testimony, and it is the same principle that was asserted here. Id.*
>
> *As Attorney General Janet Reno advised President Clinton, the "immunity such advisers enjoy from testimonial compulsion by a congressional committee is absolute and may not be overborne by competing congressional interests." So that is Attorney General Janet Reno advising President Clinton. This is not a partisan issue. This is not a Republican or Democrat issue. Administrations of both parties have asserted this principle of immunity for senior advisers. Id.* at 592.

House Reply: The OLC argument should fail because the President should not be a "judge in his own cause." As we have seen, this was one of the House Managers' most basic ethical arguments, which is to say that *those charged with unlawful behavior as a general rule cannot determine their own liability*: just as you would ignore an opinion written by a citizen about the law, you should ignore an opinion by the President's own lawyers about the law. The President had no power to dictate the rules of an impeachment any more than an individual could tell a judge what to do. They also argued that it was an improper interpretation of the closest Supreme

Court case—*United States v. Nixon*, which rejected absolute immunity for the President himself—and suggested that there should be no absolute immunity for his close advisors, either. House Manager's Reply Memorandum, 166 Cong. Rec. S374 (daily ed. Jan. 21, 2020). We will consider the *Nixon* executive privilege case more fully below, and it is reprinted in Chapter 5.

3. Future Precedent

The President's arguments about future consequences relate to the future functioning of the Presidency.

> *And why does it matter? It matters because the Supreme Court has explained that the fundamental principle behind executive privilege is that it is necessary to have confidentiality in communications and deliberations in order to have good and worthwhile deliberations, in order to have people provide their candid advice to the President. Because if they knew that what they were going to say was going to be on the front page of the Washington Post the next day or the next week, they wouldn't tell the President what they actually thought. If you want to have good decision making, there has to be that zone of confidentiality.* 166 Cong. Rec. S592 (daily ed. Jan. 27, 2020) (statement of Mr. Philbin).

> *This is the way the Supreme Court put it: "Human experience teaches that those who expect public dissemination of their remarks may well temper candor with a concern for appearances and for their own interests to the detriment of the decision-making process." That was also from* United States v. Nixon. *Id.*

House Reply: The *Nixon* case (reprinted in Chapter 5) did *not* create an absolute privilege. It rejected claims of absolute immunity for the President himself. As we will see below, *Nixon* does not necessarily decide the issue because it involved a criminal proceeding, not an impeachment. The House also emphasized the consequences if the President could stonewall an impeachment. As noted above, earlier Presidents had complied, in part, with congressional demands. The Trump precedent now provides future Presidents with a reason to refuse to cooperate.

4. Structure

As we have seen before, the structural relationship of the institutions was invoked by **the President's lawyers**, namely the "separation of powers."

There are important rationales behind this immunity. One is that the President's most senior advisers are essentially his alter egos, and allowing Congress to subpoena them and compel them to come testify would be tantamount to allowing Congress to subpoena the President and force him to come testify, but that in separation of powers would not be tolerated. Congress could no more do that with the President than the President could force Members of Congress to come to the White House and answer to him. 166 Cong. Rec. S591–92 (daily ed. Jan. 27, 2020) (statement of Mr. Philbin).

There is also a second and important rationale behind this immunity, and that relates to executive privilege. The immunity protects the same interests that underlie executive privilege. The Supreme Court has recognized executive privilege that protects the confidentiality of the communications with the President and deliberations within his executive branch. As the Court put it in United States v. Nixon, "The privilege is fundamental to the operation of government and inextricably rooted in the separation of powers under the Constitution." So the Supreme Court has recognized the executive needs this privilege to be able to function. It is rooted in the separation of powers. Id. at S592.

House Reply: The House Managers argued that the President's lawyers were not being accurate in stating the rule set forth in the *Nixon case*—that there was no absolute immunity, only qualified immunity. They also argued that the separation of powers was undermined—rather than supported—by adopting absolute immunity, because the President's argument would not permit the Congress to check the President, which is the Congress's role under the separation of powers. These reflect two very different theories of the separation of powers—one which emphasizes the concept of separate institutions and the other that emphasizes checking institutions. (*See* Chapter 2 on separation of powers theories).

5. Shared Constitutional Norms

The Presidents' lawyers employed an **ethics of confidentiality** argument, as we have seen above: that if the President was to do a faithful job, then his close advisors needed to be able to provide him with candid advice, which, if revealed, might be damaging. Compelling such testimony would mean that fear of future disclosure would mean aides might not assert unpopular positions that may be in the President's, and the country's, interest.

House Reply: The House argued the **ethics of "who decides,"** which is to say that the President should not be the final decisionmaker on the constitutionality of his own actions. The idea that one should not be a "judge in one's own cause" is an old idea going back to the Founders. It is one basis for our constitutional structure which divides power the better to check abuse.

QUESTIONS AND NOTE ON ABSOLUTE IMMUNITY

What Role Should Judicial Decisions Play?: As we have seen before, an institutional clash between the Congress and the President raises the question of "who decides." The House Managers claimed that the courts had decided against absolute immunity in the *Nixon* case and the President could not decide the immunity of his own aides. But the House also claimed that *it* should be the ultimate arbiter of that immunity. Is that lawless? The President's lawyers argued at various points that the House Managers were avoiding their obligations "under the law," by which they were referring to "judicial" decision on the law. Simply as a matter of settling the dispute, should not both sides have recourse to "the law," meaning to the courts? Later in this Chapter, we will consider deeper questions about whether judicial precedents should govern in an impeachment. In the case of absolute immunity for the President's advisors, as we will see, judicial guidance has been *very slow in arriving*.

What Happens if Courts Don't Decide?: Turning to courts may sound like a good idea, but that can take time, far longer than an average impeachment trial. The question whether presidential advisers are absolutely immune has not been resolved, and may never be resolved by the Supreme Court. Consider the following train of events involving Congress's request to the President's Counsel, Don McGhan, which was pending during the First and Second Trump Impeachment trials. McGahn's testimony was sought by the House based on reports that he had dissuaded the President from firing Special Counsel Mueller.

At the time of the First Impeachment trial, there were two district court[8] cases directly addressing absolute immunity of the President's close advisors and both had decided *against that* immunity. One involved congressional testimony by George W. Bush's White House counsel, Harriet Miers. *Committee on the Judiciary v. Miers*, 558 F. Supp. 2d 53 (D.D.C. 2008).[9] The other involved congressional requests for McGahn's testimony. *See Committee on the Judiciary v. McGahn*, 415 F. Supp.3d 148 (D.D.C.

[8] District courts are the lowest level of federal courts. They are supervised by appellate courts. Appellate courts can be reversed by the Supreme Court.

[9] The *Miers* district court order was stayed during appeal, the appellate court specifically noting that it would be mooted upon the installation of a new Congress. *Comm. on Judiciary v. Miers*, 542 F.3d 909, 911 (D.C. Cir. 2008) (holding that, even if expedited, the appeal would continue until after the end of the term of the 110th Congress, at which point the Committee would cease to be a legal entity and the suit would be rendered moot). In fact, the President and the Congress in *Miers* reached an agreement to reveal various documents and the appeal was dismissed at the request of the parties. *Comm. on the Judiciary v. Miers*, 2009 WL 3568649 (Oct. 14, 2009).

2019), *rev'd on other grounds*, 951 F.3d 510 (D.C. Cir. 2020), *rev'd and remanded*, 968 F.3d 755 (D.C. Cir. 2020) (*en banc*), *rev'd on other grounds*, 973 F.3d 121 (D.C. Cir. 2020), *vacated pending reh'g en banc*, No. 19-5331 (Oct. 15, 2020). In both cases, district courts had rejected absolute immunity as inconsistent with the Supreme Court's decisions in *United States v. Nixon*, 418 U.S. 683 (1974) (Chapter 5) which denied absolute immunity to the President, and *Clinton v. Jones*, 520 U.S. 681 (1977) (Chapter 2), which held that the President was not immune from a civil lawsuit.

Relying upon *Miers*, the district court judge in the *McGhan* case, Judge Ketanji Brown Jackson, reasoned that the Justice Department had essentially *invented* the doctrine of absolute immunity:

> To make the point as plain as possible, it is clear to this Court * * * * with respect to senior-level presidential aides, absolute immunity from compelled congressional process simply *does not exist*. Indeed, absolute testimonial immunity for senior-level White House aides appears to be a fiction that has been fastidiously maintained over time through the force of sheer repetition in OLC opinions, and through accommodations that have permitted its proponents to avoid having the proposition tested in the crucible of litigation. *Committee on the Judiciary v. McGahn*, 415 F. Supp. 3d 148, 214 (D.D.C. 2019) (emphasis added).

Judge Jackson (an Obama appointee) relied upon the reasoning of Judge Bates (a Bush appointee) ten years earlier in the *Miers* case, which in turn relied upon the Supreme Court's decisions. Judge Jackson wrote that the President's close advisors had a duty to the United States to protect the Constitution, and that the aide needed to appear before Congress and lawfully execute any claim of executive privilege on a question-by-question basis.

> Stated simply, the primary takeaway from the past 250 years of recorded American history is that Presidents are not kings. *See* The Federalist No. 51 (James Madison); The Federalist No. 69 (Alexander Hamilton); 1 Alexis de Tocqueville, *Democracy in America* 115–18 (Harvey C. Mansfield & Delba Winthrop eds. & trans., Univ. of Chicago Press 2000) (1835). This means that they do not have subjects, bound by loyalty or blood, whose destiny they are entitled to control. Rather, in this land of liberty, it is indisputable that current and former employees of the White House work for the People of the United States, and that they take an oath to protect and defend the Constitution of the United States. * * * *
>
> To be sure, there may well be circumstances in which certain aides of the President possess confidential, classified, or privileged information that cannot be divulged in the national interest and that such aides may be bound by statute or executive order to protect. But, in this Court's view, the withholding of such information from the public square in the national interest and at

> the behest of the President is a duty that the aide herself possesses. Furthermore, as previously mentioned, in the context of compelled congressional testimony, such withholding is properly and lawfully executed *on a question-by-question basis* through the invocation of a privilege, where appropriate. *Id.* (emphasis added).

On appeal, the D.C. Circuit reversed Judge Jackson's decision in an opinion written by Judge Thomas B. Griffith, concluding that the courts *had no power to even decide the case.* The specific doctrine invoked was one of "standing," which is a legalism for having an "injury." Judge Griffith argued that there was no individual right at stake[10] and therefore that the courts had no jurisdiction to decide a debate between the Congress and the President, particularly in light of the fact that there was a pending impeachment. The Griffith opinion was promptly overturned by the full D.C. Circuit, all of its judges, known as an "en banc" court. *Committee on the Judiciary v. Donald F. McGahn*, 968 F.3d 755 (D.C. Cir. Aug. 7, 2020) (en banc). The D.C. Circuit emphasized Congress's need for information:

> The Constitution charges Congress with certain responsibilities, including to legislate, to conduct oversight of the federal government, and, when necessary, to impeach and remove a President or other Executive Branch official from office. Possession of relevant information is an essential precondition to the effective discharge of all of those duties. Congress cannot intelligently legislate without identifying national problems in need of legislative solution and relying on testimony and data that provide a deeper understanding of those problems, their origins, and potential solutions. It likewise cannot conduct effective oversight of the federal government without detailed information about the operations of its departments and agencies. And it cannot undertake impeachment proceedings without knowing how the official in question has discharged his or her constitutional responsibilities. *Id.* at 761.

Id. On remand, Judge Griffith found again that the courts had no power to decide because there was no statute authorizing the Congress to go to court. Again, the full D.C. Circuit vacated the Griffith panel's judgment and agreed to rehear the case, *en banc*, for a second time. *Committee on the Judiciary v. McGahn*, 973 F.3d 121 (D.C. Cir., 2020), *vacated pending reh'g en banc*, No. 19-5331 (Oct. 15, 2020). As of the drafting of this Chapter, oral argument had been moved to April 2021.

---

[10] Critics claimed that Judge Griffith's conclusion would not really avoid so-called "political" questions: in the very distant past, Congress had simply arrested individuals who refused to testify. *McGrain v. Daugherty*, for example, was an appeal by "a recusant witness held in custody under process of attachment issued from the United States Senate in the course of an investigation." 273 U.S. 135, 150 (1927). If Congress could not sue to enforce its subpoena power, it could simply arrest Mr. McGahn, who would seek a writ of habeas corpus (meaning "release the body"), and the standing issue would disappear because Mr. McGahn would have suffered an injury by confinement.

Given this history, is the argument that the House Managers should wait for courts compelling or an evasion?

B. Executive Privilege?

The President's lawyers argued that the President could not be impeached for obstructing Congress because his failure to provide the documents and testimony was lawful under the doctrine of "**executive privilege**." The House responded that many of the documents were not protected by executive privilege and that, in any event, the President had not claimed privilege. The President's lawyers contended:

> *The idea that asserting defenses and immunity—legal defenses and immunity in response to subpoenas, acting on advice of the Department of Justice—is an impeachable offense is absurd and is dangerous for our government.* 166 Cong. Rec. S593 (daily ed. Jan. 27, 2020) (statement of Mr. Philbin).
>
> *House Democrats' obstruction theory is wrong first and foremost because, in a government of laws, asserting privileges and rights to resist compulsion is not obstruction; it is a fundamental right. In Bordenkircher v. Hayes,*[11] *the Supreme Court explains that to "punish a person because he has done what the law plainly allows him to do is a due process violation of the most basic sort, and for an agent of the State to pursue a course of action whose objective is to penalize a person's reliance on his legal rights is patently unconstitutional." Id.*

House Reply: The President had no legal right to withhold information in an impeachment proceeding. The *Nixon* case, 418 U.S. 683 (1974) (reprinted Chapter 5) decided that the President could, in some circumstances, exert executive privilege but in a different kind of case—a criminal proceeding, not an impeachment. No court has ever held that there is executive privilege on questions relating to an impeachment.

1. *Text and Founders' Meaning*

There is no constitutional text on the precise question of executive privilege.[12] This has caused some conservative theorists to argue that the President has *no* executive privilege whatsoever,

---

[11] *Bordenkircher v. Hayes*, 434 U.S. 357, 363 (1978) (holding that the Due Process clause of the 14th Amendment is not violated when a prosecutor exercises her discretion in whether or not to prosecute and on what charges, so long as such discretion is not intentionally discriminatory).

[12] Raoul Berger, Executive Privilege: A Constitutional Myth (1974).

and that *Nixon* was wrongly decided.[13] **The President's lawyers** could not argue that any constitutional text supported such a privilege. But they did argue that the House Managers' argument based on text was inconclusive.

> *What that is essentially saying—they point to the fact that article I, section 2, gives the House "the sole Power of Impeachment," and they claim because it has the sole power of impeachment, the courts have no role; the House is the final word; it is the judge of its own powers. But that is contrary to constitutional design. There is no power that is unchecked in the Constitution. The sole power of impeachment given to the House simply means that power is given solely to the House, not anywhere else.* 166 Cong. Rec. S593 (daily ed. Jan. 27, 2020) (statement of Mr. Philbin).

> *Madison explained that where the executive and legislative branches come into conflict, in Federalist No. 49, "[neither] of them, it is evident, can pretend to exclusive or superior right of settling the batteries between their respective powers." But that is exactly what the House managers have asserted in this case. They have said that the House becomes supreme. There is no need for them to go to court. The Executive must be wrong. Any resistance to their subpoena is obstruction. If you claim that our subpoena is invalid, we don't have to do anything to address that concern; we will just impeach you because resistance is obstruction of Congress. Id.*

Notice that this sounds like a structural argument. It is not infrequent that, in the absence of a clear text, textualists will resort to vaguer structural arguments. The idea is that the House cannot be the sole judge of executive privilege since it is a party in the case. The President's lawyers also invoked the Founders on the basic constitutional structure, arguing that the Founders expected friction; in other words, that the President and the Congress would disagree about their constitutional powers.

The House Managers replied that the only relevant constitutional text gave them the "sole" power to impeach which would be useless without information. That text revealed that the Founders expected the Congress to use the power of impeachment.

---

[13] Saikrishna Bangalore Prakash, *A Critical Comment on the Constitutionality of Executive Privilege*, 83 Minn. L. Rev. 1143, 1145–8 (1999) ("there are reasons to doubt that the Constitution itself conveys a unilateral right to conceal executive communications * * * * while favoring a narrow executive privilege, I believe that Congress must confer such a privilege").

2. *Past Precedent*

The President's lawyers argued that, during the Clinton impeachment, Democrats had maintained that invoking privileges was not an impeachable offense.

> *This is a principle that in the past, in the Clinton impeachment, was recognized across the board, that it would be improper to suggest that asserting rights is an impeachable offense. Harvard law professor Laurence Tribe said: "The allegation that invoking privileges and otherwise using the judicial system to shield information* * * *is an abuse of power that should lead to impeachment and removal from office is not only frivolous, but also dangerous."* 166 Cong. Rec. S593 (daily ed. Jan. 27, 2020) (statement of Mr. Philbin).

House Reply: The House replied that there was no valid executive privilege being made in the Trump Impeachment: in fact that the President had "never" asserted executive privilege. The way to assert that privilege, they argued, was for the President and his advisors to respond to *specific questions* not to direct a wholesale refusal to comply. There could be no claim of "generalized" privilege, but only with respect to specific documents or questions. 166 Cong. Rec. S544 (daily ed. Jan. 24, 2020) (statement of Rep. Lofgren).

The President's lawyers also argued that the D.C. Circuit (judicial precedent) had held that the branches owed each other a duty to accommodate each other's information requests,[14] and that the House had failed to engage in that accommodation.

House Reply: The impeachment power is an express power in the Constitution and it would mean nothing if the President could refuse to comply with information requests related to the impeachment. Court decisions on regular interbranch encounters (when Congress was seeking information regarding legislation) were not relevant since they were not requests involving impeachment. In any event, it was not for the D.C. Circuit to decide how an impeachment should be run—the Constitution gives Congress the "sole" right of impeachment. In short, the kind of accommodation that might apply in a normal interbranch encounter was contrary to the Congress's "sole" power of impeachment.

---

[14] *U.S. v. American Tel. & Tel. Co.*, 567 F.2d 121, 127 (D.C. Cir. 1977). ("[R]ather, each branch should take cognizance of an implicit constitutional mandate to seek optimal accommodation through a realistic evaluation of the needs of the conflicting branches in the particular fact situation.").

3. *Structure and Future Precedent*

The President's lawyers argued that executive privilege was a necessary structural "check" on the Congress. Counsel Philbin argued that supporting the Second Article of Impeachment, without accommodation, would mean that the House would be more powerful than the President in future impeachment disputes. The House would automatically be entitled to any possible document request.

> *Impeachment under the Constitution is the thermonuclear weapon of interbranch friction, and where there is something like a rifle or a bazooka at the House's disposal to address some friction with the executive branch, that is the next step. It is incrementalism in the Constitution—not jumping straight to impeachment—that is the solution. If the House could jump straight to impeachment, that would alter the relationship between the branches. It would suggest that the House could make itself superior over the Executive to dangle the threat of impeachment over any demand for information made to the Executive.* 166 Cong. Rec. S593 (daily ed. Jan. 27, 2020) (statement of Mr. Philbin).
>
> *This is checks and balances, this friction, this clashing between the branches. It is not evidence of an impeachable offense. It is the separation of powers in its practical operation. It is part of the constitutional design. Id.*

The House Managers argued that the text of the Constitution did in fact make the House powerful in cases of impeachment. Nothing in the nontextual principle of the separation of powers suggested anything different. Courts were not more powerful than the Congress in an impeachment.

4. *Shared Constitutional Norms*

The President's lawyers made ethical arguments based on the notion that "rights" cannot be "wrongs." If the President has a "right" to resist demands from Congress, then this could not constitute an impeachable offense—where the term "right" is being used not in a legal, but a moral sense. **The House Managers** replied that there was no such right to withhold information, either morally or legally.

QUESTIONS AND NOTE ON EXECUTIVE PRIVILEGE

Hardball in Soft Guise?: In the First Trump Impeachment trial, the President's lawyers relied heavily on the claim that the President and Congress generally tend, in the normal case, to work out claims of executive privilege by negotiation. And that is true in a normal case. But there are differences that arise in an impeachment trial. First, the idea that judicial practice in a normal case should dictate procedure in an impeachment is inconsistent with Supreme Court precedent which holds that Congress has control over its processes, and that courts will not interfere in impeachments. *Walter Nixon v. United States*, 506 U.S. 224 (1993) (reprinted Chapter 2). Second, the judicial precedents are clear that generalized claims of privilege—the kind the President's lawyers made when saying "no documents whatsoever"—are not good enough. The President and his officials must make particularized claims—meaning that they must focus on particular documents. Generalized claims, as were made in *United States v. Nixon*, 418 U.S. 683 (1974) (reprinted in Chapter 5) have not been considered sufficient by the lower courts. Is this a case of impeachment "hardball"—moving well beyond the accepted legal precedents requiring a particularized showing—wrapped in something that sounds tamer (negotiation and "incrementalism")?

Textualism and Executive Privilege: The President relied upon many highly textual arguments in arguing against the first Article of Impeachment. His lawyers were very precise. But notice that, in the case of executive privilege, as well as absolute immunity for close advisors, the President did not make a textual argument because there is no text that says either the President has executive privilege, or his advisors have absolute immunity. Is this methodologically insincere or inconsistent? If text controls in one case, why should not the lack of text mean that he has no executive privilege? Some conservatives believe that in fact there is no such thing.[15] Some textualists believe that if something is not expressly provided in the Constitution, then the power or privilege does not exist. If that is correct, was it right for the President to insist upon constitutional text in arguing about Impeachment Article I, but not in Impeachment Article II?

Bait and Switch—Institutional Arbitrage Once More: As we noted above, when more than one institution is involved, the disputing parties may take advantage of that situation. A party takes one position when circumstances favor it, and then another in another context, to make it impossible for the other party to win. It is more than inconsistency: it is a "heads you lose, tails you lose" kind of argument. The President's lawyers argued that the House had to go to court to determine executive privilege questions *before* the House could impeach. *See* 166 Cong. Rec. S384 (daily ed. Jan. 21, 2020) (statement of Mr. Sekulow). But, at the same time, the President's lawyers were arguing in the *McGahn* case that the courts had no power to decide the case. Brief for Defendant-Appellant at 14, *Committee on the Judiciary v. McGahn*, 951 F.3d 510 (D.C. Cir. 2020) (No. 19-5331) ("the Committee fails to satisfy these bedrock requirements of Article III standing"). If both those positions were correct, the House would fail; first because the courts should decide, and second because the courts would refuse to decide.

---

[15] Saikrishna Bangalore Prakash, *A Critical Comment on the Constitutionality of Executive Privilege*, 83 Minn. L. Rev. 1143, 1145–8 (1999) ("there are reasons to doubt that the Constitution itself conveys a unilateral right to conceal executive communications * * * *while favoring a narrow executive privilege, I believe that Congress must confer such a privilege").

What Role Should Judicial Opinions Play in an Impeachment?: The Constitution gives the "sole" power of impeachment to the Congress. And the Supreme Court has recognized that this means "sole," which is to say that the Congress's procedures, at least, should not be second-guessed. *Walter Nixon v. United States*, 506 U.S. 224 (1993) (reprinted Chapter 2). *This raises a very serious question about constitutional decision-making outside the courts.* Some legal academics have argued that the courts have the "final say" on matters constitutional, a position called "judicial supremacy." But can that possibly hold in a case where the Constitution appears to give the final word to the Congress? If House Members were to say that the Court's decisions had no bearing, how would the public have reacted? The public is accustomed to thinking that courts are neutral arbiters. There are good constitutional arguments, both from the text and the Supreme Court itself, that Congress has enormous power in an impeachment, but would it have been wise for Members of Congress to pronounce judicial decisions entirely irrelevant?

The Case for Some Judicial Review: One can certainly imagine Congress might abuse its powers in ways lawyers would immediately suspect are "unconstitutional" in an impeachment. Some have suggested, for example, that a *presidential* impeachment should not proceed by congressional committee despite the holding of the *Walter Nixon* case that a *judicial* impeachment by that means would not be second-guessed by the courts. *Walter Nixon v. United States*, 506 U.S. 224 (1993) (reprinted Chapter 2). The constitutional argument against such a process for a presidential impeachment goes like this: Since a President is the nation's leader, ousting him by committee raises constitutional issues. Why should a small set of representatives from a few states have the power to determine the fate of the leader of the nation as a whole? (This is a good example of structural argument, of the kind Professor Charles L. Black Jr. pioneered).

The President's lawyers seemed to suggest that there had to be judicial review of the executive privilege claims. The hypothetical noted in the paragraph above could suggest support for that view. But one should pause before reaching that conclusion, at least in the First Trump Impeachment. Hypotheticals, however beloved by law professors, are just that: theoretical constitutional conflicts, not real ones. Impeachment of a President by committee? An interesting question, but one likely never to arise. Why would any single Senator tolerate exclusion from such a momentous process? Surely, Senators would imagine that their political opponents at the next election would charge them with dereliction of duty. My point: When one is faced with constitutional hypotheticals, it is worth considering that there may be more immediate remedies: in this case, basic political incentives can operate to make the hypothetical constitutional violation just that, hypothetical.

Chapter Five

JUDICIAL REASONING AND IMPEACHMENT

We have seen how Congress and the President reason about the Constitution during an impeachment. In this Chapter, we consider what the *courts* have to say, how they reason differently, and whether it should matter in an impeachment.

We know, from Chapter 2, that courts have generally refused to consider questions arising in an impeachment. If the Trump lawyers had gone to court to ask whether the President could be impeached for an abuse of power, the court is most likely to have refused to decide that question based on its decision in *Walter Nixon*, 506 U.S. 224 (1993), that the question was left "solely" to the Congress. But both parties in the impeachment, particularly when it came to Article II, argued that judicial cases were relevant on the question of Congress's powers of inquiry and the President's executive privilege.

In this Chapter, we reprise our analysis of legal argument by looking at the actual cases to ask whether the President or the House were accurately reflecting the law. The first case, *McGrain v. Daugherty*, 273 U.S. 135 (1927), discusses Congress's oversight powers. The second case, *United States v. Nixon*, 418 U.S. 683 (1974), examines the President's executive privilege. Neither resolves the questions raised in the First Trump Impeachment, but they provide the judicial background against which both the President and the House Managers argued.

As you read these materials, ask yourself whether the lawyers were playing fast and loose with the law? In Chapter 3, we saw that the President's lawyers were playing what we might call legal "hardball," meaning that he was arguing contrary to a wide legal consensus, that an ordinary "crime" was necessary to impeach. Were the President's lawyers doing that when it came to Article II of the Impeachment? What about Congress? Were they assuming too much about Congress's own powers? What role should judicial precedents play in the impeachment? Should they matter at all? Should they be persuasive because they are issued outside the political drama of the day? Should they be persuasive because they are issued by a more neutral, unelected body? Should they control the lawyers in the impeachment?

Finally, and most importantly, *compare the kinds of arguments you see in these cases with the kinds of arguments made by Members of Congress and by the President and their lawyers*. How are they different or the same? We will return to that question at the end of the Chapter.

I. CONGRESSIONAL OVERSIGHT POWERS

Despite a long history of congressional "oversight" of the executive, it was not until the 1920s that the Supreme Court addressed the question of congressional oversight powers under the Constitution. In the following case, *McGrain v. Daugherty*, Congress sought information from the brother of a former Attorney General to assess whether the Attorney General had failed in his duties to execute the law "faithfully." U.S. Const. art. IV, cl. 3. Congress charged the Attorney General with failing to prosecute corruption, including bribery of federal officials.

Vocabulary: Subpoena—order to produce a person or documents; **Attached**—archaic meaning arrested here; **Committed**—put in custody/jail; **Implied power**—one that is not expressly stated in the Constitution's text but is implied from general powers granted; **Practical construction**—the meaning that the Constitution has been given in practice over time by constitutional actors.

MCGRAIN V. DAUGHERTY

United States Supreme Court
273 U.S. 135 (1927)

MR. JUSTICE VAN DEVANTER delivered the opinion of the Court.

[A Senate committee subpoenaed Mally Daugherty, the brother of the former Attorney General, Harry M. Daugherty, for his testimony in regard to his financial dealings. The full Senate voted to enforce the subpoena—an order to appear—and directed its law enforcement officer, the Sergeant at Arms, to enforce its order. The Sergeant of Arms arrested Daugherty in Ohio, but Daugherty appealed his detention to a court, and that court held that the Senate had no lawful grounds for its order. The Senate was investigating whether the former Attorney General had failed to prosecute individuals involved in the scandal known as Teapot Dome, in which executive branch officials defrauded taxpayers by leasing federal oil fields in Wyoming far below fair market-rates in return for bribes from oil barons. The subpoena ordered Daugherty to provide a wide array of financial documents, but the issue in the case concerned whether he could be forced to appear in person before Congress.]

[Mally Daugherty] is asserting—and is standing on his assertion—that the Senate is without power to interrogate him, even if the questions propounded be pertinent and otherwise legitimate, which for present purposes must be assumed.

* * * *

[The Court began its analysis with the text of the Constitution]

The Constitution provides for a Congress, consisting of a Senate and House of Representatives, and invests it with "**all legislative powers**" granted to the United States, and with power "to make all laws which shall be **necessary and proper**" for carrying into execution these powers and "all other powers" vested by the Constitution in the United States or in any department or officer thereof. Article 1, §§ 1, 8. * * * *(emphasis added).

But there is no provision expressly investing either house with power to make investigations and exact testimony, to the end that it may exercise its legislative function advisedly and effectively. So the question arises whether this power is so far incidental to the legislative function as to be implied.

[It then turned to precedent—how legislatures had acted in the past]

In actual legislative practice, power to secure needed information by such means has long been treated as an attribute of the power to legislate. It was so regarded in the British Parliament and in the colonial Legislatures before the American Revolution, and a like view has prevailed and been carried into effect in both houses of Congress and in most of the state Legislatures.

[More specifically, the Court looked at early congressional precedent—the history of Congress's investigations]

This power was both asserted and exerted by the House of Representatives in 1792, when it appointed a select committee to inquire into the St. Clair expedition and authorized the committee to send for necessary persons, papers and records. Mr. Madison, who had taken an important part in framing the Constitution only five years before, and four of his associates in that work, were members of the House of Representatives at the time, and all voted for the inquiry. * * * *

Among those by the Senate, the inquiry ordered in 1859 respecting the raid by John Brown and his adherents on the armory and arsenal of the United States at Harper's Ferry is of special significance. The resolution directing the inquiry authorized the committee to send for persons and papers, to inquire into the facts pertaining to the raid and the means by which it was organized and supported, and to report what legislation, if any, was necessary to preserve the peace of the country and protect the public property. * * * *

Later on the committee reported that Thaddeus Hyatt, although subpoenaed to appear as a witness, had refused to do so; whereupon the Senate ordered that he be attached and brought before it to answer for his refusal. When he was brought in, he answered by challenging the power of the Senate to direct the inquiry and exact testimony to aid it in exercising its legislative function. The question of power thus presented was thoroughly discussed by several senators—Mr. Sumner of Massachusetts taking the lead in denying the power, and Mr. Fessenden of Maine in supporting it. * * * * The vote was taken on a resolution pronouncing the witness' answer insufficient and directing that he be committed until he should signify that he was ready and willing to testify. The resolution was adopted—44 senators voting for it and 10 against.

[The Court noted Congress's own precedent and debates about its power]

The arguments advanced in support of the power are fairly reflected by the following excerpts from the debate: Mr. Fessenden of Maine: * * * * "We propose to legislate upon a given state of facts, perhaps, or under a given necessity. Well, sir, proposing to legislate, we want information. We have it not ourselves. It is not to be presumed that we know everything * * * * We want information on certain subjects. How are we to get it? The Senator says, ask for it. I am ready to ask for it; but suppose the person whom we ask will not give it to us: what then? Have we not power to compel him to come before us? Is this power, which has been exercised by Parliament, and by all legislative bodies down to the present day without dispute—the power to inquire into subjects upon which they are disposed to legislate—lost to us? Are we not in the possession of it? Are we deprived of it simply because we hold our power here under a Constitution which defines what our duties are, and what we are called upon to do? Congress have appointed committees after committees, time after time, to make inquiries on subjects of legislation. Had we not power to do it? Nobody questioned our authority to do it. We have given them authority to send for persons and papers during the recess. Nobody questioned our authority. We appoint committees during the session, with power to send for persons and papers. Have we not that authority, if necessary to legislation?" * * * *

Mr. Crittenden of Kentucky: * * * * "We have a right, in consequence of it, a necessary incidental power, to summon witnesses, if witnesses are necessary. * * * * The means of carrying into effect by law all the granted powers, is given where legislation is applicable and necessary; but there are subordinate matters, not amounting to laws; there are inquiries of the one house or the other house, which each house has a right to conduct; which each has, from the beginning, exercised the power to conduct; and each has, from the beginning, summoned witnesses. This has been the practice of the government from the beginning; and if we have a right to summon the witness, all the rest follows as a matter of course."

[The Court went on to consider precedent in the state courts]

The state courts quite generally have held that the power to legislate carries with it by necessary implication ample authority to obtain information needed in the rightful exercise of that power, and to employ compulsory process for the purpose.

In Burnham v. Morrissey, 14 Gray, 226, 239, (74 Am. Dec. 676), the Supreme Judicial Court of Massachusetts, in sustaining an exertion of this power by one branch of the Legislature of that commonwealth, said:

> The House of Representatives has many duties to perform, which necessarily require it to receive evidence, and examine witnesses. * * * * It has often occasion to acquire a certain knowledge of facts, in order to the proper performance of legislative duties. We therefore think it clear that it has the constitutional right to take evidence, to summon witnesses, and to compel them to attend and to testify. This power to summon and examine witnesses it may exercise by means of committees.

In Wilckens v. Willet, 40 N.Y. (Keyes) 521, 525, a case which presented the question whether the House of Representatives of the United States possesses this power, the Court of Appeals of New York said:

> That the power exists there admits of no doubt whatever. It is a necessary incident to the sovereign power of making laws; and its exercise is often indispensable to the great end of enlightened, judicious, and wholesome legislation.

In People v. Keeler, 2 N.E. 615, 624 (52 Am. Rep. 49), where the validity of a statute of New York recognizing and giving effect to this power was drawn in question, the Court of Appeals approvingly quoted what it had said in *Wilckens v. Willet*, and added:

> It is difficult to conceive any constitutional objection which can be raised to the provisions authorizing legislative committees to take testimony and to summon witnesses. In many cases it may be indispensable to intelligent and

> effectual legislation to ascertain the facts which are claimed to give rise to the necessity for such legislation, and the remedy required, and irrespective of the question whether in the absence of a statute to that effect either house would have the power to imprison a recusant witness, I cannot yield to the claim that a statute authorizing it to enforce its process in that manner is in excess of the legislative power. To await the slow process of indictment and prosecution for a misdemeanor, might prove quite ineffectual, and necessary legislation might be obstructed, and perhaps defeated, if the legislative body had no other and more summary means of enforcing its right to obtain the required information. That the power may be abused, is no ground for denying its existence. It is a limited power, and should be kept within its proper bounds; and, when these are exceeded, a jurisdictional question is presented which is cognizable in the courts. * * * * Throughout this Union the practice of legislative bodies, and in this state, the statutes existing at the time the present Constitution was adopted, and whose validity has never before been questioned by our courts, afford strong arguments in favor of the recognition of the right of either house to compel the attendance of witnesses for legislative purposes, as one which has been generally conceded to be an appropriate adjunct to the power of legislation, and one which, to say the least, the state Legislature has constitutional authority to regulate and enforce by statute.

[The Supreme Court then turned to its own precedents]

The first decision was in Anderson v. Dunn, 6 Wheat. 204, 5 L. Ed. 242. The question there was whether, under the Constitution, the House of Representatives has power to attach and punish a person other than a member for contempt of its authority—in fact, an attempt to bribe one of its members. The court regarded the power as essential to the effective exertion of other powers expressly granted, and therefore as implied. The argument advanced to the contrary was that as the Constitution expressly grants to each house power to punish or expel its own members and says nothing about punishing others, the implication or inference, if any, is that power to punish one who is not a member is neither given nor intended. The court answered this by saying:

> Page 225: "There is not in the whole of that admirable instrument, a grant of powers which does not draw after it others, not expressed, but vital to their exercise; not

substantive and independent, indeed, but auxiliary and subordinate."

Page 233: "This argument proves too much; for its direct application would lead to the annihilation of almost every power of Congress. To enforce its laws upon any subject, without the sanction of punishments, is obviously impossible. Yet there is an express grant of power to punish in one class of cases, and one only, and all the punishing power exercised by Congress, in any cases, except those which relate to piracy and offenses against the laws of nations, is derived from implication. Nor did the idea ever occur to any one, that the express grant in one class of cases repelled the assumption of the punishing power in any other. The truth is, that the exercise of the powers given over their own members, was of such a delicate nature, that a constitutional provision became necessary to assert or communicate it. Constituted, as that body is, of the delegates of confederated states, some such provision was necessary to guard against their mutual jealousy, since every proceeding against a representative would indirectly affect the honor or interests of the state which sent him."

[The Court went on to distinguish cases that appeared to hold that Congress had more limited powers in some situations; these have been omitted for space reasons]

* * * *

While these cases are not decisive of the question we are considering, they definitely settle two propositions which we recognize as entirely sound and having a bearing on its solution: One, that the two houses of Congress, in their separate relations, possess, not only such powers as are expressly granted to them by the Constitution, but such auxiliary powers as are necessary and appropriate to make the express powers effective; and the other, that neither house is invested with "general" power to inquire into private affairs and compel disclosures, but only with such limited power of inquiry as is shown to exist when the rule of constitutional interpretation just stated is rightly applied. * * * *

[The Court concluded its reasoning by referring to the Founding and the history of Congress]

We are of opinion that the power of inquiry—with process to enforce it—is an essential and appropriate auxiliary to the legislative function. It was so regarded and employed in American Legislatures before the Constitution was framed and ratified. Both houses of

Congress took this view of it early in their history—the House of Representatives with the approving votes of Mr. Madison and other members whose service in the convention which **framed the Constitution** gives special significance to their action—and both houses have employed the power accordingly up to the present time. The acts of 1798 and 1857, judged by their comprehensive terms, were intended to recognize the existence of this power in both houses and to enable them to employ it "more effectually" than before. So, when their practice in the matter is appraised according to the circumstances in which it was begun and to those in which it has been continued, it falls nothing short of a practical construction, long continued, of the constitutional provisions respecting their powers, and therefore should be taken as fixing the meaning of those provisions, if otherwise doubtful. * * * *

A legislative body cannot legislate wisely or effectively in the absence of information respecting the conditions which the legislation is intended to affect or change * * * *. Experience has taught that mere requests for such information often are unavailing, and also that information which is volunteered is not always accurate or complete; so some means of compulsion are essential to obtain what is needed. All this was true before and when the Constitution was framed and adopted. In that period the power of inquiry, with enforcing process, was regarded and employed as a necessary and appropriate attribute of the power to legislate—indeed, was treated as inhering in it. Thus there is ample warrant for thinking, as we do, that the constitutional provisions which commit the legislative function to the two houses are intended to include this attribute to the end that the function may be effectively exercised.

The contention is earnestly made on behalf of the witness that this power of inquiry, if sustained, may be abusively and oppressively exerted. If this be so, it affords no ground for denying the power. The same contention might be directed against the power to legislate, and of course would be unavailing. We must assume, for present purposes, that neither houses will be disposed to exert the power beyond its proper bounds, or without due regard to the rights of witnesses. * * * * And it is a necessary deduction from [prior] decisions * * * that a witness rightfully may refuse to answer where the bounds of the power are exceeded or the questions are not pertinent to the matter under inquiry.

[Finally, the Court addressed whether Congress had a legislative purpose for seeking the information in the case of Mally Daugherty]

We come now to the question whether it sufficiently appears that the purpose for which the witness' testimony was sought was to obtain information in aid of the legislative function. The court below [concluded that the legislative purpose was a pretext for **judging** and **investigating** the Attorney General, Mally Daugherty's brother], as is shown by the following excerpts from its opinion: * * * *

> The Senate's action is invalid and absolutely void, in that, in ordering and conducting the investigation, it is exercising the judicial function, and power to exercise that function, in such a case as we have here, has not been conferred upon it expressly or by fair implication. What it is proposing to do is to determine the guilt of the Attorney General of the shortcomings and wrongdoings set forth in the resolutions. It is 'to hear, adjudge, and condemn.' It so doing it is exercising the judicial function. * * * *. This it has no power to do.

[The Supreme Court then rejected the lower court's position and found that Congress had a legislative purpose]

We are of opinion that the court's ruling on this question was wrong, and that it sufficiently appears, when the proceedings are rightly interpreted, that the object of the investigation and of the effort to secure the witness' testimony was to obtain information for legislative purposes.

It is quite true that the resolution directing the investigation does not in terms avow that it is intended to be in aid of legislation; but it does show that the subject to be investigated was the administration of the Department of Justice—* * * * whether the Attorney General and his assistants were performing or neglecting their duties in respect of the institution and prosecution of proceedings to punish crimes and enforce appropriate remedies against the wrongdoers; specific instances of alleged neglect being recited. Plainly the subject was one on which legislation could be had and would be materially aided by the information which the investigation was calculated to elicit. This becomes manifest when it is reflected that the functions of the Department of Justice, the powers and duties of the Attorney General, and the duties of his assistants are all subject to regulation by congressional legislation, and that the department is maintained and its activities are carried on under such appropriations as in the judgment of Congress are needed from year to year.

The only legitimate object the Senate could have in ordering the investigation was to aid it in legislating, and we think the subject-matter was such that the presumption should be indulged that this was the real object. An express avowal of the object would have been better; but in view of the particular subject-matter was not indispensable. * * * *

We think the resolution and proceedings give no warrant for thinking the Senate was attempting or intending to try the Attorney General at its bar or before its committee for and crime or wrongdoing. Nor do we think it a valid objection to the investigation that it might possibly disclose crime or wrongdoing on his part. * * * *

We conclude that the investigation was ordered for a legitimate object; that the witness wrongfully refused to appear and testify before the committee and was lawfully attached; that the Senate is entitled to have him give testimony pertinent to the inquiry, either at its bar or before the committee; and that the district court erred in discharging him from custody under the attachment. * * * *

What has been said requires that the final order in the district court discharging the witness from custody be **reversed**.

QUESTIONS ON CONGRESS'S POWER TO INVESTIGATE

Did the House Exaggerate Its Powers?: Having now read *McGrain*, what do you think of the House Managers' arguments that they were clearly entitled to documents from the President? Congress won the *McGrain* case even though it was pretty clear that they were seeking to "check" a top executive branch official by revealing whether he was faithfully executing the law (or aiding the commission of a crime). If Congress can check a top executive branch official, why not the President? Does the fact that the House Managers were exercising the *impeachment power*, rather than the *legislative power*, make their case stronger or weaker? Or both? It could make it stronger because the impeachment power is an express power: it is specifically stated in the Constitution. But could it also make it weaker? As we will see in the next case and the notes that follow, the President has always been viewed as deserving of special respect as leader of the nation.

Did the President's Lawyers Diminish Congress's Powers Inconsistent with the Caselaw?: *McGrain* was decided nearly 100 years ago. Since then, the Supreme Court has repeatedly reaffirmed the power of Congress to subpoena documents from individuals and corporations and executive branch officials if there is a proper "legislative purpose." *See, e.g., Barenblatt v. United States*, 360 U.S. 109, 111 (1959) ("the scope of the [congressional] power of inquiry, in short, is as penetrating and far-reaching as the potential power to enact and appropriate under the Constitution"); *Eastland v. U.S. Servicemen's Fund*, 421 U.S. 491, 504 (1975) ("this Court has often noted that the power to investigate is inherent in the power to make laws"). After the First Trump Impeachment, the breadth of this power was reaffirmed in 2020 in a case involving President Trump's personal pre-presidential financial documents: *Trump v. Deutsche Bank AG*, 943 F.3d 627 (2nd Cir. 2019), *rev'd*, *Trump v. Mazars USA, LLP*, 140 S.Ct. 2019 (2020); *Trump v. Committee on Oversight*, 380 F.Supp.3d 76 (D.C. Circ. 2019), *rev'd*, *Trump v. Mazars USA*,

LLP, 140 S.Ct. 2019 (2020). Were the President's lawyers correct to imply that the Congress had no power to investigate the President?

Was the President Correct That Presidential Oversight Is Different?: During the First Trump Impeachment, the President's lawyers argued that oversight over the President should be treated differently from oversight over private citizens. Just because every corporation and citizen is required to comply with congressional subpoenas does not mean that the President must. Is this consistent with the principle that the President is not above the law? (*See* Chapter 2 and the discussion of *Clinton v. Jones*, 520 U.S. 681 (1997)). Is it consistent with the impeachment power?

After the impeachment was over, the Supreme Court appeared to affirm the principle that presidential oversight is different, even when it comes to the President's personal affairs. Congress had subpoenaed President Trump's and the Trump family's financial documents for the purpose of drafting legislation on money laundering and bank fraud. In a pair of cases, the Supreme Court appeared to agree with the President that presidential oversight is different. They required that President Trump reveal his personal finances, but imposed a higher standard for Congress's requests than for a prosecutor's requests. *Trump v. Deutsche Bank AG*, 943 F.3d 627 (2nd Cir. 2019), *rev'd*, *Trump v. Mazars USA, LLP*, 140 S. Ct. 2019 (2020); *Trump v. Committee on Oversight*, 380 F.Supp.3d 76 (D.C. Circ. 2019), *rev'd*, *Trump v. Mazars USA, LLP*, 140 S. Ct. 2019 (2020).

The Supreme Court held in *Mazars*—the case involving congressional requests—that the President is entitled to a higher standard of review, at least as far as the President's personal documents. 140 S. Ct. 2019, 2035–36 (2020). Courts must "carefully assess whether the asserted legislative purpose warrants the significant step of involving the President and his papers." *Id.* at 2035. Specifically, congressional subpoenas for the President's information must be detailed, narrow in scope, and not so burdensome as to impair the functions of the executive branch. *Id.* at 2035–36.

A different result occurred in a case brought by a New York County District Attorney, Cy Vance. In that case, the court approved the request for the President's personal financial documents, denying a higher standard to the President, under the theory that the President was not above the law, something we saw in Chapter 2, in *Clinton v. Jones*, 520 U.S. 681 (1997). *Trump v. Vance*, 140 S. Ct. 2412, 2429–2430 (2020). *Mazars* was not decided at the time of the First Trump Impeachment. If it had been, would it have helped the President? What would Congress have argued? (Hint: does *Mazars* involve an impeachment?)

Executive Branch Wrongdoing and Legislative Purposes: Many congressional investigations purport to uncover executive "wrongdoing," meaning the failure of the Executive to faithfully execute the laws. In *McGrain*, Congress was worried that executive branch officials were pocketing bribes. The Supreme Court's oversight decisions, however, have focused on Congress's need for information to *legislate*. In *Mazars*, for example, the Court accepted the idea that Congress was seeking the President's financial records to "help guide legislative reform in areas ranging from money laundering and terrorism to foreign involvement in a U.S. election," 140 S. Ct. at 2026, even though the records could also contain evidence of a crime. Everyone knows that the real reason for these subpoenas, of course, is to reveal wrongdoing (or in some cases political embarrassment). Would it be better if courts acknowledged this? Presumably, the Congress has a constitutional argument that it has the power to see that the President and his agents, "faithfully" execute the law, *particularly in cases where the President's own agents (the Department of the Justice) have provided no investigation.* After all, the President has a conflict of interest making it unlikely he will investigate himself or his agents. That power relies upon a "checking" vision of the separation of powers, however, not the idea that Congress needs the information to legislate. At the same time, Presidents have a similar argument that Congress should not be the judge in its own cause about its own investigative powers. History is full of examples of congressional investigations that were abusive to individuals (*see* the McCarthy anti-communist hearings in the 1950s) or simply highly repetitive, led by both Republican and Democratic committees alike.

Were Judicial Precedents Relevant?: The Supreme Court, as we have seen in Chapter 2, has tried to avoid deciding cases on impeachment. That means that any judicial precedent is likely to be distinguishable—the facts are different. If that is true, one should ask whether either party should have relied upon legal precedents at all. The President's lawyers could simply have said that Congress's general oversight authority did not apply to him as President since, although the cases often dealt with high officials (as in *McGrain*), none dealt with the President himself. Similarly, the Congress could say that any limits provided by the cases were equally irrelevant because the impeachment power was different. Why should or should not the lawyers for the President or the Congress rely upon these cases? Does it help their arguments to look to a body, like the courts, reputed to apply impartial views? Or does it unnecessarily cede power to the judiciary in an essentially democratic controversy—one to be decided by the people, rather than 9 wise men and women on the Court?

Is There an Asymmetric Effect to Precedent?: The judiciary has decided cases involving criminal trials and Presidents, *see United States v. Nixon*, 418 U.S. 683 (1974), as well as cases involving civil and criminal proceedings against Presidents, *see Trump v. Vance*, 140 S. Ct. 2412, 2429–30 (2020); *Clinton v. Jones*, 520 U.S. 681 (1997). The courts have also reviewed individual complaints about overzealous congressional investigations affecting individual citizens' rights. It is worth asking whether the President has easier access to the courts than does the Congress. The President's Justice Department is a frequent litigator in the Supreme Court. Individual Members of Congress typically cannot go to court; an entire House of Congress (a much larger collective effort) must vote to litigate. The transaction costs for litigating by Congress (meaning the cost of time and money in reaching agreement to go to court) may well be higher for Congress than the President. Does this difference mean that Congress is institutionally disadvantaged relative to the President? One of the most well-known sociological facts of Supreme Court practice is that those who are "repeat players" in the Court tend to have the chance to develop rules in their own favor.[1]

II. EXECUTIVE PRIVILEGE

In the 1970s, for the first time, the Supreme Court considered the idea of executive privilege, only to reject its application to then President Richard Nixon. Since that time, a number of cases in the D.C. Circuit have had to adjudicate disputes between the President and the Congress based on the premise that there is such a thing as a presidential privilege. We will consider the principal Supreme Court case on this issue, *United States v. Nixon*, 418 U.S. 683 (1974), and President Trump's legal arguments, in the First Trump Impeachment.

A. Summary of the *Nixon* Case Arguments

President Trump claimed that he could not be impeached for raising a legitimate privilege and thus the Second Article of Impeachment should fail. Executive privilege does not exist in the text of the Constitution. Nevertheless, many Presidents of both political parties have asserted such claims.

The Supreme Court first recognized an executive privilege in *United States v. Nixon,* 418 U.S. 683 (1974). Nixon had been subpoenaed by a court, not the Congress. That court was considering an indictment of the Watergate burglars, the men who actually performed the break-in of the Democratic Committee headquarters. Nixon was named as an unindicted coconspirator, meaning that he was not actually charged with a crime (the general position of Presidents is that they cannot be indicted while in office) but was somehow involved. (Evidence later showed that Nixon was involved in a complex cover-up of the burglary). Because the opinion is not succinct, I provide a summary of the basic arguments before the case.

Text: Although there is no constitutional text providing a presidential privilege, there is an express legislative privilege that prevents Members of Congress from being charged for a crime based on what they say in Congress. U.S. Const. art. I, § 6, cl. 1. The Supreme Court so acknowledges: "*Nowhere in the Constitution, as we have noted earlier, is there any explicit reference to a privilege of confidentiality.*" *U.S. v. Nixon*, 418 U.S. 683, 711 (1974).

Past Precedent: In this case, applicable precedents abound. One set of precedents involves the relationship between the Court and the President or Congress. Another involves the history of criminal

---

[1] Marc Galanter, *Why the Haves Come Out Ahead: Speculation on the Limits of Legal Change*, 9 Law & Soc'y Rev. 95 (1974).

proceedings where an individual's liberty is at stake (here, the individual Watergate burglars). A third kind of precedent addresses the nature of presidential privileges.

Structural Precedent—Courts v. President: The most famous case cited here is about the Supreme Court's own powers—*Marbury v. Madison,* 5 U.S. 137 (1803). *Marbury* is famous for announcing what many assumed at the Founding, that courts would have the power to strike down laws as unconstitutional. As we saw in Chapter 2, this is called the "power of judicial review." *Marbury* is typically known as an example of a conflict between the Courts and the Congress. In such conflicts, the Congress wants to do "X." The Court says in reply that Congress has no power to do X. This pits the Court against the other departments. At the beginning of the *Nixon* case, the Court explains on the one hand that it should defer to the constitutional judgments of the other departments, but takes that away with the other hand, explaining that the Supreme Court has rejected the constitutional judgments of both Congress and the President.

Criminal Case Precedents—the Burr Case: The Watergate burglars were being tried for a simple crime; they claimed that, in their defense, they needed information from the President. Courts are very cautious in criminal prosecutions: sending someone to jail is a serious deprivation of liberty. Many legal rules protect criminal defendants (*e.g.*, the jury must find an offense "beyond a reasonable doubt"). Although this is not immediately clear from the decision, the most important precedent was a similar case from the Founding: *United States v. Burr*, 25 F. Cas. 49 (1807), which is cited frequently. Aaron Burr was tried for treason and claimed that he needed documents from President Jefferson to prove his innocence, that he was not trying to betray the United States by waging war, but rather, he was following Jefferson's instructions.

Privileges Precedents—Distinguishing Confidentiality from National Security: This is the first case to treat a presidential claim of executive privilege outside the national security context. The Court looked to its earlier precedents on privileges that have been asserted for national security reasons. In distinguishing those cases, the Court found that, in *Nixon*, the President was asserting a "generalized" interest in confidentiality. What the Court means by a "generalized interest" is that the President is not claiming that, in the particular case, the facts dictate a privilege—as, for example, if there were an imminent threat of war or pandemic. Instead, he is claiming that there is a general rule that means he need not comply at all.

Future Precedent for the President and Courts: The Court considers whether its rule will do harm to confidential presidential advice, and finds that the harm is not great because few Presidents or their aides will be asked to testify in a criminal proceeding. *U.S. v. Nixon,* 418 U.S. 683, 712 (1974). The Court goes on to find a substantial reason to provide evidence to one who faces prison. The defendant's more specific need trumps a President's more general claims:

> On the other hand, the allowance of the privilege to withhold evidence that is demonstrably relevant in a criminal trial would cut deeply into the guarantee of due process of law and gravely impair the basic function of the courts. A President's acknowledged need for confidentiality in the communications of his office is general in nature, whereas the constitutional need for production of relevant evidence in a criminal proceeding is specific and central to the fair adjudication of a particular criminal case in the administration of justice. Without access to specific facts a criminal prosecution may be totally frustrated. The President's broad interest in confidentiality of communications will not be vitiated by disclosure of a limited number of conversations preliminarily shown to have some bearing on the pending criminal cases. *Id.*

Vocabulary: Subpoena duces tecum—an order seeking the production of documents; **Compulsory process**—the power of a court to compel a person to testify or produce documents; **Quash**—to extinguish the power of a subpoena; **In camera**—a judge's review of documents within his chambers, outside the view of others; **Third party**—refers to the fact that President Nixon was not named in the Watergate criminal proceeding; he was not under indictment.

UNITED STATES V. NIXON

United States Supreme Court
418 U.S. 683 (1974)

BURGER, C.J. delivered the opinion for the Court.

We turn to the claim that the [presidential] subpoena should be quashed because it demands "confidential conversations between a President and his close advisors * * * *"

[The Court first considered whether it had the power to hear the claim, concluding that it did]

In the performance of assigned constitutional duties each branch of the Government must initially interpret the Constitution, and the interpretation of its powers by any branch is due great respect from the others. The President's counsel, as we have noted, reads the Constitution as providing an absolute privilege of confidentiality for all presidential communications. Many decisions of this Court, however, have unequivocally reaffirmed the holding of Marbury v. Madison, 1 Cranch, 137 (1803), that "(i)t is emphatically the province and duty of the judicial department to say what the law is." * * * *

Our system of government "requires that federal courts on occasion interpret the Constitution in a manner at variance with the construction given the document by another branch." Powell v. McCormack, 395 U.S. at 549. And in Baker v. Carr, 269 U.S. at 211, the Court stated:

> (D)eciding whether a matter has in any measure been committed by the Constitution to another branch of government, or whether the action of that branch exceeds whatever authority has been committed, is itself a delicate exercise in constitutional interpretation, and is a responsibility of this Court as ultimate interpreter of the Constitution.

Notwithstanding the deference each branch must accord the others, the "judicial Power of the United States" vested in the federal courts by Art. III, s 1, of the Constitution can no more be shared with the Executive Branch than the Chief Executive, for example, can share with the Judiciary the veto power, or the Congress share with the Judiciary the power to override a Presidential veto. Any other conclusion would be contrary to the basic concept of separation of powers and the checks and balances that flow from the scheme of a tripartite government. * * * * We therefore reaffirm that it is the province and duty of this Court "to say what the law is" with respect to the claim of privilege presented in this case.

[The Court went on to consider the nature of executive privilege, and rejected the idea that the President had an absolute privilege to keep secrets if the information was needed by a court]

In support of his claim of absolute privilege, the President's counsel urges two grounds, one of which is common to all governments and one of which is peculiar to our system of separation of powers. The first ground is the valid need for protection of communications between high Government officials and those who advise and assist them in the performance of their manifold duties; the importance of this confidentiality is too plain to require further discussion. Human experience teaches that those who expect public dissemination of their remarks may well temper candor with a concern for appearances and for their own interests to the detriment of the decision-making process.

Whatever the nature of the privilege of confidentiality of Presidential communications in the exercise of Art. II powers, the privilege can be said to derive from the supremacy of each branch within its own assigned area of constitutional duties. Certain powers and privileges flow from the nature of enumerated powers; the protection of the confidentiality of Presidential communications has similar constitutional underpinnings.

The second ground asserted by the President's counsel in support of the claim of absolute privilege rests on the doctrine of separation of powers. Here it is argued that the independence of the Executive Branch within its own sphere, insulates a President from a judicial subpoena in an ongoing criminal prosecution, and thereby protects confidential Presidential communications.

However, neither the doctrine of separation of powers, nor the need for confidentiality of high-level communications, without more, can sustain an absolute, unqualified Presidential privilege of immunity from judicial process under all circumstances. The President's need for complete candor and objectivity from advisers calls for great deference from the courts. However, when the privilege depends solely on the broad, undifferentiated claim of public interest in the confidentiality of such conversations, a confrontation with other values arises.

Absent a claim of need to protect military, diplomatic, or sensitive national security secrets, we find it difficult to accept the argument that even the very important interest in confidentiality of Presidential communications is significantly diminished by production of such material for in camera inspection with all the protection that a district court will be obliged to provide.

The impediment that an absolute, unqualified privilege would place in the way of the primary constitutional duty of the Judicial Branch to do justice in criminal prosecutions would plainly conflict with the function of the courts under Article III. In designing the structure of our Government and dividing and allocating the sovereign power among three co-equal branches, the Framers of the Constitution sought to provide a comprehensive system, but the separate powers were not intended to operate with absolute independence.

While the Constitution diffuses power the better to secure liberty, it also contemplates that practice will integrate the dispersed powers into a workable government. It enjoins upon its branches separateness but interdependence, autonomy but reciprocity. Youngstown Sheet & Tube Co. v. Sawyer, 343 U.S., at 635, 72 S. Ct., at 870 (Jackson, J., concurring).

To read the Art. II powers of the President as providing an absolute privilege as against a subpoena essential to enforcement of criminal statutes on no more than a generalized claim of the public interest in confidentiality of nonmilitary and nondiplomatic discussions would upset the constitutional balance of "a workable government" and gravely impair the role of the courts under Art. III.

[The Court goes on to outline the scope of an "executive privilege"]

Since we conclude that the legitimate needs of the judicial process may outweigh Presidential privilege, it is necessary to resolve those competing interests in a manner that preserves the essential functions of each branch. The right and indeed the duty to resolve that question does not free the Judiciary from according high respect to the representations made on behalf of the President.

The expectation of a President to the confidentiality of his conversations and correspondence, like the claim of confidentiality of judicial deliberations, for example, has all the values to which we accord deference for the privacy of all citizens and, added to those values, is the necessity for protection of the public interest in candid, objective, and even blunt or harsh opinions in Presidential decisionmaking. A President and those who assist him must be free to explore alternatives in the process of shaping policies and making decisions and to do so in a way many would be unwilling to express except privately.

These are the considerations justifying a presumptive privilege for Presidential communications. The privilege is fundamental to the operation of Government and inextricably rooted in the separation of powers under the Constitution. In Nixon v. Sirica, 487 F.2d 700 (1973), the Court of Appeals held that such Presidential communications are 'presumptively privileged, and this position is accepted by both parties in the present litigation. We agree with Mr. Chief Justice Marshall's observation, therefore, that "(i)n no case of this kind would a court be required to proceed against the president as against an ordinary individual." United States v. Burr, 25 F.Cas., at 192.

But this presumptive privilege must be considered in light of our historic commitment to the rule of law. This is nowhere more profoundly manifest than in our view that "the twofold aim (of criminal justice) is that guilt shall not escape or innocence suffer." Berger v. United States, 295 U.S. at 88. We have elected to employ an adversary system of criminal justice in which the parties contest all issues before a court of law. The need to develop all relevant facts in the adversary system is both fundamental and comprehensive.

The ends of criminal justice would be defeated if judgments were to be founded on a partial or speculative presentation of the facts. The very integrity of the judicial system and public confidence in the system depend on full disclosure of all the facts, within the framework of the rules of evidence. To ensure that justice is done, it is imperative to the function of courts that compulsory process be available for the production of evidence needed either by the prosecution or by the defense. Only recently the Court restated the ancient proposition of law, albeit in the context of a grand jury inquiry rather than a trial, "that 'the public * * * * has a right to every man's evidence,'" except for those persons protected by a constitutional, common-law, or statutory privilege.

The privileges referred to by the Court are designed to protect weighty and legitimate competing interests. Thus, the Fifth Amendment to the Constitution provides that no man "shall be compelled in any criminal case to be a witness against himself." And, generally, an attorney or a priest may not be required to disclose what has been revealed in professional confidence. These and other interests are recognized in law by privileges against forced disclosure, established in the Constitution, by statute, or at common law. Whatever their origins, these exceptions to the demand for every man's evidence are not lightly created nor expansively construed, for they are in derogation of the search for truth.

In this case the President challenges a subpoena served on him as a third party requiring the production of materials for use in a criminal prosecution; he does so on the claim that he has a privilege against disclosure of confidential communications. He does not place his claim of privilege on the ground they are military or diplomatic secrets. As to these areas of Art. II duties the courts have traditionally shown the utmost deference to Presidential responsibilities. In C & S Waterman S.S. Corp, 333 U.S. 103 (1948), dealing with Presidential authority involving foreign policy considerations, the Court said:

> The President, both as Commander-in-Chief and as the Nation's organ for foreign affairs, has available intelligence services whose reports are not and ought not to be published to the world. It would be intolerable that courts, without the relevant information, should review and perhaps nullify actions of the Executive taken on information properly held secret.

In United States v. Reynolds, 345 U.S. 1 (1953), dealing with a claimant's demand for evidence in a Tort Claims Act case against the Government, the Court said:

> It may be possible to satisfy the court, from all the circumstances of the case, that there is a reasonable danger that compulsion of the evidence will expose military matters which, in the interest of national security, should not be divulged. When this is the case, the occasion for the privilege is appropriate, and the court should not jeopardize the security which the privilege is meant to protect by insisting upon an examination of the evidence, even by the judge alone, in chambers.

No case of the Court, however, has extended this high degree of deference to a President's generalized interest in confidentiality. Nowhere in the Constitution, as we have noted earlier, is there any explicit reference to a privilege of confidentiality, yet to the extent this interest relates to the effective discharge of a President's powers, it is constitutionally based.

The right to the production of all evidence at a criminal trial similarly has constitutional dimensions. The Sixth Amendment explicitly confers upon every defendant in a criminal trial the right "to be confronted with the witnesses against him" and "to have compulsory process for obtaining witnesses in his favor." Moreover, the Fifth Amendment also guarantees that no person shall be deprived of liberty without due process of law. It is the manifest duty of the courts to vindicate those guarantees, and to accomplish that it is essential that all relevant and admissible evidence be produced.

In this case we must weigh the importance of the general privilege of confidentiality of Presidential communications in performance of the President's responsibilities against the inroads of such a privilege on the fair administration of criminal justice. The interest in preserving confidentiality is weighty indeed and entitled to great respect. However, we cannot conclude that advisers will be moved to temper the candor of their remarks by the infrequent occasions of disclosure because of the possibility that such conversations will be called for in the context of a criminal prosecution.

On the other hand, the allowance of the privilege to withhold evidence that is demonstrably relevant in a criminal trial would cut deeply into the guarantee of due process of law and gravely impair the basic function of the courts. A President's acknowledged need for confidentiality in the communications of his office is general in nature, whereas the constitutional need for production of relevant evidence in a criminal proceeding is specific and central to the fair adjudication of a particular criminal case in the administration of justice. Without access to specific facts a criminal prosecution may be totally frustrated. The President's broad interest in confidentiality of communications will not be vitiated by disclosure of a limited number of conversations preliminarily shown to have some bearing on the pending criminal cases.

We conclude that when the ground for asserting privilege as to subpoenaed materials sought for use in a criminal trial is based only on the generalized interest in confidentiality, it cannot prevail over the fundamental demands of due process of law in the fair administration of criminal justice. The generalized assertion of privilege must yield to the demonstrated, specific need for evidence in a pending criminal trial.

[The Court then placed the power to enforce the rule on the lower courts, which would review the requested material to determine if it was relevant and admissible in the criminal trial of the Watergate burglars]

We have earlier determined that the District Court did not err in authorizing the issuance of the subpoena. If a President concludes that compliance with a subpoena would be injurious to the public interest he may properly, as was done here, invoke a claim of privilege on the return of the subpoena. Upon receiving a claim of privilege from the Chief Executive, it became the further duty of the District Court to treat the subpoenaed material as presumptively privileged and to require the Special Prosecutor to demonstrate that the Presidential material was "essential to the justice of the (pending criminal) case." United States v. Burr, 25 Fed. Cas., at 192.

Here the District Court treated the material as presumptively privileged, proceeded to find that the Special Prosecutor had made a sufficient showing to rebut the presumption, and ordered an *in camera* examination of the subpoenaed material. On the basis of our examination of the record we are unable to conclude that the District Court erred in ordering the inspection. Accordingly, we affirm the order of the District Court that subpoenaed materials be transmitted to that court. We now turn to the important question of the District Court's responsibilities in conducting the *in camera* examination of Presidential materials or communications delivered under the compulsion of the subpoena duces tecum. * * * *

Enforcement of the subpoena duces tecum was stayed pending this Court's resolution of the issues raised by the petitions for certiorari. Those issues now having been disposed of, the matter of implementation will rest with the District Court. "(T)he guard, furnished to (the President) to protect him from being harassed by vexatious and unnecessary subpoenas, is to be looked for in the conduct of a (district) court after those subpoenas have issued; not in any circumstance which is to precede their being issued." United

States v. Burr, *supra*, at 34. Statements that meet the test of admissibility and relevance must be isolated; all other material must be excised. At this stage the District Court is not limited to representations of the Special Prosecutor as to the evidence sought by the subpoena; the material will be available to the District Court. It is elementary that in camera inspection of evidence is always a procedure calling for scrupulous protection against any release or publication of material not found by the court, at that stage, probably admissible in evidence and relevant to the issues of the trial for which it is sought. That being true of an ordinary situation, it is obvious that the District Court has a very heavy responsibility to see to it that Presidential conversations, which are either not relevant or not admissible, are accorded that high degree of respect due the President of the United States. Mr. Chief Justice Marshall, sitting as a trial judge in the Burr case, supra, was extraordinarily careful to point out that "(i)n no case of this kind would a court be required to proceed against the president as against an ordinary individual."

Marshall's statement cannot be read to mean in any sense that a President is above the law, but relates to the singularly unique role under Art. II of a President's communications and activities, related to the performance of duties under that Article. Moreover, a President's communications and activities encompass a vastly wider range of sensitive material than would be true of any "ordinary individual." It is therefore necessary in the public interest to afford Presidential confidentiality the greatest protection consistent with the fair administration of justice. The need for confidentiality even as to idle conversations with associates in which casual reference might be made concerning political leaders within the country or foreign statesmen is too obvious to call for further treatment. We have no doubt that the District Judge will at all times accord to Presidential records that high degree of deference suggested in *United States v. Burr*, *supra* and will discharge his responsibility to see to it that until released to the Special Prosecutor no in camera material is revealed to anyone. This burden applies with even greater force to excised material; once the decision is made to excise, the material is restored to its privileged status and should be returned under seal to its lawful custodian. * * * *

QUESTIONS ON EXECUTIVE PRIVILEGE

Did the President's Lawyers Accurately Portray the Law?: Now that you have read the *Nixon* case, do you think that the President's lawyers were right to argue that senior presidential advisors are absolutely immune from testifying before Congress? What does *Nixon* say about absolute immunity? If the President is not absolutely immune, how can his advisors be immune? (Remember Judge Brown's claim that the Justice Department's view was a "fiction"—they had invented the immunity.) *See* Notes in Chapter 4, *Committee on the Judiciary v. McGahn*, 415 F. Supp. 3d 148, 214 (D.D.C. 2019) *rev'd on other grounds*, 951 F.3d 510 (D.C. Cir. 2020), *rev'd and remanded*, 968 D.3d 755 (D.C. Cir. 2020) (*en banc*), *rev'd on other grounds*, 973 F.3d 121 (D.C. Cir. 2020), *vacated pending reh'g en banc*, No. 19-5331 (Oct. 15, 2020). If, as many urge, the President's lawyers have an ethical duty to "faithfully" execute the law, does that "law" apply to judicial decisions? If so, how can they reconcile their claim in the impeachment (i.e. absolute immunity) with the opinion's rather flat statements against absolute immunity? Is the President playing legal "hardball" here, going against the weight of legal opinion?

Did House Members Accurately Rely Upon the Law?: House Members claimed that the President had no valid claim of executive privilege. The President had to make specific claims about specific documents, and he had not done that. This is why they urged that he had not even "asserted" executive privilege. Is that consistent with the *Nixon* case above? Is it consistent with the admission that the President, in an 8-page letter, told the Congress he was not going to comply? Remember that the House made 70 separate requests to many different agencies.[2] Did Congress make a mistake by asking for so many documents across so many agencies? Did the breadth of the request invite claims that that inquiry would divert agencies and the White House from doing their jobs (one of the points made in *Nixon* and *Clinton*). Would the House have fared better if had taken a narrower approach, asking for documents that were clearly relevant? Or was the point that "wholesale" rejection of the request looked bad to the average public, the ultimate jury in an impeachment?

Relying on the DOJ Opinions: The Justice Department (DOJ) issues its own guidance on constitutional issues through the Office of Legal Counsel (OLC). In resisting McGahn's testimony, his successor as White House counsel, Pat Cipollone (one of the President's impeachment lawyers), argued that the DOJ opinion granted absolute immunity to McGahn. *See Testimonial Immunity Before Congress of the Former Counsel to the President*, 43 Op. O.L.C. (May 20, 2019). As the Court in *Nixon* explains, each department has a duty to determine the constitutionality of its own actions. But is blanket reliance on one's own opinion appropriate? No corporate lawyer would go into a courtroom and argue that because his office had come to an opinion on a statute's constitutionality that his opinion should prevail over a court's opinion. And the Supreme Court has never held that OLC opinions are in fact "the law." The best that one can say for reliance on an OLC opinion for absolute immunity is that it has been done by Presidents of both parties. The argument is partial to the institution, then, not to political

---

[2] *See* 166 Cong. Rec. S533 (daily ed. Jan. 24, 2020) (statement of Rep. Garcia). To avoid confusion about this, executive privilege claims do not necessarily apply only to statements made by the President himself or even to the President's close advisors; they can cover inter-agency deliberations relatively far removed from the President himself. *See* Gbemende Johnson, *Adjudicating Executive Privilege: Federal Administrative Agencies and Deliberative Process Privilege Claims in U.S. Courts*, 53 Law & Soc. Rev. 823 (2019).

party. Presidents of both parties make the same argument, reflecting the power of institutional interests to dominate party considerations.

Congressional Requests v. Judicial Requests: The *Nixon* case addresses a request for presidential information by a criminal defendant in a criminal trial. In the First Trump Impeachment, Congress—not a court or individual—requested the information. Notice that the Supreme Court begins by noting that the President cannot have an absolute privilege because *the courts* must "say" what the law is, citing *Marbury v. Madison*. Put in other words, the President cannot be above the courts. But what about the Congress? And why should the courts be the final arbiter between two democratic institutions? In two recent cases, decided after the impeachment, the Supreme Court appeared to prefer judicial to congressional proceedings. The Court ordered the President to release personal financial information to a grand jury (which is supervised by a court) under one standard, but imposed a higher standard when Congress requested the very same information. *See Trump v. Mazars*, 140 S. Ct. 2019, 2035–36 (2020) (recognizing that congressional subpoenas seeking the President's private papers must satisfy a heightened standard of scrutiny); *but see Trump v. Vance*, 140 S. Ct. 2412, 2429–20 (2020) (rejecting a heightened standard of need for grand jury subpoenas seeking the President's private papers). Why should courts prefer their own institutional processes to those of the people?

III. JUDICIAL REASONING COMPARED

Now that you have seen courts reason about Congress's oversight powers and the President's executive privilege, think about how similar and/or different the courts' reasoning styles are from those offered by the Congress and the President during the impeachment trial. Here are some ideas worth considering:

Different Audiences: Congress and the courts appeal to different audiences, or at least perceive themselves as having different audiences. Members of Congress tend to speak in the vernacular; they are used to translating law to "regular people," namely voters. Remember Rep. Garcia (D-TX), a former judge, who said "there is simply no evidence—nothing, *nada*—in the record to support this baseless allegation." 166 Cong. Rec. S495 (daily ed. Jan. 23, 2020) (emphasis added). It is doubtful that, as a judge, she would written "nada" or "goose egg" in a judicial opinion. Similarly, Mr. Sekulow, the President's lawyer, hoped to obtain Senators' and perhaps television viewers' attentions when he said "Danger, Danger, Danger." 166 Cong. Reg. S621 (daily ed. Jan. 28, 2020). (For those too young to know, some may have heard a popular culture reference to a 1960s television show, *Lost in Space*). The speakers knew that their words were being heard as much as read.

Now imagine reading the *McGrain* opinion out loud. Would the average voter understand? Formality and precision are part of judicial legal reasoning; the judicial audience amounts to experts and legal elites, as a general rule.[3] In theory, formality lends itself to a kind of forced civility and insulation from partisan debate—in theory, it avoids insulting and embarrassing people. At its most ideal, it conveys to the losing party that there are reasons for their defeat. Judges take an oath to deliver impartial justice which, for them, means that they should not be talking to political audiences in their opinions. Of course, formality has the drawback of obscurity, and the potential to paper over real and important differences that the vernacular conveys.

Advocacy v. Judicial Opinions: Judicial decisions set forth the court's reasoning, based on adversary presentations. Judicial opinion-writing, like persuasive reasoning generally, aims to answer *both sides* of an argument. The judge's job, in its simplest form, is to explain her reasoning to winners and losers. At its best, an opinion has the qualities of a "persuasive dialogue," which requires the decisionmaker to, among other things: have sufficient empathy with the losing side to portray the arguments fairly, willingness to consider the opposed point of view, weigh the merits "instead of rejecting them out of hand," consider "objections to her own arguments," as well as contrary evidence.[4] This helps to explain why the *Nixon* court comes to a "balanced" solution, rejecting the President's more aggressive position of absolute immunity. It also reveals itself in the *McGrain* decision's consideration of precedents that both favor and oppose the outcome. Advocates, by contrast, as were the lawyers for the President and the Congress in the Trump Impeachments, are committed, by the ethics of the legal profession, to pursue their claims zealously.[5] They may not distort the law, but they are not required to balance their arguments.

Institutional Bent: In the First Trump Impeachment, we saw arguments that tended to bend toward the self-interest of the institutions making those arguments. For example, the House Managers argued for the constitutional checking power of the Congress against the President. Similarly, the President argued that his branch needed confidentiality to operate. But the same is also true of judicial institutions. In *Nixon* above, the Supreme Court claimed that judicial prerogative outweighed the President's generalized interest in confidentiality, and that judges should decide

[3] Laurence Baum, Judges and Their Audiences: A Perspective on Judicial Behavior (2006); Neal Devins & Laurence Baum, The Company They Keep: How Partisan Divisions Came to the Supreme Court (2019).

[4] Douglas Walton, One-Sided Arguments: A Dialectical Analysis of Bias 32 (1999).

[5] American Bar Association Rule 1.3: "A lawyer must also act with commitment and dedication to the interests of the client and with zeal in advocacy upon the client's behalf."

how to balance that interest by reviewing the documents. The same is true in *Vance* and *Mazars*: the state prosecutor in the judicial system is preferred to the Congress. Is this preferring the Court's own interest in regulating the separation of powers? Does it transform political disputes into legal ones? What will happen if, in the future, a state court charges former President Trump with a crime?

Finality: One of the central differences between judicial proceedings and impeachment is that judges generally *decide*—they come to a conclusion. Settlement is considered one of the great virtues of the law, precisely because of the alternative (constant contestation or worse, violence). As Justice Brandeis once wrote, "[i]t is usually more important that a rule of law be settled, than that it be settled right." *Burnet v. Coronado Oil & Gas Co.*, 285 U.S. 393, 406 (1932) (Brandeis, J. dissenting). In the First Trump Impeachment, individual Senators made statements about their votes on crucial questions. But there is no final Senate *decision* in an impeachment proceeding other than a raw vote total. (Imagine if that was all that resulted in the Supreme Court—just a list of numbers without an opinion—6–3, 5–4, 7–2). Because Congress does not issue a single opinion justifying the impeachment verdict, query whether impeachments lack the virtues of decision, meaning that they lead to constant contestation. Historians and pundits still differ, for example, about the validity or virtues of the impeachments of both President Andrew Johnson and President William Clinton. Is there any reason to think that there will not be contestation about the two impeachments of President Donald Trump?

Impeachment and Indecision: Precisely because there is no written decision, impeachments can be terribly unsatisfying to lawyers trained in the arts of reading judicial opinions. One can be sure that, given the First Trump Impeachment, some legal arguments will (to use the Trump/Matz phrase) return "zombie"-like[6] should another President be impeached. It also means that the parties may have an institutional interest, given the lack of finality, for making extreme arguments. Why? Given that impeachment is rare, it is in both institutions' interest to push their own claims as far as possible. (*E.g.*, to argue for absolute blanket immunity for advisors even though the best reading of the existing case law suggests that courts will not accept that argument). This may explain why some scholars have debated whether the Supreme Court was in fact right

[6] Laurence H. Tribe & Joshua Matz, To End a Presidency: The Power of Impeachment 45 (2018).

when it concluded that it should not intervene in impeachments.[7] Some worry, for example, that we have entered into a new age of impeachment[8] given the rising pace of such inquiries. No doubt, increasing political polarization increases the likelihood of impeachment, but query whether the very structure of impeachment itself leads to intensifying political divisions? Does the lack of decision force the parties to legal extremes?

Impeachment v. Judicial Precedents: Precisely because impeachments do not result in written opinions justifying the Senate's reasoning, impeachment scholars have raised questions about what impeachments decide. As Professor Frank O. Bowman III has written, in each presidential impeachment "the facts are inevitably idiosyncratic, as are the political alignments and pressures of their eras."[9] As I write, everyone appears to believe that the Richard Nixon impeachment relied upon a proper use of the impeachment power. And his resignation reflects his acknowledgment of the gravity of the offense. But beyond this, there is a range of opinion. For example, in the Andrew Johnson impeachment, did the Members vote as they did because they thought the underlying criminal law was unconstitutional, because a partisan impeachment seemed unwise, because a new election was near, or for more nefarious reasons?[10] Professor Philip Bobbitt believes that the Clinton impeachment should serve as no "precedent" because "the House indictment was decisively rejected by the Senate and because of the indictment's peculiar grounds."[11] Should the Senate's rejection of the First Trump Impeachment suggest the same result? Is it no precedent because the Senate decisively rejected it and the grounds were "peculiar"?

Or Is the Point Not to Decide—Democratic Fire Alarm Theory: It is possible to view impeachment as an extreme step in an ongoing system of electoral politics. The point of impeachment is not to undo a past election because we know in advance that removal is entirely unlikely. (This is particularly true given the malapportionment of the Senate, meaning that it only takes a small minority of Senators to block a conviction). The point of impeachment in these circumstances

---

7 *See generally* Michael J. Gerhardt, The Federal Impeachment Process: A Constitutional and Historical Analysis (2019).

8 Laurence H. Tribe & Joshua Matz, To End a Presidency: The Power of Impeachment 153 (2018) ("Modern Americans live in the post-Clinton age of a permanent impeachment campaign.").

9 Frank O. Bowman III, High Crimes and Misdemeanors: A History of Impeachment for the Age of Trump 249 (2019).

10 David O. Stewart, Impeached: The Trial of President Andrew Johnson and the Fight for Lincoln's Legacy (2009).

11 Charles L. Black Jr. & Philip Bobbitt, Impeachment: A Handbook 81 (2018).

is to sound a fire alarm that the system is in danger. In this sense, impeachments may end up previewing arguments to be made in an upcoming election by showcasing them in a highly public format. It would be wrong, however, to think that the choice to pursue impeachment is a matter of ordinary electoral politics.

Members of Congress take a serious risk in an impeachment. Speaker of the House Nancy Pelosi (D-CA) resisted the call to impeach President Trump for years. Congress only impeached President Andrew Johnson after a long course of antagonistic behavior.[12] The reason that we have had so few impeachment trials in our country's history reflects Congress's *own recognition that there are serious short-term political risks*. If the trial looks petty or a waste of time, Members will be punished at the polls. Only if the trial reveals that the democratic "fire alarm" is truly necessary will Members have made the right decision. As in many things political, history will make the judgment.

He Will Do It Again: After the impeachment and the election of President Joseph R. Biden Jr. in November 2020, President Trump claimed that there had been massive fraud in the election, but there was no evidence of that fraud. He launched dozens of lawsuits claiming fraud, all of which failed. If the measure of an impeachment is not the result (since we know that removal is almost impossible), should the measure of impeachment be whether it rightly warns of danger to the democratic system? Representative Schiff (D-CA) warned during the First Impeachment Trial that, if left in office, President Trump would "do it again," that he would try to cheat in an election. Did President Trump's post-election behavior vindicate the House effort to impeach? *See* Part Two for the Second Impeachment Trial.

---

[12] Michael Les Benedict, *A New Look at the Impeachment of Andrew Johnson* in Preserving the Constitution: Essays on Politics and the Constitution in the Reconstruction Era 43 (2006) ("the Johnson impeachment was the reluctant decision of men who felt that they had been forced to take a stand to defend the constitutional prerogatives of Congress against presidential aggression").

Part Two

THE SECOND IMPEACHMENT TRIAL OF DONALD TRUMP

Chapter One

SENATE JURISDICTION

The Second Impeachment Trial of Donald Trump involved a violent attack on the Capitol during Congress' certification of the 2020 election for his opponent, President Joseph R. Biden Jr. Chapter 2 of this Part presents the details of the attack as presented by the House Managers. Shortly after the attack, and while President Trump was in office, the House voted for an Article of Impeachment (*see* Appendix A). However, the Senate did not try the case until after President Biden was inaugurated.

In this Chapter, two legal questions are addressed: first, whether Chief Justice Roberts would preside as he had in the First Impeachment trial; and second, whether the Senate had "jurisdiction" to try the Second Impeachment charge because President Trump was no longer in office at the time of the trial.[1] "Jurisdiction" is a standard legal term in any civil or criminal judicial case meaning the power of a court to try the case and is typically resolved before trial. As in the prior Chapters, we identify arguments made based on the **text** and **Founders' meaning, past precedent, future precedent**, and **shared constitutional norms**.

I. THE PRESIDING OFFICER

Before the Second Impeachment trial began, a question arose about who would preside over the trial. In the First Trump Impeachment trial, the Chief Justice presided. The House Managers and the Senate agreed that, since President Trump was no longer in office in February 2021, the Chief Justice was not required by the Constitution to preside. The President Pro Tempore, **Senator Patrick Leahy** (D-VT), issued the following statement on Jan. 25, 2021 regarding his role as presiding officer:

> The president pro tempore has historically presided over Senate impeachment trials of non-presidents. When presiding over an impeachment trial, the president pro tempore takes an additional special oath to do impartial justice according to the Constitution and the laws. It is an oath that I take extraordinarily seriously.

---

[1] Donald Trump was not tried by the Senate while serving as President of the United States. However, this Part refers to him as "the President" or "President Trump" because he was serving as President when he was impeached by the House and when the conduct for which he was impeached took place.

> I consider holding the office of the president pro tempore and the responsibilities that come with it to be one of the highest honors and most serious responsibilities of my career. When I preside over the impeachment trial of former President Donald Trump, I will not waver from my constitutional and sworn obligations to administer the trial with fairness, in accordance with the Constitution and the laws.[2]

As a general rule, the Constitution provides that the Chief Justice must preside over an impeachment trial of the President. Article I, sec. 3, cl. 6 provides:

> The Senate shall have the sole Power to try all Impeachments. When sitting for that Purpose, they shall be on Oath or Affirmation. *When the President of the United States is tried the Chief Justice shall preside*: And no Person shall be convicted without the Concurrence of two thirds of the Members present. *Id.* (emphasis added).

However, the Chief Justice[3] does not preside over all impeachment trials, such as an impeachment trial of **executive officers or judges**. As one legal commentator remarked in January 2021, the Constitution says "President of the United States," and the "last time I checked Joe Biden is the president of the United States."[4] According to a leading impeachment expert, there have been a number of impeachments in which the Presiding Officer of the Senate, rather than the Chief Justice, has sat as the presiding officer during the trial.[5]

---

[2] Sen. Patrick Leahy, Comment on Presiding Over the Impeachment Trial Of President Donald Trump (Jan. 25, 2021), https://www.leahy.senate.gov/press/comment-on-presiding-over-the-impeachment-trial-of-president-donald-trump.

[3] Newspaper reports conflicted about whether Chief Justice Roberts had refused to preside. *See, e.g.*, Graham McNally, *Fact Check: Did Chief Justice Roberts Refuse to Preside Over Trump's Impeachment Trial?*, Newsweek (Jan. 25, 2021), https://www.newsweek.com/fact-check-did-chief-justice-roberts-refuse-preside-over-trumps-impeachment-trial-1564300 ("Newsweek found no evidence that Roberts refused or was even asked to preside over the trial, nor does he have any legal obligation to do so"). The Senate Majority Leader, Chuck Schumer (D-NY), stated that "it was up to John Roberts whether he wanted to preside with a president who's no longer sitting," but that "he doesn't want to do it." Rachel Maddow Show (MSNBC television broadcast, Jan. 25, 2021). Debra Cassens Weiss, *Chief Justice Roberts Won't Preside in Trump's Second Impeachment Trial; What Does the Constitution Say?*, ABA Journal (Jan. 26, 2021), https://www.abajournal.com/news/article/chief-justice-roberts-wont-preside-in-impeachment-trial-what-does-the-constitution-say.

[4] Steven Vladeck (@steve_vladeck), Twitter (Jan. 25, 2021, 12:36 PM), https://twitter.com/steve_vladeck/status/1353758667053674497.

[5] See Frank O. Bowman III, *The role of the chief justice in an impeachment trial*, SCOTUSBlog (Jan. 10, 2020), https://www.scotusblog.com/2020/01/the-role-of-the-chief-justice-in-an-impeachment-trial/ ("In any impeachment case other than that of the president, the vice president can preside, as Thomas Jefferson did in the very first

Some worried that the absence of the Chief Justice was constitutionally significant in the Second Trump Impeachment trial.[6] When one considers why the Chief Justice sits, it becomes clearer why Chief Justice Roberts did *not* preside over the second trial. Constitutionally, the Vice President is the President of the Senate. U.S. Const. art. I, § 3, cl. 4. If the Vice President were to sit on the impeachment trial of the President, there would be an obvious conflict of interest: if the President were removed, the Vice President would inherit the office. A self-interested Vice President might try, even unwittingly, to tilt the impeachment against the President to oust him from office. For that reason, the Constitution specifically provides that the Chief Justice should preside in an impeachment trial of a President. Once the President is out of office, however, the underlying conflict disappears.[7]

The presiding officer of the Senate, in both an impeachment trial, and more generally, performs a largely ceremonial office.[8] The President Pro Tempore of the Senate is technically the presiding officer when the Senate is conducting legislative business. Senate Rule I (2). Since 1945, the President Pro Tempore (or temporary President, as the Vice President is the formal President of the Senate), has typically been a senior member of the Majority Party.[9] At the time of the Second Trump Impeachment trial, Sen. Patrick Leahy was the President Pro Tempore. If the impeachment had been

---

impeachment, that of Senator William Blount in 1799, and as Aaron Burr later did in the 1805 trial of Justice Samuel Chase"). *See generally*, Frank O. Bowman III, High Crimes and Misdemeanors: A History of Impeachment for the Age of Trump chs. 5, 6 (2019) (impeachments of persons other than Presidents).

6 Senator Josh Hawley (R-MO) stated that the Constitution "requires the chief justice to preside." Senator John Cornyn (R-TX) stated that "The Constitution requires that the chief justice preside over the impeachment trial of a president but that's not what we're doing," and Senator Rand Paul (R-KY) stated that "If the chief justice doesn't preside, I think it's an illegitimate hearing and really goes to show that it's not really constitutional to impeach someone who's not president." Alexander Bolton and Jordain Carney, *Leahy, not Roberts, to preside over impeachment trial*, The Hill (Jan. 25, 2021), https://thehill.com/homenews/senate/535700-leahy-roberts-to-preside-over-impeachment-trial.

7 For this argument by the House Managers, *see id.* at S595 (Feb. 9, 2021) (statement of Rep. Cicilline).

8 *See* Cong. Research Serv., RS21553, Presiding Officer: Senate (2003) ("In modern practice, neither the Vice President nor the President pro tempore spends much time presiding over the Senate * * * *Vice Presidents today preside only upon ceremonial occasions or when a close vote on a measure or amendment of interest to the Administration * * * * general duties of the Senate presiding officer consist mostly of preserving order and decorum on the Senate floor and in the galleries").

9 *See* Christopher M. Davis, Cong. Research Serv., RL30960, The President Pro Tempore of the Senate: History and Authority of the Office 6 (2015) ("Of the Presidents pro tempore who have served since 1945, only one has not been the most senior Senator in his party * * * *Prior to 1945, while the parties had for the most part tended to put forward men with long senatorial service as candidates for President pro tempore, there were some notable exceptions").

of any other executive official, such as a Cabinet Member or a judge, Senator Leahy would have presided—as he did in the Second Trump Impeachment.

Although being elected President Pro Tempore is "one of the highest honors offered to a senator," the job of presiding over a legislative session is not a particularly prized one.[10] In fact, the President Pro Tempore does not typically preside over legislative sessions. Instead, the President Pro Tempore chooses the most junior Senator to act *as* the presiding officer because it is a job that few enjoy: the Senator simply announces the rules as provided to him by on slips of paper prepared by the nonpartisan Senate parliamentarian. Senate Rule I (3). Busy Senators often bristle at the waste of time spent as a temporary presiding officer.

During the Second Trump Impeachment, the President argued that a "political" judge would bend rulings against him because of his political party. Mr. Schoen, one of the President's lawyers, explained:

> *Mr. Trump now faces a situation in which the Presiding Officer will serve as both judge, with all the powers that the rules endow him with, and juror with a vote. And beyond that, the Presiding Officer* * * * * *has been Mr. Trump's vocal and adamant opponent throughout the Trump administration.* * * * *.[11] 167 Cong. Rec. S605 (daily ed. Feb. 9, 2021).

Of course, as we have seen in earlier Chapters, impeachment trials are political trials in the sense that the judges (the Senators) are elected representatives. Such trials are not governed by judicial precedent or rules of evidence. But that does not answer the claim that judges, as a general rule, should appear impartial.

The answer to worries about the presiding officer's impartiality depends upon understanding the Senate as an institution. First, all Senators, including the presiding officer, are required to take an oath of impartiality before the impeachment trial, as Senator Leahy announced on January 25, 2021.[12] Second, the presiding officer makes few if any rulings in the sense that a trial judge might make. Judges in civil and criminal cases exercise a constant and firm hand on the presentation of evidence, but in an impeachment such

---

[10] *Id.* at 1 (citing Senate President Pro Tempore Robert C. Byrd).

[11] This was couched as a "due process" argument by the President's lawyers, as well as a reason for the Senate not to exercise jurisdiction. We consider the due process objections in Chapter 2 of this Part.

[12] 167 Cong. Rec. S142 (daily ed. Jan. 26, 2021) ("Do you solemnly swear that in all things appertaining to the trial of the impeachment of Donald John Trump, president of the United States, now pending, you will do impartial justice according to the Constitution and laws, so help you god?").

decisions are rare and made by the full Senate.[13] Third, the presiding officers' rulings reflect the Senate's rules as interpreted by a nonpartisan parliamentarian[14] (so, in theory, the real judge here, the parliamentarian, must apply the rules equally to both parties). Fourth, and perhaps most importantly, any ruling by the presiding officer can be subject to debate and reversal by the entire Senate.[15]

As a result, neither the Chief Justice in the first trial, nor Senator Leahy in the second trial, made statements that were not simply written out for them by the Senate Parliamentarian, Elizabeth MacDonough. In the first trial, Chief Justice Roberts repeated the words provided by MacDonough and Senate staff, with one notable exception, when he called for order in the Chamber after Rep. Nadler (D-NY) and White House Counsel Cipollone exchanged harsh words.

> *"I think it is appropriate at this point for me to admonish both the House managers and the President's counsel in equal terms to remember that they are addressing the world's greatest deliberative body. One reason it has earned that title is because its Members avoid speaking in a manner and using language that is not conducive to civil discourse.* 166 Cong. Rec. S428 (daily ed. January 21, 2020).

So, too, as we will see later, Senator Leahy made only a brief intervention in the Second Trump Impeachment trial when the Chamber erupted in laughter over a claim made by the President's counsel.

> *I would remind everybody that we will have order in the Chamber during these proceedings.* 167 Cong. Rec. S718 (daily ed. Feb. 13, 2021).

II. THE JURISDICTIONAL DEBATE

Questions emerged before the trial, in the press, about whether President Trump could be tried by the Senate since he was a "former" President at the time of the trial.[16] Some called it a "late"

---

[13] S. Res. 47, 117th Cong. (2021).

[14] As Jonathan Gould has shown, there is an internal "law" of Congress that both sides have seen fit to follow and that law depends upon the parliamentarian's neutrality. Parliamentarians must answer to both political parties and can be dismissed. *See* Jonathan S. Gould, *Law Within Congress*, 129 Yale L.J. 1946, 1950 (2020) ("what is and is not permitted in Congress therefore often turns on parliamentary precedents * * * *made and applied by nonpartisan quasi-judicial figures in each chamber: the House and Senate parliamentarians.").

[15] S. Res. 47, 117th Cong. (2021).

[16] The leading source on the history of impeachments involving individuals who have resigned or are otherwise not in office is Brian Kalt. *See* Brian Kalt, *The*

impeachment. In fact, since impeachment is simply a legal charge under the Constitution, and that charge was made while Trump *was* President, the "late impeachment" charge is a misnomer. The better question is whether the Senate could hold a "late trial." The lawyers called this a "jurisdictional" debate. Jurisdiction is a lawyerly term used to determine whether a court has power to hear a controversy. It is typically a separate question, and does not affect a ruling on the merits of the case—namely whether or not President Trump committed a high crime or misdemeanor on January 6, 2021.

Textual and Founders' Argument

Rep. Raskin (D-MD) opened **the House Managers'** case on the question of jurisdiction:

> *The President, it is undisputed, committed his offense while he was President, and it is undisputed that we impeached him while he was President. There can be no doubt that this is a valid and legitimate impeachment, and there can be no doubt that the Senate has the power to try this impeachment.*
>
> *We know this because article I, section 3 gives the Senate the sole power to try all impeachments. The Senate has the power, the sole power, to try all impeachments. "All" means all, and there are no exceptions to the rule.*
>
> *Because the Senate has jurisdiction to try all impeachments, it most certainly has jurisdiction to try this one. It is really that simple.*
>
> *The vast majority of constitutional scholars who studied the question * * * * agree with us, and that includes the Nation's most prominent conservative legal scholars, including former Tenth Circuit Judge Michael McConnell; the cofounder of the Federalist Society, Steven Calabresi; Ronald Reagan's Solicitor General Charles Fried; luminary Washington lawyer Charles Cooper, among hundreds of other constitutional lawyers and professors.*[17] 167 Cong. Rec. S591 (daily ed. Feb. 9, 2021).

Constitutional Case for the Impeachability of Former Federal Officials: An Analysis of the Law, History, and Practice of Late Impeachment, 6 Tex. L. Rev. & Pol. 13 (2001).

[17] *See* Michael W. McConnell and Ken Gormley, *Yes, the Senate had the power to try Trump. He was impeached in office.*, Wash. Post. (Feb. 4, 2021), https://www.washingtonpost.com/opinions/2021/02/04/yes-senate-has-power-try-trump-he-was-impeached-office/; Charles Cooper, *The Constitution Doesn't Bar Trump's Impeachment Trial*, Wall St. J. (Feb. 7, 2021), https://www.wsj.com/articles/the-constitution-doesnt-bar-trumps-impeachment-trial-11612724124; Letter, Constitutional Law Scholars on Impeaching Former Officials (Jan. 21, 2021) (available at https://www.politico.com/f/?id=00000177-2646-de27-a5f7-3fe714ac0000).

Rep. Neguse (D-CO) underscored the point by quoting the key texts:

> *First, let's start with what the Constitution says about Congress's power in article I. You heard Lead Manager* RASKIN *make this point, but it is worth underscoring.*
>
> *Article I, section 2 gives the House "sole Power of Impeachment." Article I, section 3 gives the Senate the "sole Power to try all Impeachments." Based on President Trump's argument, one would think that language includes caveats, exceptions, but it doesn't. It doesn't say "Impeachment of current civil officers." It doesn't say "Impeachment of those still in office."* (caps in original).
>
> *Up on the screen, you will see article I, section 3, clause 7. With that in mind, the language says that if the Senate convicts, the judgment "shall not extend further than" removal and disqualification. That is it. The meaning is clear. The Senate has the power to impose removal, which only applies to current officials. And, separately, it has the power to impose disqualification, which obviously applies to both current and former officers. But it doesn't have the power to go any further than that.*
>
> *Now, as I understand President Trump's argument, they believe that this language somehow says that disqualification can only follow the removal of a current officer, but it doesn't. That interpretation essentially rewrites the Constitution. It adds words that aren't there. I mean, after all, the Constitution does not say "removal from office and then disqualification." It doesn't say "removal from office followed by disqualification." It simply says the Senate can't do more than two possible sentences: removal and disqualification.* 167 Cong. Rec. S593 (daily ed. Feb. 9, 2021).

Rep. Raskin (D-MD) argued that the Founders were aware of impeachments of former officials and expressed nothing negative about such impeachments at the Constitutional Convention.

> *Every single impeachment of a government official that occurred during the Framers' lifetime concerned a former official—a former official. Indeed, the most famous of these impeachments occurred while the Framers gathered in Philadelphia to write the Constitution. It was the impeachment of Warren Hastings, the former Governor-general of the British colony of Bengal and a corrupt guy.*

The Framers knew all about it, and they strongly supported the impeachment. In fact, the Hastings case was invoked by name at the convention. It was the only specific impeachment case that they discussed at the convention. It played a key role in their adoption of the high crimes and misdemeanors standard. And even though everyone there surely knew that Hastings had left office 2 years before his impeachment trial began, not a single Framer—not one—raised a concern when Virginian George Mason held up the Hastings impeachment as a model for us in the writing of our Constitution.

Given the Framers' intense focus on danger to elections and the peaceful transfer of power, it is inconceivable that they designed impeachment to be a dead letter in the President's final days in office when opportunities to interfere with the peaceful transfer of power would be most tempting and most dangerous, as we just saw. Thus, as a matter of history and original understanding, there is no merit to President Trump's claim that he can incite an insurrection and then insist weeks later that the Senate lacks the power to even hear evidence at a trial, to even hold a trial. The true rule was stated by former President John Quincy Adams when he categorically declared: "I hold myself, so long as I have the breath of life in my body, amenable to impeachment by [the] House for everything I did during the time I held any public office." 167 Cong. Rec. S591 (daily ed. Feb. 9, 2021)

The President's lawyers, here **Mr. Castor**, argued:

*I will be quite frank with you. We changed what we were going to do on account that we thought that the House managers' presentation was well done, and I wanted you to know that we have responses to those things. * * * * Some of this was shown on the screen, but article I, section 3 says:*

> Judgment in Cases of Impeachment shall not extend further than to removal from Office, and disqualification to hold.* * * * any Office of honor, Trust or Profit under the United States: but the Party convicted shall nevertheless be liable and subject to Indictment, Trial, Judgment and Punishment, according to law.

So this idea of a January amnesty is nonsense. If my colleagues on this side of the Chamber actually think that President Trump committed a criminal offense—After he is out of office, you go and arrest him. So there is no opportunity where the President of the United States can run rampant into January, the end of his term, and just go away scot-free. The Department of Justice does know what to do with such people. And so far, I haven't seen any activity in that direction.[18] * * * *

*But the section I read—"Judgment"—in other words, the bad thing that can happen—the "Judgment in Cases of Impeachment"—i.e., what we are doing—"shall not extend further than * * * * removal from Office." What is so hard about that? Which of those words are unclear?*

> Shall not extend further than removal* * * * from Office.

President Trump no longer is in office. The object of the Constitution has been achieved. He was removed by the voters. 167 Cong. Rec. S601 (daily ed. Feb. 9, 2021).

Mr. Schoen focused on the textual arguments at some length, first explaining a method typically used in court:

A true textual analysis, as the name implies, always begins with the words of the text and only resorts to legislative history or history itself if the meaning of the text is not plain. As the Supreme Court has emphasized, "[s]tatutory interpretation, as we always say, begins with the text." "In interpreting this text, we are guided by the principle that the Constitution was written to be understood by the voters; its words and phrases were used in their normal and ordinary as distinguished from technical meaning." And "[w]e must enforce plain and unambiguous statutory language according to its terms." 167 Cong. Rec. S606 (daily ed. Feb. 9, 2021).

Mr. Schoen first argued that former President Trump was not an officer and therefore did not fall within article II, section 4:

The President, Vice President and all civil Officers of the United States, shall be removed from Office on Impeachment for, and Conviction of, Treason, Bribery, or other high Crimes and Misdemeanors. * * * *

From which office shall a non-President be removed if convicted? A non-President doesn't hold an office, therefore

[18] As we noted earlier, in the First Trump Impeachment, President Trump's Justice Department had argued strenuously that a President could not be indicted while in office based on various Office of Legal Counsel (OLC) opinions. Note as well that dozens of criminal prosecutions were begun against rioters by the Justice Department and the U.S. Attorney as early as February 2021.

cannot be impeached under this clause, which provides for the removal from office of the person under the impeachment attack. Id.

Mr. Schoen went on to make what is known by lawyers as an "intratextual argument," meaning comparing language in one provision on the meaning of "President" with other language. Here he compares all references to President should be to a sitting President:

> *It is well established that "[a] term appearing in several places in a statutory text is generally read the same way each time it appears."*
>
> *If the text, "the President of the United States" in the constitutional provision requiring the Chief Justice to preside can refer only to the sitting President, and not to former presidents, then the textual identification of "[t]he President" contained in article II, section 4, which makes the President amenable to impeachment in the first place, also excludes anyone other than the sitting President.* * * * *
>
> *Only a sitting President is referred to as the President of the United States in the Constitution. And only a sitting President may be impeached, convicted, and removed upon a trial in the Senate. "The President" in article II, section 4 and "the President" in article I, section 3 identify the same person. If the accused is not "the President" in one, he is not "the President" in the other. No sound textual interpretation—I emphasize "textual interpretation"—principle permits a contrary reading.*
>
> *Unwittingly or unwillingly as it may be, Senate Democrats, in their announcement that Senator* LEAHY *will preside, have already taken their position on this matter. Id.* (caps in original).

Mr. Schoen urged that the Constitution's text provided for "removal" and that was a "factual and legal impossibility."

> *In ordinary criminal jurisprudence, a person convicted of public crimes committed while he or she was in office may still be punished even though they no longer hold that office. Not so with impeachment. In a Senate impeachment trial, conviction means and requires removal, and conviction without a removal is no conviction at all. Only upon a valid conviction and its requisite, enforceable removal may the additional judgment of disqualification plausibly be entertained.*

> [Former] *Judge Luttig relies on this textual reading for his firm conclusion that a former President cannot be impeached or convicted. Consider the alternative, as Robert Delahunty and John Yoo have: If Mr. Trump can be convicted as "the President," the language the Constitution uses, then why is he still not "the President" under the Commander in Chief clause, for example? They are joined by Professor Alan Dershowitz and University of Chicago Professor Richard Epstein in their focus and conclusion. They point out the dangers of an approach that deviates from a focus on the text.* * * * * 167 Cong. Rec. S606 (daily ed. Feb. 9, 2021).[19]

Mr. Schoen argued that conviction was required before disqualification and since President Trump could not be convicted, he could not be disqualified:

> *The managers critically ignore this language in article I, section 3, clause 7, which states that "[j]udgment in Cases of Impeachment shall not extend further than to removal from Office, and disqualification to hold and enjoy any Office of honor, Trust or Profit under the United States." Ordinarily, as in everyday English, use of the conjunctive "and" in a list means that all of the listed requirements must be satisfied, while use of the disjunctive "or" means that only one of the list of requirements needs to be satisfied.* * * * *
>
> *As* [former] *Judge Michael Luttig, again, recently argued, "The Constitution links the impeachment remedy of disqualification from future office with the remedy of removal from the office that person currently occupies; the former remedy does not apply in situations where the latter is unavailable."*[20] *Conviction and removal are inextricably entwined. If removal no longer is possible, neither is an impeachment conviction.* * * * *

---

[19] *See* J. Michael Luttig, *Once Trump leaves office, the Senate can't hold an impeachment trial,* Wash. Post (Jan. 12, 2021), https://www.washingtonpost.com/opinions/2021/01/12/once-trump-leaves-office-senate-cant-hold-an-impeachment-trial/; Robert Delahunty and John Yoo, *The Originalist Case against a Trump Impeachment Trial,* Nat'l Rev. (Jan. 27, 2021), https://www.nationalreview.com/2021/01/the-originalist-case-against-a-trump-impeachment-trial/; Alan M. Dershowitz, *No, You Can't Try an Impeached Former President,* Wall St. J. (Jan. 20, 2021), https://www.wsj.com/articles/no-you-cant-try-an-impeached-former-president-11611167113; Richard A. Epstein, *The Trial That Should Not Be,* Hoover Inst. (Jan. 19, 2021), https://www.hoover.org/research/trial-should-not-be.

[20] J. Michael Luttig, *Once Trump leaves office, the Senate can't hold an impeachment trial,* Wash. Post (Jan. 12, 2021), https://www.washingtonpost.com/opinions/2021/01/12/once-trump-leaves-office-senate-cant-hold-an-impeachment-trial/.

We heard earlier today we don't cite any scholars. Professor Philip Bobbitt is a distinguished Webster professor at Columbia University who, along with Professor Charles Black, wrote the handbook on impeachment used for many, many years. He is a constitutional expert on impeachment. He has written that "there is little discussion in the historical record surrounding the precise question of whether a person no longer a civil officer can be impeached—and in light of the clarity of the text, this is hardly surprising,' Professor Bobbitt wrote. Professor Bobbitt, by the way, who has a rich family history in the Democratic Party—LBJ—also asserted the following, as recently as January 27, 2021, arguing against holding this trial. He said: There is no authority granted to Congress to impeach and convict persons who are not "civil officers of the United States."[21] *It's as simple as that.* 167 Cong. Rec. S608 (daily ed. Feb. 9, 2021).

Argument from Precedent

Two key precedents featured in the Second Trump Impeachment trial: the 18th-century impeachment of Senator William Blount, and the 19th-century impeachment of General William Belknap. In both cases, the individuals were not holding office at the time of their impeachment trials. **The House Managers** argued:

Rep. Neguse (D-CO) explained both precedents:

Let's start with the precedent, with what has happened in this very Chamber. I would like to focus on just two cases.

One of them is the Nation's very first impeachment case, which actually was of a former official. In 1797, about a decade after our country ratified our Constitution, there was a Senator from Tennessee by the name of William Blount, who was caught conspiring with the British to try to sell Florida and Louisiana. Ultimately, President Adams caught him. He turned over the evidence to Congress. Four days later, the House of Representatives impeached him. A day after that, this body, the United States Senate, expelled him from office, so he was very much a former official.

Despite that, the House went forward with its impeachment proceeding in order to disqualify him from ever again holding Federal office. And so the Senate proceeded with the trial with none other than Thomas Jefferson presiding.

---

[21] Philip Bobbitt, *Why the Senate Shouldn't Hold a Late Impeachment Trial*, Lawfare (Jan. 27, 2021), https://www.lawfareblog.com/why-senate-shouldnt-hold-late-impeachment-trial.

> *Now, Blount argued that the Senate couldn't proceed because he had already been expelled. But here is the interesting thing: He expressly disavowed any claim that former officials can't ever be impeached. And unlike President Trump, he was very clear that he respected and understood that he could not even try to argue that ridiculous position. Even impeached Senator Blount recognized the inherent absurdity of that view. Here is what he said: "I certainly never shall contend, that an officer may first commit an offense, and afterwards avoid by resigning his office."* 167 Cong. Rec. S592 (daily ed. Feb. 9, 2021).

The Blount precedent is unusual because it applied to a Senator as opposed to an executive official or a judge. **Rep. Neguse** (D-CO) went on to discuss another 19th-century **precedent** in which the Senate had tried a former official, former Secretary of War William Belknap:

> *Fast-forward 80 years later—arguably the most important precedent that this body has to consider—the trial of former Secretary of War William Belknap. I am not going to go into all the details, but, in short, in 1876, the House discovered that he was involved in a massive kickback scheme. Hours before the House Committee had discovered this conduct, released its report documenting the scheme, Belknap literally rushed to the White House to resign, tender his resignation to President Ulysses Grant to avoid any further inquiry into his misconduct, and, of course, to avoid being disqualified from holding Federal office in the future.*
>
> *Later that day, aware of the resignation, what did the House do? The House moved forward and unanimously impeached him, making clear its power to impeach a former official. And when his case reached the Senate—this body—Belknap made the exact same argument that President Trump is making today, that you all lack jurisdiction, any power, to try him because he is a former official.*
>
> *Now, many Senators at that time, when they heard that argument—literally, they were sitting in the same chair as you all are sitting in today—they were outraged by that argument—outraged. You can read their comments in the record. They knew it was a dangerous, dangerous argument with dangerous implications. It would literally mean that a President could betray their country, leave office, and avoid impeachment and disqualification entirely. And that is why, in the end, the United States Senate decisively voted that the Constitution required them to proceed with the trial.*

> *The Belknap case is clear precedent that the Senate must proceed with this trial since it rejected pretrial dismissal, affirmed its jurisdiction, and moved to a full consideration of the merits.* 167 Cong. Rec. S592 (daily ed. Feb. 9, 2021).

The President's lawyers rebutted claims based on **precedent**. In their trial brief, the President's lawyers argued that the Blount and Belknap precedents did not actually decide the question whether the Senate had jurisdiction:

> *Significantly, neither Belknap nor Blount received the required two-thirds majority of the Senate and were acquitted so their proceedings provide no binding precedent establishing the Senate's jurisdiction to convict former officials of impeachment. "These cases cannot be read as foreclosing an argument that they never dealt with."* President's Brief at 26 (case citation omitted).[22]

As to the Blount case, they asserted it had no precedential value:

> *In a close vote, the Senate defeated a resolution asserting Blount was an impeachable civil officer. But the debate around this vote, and the text of the resolution, do not make clear whether the resolution was rejected because it was felt that a senator was not "a civil officer" or whether, having been expelled, Blount ceased to be impeachable." (quoting the House Manager's brief). Therefore, the case has little or no precedential value supporting a late impeachment. Id.* at 24.

As to the Belknap case, they urged the same, that it was irrelevant:

> *Despite Belknap's resignation, the House voted to impeach him anyway. The issue of whether an officer who had resigned could be impeached was heavily debated from May 15 to May 29th, but ultimately the Senate voted 37–29 that it had the power to hold an impeachment trial for a former officeholder and proceeded to have a trial. On August 1, 1876, Belknap was acquitted because less than 2/3 of the Senate voted for impeachment. While historical accounts suggest that few senators believed Belknap was innocent, the majority of those voting to acquit him did so because they did not think the Senate had jurisdiction to convict someone who was no longer in office. Id.* at 24–25.

---

[22] We relied upon a copy of the brief that as published by the New York Times. Future citations are to that version. *See Read Trump's Impeachment Defense Memo*, N.Y. Times (Feb. 8, 2021), https://www.nytimes.com/interactive/2021/02/08/us/trump-defense-impeachment-trial.html.

To support the latter point—that those who voted to acquit Belknap did so because they did not believe that the Senate had jurisdiction—the President's brief quoted "3 Hinds Precedents of the House of Representatives, § 2467 (1907)":

> *An analysis of the reasons given with the votes shows that of those voting "guilty," 2 believed that the Senate had no jurisdiction, but gave their verdict in good faith, since by vote jurisdiction had been assumed. Of those voting "not guilty,"3 announced that they did so on the evidence, while 22 announced that they voted not guilty because they believed the Senate had no jurisdiction. One Senator stated that he declined to vote because he believed they did not have jurisdiction.* President's Brief at 25, n.68.

Argument from Future Precedent

The House Managers argued that failing to try Trump would create a "January" exception for any future would-be demagogue. Assume, for example, that a disappointed President denied reelection in November decided to invite an enemy attack in January to prevent the peaceful transfer of power. The House argued that such an offense would clearly be a high crime or misdemeanor and that Presidents should not be able to avoid the consequences of impeachment and disqualification from future office simply by acting at the last minute.

Rep. Raskin (D-MD) explained:

> *If the President's arguments for a January exception are upheld, then even if everyone agrees that he is culpable for these events, even if the evidence proves, as we think it definitively does, that the President incited a violent insurrection on the day Congress met to finalize the Presidential election, he would have you believe there is absolutely nothing the Senate can do about it—no trial, no facts. He wants you to decide that the Senate is powerless at that point. That can't be right.* 167 Cong. Rec. S591 (daily ed. Feb. 9, 2021).

Rep. Neguse (D-CO) added:

> *Like every one of you, I was in the Capitol on January 6. I was on the floor with Lead Manager* RASKIN. *Like every one of you, I was evacuated as this violent mob stormed the Capitol's gates. What you experienced that day, what we experienced that day, what our country experienced that day was the Framers' worst nightmare coming to life. Presidents can't enflame insurrection in their final weeks and then*

walk away like nothing happened. Yet that is the rule that President Trump asks you to adopt. Id. at S594 (caps in original).

And just imagine the consequences of such an absurd interpretation of the Constitution. If President Trump were right about that language, then officials could commit the most extraordinary, destructive offenses against the American people—high crimes and mis- demeanors. They would have total control over whether they could ever be impeached and, if they are, whether the Senate can try the case. If they want to escape any public inquiry into their misconduct or the risk of dis- qualification from future office, then it is pretty simple. They could just resign 1 minute before the House impeaches or even 1 minute before the Senate trial or they could resign during the Senate trial if it is not looking so well. That would effectively erase "disqualification" from the Constitution. It would put wrongdoers in charge of whether the Senate can try them. Id. at S593.

Rep. Cicilline (D-RI) explained:

In the same vein, President Trump and his lawyers argue that he shouldn't be impeached because it will set a bad precedent for impeaching others. But that slippery slope argument is also incorrect. For centuries, the prevailing view has been that former officials are subject to impeachment. We just heard a full discussion of that. The House has repeatedly acknowledged that fact. But in the vast majority of cases, the House has rightly recognized that an official's resignation or departure makes the extraordinary step of impeachment unnecessary and maybe even unwise. * * * *

President Trump's case, though, is different. The danger has not "gone by." His threat to democracy makes any prior abuse by any government official pale in comparison. Moreover, allowing his conduct to pass without the most decisive response would itself create an extraordinary danger to the Nation, inviting further abuse of power and signaling that the Congress of the United States is unable or unwilling to respond to insurrection incited by the President. Think about that.

To paraphrase Justice Robert Jackson, who said that precedent that I just described would lie about like a loaded weapon, ready for the hand of any future President who decided in his final months to make a play for unlimited power—think of the danger. Id. at S595.

The President's lawyers argued that impeaching former President Trump would create a radical precedent, allowing the impeachment of former officers in the future.

Mr. Schoen stated:

*Let's be perfectly clear. If you vote to proceed with this impeachment trial, future Senators will recognize that you bought into a radical, constitutional theory that * * * *any civil officer who ever dares to want to serve his or her country must know that they will be subject to impeachment long after their service in office has ended, subject only to the political and cultural landscape of the day that is in operation at any future time. This is exactly the position taken by the House managers at page 65 of their brief—unprecedented, radical position. They unabashedly say so. Imagine the potential consequences for civil officers you know and who you believed served so honorably but who, in the view of a future Congress, might one day be deemed to be impeachment worthy. Imagine it now because your imagination is the only limitation. The House managers tell you a correct reading of the impeachment power under the Constitution is that it has no temporal limit and can reach back in time without limitation to target anyone who dared to serve our Nation as a civil officer. Id.* at S602 (daily ed. Feb. 9, 2021).

Shared Constitutional Norms

The House Managers argued that a trial was necessary to maintain democracy and hold the former President to account. **Rep. Cicilline** (D-RI) invoked democracy as the central reason to hold an impeachment trial:

*Fundamentally, impeachment exists * * * * to safeguard our democracy. It achieves that by deterring abuse of the extraordinary power that we entrust to our Presidents from the very first day in office to the very last day. It also ensures accountability for Presidents who harm us or our government. In the aftermath of a tragedy, it allows us an opportunity to come together and to heal by working through what happened and reaffirming our constitutional principles, and it authorizes this body and this body alone to disqualify from our political system anybody whose conduct in office proves that they present a danger to the Republic.* 167 Cong. Rec. S594 (daily ed. Feb. 9, 2021).

> *Here is the rare case in which love of the Constitution and commitment to our democracy required the House to impeach. It is for the same reason, the Senate can and must try this case. Id.* at S595.

Rep. Raskin (D-MD) closed the jurisdictional portion of the trial by linking democracy to his own family's experience the day of the attack. He had brought his family to the Capitol on Jan. 6 because his son had just died that week. His family hid under desks while the Capitol was ransacked.

> *This trial is personal indeed for every Senator, for every Member of the House, every manager, all of our staff, the Capitol Police, the Washington, DC, Metropolitan Police, the National Guard, the maintenance and custodial crews, the print journalists and TV people who were here, and all of our families and friends. I hope this trial reminds America how personal democracy is and how personal is the loss of democracy too.* 167 Cong. Rec. S592 (daily ed. Feb. 9, 2021).
>
> *People died that day. Officers ended up with head damage and brain damage. People's eyes were gouged. An officer had a heart attack. An officer lost three fingers that day. Two officers have taken their own lives. Senators, this cannot be our future. Id.* at S597.
>
> *This cannot be the future of America. We cannot have Presidents inciting and mobilizing mob violence against our government and our institutions because they refuse to accept the will of the people under the Constitution of the United States. Much less can we create a new January exception in our precious, beloved Constitution that prior generations have died for and fought for. Id.*

The President's lawyers argued that the impeachment was an attempt by elitists who hated Donald Trump to deny him the ability to run for future office:

> *This is a process fueled irresponsibly by base hatred by these House managers and those who gave them their charge, and they are willing to sacrifice our national character to advance their hatred and their fear that one day they might not be the party in power.* * * * *
>
> *They have a very different view of democracy and freedom. This is nothing less than the political weaponization of the impeachment process—pure, raw sport, fueled by the misguided idea of party over country when, in fact, both will*

> *surely suffer.* * * * * 167 Cong. Rec. 602 (daily ed. Feb. 9, 2021) (statement by Mr. Schoen).
>
> *They say you need this trial before the Nation can heal, that the Nation cannot heal without it. I say our Nation cannot possibly heal with it. With this trial, you will open up new and bigger wounds across the Nation, for a great many Americans see this process for exactly what it is: a chance by a group of partisan politicians seeking to eliminate Donald Trump from the American political scene and seeking to disenfranchise 74 million-plus American voters and those who dare to share their political beliefs and vision of America. They hated the results of the **2016** election and want to use this impeachment process to further their political agenda.*
>
> *These elitists have mocked them for 4 years. They called their fellow Americans who believe in their country and their Constitution "deplorables." And the latest talk is that they need to deprogram those who supported Donald Trump and the Grand Old Party. But at the end of the day, this is not just about Donald Trump or any individual. This is about our Constitution and abusing the impeachment power for political gain. They tell us that we have to have this impeachment trial, such as it is, to bring about unity, but they don't want unity. And they know this so-called trial will tear the country in half, leaving tens of millions of Americans feeling left out of the Nation's agenda, as dictated by one political party that now holds the power in the White House and in our national legislature. Id.* at S601.

On the first Day of the trial, the Senate voted 56–44 to reject the jurisdictional arguments. 167 Cong. Rec. S609 (daily ed. Feb. 9, 2021). Six Republicans, Members of the former President's party, joined the 50 Democrats: Sen. Cassidy (R-LA), Sen. Collins (R-ME), Sen. Murkowski (R-AK), Sen. Romney (R-UT), Sen. Sasse (R-NE) and Sen. Toomey (R-PA).

QUESTIONS ON THE JURISDICTIONAL ARGUMENTS

Text

Picking and Choosing Text: One of the problems with textual arguments is that they can effectively "gerrymander" the text, meaning that they can "pick and choose" particular provisions. *See* William N. Eskridge, Jr. & Victoria F. Nourse, *The Gerrymandered Text: The Eclipse of Republican Government in an Era of Statutory Populism* (forthcoming N.Y.U. L. J. 2021). The President's lawyers, for example, argued that the Constitution prevented the Senate from doing anything other than "removing" a sitting President as follows:

> *But the section I read—"Judgment"—in other words, the bad thing that can happen—the "Judgment in Cases of Impeachment"—i.e., what we are doing—"shall not extend further than * * * * removal from Office." What is so hard about that? Which of those words are unclear? Shall not extend further than removal * * * * from Office.* 167 Cong. Rec. S601 (daily ed. Feb. 9, 2021) (statement of Mr. Castor) (ellipses in original)

Notice that this argument *truncates the actual text,* which provides as follows:

> Judgement in Cases of Impeachment shall not extend further than to removal from Office, **and disqualification to hold and enjoy any Office of honor, Trust or Profit under the United States**: but the Party convicted shall nevertheless be liable and subject to Indictment, Trial, Judgement and Punishment, according to Law. U.S. Const. art. I, § 2, cl. 7 (emphasis added).

Different Texts: Notice that the House Managers' argument emphasized some constitutional provisions and the President's lawyers emphasized other constitutional texts. The House Managers urged that Article I gave the Senate power to try "all" impeachments, that the President had been impeached "while in office," and that Article II provided the Senate with the power not only to remove but also to "disqualify" the former President from future office.

> *"All" means all, and there are no exceptions to the rule. Because the Senate has jurisdiction to try all impeachments, it most certainly has jurisdiction to try this one. It is really that simple.* 167 Cong. Rec. S591 (daily ed. Feb. 9, 2021) (statement of Rep. Raskin).

Meanwhile, the President's lawyers argued that removal, as provided in Article II, was what lawyers call a "condition precedent," meaning a necessary condition for disqualification, and thus limited the power of the Senate to try the impeachment. Disqualification had to follow, in time, removal.

> *The Constitution links the impeachment remedy of disqualification from future office with the remedy of removal from the office that person currently occupies; the former remedy does not apply in situations where the latter is "unavailable." Conviction and removal are inextricably entwined. If removal no longer is possible, neither is an impeachment conviction. Id.* at S608 (statement of Mr. Schoen) (quoting Judge J. Michael Luttig).[23]

The weight of the opinion by constitutional commentators who wrote prior to the Second Trump Impeachment was on the side of the House Managers: that the most relevant provision was that of Article I determining the

---

[23] *See* Cong. Research Serv., LSB10565, The Impeachment and Trial of a Former President 2 (2021).

Senate's power to try the case.[24] The President was impeached while in office so there was no real issue that it was a "late impeachment." The question was whether there was a "late trial" by the Senate. On that question, the Constitution says both that the Senate may try all impeachments, without time limitation. U.S. Const. art. I, § 3, cl. 6. ("The Senate shall have the sole Power to try all Impeachments."). Query whether this reading of "all" goes too far, if it is taken out of context of other provisions. Would the Senate be authorized to try a former President who the House had *not* been impeached while in office, but after he left office?[25]

Harmonizing Texts: The best reading of any text makes sense of *more* rather than *less* text. Why? To avoid cutting the text into tiny pieces like "all" or "and" as we will see below, which inevitably takes words *out of context*. No interpreter, including a stringent textualist, believes that words should be taken out of context. If one were to take all the impeachment provisions together, and wanted to give each maximum effect, what would you do? The Senate does have power to try *all* "impeachments." U.S. Const. art. I, § 3, cl. 6 and it has the power to create the "rules of its own proceedings." *Id.* art. I, § 5, cl. 2. If the Senate were to enact a Senate Rule saying that it could try impeachments issued by the House within three months of the end of a President or officer's term, would the Supreme Court reject that rule as unconstitutional? Remember, as well, from Part One, Chapter 5 that the Senate has broad investigatory powers and could choose to hold an investigation in any form, including one that required all Senators to attend. As we know from Part One, Chapter 2, the Supreme Court has been highly deferential to the Senate's rules governing impeachment trials. *See Walter Nixon v. United States*, 506 U.S. 224 (1993).

The Meaning of "and": Linguists debate the question of "and." (Yes, 'tis true). In fact, when it came to a key clause in Article I, the House Managers and the President's lawyers were deploying different meanings of "and." U.S. Const. art. I, § 3, Clause 7 provides that: "Judgement in Cases of Impeachment shall not extend further than to removal from Office, *and* disqualification to hold and enjoy any Office of honor, Trust or Profit under the United States." (emphasis added). The House Managers argued that this gave the Senate two powers, one to remove and the other to disqualify. To them, "and" meant "both."

> *The meaning is clear. The Senate has the power to impose removal, which only applies to current officials. And, separately, it has the power to impose disqualification, which obviously applies to both*

---

[24] *See* 167 Cong. Rec. S591 (daily ed. Feb. 9, 2021) (statement of Rep. Raskin) (citing Letter, Constitutional Law Scholars on Impeaching Former Officials (Jan. 21, 2021) (available at https://www.politico.com/f/?id=00000177-2646-de27-a5f7-3fe714ac0000)).

[25] Senator John Cornyn (R-TX), for example, asked "could we go back and try President Obama?" after the House delivered its Article of Impeachment against Donald Trump after he had left office. Lisa Mascaro and Mary Clare Jalonick, *Trump impeachment goes to Senate, testing his sway over GOP*, Associated Press (Jan. 25, 2021), https://apnews.com/article/senate-gop-oppose-trump-impeachment-f4b8bf18ce0e23b877ba945545c3e257.

> *current and former officers.* 167 Cong. Rec. S593 (daily ed. Feb. 9, 2021) (statement of Rep. Neguse).

The President's lawyers were using a different view of "and"—meaning "if and only if" or "thereafter in time." To them, President Trump could only be disqualified if he had been convicted of an impeachable offense while he was the President, and after he had been removed from office.

> *In a Senate impeachment trial, conviction means and requires removal, and conviction without a removal is no conviction at all. Only upon a valid conviction and its requisite, enforceable removal may the additional judgment of disqualification plausibly be entertained. Id.* at S606 (statement of Mr. Schoen).

Is there any way to determine, based on the text alone, which meaning is better? Could you argue that the "if and only if" meaning undermines the Senate's power to try "all" impeachments? Linguists distinguish between "and-as-both" and "and-as-thereafter" by asking whether you can reverse the sentence and still have it make sense. If so, "thereafter" readings are disfavored. What if the clause read: "Judgement in Cases of Impeachment shall not extend further than disqualification to hold and enjoy any Office of Honor, Trust or Profit under the United States and removal from office"? *See* Victoria Nourse, *Picking and Choosing Text: Lessons for Statutory Interpretation from the Philosophy of Language*, 69 Fla. L. Rev. 1409, 1414–1415 (2017) (describing the test used by linguists to distinguish between different meanings of "and").

The Meaning of "President": President Trump's lawyers also deployed a novel argument akin to "intratextualism." For a sophisticated version of this argument, *see* Akhil Amar, *Intratextualism*, 112 Harv. L. Rev. 747 (1999). Less sophisticated versions of the argument assume that the Constitution is like a dictionary, whose words have consistent meanings throughout. The President's lawyers argued that the meaning of "President" in Article I, Section 3, Clause 6—requiring the Chief Justice to preside over a Senate impeachment trial when the President of the United States is tried—had to mean "sitting President." Since "President" in that clause must mean "sitting President," then *every other reference* to "the President" in the Constitution also means "sitting President." One should therefore read the impeachment clauses as limited to "sitting Presidents." (Of course, the word "*sitting* President" is nowhere in the actual Constitution.)

If you disagree with the President's lawyers, why? One reason may be that the underlying reasons for the provisions differ. As we noted above, the Chief Justice sits to avoid having the Vice President determine the outcome of an impeachment trial from which the Vice President could profit by becoming the next President. Is that the same reason for the clause allowing the Senate to disqualify impeached Presidents from future office? U.S. Const. art. I, § 3, cl. 7. Linguists, and textualists, agree that text can only be determined by context. The problem is that context can radically change meaning. Take for example the word "states." Does that term mean the same thing everywhere in the Constitution? (Hint, sometimes it means "United States" or the federal government, and sometimes it means the individual states—like Alaska or Kentucky or Massachusetts. In theory, the word "state" might also mean another country since, in international law, countries are often called "states.") If relevant context includes the reasons for having particular provisions, then why shouldn't terms differ in meaning throughout the Constitution if the reasons for those provisions differ?

Intratextualism should not be easily dismissed: Chief Justice Roberts is a fan of intratextual analysis. In *Arizona State Legislature v. Arizona Independent Redistricting Commission*, the Supreme Court held that the Elections Clause of the Constitution does not prohibit the people of Arizona from appointing an independent commission, via ballot initiative, to draw congressional districts to reduce partisan gerrymandering. 576 U.S. 787 (2015). The Elections Clause states that "the Times, Places and Manner of holding Elections for Senators and Representatives, shall be prescribed in each State by the Legislature thereof* * * *". U.S. Const. art. I, § 4, cl. 1 (emphasis added). Justice Ruth Bader Ginsburg wrote for the majority that, since "legislatures" exist to express the will of the people and make laws, that term cannot be interpreted to preclude the people from expressing their will or making laws, themselves, when they are permitted to do so under state law—just as the Arizona state constitution permits the people to "bypass their elected representatives and make laws directly through the initiative." 576 U.S. at 796. Chief Justice Roberts dissented. Relying on intratextualism, he opined that the Elections Clause requires that state legislatures, and state legislatures alone, oversee redistricting:

> The unambiguous meaning of "the Legislature" in the Elections Clause as a representative body is confirmed by other provisions of the Constitution that use the same term in the same way. When seeking to discern the meaning of a word in the Constitution, there is no better dictionary than the rest of the Constitution itself. * * * * The Constitution includes seventeen provisions referring to a State's "Legislature." * * * * Every one of those references is consistent with the understanding of a legislature as a representative body. More importantly, many of them are only consistent with an institutional legislature—and flatly incompatible with the majority's reading of "the Legislature" to refer to the people as a whole. [Among these provisions are Article I, Sections 2 and 3; Article IV, Section 4; and Article VI.] *Id.* at 829–31 (Roberts, C.J. dissenting).

Intratextualism, like textualism more generally, tends to reject arguments based on precedent. The claim is that if the text means one thing, then it does not matter if other persons, in the past, viewed it differently. The President's lawyers in this case attempted to deploy the text to reject past precedents, explained below, in which the Congress had proceeded to impeach and try individuals who had resigned from office.

Past Precedent

Were the Blount and Belknap Precedents Controlling?: The House Managers relied upon past congressional precedent to argue that the Senate had the right to try President Trump. In two cases, summarized earlier, the

Senate had tried impeachments of those who were no longer in office.[26] Lawyers typically invoke precedent as guides for decision. Precedents allow judges to maintain continuity and impartiality. We are all subject to the emotions of the day and to cognitive bias. One way to prevent those emotions from biasing our judgments and to maintain continuity in law is to look at what people outside of those circumstances considered. If someone in another time and age decided "X" in a similar situation, then that helps a judge resist her political biases for or against any particular outcome.

The House Managers considered the Blount and Belknap cases as good reasons to hold a trial even after President Trump left office. 167 Cong. Rec. S592–3 (daily ed. Feb. 9, 2021) (statement of Rep. Neguse). The basic gist of the argument: other Congresses, under entirely different political circumstances, had done the same thing. Lawyers view precedents as "controlling" when they depend upon similar factual circumstances. In both cases, Blount and Belknap, the Senate proceeded to a trial after the official was no longer in office. The precedential effects of prior Senate practices are sometimes considered weaker than judicial precedent because the Senate could, in theory, vote to overturn them. But, as Jonathan Gould has shown, there are good reasons, including institutional self-interest, that explain why the Senate follows its own precedents as a general rule, even when it might, in theory, ignore them. *See* Jonathan S. Gould, *Law Within Congress*, 129 Yale L.J. 1946, 1994–1997 (2020) (explaining the system of legislative precedent operating within the Congress).

Were the Blount and Belknap Precedents Irrelevant, as President Trump's Lawyers Argued?: The House Managers seemed aghast that the President's lawyers spent little time on these precedents in the actual trial. In their briefs, the President's lawyers argued that the cases were not relevant because nothing had been decided. President's Brief at 23–26. At least in the Belknap case, however, no one disputed that the Senate had spent two weeks on the jurisdictional question and that the Senate voted on the jurisdictional question in favor of trying a former officer who had resigned his office. (Technically, the Belknap case was even further removed from a standard impeachment because Belknap resigned before the House could impeach and the Senate still went on to try him; by contrast, President Trump was impeached while he was still in office, but the question was whether the Senate could proceed to a trial.) How could the jurisdictional question not have been decided? For most lawyers, in a traditional case, that would have been enough. But the President's lawyers argued that Belknap was acquitted and that many Senators voted to acquit and made statements that they did so on the basis that "they did not think the Senate had jurisdiction to convict someone who was no longer in office." *Id.* at 25.

The House Managers were dismissive of this argument because lawyers make strong distinctions between procedural motions about jurisdiction (arguing the court has no power to try the case) and verdicts (the end result

---

[26] For full consideration of the Blunt and Belknap cases, *see* Brian Kalt, *The Constitutional Case for the Impeachability of Former Federal Officials: An Analysis of the Law, History, and Practice of Late Impeachment*, 6 Tex. L. Rev. & Pol. 13 (2001).

in a case) which adjudge liability or guilt. House Managers Brief at 72–73.[27] Even a first-year law student would not confuse a ruling on a jurisdictional motion with a jury verdict. After the Senate voted to take jurisdiction, by a margin of 56 to 44, the House Managers insisted that the jurisdictional issue was decided. The jurisdictional dispute between the House Managers and the President's lawyers reveals the differences between a standard judicial trial and a Senate impeachment trial. In a standard trial, juries must typically be unanimous. Juries do not issue statements, as a general rule, explaining their reasoning. Judges may explain their reasoning; but once a judge makes a decision, that is typically the end of the matter until after a verdict is reached (at which point, there may be grounds for an appeal). In an impeachment trial, however, Senators do not always make statements explaining their votes—as they did in the Belknap trial. And Senators are not required to abandon their jurisdictional qualms, even after a Senate vote is taken against their position. Not surprisingly, therefore, the President's lawyers continued to argue that Senators could acquit President Trump for any reason, including lack of jurisdiction.

Why would Senators relitigate the jurisdictional question in the Belknap trial after the evidence was presented and a vote on jurisdiction was concluded? Was it pure political expediency? Was it easier for the Senators to say that the case should never have been tried, rather than to say that Belknap was not guilty of the underlying misbehavior? Note that this occurred in the Second Trump Impeachment trial as well. Even though the Senate voted to take jurisdiction, Senators who ultimately voted to acquit Trump claimed that they did so because they worried about whether the Senate should have tried the case. When Senator Mitch McConnell (R-KY), the Republican leader, explained why he voted to acquit, he stated that it was partly because of "the loss of jurisdiction" following Donald Trump's departure from office. 167 Cong. Rec. S736 (daily ed. Feb. 13, 2021). Senator Ted Cruz (R-TX) released a statement explaining that he "was against the Senate taking jurisdiction in this trial from the start."[28] And Senator Mike Lee (R-UT) explained in a statement of his own that "the Senate should never have exercised jurisdiction over this Article in the first place."[29] Does this mean that there really are no precedents in Senate impeachment trials?

Senatorial Bad Faith on Trial Timing?: After the trial was over, at a press conference, Speaker of the House Nancy Pelosi (D-CA) contended that the Senate had acted in bad faith. Senator Mitch McConnell (R-KY) justified his vote for acquittal on the grounds that "former President Trump is not constitutionally eligible for conviction" because a trial could not be conducted

---

[27] We relied upon a copy of the brief that as published by the New York Times. Future citations are to that version. *See Read the House Impeachment Managers' Memo*, N.Y. Times (Feb. 8, 2021), https://www.nytimes.com/interactive/2021/02/08/us/house-managers-trump-impeachment-trial.html.

[28] Press Release, Senator Ted Cruz, Statement On Vote To Acquit Former President Donald Trump (Feb. 13, 2021) (https://www.cruz.senate.gov/?p=press_release&id=5617).

[29] Press Release, Senator Mike Lee, Statement on Acquittal of Former President Trump (Feb. 13, 2021) (https://www.lee.senate.gov/public/index.cfm/2021/2/sen-lee-statement-on-acquittal-of-former-president-trump).

before he left office: "a Senate verdict before Inauguration Day was never possible." 167 Cong. Rec. S736 (daily ed. Feb. 13, 2021). The House Speaker claimed that the House Managers had attempted to deliver the Article of Impeachment to the Senate between January 13th, when the Article was passed by the full House, and January 20th, when President Biden was inaugurated. If the Senate had tried President Trump before January 20th, no one could have claimed that there was a "late" impeachment. Speaker Pelosi essentially accused Senator McConnell of purposely delaying the case to help the President's defense.[30] What do you think of the Speaker's accusation? It is worth noting that, in the same floor statement in which he said that the Senate had no jurisdiction to try Trump, Senator McConnell issued a blistering indictment that the former President was "practically and morally" responsible for the attack on the Capitol. 167 Cong. Rec. S736 (daily ed. Feb. 13, 2021).

Will the Trump Verdict Stand as a Precedent Overruling Belknap?: The Senate voted to acquit in the Second Trump Impeachment. 167 Cong. Rec. S733 (daily ed. Feb. 13, 2021). As noted above, Republican Senators, like McConnell (R-KY), made specific statements that would support the view that the Senate did not have jurisdiction. Imagine that in the future, there is an impeached judge who resigns to avoid a trial in the Senate. Will he be able to argue that the Senate lacks jurisdiction over his case using the Second Trump Impeachment trial as precedent—that, since some Senators voted to acquit Trump based on jurisdiction, even after the Senate voted to take jurisdiction, the Senate generally lacks jurisdiction over an impeached official who leaves office? Or is the resignation issue different? In the case of an official who resigns, the alleged miscreant has acted to avoid justice, in effect profiting from his own wrong. It is a general principle in law that individuals should not be able to avoid justice in such a manner—no corporate head would be able to avoid a criminal prosecution by resigning his office. By contrast, President Trump was voted out of office. Should that matter? Would it be helpful to know that a corporate CEO who had committed an offense against the corporation, and was voted out by the Board of Directors, could still be held liable in some circumstances under both civil and criminal law?

Future Precedent

The House Managers insisted that failure to take jurisdiction would mean that there was a "January exception"—that a President could stage a coup or commit some other impeachable offense, and Congress could not remove him if he did it late enough in his term. 167 Cong. Rec. S590 (daily ed. Feb. 9, 2021) (statement of Rep. Raskin). They also emphasized that President Trump had been impeached while in office, so that his trial would not create precedent that would allow impeachment and trial of former Presidents or former Cabinet Members. House Managers Brief at 49. The President's lawyers were just as insistent that, if the Senate could try an impeached former President like Trump, then Congress could impeach and

---

30 *See Speaker Pelosi Blames Senator McConnell for Delaying Impeachment Trial until After January 20*, CSPAN (Feb. 13, 2021), https://www.c-span.org/video/?c4946118/speaker-pelosi-blames-senator-mcconnell-delaying-impeachment-trial-january-20.

try all sorts of other former officials—like the former Attorney General under President Obama, Eric Holder. *Id.* at S599 (statement of Mr. Castor).

Testing the Impeaching Former Officials Argument: We have seen "slippery slope" arguments before. Lawyers allege that something terrible will happen if a ruling is made against them. These arguments are often overstated.[31] The President's lawyers argued that there would be dire consequences since this precedent would allow the "late" impeachment of any civil officer. If true, that would be a serious consequence. The value of an argument about future precedent is that it sticks to the facts. Would the Senate be able to impeach Hillary Clinton tomorrow because of her purported bad acts in office as Secretary of State, based on the Trump precedent? Is this a likely consequence? Or is this exaggerated? Remember that the House voted to impeach Trump *while he was in office* immediately after the events. So, the precedent would only extend to those who committed an act while in office and were impeached by the House near the end of their term. Since former Secretary of State Hillary Clinton was not impeached while she was in office, the hypothetical would not be analogous.

What About Former Officials Impeached by the House at the End of Their Terms?: Assuming that any future precedent would be limited to those officials impeached by the House at the end of their term, would this be a dangerous future precedent? Note that new Presidents are typically inaugurated on January 20th, but that new Congresses are typically convened on January 3rd.[32] Since 1993, every outgoing President has served out the final days of his term with new congressional majorities of the opposite party.[33] What if the Republican 115th Congress—led by House Speaker Paul Ryan (R-WI) and Senate Majority Leader Mitch McConnell (R-KY)—had waited until mid-January to impeach President Obama, and tried him after President Trump's inauguration? What if the Democratic 111th Congress—led by House Speaker Nancy Pelosi (D-CA) and Senate Majority Leader Harry Reid (D-NV) had waited until the end of George W. Bush's presidency, impeached him in January, and tried him during the Obama administration? Is the real danger here an impeachment "late" in a President's term or an impeachment, shortly after an election, by a new, emboldened Congress? What incentive would a new Congress have to impeach an outgoing President? Presumably, a vindictive Congress could seek to punish an outgoing President, prevent him running again (disqualification), or distract from the new President's agenda. But, as we see below, there are political costs to impeachment—any House Member

---

[31] Mr. Castor, for example, not only argued that "the slippery-slope principle will have taken hold if [the Senate] continue[d] to go forward" with a second Trump impeachment, but that "the floodgates will open" if he is tried and a trial would "release the whirlwinds." 167 Cong. Rec. S599 (daily ed. Feb. 9, 2021).

[32] U.S. Const. amend. XX ("The terms of the President and the Vice President shall end at noon on the 20th day of January, and the terms of Senators and Representatives at noon on the 3rd day of January* * * *and the terms of their successors shall then begin").

[33] When Bill Clinton left office, there was a 50/50 split in the Senate, but a Republican House. Since Gore was his VP, the Senate was technically Democratic. In all other cases, both the House and Senate had flipped.

would have to ask herself whether she was willing to risk that the voting public would consider it wasted time or pure political vendetta.

The "Political Safeguards" of Impeachment: There have been very few impeachments over 200 plus years of U.S. history. Arguments about future precedent must contend with this hard fact. The President's lawyers in both the First and Second Trump Impeachments suggested that the trials reflected political vendettas and amounted to a "witch hunt." If policy differences or even partisan politics were enough to prompt impeachment, we would expect to see impeachments on a regular basis, but *the numbers belie that fact*. Why? Because of what I call the "political safeguards" of impeachment. We know that the President is highly unlikely to be impeached if the House is held by his own party. But party differences are not enough to explain the dearth of impeachments. If party differences, or even policy differences, were determinative, Presidents would be regularly impeached. But they are not.

What explains the low numbers? The short answer: there are political costs to impeachment. The collective action costs alone are tremendous—the time and energy of getting a majority of House Members (218) to agree on a highly momentous action. Each Member will have to think how such a publicly salient vote will affect voters in the 5th district of Pennsylvania or the 4th of Alaska. Individual representatives have a far greater incentive, particularly those in any swing district, to focus on their constituents' priorities, like roads and tax reform. Party leaders worry that American voters of both parties punish those who spend more time on political vendettas than on improving citizens' lives. The First Trump Impeachment only received a positive full chamber vote, as we saw in Part One, when *moderate Members* decided that impeachment was necessary to protect national security. Finally, everyone knows that the impeached individual is unlikely to be convicted, because it requires a 2/3 Senate vote. Given all these costs, are you convinced by President Trump's arguments that impeachment will become more common in the future?

Shared Constitutional Norms

The House Managers claimed that President Trump had attempted a near-coup by inciting an attack on Congress as it met to certify the 2020 presidential election. The President's lawyers distanced the President from responsibility for the rioters' actions. Notice, however, that the President's lawyers were also making a "populist" argument. They were arguing that the people had the right to take back their government from dangerous elites who simply "hated" the President and were "weaponizing" the political process. As Mr. Schoen said:

> *These elitists have mocked [the Trump voters] for 4 years. They called their fellow Americans who believe in their country and their Constitution "deplorables." And the latest talk is that they need to deprogram those who supported Donald Trump and the Grand Old Party. But at the end of the day, this is not just about Donald Trump or any individual. This is about our Constitution and*

> *abusing the impeachment power for political gain.* 167 Cong. Rec. S601 (daily ed. Feb. 9, 2021).
>
> *This is a process fueled irresponsibly by base hatred by these House managers and those who gave them their charge, and they are willing to sacrifice our national character to advance their hatred and their fear that one day they might not be the party in power.* * * * *
>
> *They have a very different view of democracy and freedom. This is nothing less than the political weaponization of the impeachment process—pure, raw sport, fueled by the misguided idea of party over country when, in fact, both will surely suffer. Id.* at S602.

Democracy v. America: One of the interesting rhetorical aspects of the President's defense was the lawyers' appeal to *American* interests rather than *Democracy*. This reflects President Trump's own tendency to embrace slogans like "America First." But it also reflects a subtle shift toward populist themes. One of the basic dangers of populism, as reflected in the political science literature, is that it speaks in the name of the average person but, in truth, sets up an apocalyptic struggle between individuals versus elites and existing institutions. The term "America" appeals to a particular imagined and unified people; the term "democracy' to an institutional form of government that seeks to represent divergent views. As Professor Samuel Issacharoff has written, there are several characteristics of populism including its often apocalyptic vision:

> There "can be no populism * * * *without someone speaking in the name of the people as a whole." Populist impulses shorten the time frame and turn everything into a binary choice, a political life at the knife's edge. Us or them, success or perfidy, the people or the oligarchs, Americans or foreigners. There can be no spirit of partial victory, of legitimate disagreement, or even of mutual gain through engagement.

Sam Issacharoff, *Democracy's Deficits*, 85 Chi. L. Rev. 485, 486 (2018) (quoting Jan-Werner Mueller, What is Populism? 43 (2018)). We will return to this basic question in Chapter 2.

PROBLEM 1-1

This Chapter addressed the question of **when** the Senate can try impeachments. Imagine that the House of Representatives has a majority of Republicans in 2024. Imagine as well that the current Speaker of the House, Nancy Pelosi (D-CA), decides to retire and is no longer there in 2024. The new Republican Speaker of the House seeks to impeach a variety of former Democratic politicians, including Pelosi and former Obama Attorney General Eric Holder. You are a lawyer in the Speaker's office. What do you tell her about the legal bases for these actions and their likely results? Hint: Can a former Member of Congress be impeached? To be sure, we saw Senator Blount was impeached but, as a general rule today, Congress follows its own rules for expelling Members rather than starting impeachment proceedings.[34] Take a look at the text of the Constitution, Article I, § 5 to see one reason why Congress does not impeach its own Members. What about a former Member? And what about a former Attorney General?

[34] On the legal question of whether Members of Congress can be impeached, see Frank O. Bowman III, High Crimes and Misdemeanors: A History of Impeachment for the Age of Trump ch. 5 (2019).

Chapter Two

THE SECOND IMPEACHMENT TRIAL

In this Chapter, we consider the House Managers' substantive case against the President and the President's defense. A good deal of the case made by the House Managers recounts the events leading to violence inside the U.S. Capitol on January 6, 2021. For ease of understanding, we break the factual case into central arguments. After we consider the House Managers' case, we turn to the President's defense, and the House Managers' rebuttal. Finally, we consider the President's principal legal arguments against impeachment: the Constitution's First Amendment and Due Process clause.

I. THE HOUSE MANAGERS' CASE

Once the jurisdictional vote was taken, the House Managers proceeded to present a case showing that former President Trump had incited the storming of the Capitol and then did nothing to stop it. The President's lawyers did not focus, as their predecessors had during the First Trump Impeachment, on the meaning of "high Crimes and Misdemeanors." Instead, they argued (1) that the rioters were acting on their own and, consequently, that the President was not responsible for their actions; (2) that the President's actions were protected by the First Amendment; and (3) that the Due Process Clause made the Senate trial unlawful.

A. The Factual Presentation

Because the House Managers used a good deal of video, which is then transcribed in the Congressional Record, the video transcriptions of statements made by persons other than the House Managers appear without italics to mark them as distinct. Note as well that the Congressional Record capitalizes the names of Members of Congress.

The President Incited Violence

Rep. Raskin (D-MD) opened by explaining the importance of the trial and rejecting the notion that it was simply about politics:

> *Some people think this trial is a contest of lawyers or, even worse, a competition between political parties. It is neither. It is a moment of truth for America.* * * * **America needs the truth about ex-President Trump's role in inciting the*

insurrection on January 6 because it threatened our government, and it disrupted—it easily could have destroyed—the peaceful transfer of power in the United States for the first time in 233 years. * * * * 167 Cong. Rec. S615 (daily ed. Feb. 10, 2021).

The evidence will show you that ex-President Trump was no innocent bystander. The evidence will show that he clearly incited the January 6 insurrection. * * * **The evidence will show you that he saw it coming and was not remotely surprised by the violence.* * * * * *Id.* at S626.

[W]e will show you that he completely abdicated his duty as Commander in Chief to stop the violence and protect the government and protect our officers and protect our people. He violated his oath of office to preserve, protect, and defend the Constitution, the government, and the people of the United States. Id.

Trump incited the January 6 attack, and when his mob overran and occupied the Senate and attacked the House and assaulted law enforcement, he watched it on TV like a reality show. He reveled in it, and he did nothing to help us as Commander in Chief. Instead, he served as the "inciter in chief," sending tweets that only further incited the rampaging mob. He made statements lauding and sympathizing with the insurrectionists. Id.

At 4:17 p.m.—over 3 hours after the beginning of the siege—for the very first time, he spoke out loud—not on Twitter. He spoke out loud to the American people. Here is what he said:

(Text of video presentation of 1-6-2021.)

> President TRUMP. I know your pain. I know you're hurt. We had an election that was stolen from us. It was a landslide election, and everyone knows it, especially the other side.

If anyone ever had a doubt as to his focus that day, it was not to defend us; it was not to console us. It was to praise and sympathize and commiserate with the rampaging mob. It was to continue to act as "inciter in chief," not Commander in Chief, by telling the mob that their election had been stolen from them. Id.

The President Did Not Just Make a Speech, He Planned to Attack the Election

Rep. Neguse (D-CO) placed the former President's actions in the context of a pattern of lying about the election beginning months *before* November:

> *Now, some have said that President Trump's remarks, his speech on January 6, was just a speech. Well, let me ask you this: When in our history has a speech led thousands of people to storm our Nation's Capitol with weapons, to scale the walls, break windows, kill a Capitol Police officer?*
>
> *This was not just a speech.* * * * *
>
> *And how do we know this? Because in the weeks prior to, during, and after the election, he used the same words over and over and over again. You will hear over and over three things—you can see them on the screens—first,* * * * * *the "big lie," that the "election was stolen, full of fraud, rigged."*
>
> *You will hear over and over him using that lie to urge his supporters to "never concede" and "stop the steal." Finally, you will hear the call to arms, that it was his supporters' patriotic duty to fight like hell. To do what? To stop the steal. To stop the election from being stolen by showing up in this very Chamber. To stop you. To stop us.* * * * *
>
> *[Mr. Trump] didn't just tell them to fight like hell; he told them how, where, and when. He made sure they had advance notice, 18 days' advance notice. He sent this "save the date" for January 6. He told them to march to the Capitol and fight like hell on January 6,* * * * * *the exact same day we were certifying the election results. What time was that rally scheduled for? The exact same time that this Chamber was certifying the election results in joint session. When did he conclude his speech? Literally moments before Speaker* PELOSI *had gaveled us into session.*
>
> *Let's take just a minute and really look at his words on January 6 as he spoke at the Save America rally. Remember, I told you you would hear three phrases: "The election was stolen," "Stop the Steal," and "Fight like hell." Let's start with that first phrase.*
>
> (Text of video presentation of 1-6-2021.)
>
> > President TRUMP. All of us here today do not want to see our election victory stolen. There has never been anything like this. It is a pure theft in American history. Everybody knows it. Make no mistake, this

election was stolen from you, from me, and from the country.

Now, of course, each of you heard those words before. So had the crowd. The President had spent months telling his supporters that the election had been stolen, and he used this speech to incite them further, to inflame them, to stop the steal, to stop the certification of the election results. * * * * 167 Cong. Rec. S618 (daily ed. Feb. 10, 2021).

The President Failed to Defend the Capitol

Rep. Neguse (D-CO) continued:

I do want to be clear about what also happened during that terrible attack, and that is this: that President Trump, once again, failed us because when the violence erupted, when we and the law enforcement officials protecting you were under attack, as each of you were being evacuated from this Chamber from a violent mob, as we were being evacuated from the House, he could have immediately and forcefully intervened to stop the violence. It was his duty as Commander in Chief to stop the violence, and he alone had that power, not just because of his unique role as Commander in Chief but because they believed that they were following his orders. They said so. Id.

You will hear evidence tonight, tomorrow, throughout the trial, about his refusal as Commander in Chief to respond to numerous desperate pleas on the phone, across social media, begging him to stop the attack. And you will see his relentless attack on Vice President PENCE, *who was at that very moment hiding with his family as armed extremists were chanting, "Hang Mike Pence," calling him a traitor.* * * * *

Think for a moment—just a moment—of the lives lost that day, of the more than 140 wounded police officers, and ask yourself if, as soon as this had started, President Trump had simply gone onto TV, just logged onto Twitter and said "Stop the attack." If he had done so with even half as much force as he said "Stop the steal," how many lives would we have saved? Sadly, he didn't do that.

Five people lost their lives on that terrible, tragic day. A woman was shot dead 50 feet from where we later certified the election results. And for those who question just how bad it was, criminal complaints recently unsealed by the Department of Justice are more than revealing. You all see one of these documents on the screen. In the charging *affidavit of one of the leaders of the Proud Boys, we learned that members of this group "said that they would have killed * * * * Mike Pence if given the chance." * * * * Id.* at S619.

*In another, we learned of the tweet in real time while they were in the building stating: "We broke into the Capitol * * * * we got inside, we did our part. We were looking for Nancy [Pelosi] to shoot her in the friggin' brain but we didn't find her." Id. at* S620.

The President Claimed the Election Would Be Stolen Months Before November

Rep. Castro (D-TX) explained the lead-up to the January 6 attack, including the President's refusal to commit to a peaceful transfer of power if he lost the election.

Beginning in the spring of 2020, President Trump began to fall behind in the polls, and by July, President Trump had reached a new low. He was running 15 points behind his opponent, and he was scared. He began to believe that he could legitimately lose the election, so he did something entirely unprecedented in the history of our Nation. He refused to commit to a peaceful transition of power. Here is what he said:

(Text of videotape presentation.)

Mr. WALLACE: Can you give a direct answer you will accept the election?

Mr. TRUMP. I have to see. Look, I have to see. No, I'm not just going to just say yes. I'm not going to say no.

Mr. WALLACE. Do you commit to making sure that there is a peaceful transfer of power?

Mr. TRUMP. Get rid of the ballots and you'll have a very peaceful—there won't be a transfer, frankly. There will be a continuation * * * *

Senators, the President of the United States said: There won't be a transition of power, frankly. There will be a continuation. President Trump was given every opportunity to tell his supporters: Yes, if I lose, I will peacefully transfer power to the next President. Instead, he told his supporters the only way he could lose the election is if it were stolen.

In tweet after tweet, he made sweeping allegations about election fraud that couldn't possibly be true. But that was the point. He didn't care if things were true. He wanted to make sure that his supporters were angry, like the election was being ripped away from them.

On May 24, 6 months before the election, he tweeted:

> It will be the greatest Rigged Election in history.

How could he possibly know it would be the greatest rigged election in history 6 months before the election happened.

And, on June 22, more of the same:

> RIGGED 2020 ELECTION: IT WILL BE THE SCANDAL OF OUR TIMES![1]

Again—about an election that had not even happened. On July 30:

> 2020 will be the most INACCURATE & FRAUDULENT Election in history.* * * *

Now, these were just a few of the many times President Trump tweeted about this, and he did it in speeches, in rallies, and on television, too.

(Text of video presentation of 7-31-2020.)

> President TRUMP: This is going to be the greatest election disaster in history. Because the only way we are going to lose this election is if the election is rigged. Remember that.
>
> The only way they can take this election away from us is if this is a rigged election. We are going to win this election.
>
> It's a rigged election. That's the only way we are going to lose.
>
> But this will be one of the greatest fraudulent—most fraudulent elections ever. 167 Cong. Rec. S620 (daily ed. Feb. 10, 2021).

The President Refused to Accept the Results of the Election

Rep. Castro (D-TX) continued:

*Let us turn now to the election. * * * *[B]y November 7, major news networks, including FOX News, reported that, once the remaining votes were counted, Joe Biden would be the likely victor. So President Trump began urging his*

---

[1] Capitalization appears in the congressional record, as a verbatim recording of President Trump's tweets.

*supporters to stop the count. * * * *. He said at 12:49 a.m. on election night:*

> They are trying to STEAL the Election. We will never let them do it.

A little over an hour later, at, roughly, 2:30 in the morning, before all the votes were even close to being counted, he goes even further and actually declares victory. Take a look.

(Text of video presentation of 11-4-2020.)

> President TRUMP. This is a fraud on the American public. This is an embarrassment to our country. We were getting ready to win this election. Frankly, we did win this election. * * * *

On November 5, he tweeted, in all capital letters, as if shouting commands:

STOP THE COUNT! STOP THE FRAUD!

The same day as those tweets— * * *—around 100 Trump supporters showed up in front of the Maricopa County elections center in Phoenix, some of them carrying rifles, literally trying to intimidate officials to stop the count just as President Trump had commanded. * * * *

*In Philadelphia * * * * police investigated an alleged plot to attack the city's Pennsylvania Convention Center, where votes were being counted. Police took at least one man into custody who was carrying a weapon * * * *. This happened all over. In Atlanta, in Detroit, and in Milwaukee, his supporters used armed force to try to disrupt the lawful counting of votes because they bought into Trump's big lie that the election was stolen from them.*

*President Trump's months of inflaming and inciting his supporters had worked. They believed it was their duty to, quite literally, fight to stop the count. So they showed up at election centers across the country to do just that. * * *.* 167 Cong. Rec. S621 (daily ed. Feb. 10, 2021) (statement of Rep. Castro) (caps in original).

The President Failed to Accept His Electoral Loss

Rep. Swalwell (D-CA) detailed President Trump's attempts to challenge the election from November 3, 2020 until January 6, 2021:

*Day after day, he told his supporters false, outlandish lies that the victory—that the election outcome was taken and it was rigged. * * * **

On November 15, he stated:

> I concede NOTHING! We have a long way to go. This was a RIGGED ELECTION!

* * * *

November 17, in a Twitter statement:

> "DEAD PEOPLE VOTED" * * * *

November 28, Twitter statement:

> "We have found many illegal votes. Stay tuned!"

* * * **These are just a few of the hundreds of Twitter statements that President Trump sent. * * * *[H]e was dialing into meetings, holding rallies, appearing on television, continuing to spread the big lie that his election victory was stolen.* * * * *

President Trump cannot say: I didn't know what I was inciting. * * * *. *He could have very easily told his supporters: Stop threatening officials.* * * * **But each time, he didn't. Instead, in the face of escalating violence, he incited them further.* * * * *

But on December 14, despite all of President Trump's efforts to stop, the electors cast their votes according to the will of the American people, and Joe Biden was certified as having won 306 electoral college votes.

You will see here, in mid-December, President Trump announced the release of ads, including ones entitled "The Evidence is Overwhelming—FRAUD!" "STOP THE STEAL."

He spent $50 million from his legal defense fund on these ads to stop the steal and amplify his message. They were released nationally, played in video ads, online advertising, and targeted text messages. * * * *

Donald Trump would issue a deliberate call to action, and just like in his ads, that action was centered around January 6.

On December 19, at 1:42 in the morning, our Commander in Chief tweeted:

> Big protest in D.C. on January 6th. Be there, will be wild!

"Will be wild!" We know why he picked this day. It wasn't random. It was his last chance to stop a peaceful transition

of power, and he gave his supporters plenty of time to plan. 167 Cong. Rec. S622 (daily ed. Feb. 10, 2021).

*This was the save-the-date sent out 18 days before the event on January 6, and it wasn't a casual one-off reference or a single invitation. * * * * Id.* at S623 (daily ed. Feb. 10, 2021).

*President Trump's conduct leading up to January 6 was deliberate, planned, and premeditated. This was not one speech, not one tweet. It was dozens in rapid succession with the specific details. * * * **

This was never about one speech. He built this mob over many months with repeated messaging until they believed that they had been robbed of their votes and they would do anything to stop the certification. He made them believe that their victory was stolen and incited them so he could use them to steal the election for himself. Id.

(Text of videotape presentation.)

President TRUMP. This election was rigged.

Unidentified Speaker. This is tyranny against the people of the United States, and we are not standing for it any more.

President TRUMP. If we don't root out the fraud—the tremendous and horrible fraud that has taken place in our 2020 election, we don't have a country anymore.

The Left lies. They cheat, and they steal. They are ruthless, and they are hell-bent on getting power and control by any means necessary. * * * *

President TRUMP. The Democrats are trying to steal the White House. You cannot let them. *Id.* (caps in original).

The President's 60+ Legal Challenges Failed and He Intimidated Election Officials to Overturn the Results

Rep. Dean (D-PA) **and Rep. Lieu** (D-CA) argued that the President's efforts to challenge the election through the courts were frivolous and that he had intimidated election officials.

President Trump and his allies filed 62 separate lawsuits in Federal courts across more than half a dozen States and the District of Columbia, including Pennsylvania, my home State, as well as Arizona, Georgia, Michigan, Minnesota, Nevada, and Wisconsin.

Of the 62 postelection legal challenges, he lost 61. Only one was successful, and that case involved ballot curing in Pennsylvania and had no impact on President Biden's 80,555-vote victory in our Commonwealth. To be clear, not a single court, not a single judge agreed that the election results were invalid or should be invalidated.

Instead, court after court reviewing these challenges said these cases were "not credible," "without merit," "based on nothing but speculation," and "flat out wrong." * * * *

Judge Stephanos Bibas, a Trump appointee * * * **wrote:*

> The Campaign's claims have no merit. The number of ballots it specifically challenges is far smaller than the roughly 81,000-vote margin of victory. And it never claims fraud or that any of the votes were cast by illegal voters. Plus, tossing out millions of mail-in ballots would be drastic and unprecedented, disfranchising a huge swath of the electorate and upsetting all down-ballot races.* * * *.

In other words, Donald Trump was asking the judiciary to take away votes from Americans so that he could steal the election for himself. 167 Cong. Rec. S625 (daily ed. Feb. 10, 2021) (statement of Rep. Dean).

Rep. Dean (D-PA) explained that Trump put pressure on election officials in Michigan and Pennsylvania. She went on to explain pressure on a Georgia official, Brad Raffensperger, who had certified Georgia's election, and a recount, against Trump:

In all, Trump tweeted at Raffensperger 17 times in the coming weeks—there are just a few—calling him a "disaster," "obstinate," not having a clue, being played for a fool, and being a "so-called Republican," * * * *

Mr. Raffensperger and his family received death threats * * * **After these death threats, on November 25, Mr. Raffensperger wrote an op-ed, where he said:*

> My family voted for [Trump], donated to him and are now being thrown under the bus by him. * * * *

What did Trump do? Did he stop? Did he say: No, no, supporters; that isn't what I meant? No. He doubled down. * * * *

(Text of audio presentation of 11-26-2020.)

> President TRUMP. This was a massive fraud. This should never take place in this country. We're like a

> third world country. Look at—look at Georgia. But I understand the secretary of state who is really, uh, uh, he's an enemy of the people. The secretary of state—and whether he's Republican or not, this man, what he's done * * * *this character in Georgia, who is a disaster. * * * *

On January 5, the Washington Post released a recording of [the Brad Raffensperger] *call which had occurred on January 2—remember, just 4 days before the attack on the Capitol. Here is what President Trump said:*

(Text of audio presentation of 1-2-2021.)

> President TRUMP. It's more illegal for you than it is for them because you know what they did and you're not reporting it. That's the—you know, that's a criminal—that's a criminal offense. And you know, you can't let that happen. That's—that's a big risk to you and to Ryan, your lawyer. That's a big risk. * * * *

Remember, President Biden won Georgia by 11,779 votes. In his own words, Trump said:

> All I want to do is this. I just want to find 11,780 votes.

167 Cong. Rec. S625 (daily ed. Feb. 10, 2021).

The President Pressured His Vice President to Refuse to Certify the Election

Rep. Lieu (D-CA) argued that President Trump had lambasted members of the Republican Party, and pressured Attorney General William Barr and Vice President Mike Pence to reverse the results of the election.

Trump also pressured our Justice Department to investigate the false claims that the election was stolen. At the President's direction, Attorney General William Barr, a loyal member of the President's Cabinet, authorized Federal prosecutors to pursue "substantial allegations of voting and vote tabulation irregularities.' " * * * *

[A]fter his investigation, this is what he found:

> [W]e have not seen fraud on a scale that could have effected a different outcome in the election. * * * *

According to a news report, Bill Barr, the highest law enforcement official in the land, told President Donald Trump to his face that his theories of election fraud were "bullshit." * * * *

Finally, in his desperation, [Trump] turned on his own Vice President. He pressured Mike Pence to violate his constitutional oath and to refuse to certify the vote. President Trump had decided that Vice President Pence, who presided over the certification, could somehow stop it.

As Pence later confirmed, the Vice President does not have that power in the Constitution. And President Trump never tried to explain why he thought the Vice President could block the certification of the election results; he just began relentlessly attacking the Vice President.

Publicly, President Trump attacked Pence on social media and at rallies, getting his supporters to believe that Mike Pence could stop the certification on January 6. * * * *

(Text of video presentation of 1-4-2021.)

> President TRUMP. And I hope Mike Pence comes through for us, I have to tell you. I hope that our great Vice-President, our great Vice-President comes through for us. He's a great guy. Of course, if he doesn't come through, I won't like him quite as much.

On the morning of the rally on January 6, President Trump tweeted:

> All Mike Pence has to do is send them back to the States, AND WE WIN. Do it Mike, this is a time for extreme courage!

President Trump later went on to attack Pence nearly a dozen times in his speech at the Save America March. 167 Cong. Rec. S626 (daily ed. Feb. 10, 2021).

Privately, in person, before Pence headed to oversee the joint session on January 6, President Trump again threatened Pence. "You can either go down in history as a patriot," Mr. Trump told him, according to two people briefed on the conversation, "or you can go down in history as a pussy." * * * *. *Id.* at S627 (caps in original).

The President Knew That His Followers Could Be Violent and Included White Supremacists

Rep. Plaskett (D-VI, delegate) focused on the day of the violence, January 6, 2021, in anticipation of President Trump's arguments that the he was not aware of his followers' violent tendencies:

Some of you have said there is no way the President could have known how violent the mob would be. * * * **I want to*

> *show you why this violence was foreseeable and why Donald Trump was different than any other politician just telling their fighters, their supporters to fight for something.* * * * *
>
> *You will see that Donald Trump knew the people he was inciting, he saw the violence that they were capable of, and he had a pattern and practice of praising and encouraging that violence, never ever condemning it.*
>
> *Now, if the President had only said something once about fighting to stop the steal, and violence erupted, there would be no way to know he intended to incite it or saw it coming. But just as the President spent months spreading his big lie of the election, he also spent months cultivating groups of people who, following his command, repeatedly engaged in real, dangerous violence. And when they did, when the violence erupted as a response to his calls to fight against the stolen election, he did not walk it back. He did not tell them no. He did the opposite—the opposite. He praised and encouraged the violence so that it would continue. He fanned the flame of violence and it worked.* * * * *
>
> *Let's start with President Trump's incitement of the Proud Boys. Many of you have heard of this group, which since 2018 has been classified by the FBI as an extremist organization. Since that classification, the group has repeatedly engaged in serious acts of violence, including at pro-Trump rallies. In one such act on September 7, the Proud Boys attacked a man with a baseball bat and then punched him while he was down on the ground.*
>
> *On September 29, during a Presidential debate, President Trump was asked specifically if he was willing to condemn White supremacy and militia groups, if he was willing to tell them to stand down and stop the violence.* * * * * 167 Cong. Rec. S627 (daily ed. Feb. 10, 2021).
>
> *When asked to condemn the Proud Boys and White supremacists, what did our President say? He said: "Stand back and stand by."* *Id.* at S628.

Rep. Plaskett (D-VI, delegate) then played a video showing a group of Trump supporters attempting to drive a Biden campaign bus off the road on its way to Austin, Texas.

> *The President of the United States tweeted a video of his supporters trying to drive a bus off of the road.* * * * *

Well, the [video] he tweeted had a fight theme song placed to it that the President—the President—put that music to that video and he added at the top: "I LOVE TEXAS!"

Now, our President, Donald Trump, could have said: OK, I didn't realize how bad that was. This was very violent. Please stop. But he didn't. He saw the investigation and made a statement in defense of his supporters' attack on the bus writing:

In my opinion, these patriots did nothing wrong.

* * * * 167 Cong. Rec. S628 (daily ed. Feb. 10, 2021) (caps in original).

Rep. Plaskett (D-VI, delegate) argued that the President must have known about potential violence since the Proud Boys had previously engaged in violence, in December 2020, at a rally organized by the same group that would organize the Save America Rally on January 6th:

After the election on December 12, Trump supporters gathered in mass to protest the "stolen" election in DC. It was billed by his loyalists as the second Million MAGA March. The rally was organized by Women for America First, the same group that you will see later secured the permit for the January 6 rally. And who else was there? The Proud Boys, standing by. * * * *

The Proud Boys, after that rally, engaged in serious acts of violence in downtown DC. Some Trump supporters and self-identified Proud Boys vandalized churches after that rally.

If we look at these events, it is clear how we got here because what did the President do after that? He turned right around, and a little over a week later, he began coordinating the January 6 Save America rally with the same people who had planned the second Million MAGA March. * * * *

On December 19, President Trump tweeted his save the date for January 6. He told his supporters to come to DC for a "big protest" that day, billing it as "wild." * * * *

Donald Trump, over many months, cultivated violence, praised it, and then, when he saw the violence his supporters were capable of, he channeled it to his big, wild, historic event. He organized January 6 with the same people who had just organized the rally resulting in substantial violence, and he made absolutely sure, this time, these violent rally-goers wouldn't just remain in place. He made sure that those violent people would literally march right

> *here, to our steps, from the Ellipse to the Capitol, to stop the steal—his cavalry. This was deliberate. Id.* at S629.

The President Had to Know the Potential for Violence Because the Insurgents Planned Their Attack on Public Social Media Before January 6

Finally, **Rep. Plaskett** (D-VI, delegate) argued that the President had to know of the violence because the plans appeared on public websites and because the media predicted violence immediately prior to the January 6th rally.

> *The insurgents were not shy about their planning. They believed they were following the orders of the Commander in Chief. They were, as with the tweet we just saw, quite literally, his cavalry. So they posted exact blueprints of the attack openly, loudly, proudly, and they did this all over public forums. They were not just hidden posts on a dark website that Trump would not have seen. Quite the opposite. We know that President Trump's team monitored these websites. We know this because his advisers confirmed it.* 167 Cong. Rec. S629–S630 (daily ed. Feb. 10, 2021).
>
> *They actively monitored the exact sites, like TheDonald.win, on which these insurrectionists wrote their posts.* * * * *
>
> *A third-party site captured a post on TheDonald.win, where one user posted:*
>
> > This cannot simply be a protest. It has to be the establishment of the MAGA militia with command offices set up, with all further militia tactical missions spreading from there.
>
> *Another user said in response:*
>
> > We will have to achieve an actual tactical victory like storming and occupying [the Capitol] to have the intended effect.
>
> *That is what they understood Donald Trump to want—there it is in black and white—and they explained why they felt justified in this.*
>
> *Another poster on the forum TheDonald.win wrote on January 4:*
>
> > If Congress illegally certifies Biden * * * *Trump would have absolutely no choice but to demand us to storm Congress and kill/beat them up for it.* * * * *Id.* at S630.

Here is another. When discussing how to carry guns into DC, one noted:

> Yes, it's illegal, but this is war, and we're clearly in a post-legal phase of our society.

What? They treated it as a war, and they meant it. On the morning of the attack, under a thread titled "Today, I told my kids goodbye," one poster wrote:

> Today I had the very difficult conversation with my children, that daddy might not come home from DC.

Within a matter of hours, that post amassed 4,000 "likes." * * * *

These supporters didn't just rely on entering the Capitol with guns haphazardly. They had maps of this building. They talked through which tunnels to use and how to get to the Senate Chamber. Some posted specific floor plan layouts of the Capitol alongside hopes of overwhelming law enforcement to "find the tunnels; arrest the worst traitors."

Posters also fixated on what they saw as their ability to easily overwhelm the Capitol Police as "there are only around 2k of them," and, again, they urged "the capitol is our goal. Everything else is a distraction."

There were hundreds of these posts—hundreds—monitored by the Trump administration, and these posts were chillingly accurate right down to communication devices. * * * *

A third-party site captured a post on TheDonald.win—again, the site monitored by Trump's team.

> He [meaning Donald Trump in this instance] can order the NAT guard to stand down if needed. Unfortunately, he has no control over the Capitol Police * * * * but there are only around 2k of them and a lot are useless fat asses or girls.

* * * * *This was reported in the NBC News and the Washington Post, with headlines like: "Violent threats ripple through far-right internet forums ahead of protest." "Pro-Trump forums erupt with violent threats ahead of Wednesday's rally against the 2020 election."*

FOX News also reported that the Proud Boys would come to the January 6 rally prepared for violent action, even quoting a Proud Boy member who said they would be "incognito" and "spread across downtown DC in smaller numbers."

City officials, seeing these same warnings, also publicly warned about the violence and unlawful weapons at the event. DC Mayor Muriel Bowser cautioned residents of the District of Columbia to avoid the downtown area while the rally attendees were in town. Federal law enforcement warned of these threats also. On January 3, a Capitol Police intelligence report warned of a violent scenario in which "Congress itself" could be the target of the angry supporters of President Trump on January 6. According to that report, obtained by the Washington Post:

> Supporters of the current president see January 6, 2021, as the last opportunity to overturn the results of presidential election * * * * This sense of desperation and disappointment may lead to more * * * * to become violent. Unlike previous post-election protests, the targets of the pro-Trump supporters are not necessarily the counter-protesters as they were previously, but rather Congress itself is the target [for January 6]. (ellipses in original)

The day before the rioters stormed the Congress, an FBI office in Virginia also issued an explicit warning that extremists were preparing to travel to Washington to commit violence and "war," according to internal reports. The FBI report cited to an online post where the user declared that Trump supporters should go to Washington and get violent. The supporter said:

> Stop calling this a march, or rally, or a protest. Go there ready for war. We get our President or we die.* * * * *Id.*

And yet, in the face of all this—these credible warnings of serious, dangerous threats to our Capitol—when those thousands of people were standing in front of President Trump, ready to take orders and attack, this is what he said:

> We're going to the Capitol. And we fight. We fight like hell. And if you don't fight like hell, you're not going to have a country anymore.

And that is why this is different. That is why he must be convicted and disqualified. And that is why this is different. That is why he must be convicted and disqualified. *Id.* at S631.

The President Heard the Crowd Chanting That They Would "Storm the Capitol"

Rep. Dean (D-PA) repeated the key elements of Trump's speech to rebut claims that the President sought only peace:

> *One of President Trump's key defenses focused on what he said for a few seconds, 15 minutes into the speech.*
>
> (Text of videotape presentation of 1-6-2021.)
>
> President TRUMP. I know that everyone here will soon be marching over to the Capitol building, to peacefully and patriotically make your voices heard.
>
> *In a speech spanning almost 11,000 words—yes, we did check—that was the one time, the only time President Trump used the word "peaceful" or any suggestion of nonviolence. * * * * President Trump used the word "fight" or "fighting" 20 times, including telling the crowd they needed to "fight like hell" to save our democracy.*
>
> *We know how the crowd responded to Donald Trump's words, and he knew how they responded to his speech. Here is the evidence of how the crowd reacted.*
>
> (Text of video presentation of 1-6-2021.)
>
> (People cheering.)
>
> President TRUMP. We are going down to the Capitol—
>
> (People cheering.)
>
> President TRUMP * * * * weakness, you have to show strength—
>
> Unidentified Speaker. Yes. Right.
>
> (People chanting: "Take the Capitol.")
>
> (People chanting: "Taking the Capitol right now.")
>
> (People chanting: "Invade the Capitol.")
>
> (People chanting: "Storm the Capitol.")
>
> President TRUMP. Make your voices heard (ellipses in original).
>
> *"Storm the Capitol." "Invade the Capitol." "Fight, fight, fight." "Take the Capitol right now."*
>
> *These were the words of the crowd. Trump was telling them to fight, and he would keep telling them to fight throughout the rest of his speech. These are not only words of aggression,*

they are words of insurrection, and if you have any doubt, listen to what he says next. * * * *

> President TRUMP. When you catch somebody in a fraud, you are allowed to go by very different rules. So I hope Mike has the courage to do what he has to do. * * * *

We told you that context matters. Here is the context: This was not just one reference or a message to supporters by a politician to fight for a cause. He had assembled thousands of violent people, people he knew were capable of violence, people he had seen be violent. They were standing now in front of him. And then he pointed to us, lit the fuse, and sent an angry mob to fight the perceived enemy—his own Vice President and the Members of Congress as we certified an election. 167 Cong. Rec. S632 (daily ed. Feb. 10, 2021).

The Mob Threatened the Vice President and Speaker of the House

Rep. Plaskett (D-VI, delegate) described the attack on January 6th and showed video taken from inside the Capitol during the attack. The video showed offices ransacked. Senator Romney (R-UT) was seen being warned by a Capitol police officer of an approaching mob. Staffers and Senators were shown rushing to hide. The video showed armed officers barricading the House chamber from the inside. An officer was shown shooting a woman trying to forcibly enter the House chamber. House Members were shown hiding in the galleries above the House floor, with gas masks on. The Speaker of the House, Nancy Pelosi (D-CA), was shown being ushered out of the House by Capitol Police officers, and Vice President Mike Pence was shown being ushered by Secret Service agents out of his hiding place near the Senate floor. 167 Cong. Rec. S633–S638 (daily ed. Feb. 10, 2021). This account emphasized threats to those who lie in the direct line of succession to the Presidency: the Vice President and the Speaker of the House.[2]

You can hear the security alarm through the door in the background. And you can hear the mob calling for the death of the Vice President of the United States.

(Text of video presentation of 1-6-2021.)

(People chanting: "Hang Mike Pence.") * * * *

---

[2] 3 U.S.C. § 19(a)(1) (2006) ("If* * * *there is neither a President or Vice President to discharge the powers and duties of the office of President, then the Speaker of the House of Representatives shall, upon his resignation as Speaker* * * *act as president").

Here is another example of the crowd outside yelling: "Bring out Pence, bring him out."

> (People chanting: "Bring him out.") (People chanting: "Bring out Pence.").

* * * *

Listen to this man explain.

> (Text of video presentation of 1-6-2021.)
>
> Unidentified Speaker. * * * * Pence lied to us. He is a total treasonous pig. And his name will be mud forever. Now the real battle begins. And it looks like the American people are very pissed. So good luck with that. Peace out.

* * * * *The mob also went after the Speaker of the House, who alongside the Vice President, was presiding over the joint session of the certification in the House Chamber.* * * * *

I have already discussed Proud Boys member Dominic Pezzola, who has since been charged with eight Federal crimes for his conduct on January 6. As you will recall, according to the FBI agent's affidavit submitted to the court, the group he attacked the Capitol with confirmed that "anyone they got their hands on they would have killed, including NANCY PELOSI. * * * *. (caps in original).

William Calhoun, a lawyer, from Georgia, also participated in the insurrection. * * * **Calhoun wrote about his involvement on his own Facebook page. Here is the post. Calhoun stated:*

> And get this—the first of us who got upstairs kicked in Nancy Pelosi's door and pushed down the hall towards her inner sanctum, the mob howling with rage—Crazy NANCY probably would have been torn into little pieces, but she was nowhere to be seen. "Crazy NANCY"—that is Trump's nickname for the Speaker of the House. Then he explains that he and his group only abandoned their claim to the Speaker's office when "a SWAT team showed up." * * * * 167 Cong. Rec. S635 (daily ed. Feb. 10, 2021) (caps in original).

At 2:50 p.m., several rioters, including Richard "Bigo" Barnett, entered Speaker PELOSI*'s office. The world is all now too familiar with the images from these slides. If you look closely, however, at the now-infamous pictures of*

Barnett with his feet on the desk, you might see something that you didn't notice previously. Here is a better look. As this photo highlights, he is carrying a stun gun tucked into his waistband. The FBI identified the device as a ***950,000-*** *volt stun gun walking stick. The weapon could have caused serious pain and incapacitated anyone Barnett had used it against. Id.* at S636.

The President Knew of Violence at the Capitol but Did Nothing to Stop It

Rep. Cicilline (D-RI) presented a timeline of events from the close of President Trump's speech to the start of the violence at the Capitol:

*Within 10 minutes, at 1:11 p.m. * * * *Donald Trump concluded his speech with his final reminder to the thousands gathered there: It was time to go to the Capitol.* * * * *

[B]y 1:15, an explosive device had been found at the DNC, and a pipe bomb had been found at the RNC about 15 minutes earlier. The House Sergeant at Arms had called for immediate assistance. At 1:34 p.m., the mayor of Washington, DC, called for additional National Guard troops. * * * *

*We didn't hear anything from Donald Trump until 1:49 p.m., when, while all of this is unfolding, President Trump sent out a tweet. * * * *. What was that tweet? * * * * Donald Trump released a propaganda reel of his "Save America" speech that he had given an hour before.* 167 Cong. Rec. S639 (daily ed. Feb. 10, 2021).

Even if President Trump claims he didn't know the extent of the violence that would follow his speech, it was now happening in plain view, broadcast on television. His supporters were attacking law enforcement. The mayor and the police chief were calling for help. Members of Congress and the Vice President were inside scared for their lives.

He doesn't send help, and he doesn't try to stop it. He doesn't even acknowledge the attack. Instead, our Commander in Chief tweeted the video of the speech that he had given before, that included language like "our country has had enough. We will not take it anymore and that's what this is all about. You have to be strong."

Those around Donald Trump—this was later reported—were disgusted. His close aides, his advisers, those working for him, former officials, and even his family were begging him to do something. Kellyanne Conway, the President's close adviser, called to "add her name" to the chorus of aides urging Donald Trump to take action. Ivanka Trump, the President's own daughter, went to the Oval Office "as soon as" the rioting escalated, and as was confirmed by Senator GRAHAM, *"trying to get [Trump] to speak out, to tell everyone to leave." Id.* (caps in original).

Minority Leader KEVIN MCCARTHY called *Jared* Kushner [the President's son-in-law], *"pleading with him to persuade Trump to issue a statement" or to do something. And Kushner, too, went down to the White House after that call. * * * * Members of Congress from both parties, who were trapped here, were calling the White House to ask for help. Some Members even appealed directly to Donald Trump. Id.* (caps in original).

Now, the extent of how many people tried to reach the President to get him to act is not known. But what is clear, what we know without any doubt, is that from the very beginning, the people around Donald Trump lobbied him to take command. What is also clear is what Donald Trump, our Commander in Chief, did in those initial hours to protect us. Nothing. Not a thing. He knew it was happening. The attack was on TV. We all know that President Trump had the power to stop these attacks. He was our Commander in Chief. He had the power to assess the security situation, send backup, and send help. * * * *

The President, as reported by sources at the time, was delighted. As he watched the violence unfold on television, President Trump was reportedly "borderline enthusiastic because it meant the certification was being derailed." * * * *

[H]is singular focus that day—the day we were attacked—was not protecting us, was not protecting you, was not protecting the Capitol, but it was stopping the certification of the election results.

The evidence is clear. Shortly after 2 p.m., as the siege was fully under way, then-President Trump made a call. This is the first call that we are aware he made to anyone inside the Capitol during the attack. He didn't call the Vice President to ask how he could help defend the Capitol. He didn't call the next two in line to succession of the Presidency to check on their safety or well-being. * * * *

*Let's be clear. At roughly 2 p.m., when Donald Trump was walking around the White House watching the TV delighted and spent 5 to **10** minutes talking to Senator* TUBERVILLE, *urging him to delay the election results, this is what was happening in the Capitol.* [Ed: Video presentation omitted.] * * * * 167 Cong. Rec. S640 (daily ed. Feb. 10, 2021) (caps in original).

By 2:15 p.m., the crowd was chanting in unison "Hang Mike Pence" outside the very building he had been evacuated from with his family. * * * *

*At 2:24 p.m., [*the President*] tweeted*

> Mike Pence didn't have the courage to do what should have been done to protect our country and our Constitution. * * * *

Over an hour and a half into the attack, and this is what he tweeted. And he still, even at this point, did not acknowledge the attack on the Capitol, let alone condemn it. Instead, he further incites the mob against his own Vice President, whose life was being threatened.

Well, some of you may say: Well, who was paying attention anyway? Well, that mob was paying attention.

(Text of video presentation.)

> Unidentified Speaker. Mike Pence didn't have the courage to do what should have been done to protect our country and our Constitution, giving States a chance to certify or correct a set of facts, not (inaudible) defraud ones or inaccurate ones, which they were asked to previously certify. U.S. demands the truth.
>
> Unidentified Speaker. Mike Pence, anarchist. Mike Pence, anarchist.
>
> Unidentified Speaker. (Inaudible.) Can I speak to Pelosi? Yeah, we're coming, bitch. Oh, Mike Pence, we're coming for you, too, fucking traitor.
>
> Unidentified Speaker. Donald J. Trump better (inaudible).
>
> Unidentified Speaker. Full house.
>
> Unidentified Speaker. (Inaudible) Mike Pence let us down. Mike Pence let us down, people. If you want to get something done, you are going to have to do it yourself. * * * *

*It wasn't until 2:38 p.m. * * * * that Donald Trump even acknowledged the attack. And when he finally did acknowledge the attack, here is what he said * * * *:*

> Please support our Capitol Police and Law Enforcement. They are truly on the side of our Country. Stay peaceful!

Much has been made of the fact that in this tweet he says, "Stay peaceful." Senators, "Stay peaceful"? Think about that for a second. These folks were not peaceful. They were breaking windows, pushing through law enforcement officers, waving the flag as they invaded this Capitol Building. This was a violent, armed attack. "Stay peaceful"? How about: Stop the attack. Stop the violence. "Stay peaceful"? How about you say: Immediately leave. Stop. * * * *

By 2:45 p.m., the warnings were tragically proven correct. Ashli Babbitt was shot by an officer as she tried to break through a glass door to reach the Speaker's Lobby. At this point, the pleas to Donald Trump, publicly and privately, grew even more desperate. Id. at S641.

At 2:54 p.m., Alyssa Farah, a former strategic communications director, begged the President:

> Condemn this now. You are the only one they will listen to. For our country!

Mick Mulvaney, the President's former Chief of Staff, his right-hand man at one point, tweeted at 3:01:

> The President's tweet is not enough. He can stop this now and needs to do exactly that. Tell these folks to go home. He can stop this now. Tell these folks to go home.

At 3:06 p.m., Representative MCCARTHY *appeared on FOX News. Here is what he said.*

(Text of video presentation of 1-6-2021.)

> Mr. MCCARTHY. I could not be sadder or more disappointed with the way our country looks at this very moment. People are getting hurt. Anyone involved in this, if you're hearing me, hear me very loud and clear: This is not the American way.

He is saying on FOX News, which the President watches: This is not the American way. Stop the attack.

Representative GALLAGHER [R-WI], *at 3:11 p.m., while secured in his own office, posted a video to Twitter.*

(Text of video presentation of 1-6-2021.)

Mr. GALLAGHER. Mr. President, you have got to stop this. You are the only person who can call this off. Call it off.

And then, when the President didn't answer his pleas on Twitter, Representative GALLAGHER went on live television.

(Text of video presentation of 1-6-2021.)

Mr. GALLAGHER. I mean, this is insane. I mean—I—I have not seen anything like this since I deployed to Iraq in 2007 and 2008. I mean, this is America, and this is what is happening right now. We need—the President needs to call it off. Like, call it off. Call it off. * * * *

The message around the President was clear, from everyone: You need to call this off. Stop it. But does he? No. His next tweet was not until about 3:13 p.m. Once again, it is important to consider what was happening between Donald Trump's 2:38 p.m. tweet and his next tweet at 3:13 p.m.

You will see footage from the attack during that time on the right and Donald Trump's tweet on the left. [Ed: The video shows violence, and the tweet shows Donald Trump thanking his supporters.]

You will notice one of the things he says to his mob, to these insurrectionists, rather than to stop or to leave, was to say thank you. Thank you. Thank you for what? Thank you for shattering the windows and destroying property? Thank you for injuring more than 140 police officers? Thank you for putting in danger all of our lives and the lives of our families?

How about, instead of "thank you," Donald Trump, on that day, acted like our Commander in Chief and stopped this, as only he could, and told those people to leave. Id. at S642.

The Insurrectionists Understood President Trump's Call to Action as a Call for Violence

Rep. DeGette (D-CO) replayed the tape of Trump's speech on January 6, in which members of the crowd replied to the President's call to "fight" that they would "storm the capitol." She continued:

Footage from inside the Capitol shows when the insurrectionists first got into the building and confronted police, the mob screamed at the officers that they were listening to President Trump.

(Video presentation of 1-6-2021.)

> Unidentified Speaker. Stand down. You're outnumbered. There's a fucking million of us out there, and we are listening to Trump, your boss.

The insurrectionists argued with law enforcement that they shouldn't even be fighting them because they believed that the Commander in Chief was ordering this. * * * *

When President-Elect Biden went on television that day to demand an end to the siege, one woman asked this:

(Video presentation of 1-6-2021.)

> Unidentified Speaker. Does he not realize President Trump called us to siege the place?

* * * * 167 Cong. Rec. S646 (daily ed. Feb. 11, 2021).

Another Trump supporter who has been federally charged is Texas real estate agent Jennifer Ryan. * * * *

(Text of video presentation.)

> Ms. RYAN. Personally, I do not feel a sense of shame or guilt from my heart for what I was doing. I thought I was following my President. I thought I was following what we were called to do. He asked us to fly there. He asked us to be there. So I was doing what he asked us to do.
>
> Ultimately, yes, we were going in solidarity with President Trump. President Trump requested that we be in DC on the 6th, so this was our way of going and stopping the steal.
>
> If it comes down to work—guess what—I'm going to be there. We're all going to be up here, and we're going to be breaking those windows.

* * * *

(Text of video presentation of 1-6-2021.)

> Unidentified Speaker. We were invited here. We were invited. Hey, we were invited here. We were invited by the President of the United States. *Id.* at S646–S647.

The Call to Violence Was Part of a Pattern of Conduct in Which the President Embraced and Incited Violence

Rep. Raskin (D-MD) argued that President Trump's actions leading to January 6th formed part of a larger pattern of violent activity going back to a 2017 rally by white supremacists in Charlottesville, Virginia—after which the President appeared to endorse white supremacy by stating that the attendees were "very fine people."[3] During the 2020 presidential campaign, in an interview by television host Savannah Guthrie, the President refused to disavow white supremacist groups.[4] Rep. Raskin emphasized events in Michigan during the campaign as a "dress rehearsal" for the assault on the Capitol.

> *On March 27, [President Trump tweeted criticisms of the Michigan Governor]:*
>
> > I love Michigan, one of the reasons we are doing such a GREAT job for them during this horrible Pandemic. Yet your Governor, Gretchen "Half" Whitmer is way in over her ahead, she doesn't have a clue. Likes blaming everyone for her own ineptitude! #MAGA. (caps in original).
>
> *By April, Trump's rhetorical attacks and name-calling turned to calls for mass mobilization of his supporters. This was a sign of things to come. On April 17, 2020, he tweeted:*
>
> > LIBERATE MICHIGAN (caps in original).
>
> *Not even 2 weeks later, on April 30, his supporters marched on the Michigan State capitol in Lansing. They stormed the building. Trump's marching orders were followed by aggressive action on the ground.*
>
> (Text of video presentation.)
>
> > Unidentified Speaker. We have a right. Let us in.
> >
> > (People chanting: "Let us in.")
> >
> > Unidentified Speaker. Heil Hitler! Heil Hitler.
> >
> > Unidentified Speaker. You policemen are all cowards. You betrayed us. The police have betrayed the people.

---

[3] Glenn Thrush and Maggie Haberman, *Trump Gives White Supremacists an Unequivocal Boost*, N.Y. Times (Aug. 15, 2017), https://www.nytimes.com/2017/08/15/us/politics/trump-charlottesville-white-nationalists.html.

[4] Laura Egan, *Trump clashes with Guthrie after question about white supremacy*, NBC News (Oct. 15, 2020), https://www.nbcnews.com/politics/2020-election/live-blog/trump-biden-town-halls-start-time-how-watch-live-updates-n1243511/ncrd1243626#blogHeader.

(People chanting: "Lock her up up.")

[This attack] was effectively a State-level dress rehearsal for the siege of the U.S. Capitol that Trump incited on January 6. It was a preview of the coming insurrection.

President Trump's response to these two events was strikingly similar. Following the armed siege in Lansing, President Trump refused to condemn the attacks on the Michigan capitol or denounce the violent lawbreakers. * * * * 167 Cong. Rec. S648 (daily ed. Feb. 11, 2021).

Two weeks later, on May 14, Trump's mob again stormed the State capitol. This time, as you can see here, one man brought a doll with a noose around the neck, foreshadowing the appearance of the large gallows erected outside of this building, downstairs from here, on January 6, as the crowd chanted—and I still can hear the words ringing in my ear—"Hang Mike Pence. Hang Mike Pence. Hang Mike Pence."

Over the coming months, even after a crowd threatening Governor Whitmer stormed the capitol, Trump continued to assail her in public. * * * *

Then, on October 8, the precise consequences of the President's incitement to violence were revealed to the whole world.

(Video presentation.)

> Thirteen men were arrested by the FBI for plotting to storm the Michigan State capitol building, launch a civil war, kidnap Governor Whitmer, transport her to Wisconsin, and then try and execute her.

This was an assassination conspiracy, a kidnapping conspiracy. * * * *

In the charging document, the FBI reported that one of the conspirators said he needed "200 men" to storm the capitol building and take political hostages, including the Governor. The suspect called it a "snatch and grab, man. Grab the [f'ing] Governor." 167 Cong. Rec. S646 (daily ed. Feb. 11, 2021).

He did it again on October 27 during a preelection rally speech in Lansing, MI, where the capitol had been stormed. Trump openly joked with the crowd about critics saying his words had provoked the violent plot against Governor Whitmer. * * * *

(Text of video presentation.)

President TRUMP. We got to get her going. I don't think she likes me too much.

(People chanting: "Lock her up.")

President TRUMP. See, I don't comment to that because every time, if I make just even a little bit of a nod, they say: "The President led them on." No, I don't have to lead you on. Even a little nod, they say: "The President said." * * * *Now, your Governor—I don't think she likes me too much. Hey, hey, hey, hey, I'm the one. It was our people that helped her out with her problem. I mean, we have to see if it is a problem, right? People are entitled to say maybe it was a problem, maybe it wasn't. It was our people—my people—our people that helped her out.

So President Trump offered them a little winking inside joke about his constant incitement of the mob and how much can actually be communicated by him with just a little nod—just a little nod. * * * *

Trump knew exactly what he was doing in inciting the January 6 mob—exactly. He had just seen how easily his words and actions inspired riots in Michigan. He sent a clear message to his supporters. He encouraged planning and conspiracies to take over capitol buildings and threaten public officials who refused to bow down to his political will. Is there any chance Donald Trump was surprised by the results of his own incitement? * * * * *Id.*

My dear colleagues, is there any political leader in this room who believes that if he is ever allowed by the Senate to get back into the Oval Office, Donald Trump would stop at inciting violence to get his way? Would you bet the lives of more police officers on that? Would you bet the safety of your family on that? Would you bet the future your democracy on that? Id. at S650.

Impeachment Is Not a Partisan Exercise: Republicans Have Condemned Trump's Incitement of Violence

Rep. Lieu (D-CA) arrayed a long list of Republican officials who condemned the attack to rebut the claim that the impeachment was a partisan exercise:

People in his own party—State officials, former officials, current officials, Members of Congress—have, unambiguously and passionately, said that what Donald

Trump did was "disgraceful," "shameful," and have called his behavior "existential" and "wrong," and they have said that his actions gave rise to one of the darkest chapters in United States' history. * * * * 167 Cong. Rec. S651 (daily ed. Feb. 11, 2021).

(Text of video presentation of 1-7-2021.)

> Mr. DeWine. [Republican Governor from Ohio] President Trump's continued refusal to accept the election results without producing credible evidence of a rigged election has stirred the fire that has threatened to burn down our democracy. This incendiary speech yesterday, the one he gave preceding the march, that he gave to the protesters, served only to fan those flames.

(Text of video presentation of 1-7-2021.)

> Mr. Hogan [Republican Governor of Maryland]: I proudly stood by my father's side at age 12 on the floor of the House Chamber as we both took the oath of office, an oath to support and defend the Constitution of the United States. It's clear to me that President Trump has abandoned this sacred oath.

(Text of video presentation of 1-7-2021.)

> Mr. Scott [Republican Senator from South Carolina]. Seeing our Capitol, a symbol of democracy around the world, stormed by an angry mob was heartbreaking. And let me be clear: These actions were not patriotic, and these people are not patriots. The fact that these flames of hate and insurrection were lit by the President of the United States will be remembered as one of the darkest chapters in our Nation's history.

* * * * *Former members of the Trump administration, longstanding Republicans, also made clear that President Trump incited this insurrection and that it went against our democracy. The President's former Secretary of Defense, James Mattis, declared:*

> [T]oday's violent assault on our Capitol, an effort to subjugate American democracy by mob rule, was fomented by Mr. Trump.

Former White House Chief of Staff John Kelly spoke on this as well, and I would like to play an audio clip of what he said.

(Text of audio presentation of 1-7-2021.)

Mr. Kelly. [W]hat happened on Capitol Hill * * * *was a direct result of him poisoning the minds of people with the lies and the fraud. * * * *

Former [Republican] *Speaker of the House John Boehner declared:*

[T]he invasion of our Capitol by a mob, incited by lies from some entrusted with power, is a disgrace to all who sacrificed to build our Republic.

This was echoed by former Trump official after former Trump official. Here is what former National Security Advisors John Bolton and H.R. McMaster, former White House Communications Director Alyssa Farah, and former Chief of Staff Mick Mulvaney said:

(Text of video presentation of 1-7-2021.)

Mr. Bolton. * * * * Look, I agree with Bill Barr. I think he did incite this mob with the clear intention of having them disrupt the electoral college certification and delay it to give him more time. I don't think there's any question about it.

(Text of video presentation of 1-7-2021.)

Mr. McMaster. There are many reasons for this assault on the Capitol, but foremost among them was the President's exhortations, was the President's sustained disinformation. * * * *

(Text of video presentation of 1-8-2021.)

Mr. Mulvaney. I think everybody recognizes that what happened on Wednesday is different. You can go down the long litany of things that people complained about with Donald Trump, and I could probably defend almost all of them. Many of them were policy differences; many of them were stylistic differences, but Wednesday was different. Wednesday was existential. Wednesday is one of those things that struck to the very heart of what it means to be an American, and it was wrong.

This sentiment was echoed not just from people outside the administration but from people inside the Trump administration. Perhaps the most telling was the flood of resignations from people inside President Trump's administration with firsthand access to President Trump.

His own officials felt so betrayed by his conduct that numerous officials resigned in protest days before the end of President Trump's term. Sixteen officials resigned in protest—16. They all took this dramatic action of resigning because they saw the clear link between President Trump's conduct and the violent insurrection. * * * * *Id.* at S652.

Impeachment Was Necessary to Protect Democracy

Rep. Cicilline (D-RI) discussed the consequences of the Capitol riot—the loss of life, the trauma to the Members on the floor of the House and Senate, and the effect on police officers from violence and racial slurs. Ultimately, he concluded that it was an "attack on democracy."

The attack we saw had a purpose: Stop the certification. Stop our democratic process. Fortunately, they did not prevail.

Newspapers across America on January 21, the day after the inauguration, proclaimed: Democracy has prevailed. 167 Cong. Rec. S656 (daily ed. Feb. 11, 2021).

Think about that for a moment. What if President Trump had been successful? What if he had succeeded in overturning the will of the people and our constitutional processes? Who among us is willing to risk that out-come by letting Trump's constitutional crimes go unanswered?

The Founders included impeachment in our Constitution, not as a punishment but to prevent. We have to prevent every President—today, tomorrow, or anytime in the future—from believing that this conduct is acceptable. Today, we have to stand up for our democracy and ensure we remain a country governed by the people, for the people by telling Donald Trump and people all across this country and all across the world that his crimes will not and cannot stand. Id. at S657.

The Attack Was a Gift to Democracy's Enemies

Rep. Castro (D-TX) explained the harm caused by the Capitol riot to national security:

According to charging documents, Riley Williams allegedly helped steal a laptop from Speaker PELOSI*'s office to "send the computer device to a friend in Russia, who then planned to sell the device to SVR, Russia's foreign intelligence service."*

While we can't be certain if or how many foreign spies infiltrated the crowd or at least coordinated with those who did, we can be sure that any enemy who wanted access to our secrets would have wanted to be part of that mob inside these halls.

The point is this: Many of the insurrectionists that President Trump incited to invade this Chamber were dangerous—people on the FBI watch list, violent extremists, White supremacists. And these insurrectionists incited by President Trump threatened our national security. Stealing laptops, again, from Speaker PELOSI'*s office; taking documents from Leader* MCCONNELL'*s desk; snapping photographs, as you saw in the videos earlier, in sensitive areas; ransacking your offices; rifling through your desks.* * * * * (caps in original).

Senator RUBIO *made this point well.*

(Text of video presentation.)

> Mr. RUBIO. If you're a terrorist right now and you're sitting out there watching this, you're saying to yourself, hey, it's not that hard to get into the Capitol. Maybe it's not hard to get into the White House or the Supreme Court building or somewhere else. * * * * 167 Cong. Rec. S657 (daily ed. Feb. 11, 2021).

Russia has also seized on this violent attack against our government, decrying that democracy is "over." The chairman of the Russian upper house of Parliament's International Affairs Committee said:

> The celebration of democracy is over. This is, alas, actually the bottom. I say this without a hint of gloating. America is no longer charting the course, and therefore has lost all its rights to set it. And especially to impose it on others.

They are using President Trump's incitement of an insurrection to declare that democracy is over. In Iran, the Supreme Leader is using President Trump's incitement of an insurrection to mock America. He said of the situation in the United States:

> This is their democracy and human rights, this is their election scandal, these are their values. These values are being mocked by the whole world. Even their friends are laughing at them.* * * *

And that is true. For generations, the United States has been a North Star in the world for freedom, democracy, and human rights because America is not only a nation for many, it is also an idea. It is the light that gives hope to people struggling for democracy in autocratic regimes, the light that inspires people fighting across the world for fundamental human rights, and the light that inspires us to believe in something larger than ourselves. Id. at S658.

B. An Evidentiary Offer

At the end of **the House Managers'** presentation, which had taken 4 days, on Saturday, Feb. 13, 2021, they offered to introduce into the trial record a statement by Rep. Jaime Herrera Beutler (R-WA)—who, on the evening of February 12th, 2021, confirmed that "in the middle of the insurrection, when House Minority Leader KEVIN McCARTHY called the President to beg for help, President Trump responded: "Well, Kevin, I guess these people are more upset about the election than you are." 167 Cong. Rec. S717 (daily ed. Feb. 13, 2021) (statement of Mr. Raskin) (caps in original).

The House Managers stated that Rep. Beutler had invited other "patriots" to come forward to affirm those facts, and the House Managers indicated that they would want to take depositions of any such "patriots" as well. *Id.* at S718. The inference was that the President knew and approved of anything that would hold up certifying the election. In past impeachments, such as the Clinton impeachment, the Senate had stopped its proceedings to take depositions.

The President's lawyer, Mr. Van Der Veen, responded angrily that he "would need at least over 100 depositions, not just 1," if the Senate permitted the House Managers to depose witnesses. *Id.* at S717. He had hoped to "close this case out today," and enter into a stipulation that there would be no witnesses. *Id.* He went on:

So for the House managers to say we need depositions about things that happened after, it is just not true. But—but if he does, there are a lot of depositions that need to be happening. Nancy Pelosi's deposition needs to be taken. Vice President Harris's deposition absolutely needs to be taken, and not by Zoom. None of these depositions should be done by Zoom. These depositions should be done in person, in my office, in Philadelphia. That is where they should be done.

(Laughter.)

Mr. Van Der Veen appeared taken aback by the laughter from the Senators. He responded by raising his voice.

I don't know how many civil lawyers are here, but that is the way it works, folks. When you want somebody's deposition,

> *you send a notice of deposition, and they appear at the place where the notice says. That is civil process.*
>
> *I don't know why you are laughing. It is civil process. That is the way lawyers do it.*

This prompted Senator Leahy (D-VT), the presiding officer, to call for order.

> *I would remind everybody that we will have order in the Chamber during these proceedings.*

The laughter reflected the fact that Mr. Van der Veen was suggesting to the Senators that the rules of civil law practice applied in an impeachment proceeding.[5] *Id.*

Shortly thereafter, a vote was taken to "consider and debate" whether to subpoena documents. *Id.* at S719. The Senate voted 55–45 to admit such evidence. The House Managers and the President's lawyers then negotiated an agreement to "stipulate" that, were Rep. Beutler (R-WA) to testify, she would have repeated her written statement of Feb. 12, 2021:

> *When McCarthy finally reached the president on January 6 and asked him to publicly and forcefully call off the riot, the president initially repeated the falsehood that it was antifa that had breached the Capitol. McCarthy refuted that and told the president that these were Trump supporters. That's when, according to McCarthy, the president said: 'Well, Kevin, I guess these people are more upset about the election than you are.' Id.* (statement inserted into record).

In doing so, the parties avoided a lengthy period of depositions. Senate Majority Leader Schumer (D-NY) noted, however, that the rules of the trial—set forth in Senate Resolution 47 and reprinted here in Appendix D—provided that "the admission of this evidence does not constitute a concession by either party as to the truth of the matters asserted by the other party and that each Senator shall decide for him or herself the weight to be given such evidence." *Id.* at S720.

---

5 The laughter may have also reflected the fact that Mr. Van Der Veen, a resident of Philadelphia, employs a unique pronunciation of the name of that city: "Philly-delphia." In a later interview, he explained that "Philly-delphia is something I say often * * * * to make an effective point. Folks in my office or my kids will tell you I always talk about Philly-delphia." Pat Ralph, *Trump's impeachment lawyer explains 'Philly-delphia' mispronunciation*, Philly Voice (Feb. 16, 2021), https://www.phillyvoice.com/michael-van-der-veen-phillydelphia-donald-trump-impeachment-attorney/.

QUESTIONS ON THE HOUSE MANAGERS' PRESENTATION

Why Did the Lawyers Not Argue That an Ordinary Crime Was Necessary to Impeach, as They Had in the First Impeachment Trial?: Unlike the First Trump Impeachment trial, neither the House Managers nor the President's lawyers discussed whether an ordinary crime was necessary to impeach. As we explained at length in Chapters 3 and 4 in Part One, with regard to the First Trump Impeachment, the weight of authority holds that an ordinary crime need not occur for a constitutionally proper impeachment. In the Second Trump Impeachment, the House Managers presented a case that the President had abused his power by inciting a violent attack on the Capitol to prevent certification of the presidential election. No one denied that the attack was serious or that the attackers had committed crimes. Nor did they deny that, had the President been guilty of the crime of incitement, he would have committed acts barred by existing law.

Incitement of Violence: "Incitement" is a legal term. It is a crime under federal and state law. It is difficult to prove because it typically involves speech and the First Amendment typically shields even aggressive speech. *See Brandenburg v. Ohio*, 395 U.S. 444, 448 (1969). The First Amendment *does not mean* that speech itself cannot be prosecuted, however. If you threaten to kill the Vice President or other public officials, for example, that can be a crime even though the crime is made up of words alone. *See R.A.V. v. City of St. Paul, Minnesota*, 505 U.S. 377, 388 (1992). So, too, if you ask someone else to commit a crime, even though those are only words, that can be a crime. *See* 18 U.S.C. § 373 (1994) ("Solicitation to commit a crime of violence"). Incitement requires a showing that the speaker both (1) intended to cause immediate lawless violence and (2) the speech is likely to cause such action. We will examine the First Amendment argument in greater depth in the next section of this Chapter.

Failure to Protect: The House Managers emphasized the President's *actions* planning the speech on the day of election certification. Further, they argued that the President knew of the attack, watched it on TV, and *failed to do anything*. The criminal law does not generally impose a duty to rescue. A private citizen who heard the President's speech, or heard the rioters plan to storm the Capitol, and failed to do anything would not be charged with a crime. On the other hand, the criminal law can be deployed when an individual has a duty to act.[6] So, for example, parents who have failed to feed their children have been charged with certain forms of homicide because they violated their duty to protect.[7] There is no question that the President has a legal "duty" to defend the Constitution and the Congress from physical assault, under his duty to "take care" the laws be faithfully executed and from his oath of office. U.S. Const. art. II, § 3 ("he shall take Care that the

---

[6] *See, e.g., Commonwealth v. Twitchell*, 416 Mass. 114, 617 N.E.2d 609 (Mass. 1993) ("a parental duty of care has been recognized in the common law of homicide in this Commonwealth.").

[7] *See, e.g.,* Deanna Paul, *Florida couple arrested for manslaughter after 18-month-old son dies of malnourishment*, Wash. Post (Nov. 22, 2019), https://www.washingtonpost.com/nation/2019/11/22/baby-kept-vegan-diet-died-his-parents-have-been-charged-with-manslaughter/.

Laws be faithfully executed"). The House Managers emphasized that the President had failed in his duty. Politicians have been charged with crimes when they know of harms they do nothing to prevent. For example, Michigan's former Governor, Rick Snyder, was charged with two counts of willful neglect of duty for failing to prevent lead from tainting Flint, Michigan's water supply.[8] Is President Trump's failure to act a stronger argument for impeachment than incitement?

What Did the President Know and When Did He Know It?: One of the most famous questions arising during the Nixon impeachment was, in the words of Senator Howard Baker, "what did the President know and when did he know it?" 160 Cong. Rec. S4235 (daily ed. Jul. 8, 2014) (statement of Sen. Lamar) (quoting Sen. Howard Baker). This question emerged when it became clear that there were ties between the Nixon administration and the Watergate burglars. When tapes made of President Nixon's conversations became public, the public suddenly "knew" that he took an active role in covering up the burglary, among other things. The Second Trump Impeachment trial presents a variety of evidence that President Trump knew that the Capitol, including his own Vice President, was under attack, but the evidence is "circumstantial." For example, we do not have an actual videotape or audio recording showing President Trump watching television and cheering the rioters.

Most criminal and civil cases depend upon "circumstantial" evidence—a technical legal term meaning that the evidence was "not direct." Direct evidence would be from a person who was with the President at the time of the attack, or an authentic video or audio recording of the President's actions after the speech. The House Managers relied upon the President's own tweets, calls during the attack to the President by the House Minority leader McCarthy (R-CA), and calls by the President to Senator Tuberville (R-AL). In a court of law, however, these would all be "hearsay," since they were statements made outside of a courtroom (although they might fall within one of many hearsay exceptions).[9] The bottom line: if you were a lawyer wanting to know of President Trump's actions on the day of the attack, you would want to find people who were in the White House with him, and any recording of phone calls that he made or were made to him at the time of the attack. Future historians, and reporters, will surely be scouring White House records to find such evidence.

Conspiracy Against the United States: A conspiracy against the United States is a federal offense under 18 U.S.C. § 371. It is said that the conspiracy charge is a prosecutor's best friend because it is easy to prove. Conspiracy is a charge that someone agreed with one or more persons to commit an unlawful act. All one has to show is that a person *agreed* with another person, and did some *overt act* in furtherance of the conspiracy. If I agree with you to steal a statue from the Capitol, even if I do not actually go to the Capitol

[8] Brakkton Booker, *Ex-Michigan Gov. Rick Snyder And 8 Others Criminally Charged In Flint Water Crisis*, NPR (Jan. 14, 2021), https://www.npr.org/2021/01/14/956924155/ex-michigan-gov-rick-snyder-and-8-others-criminally-charged-in-flint-water-crisis.

[9] *See* Fed. R. Evid. 801–803.

and all I do is provide you with plans that help you steal the statue, I am guilty of conspiracy. Defendants in the Mueller investigation were convicted of this crime.[10] Was Donald Trump guilty of conspiracy against the United States? To know that, a prosecutor would have to determine whether a jury would find beyond a reasonable doubt that President Trump: (1) knew that the protestors would be violent; (2) agreed in some fashion (tacitly or not) to an unlawful act; and (3) did something, however small, to encourage that unlawful action.

Lawsuits, Civil and Criminal: As of the writing of this book, many criminal prosecutions had been brought against individuals rioting in the Capitol. In addition, civil suits have been filed against former President Trump. *See, e.g.*, *Swalwell v. Trump*, No. 1:21-CV-00586 (filed U.S.D.C. March 5, 2021) (suit by a House Member who alleges various legal violations, including violation of D.C. law); *Blassingame v. Trump*, No. 21-cv-00585 (D.D.C. filed Mar. 30, 2021) (suit by Capitol police officers injured in the riot). A civil law suit seeks money damages; it does not result in a prison sentence. The point of these lawsuits may be less to obtain damages than to reveal facts not apparent in the impeachment, to preserve evidence, and to create a judicial record of President Trump's connections to white supremacists. There is no guarantee that President Biden's Department of Justice will charge former President Trump with a crime. As we learned during the Mueller investigation and the First Trump Impeachment, the Justice Department has a policy of not charging Presidents during their time in office. Nothing in that policy bars a future criminal prosecution of former President Trump, however.

President Biden has publicly stated he will leave the criminal prosecution decision to his Attorney General, former Judge Merrick Garland.[11] There are reasons to believe that any criminal case would be legally difficult because it is always difficult to prove incitement.[12] Moreover, Presidents have political incentives to move on to correct the country's problems, rather than to stir up old controversies.[13] They worry that they will reinjure the country, and make martyrs of those being tried. This may

---

10 *See* Ryan Teague Beckwith, *Here Are All of the Indictments, Guilty Pleas and Convictions from Robert Mueller's Investigation*, Time (Nov. 15, 2019), https://time.com/5556331/mueller-investigation-indictments-guilty-pleas/.

11 Carrie Johnson, *One Tough Question For DOJ If Biden Is Elected: Whether To Prosecute Trump*, NPR (Aug. 13, 2020), https://www.npr.org/2020/08/13/901679755/one-tough-question-for-doj-if-biden-is-elected-whether-to-prosecute-trump ("I will not interfere with the Justice Department's judgment of whether or not they think they should pursue a prosecution").

12 Brent Kendall, *Incitement Case Against Trump for Capitol Riot Would Present Challenges*, Wall St. J. (Feb. 21, 2021), https://www.wsj.com/articles/incitement-case-against-trump-for-capitol-riot-would-present-challenges-11613916000.

13 Carol E. Lee, Kristen Welker, and Mike Memoli, *Biden hopes to avoid divisive Trump investigations, preferring unity*, NBC (Nov. 17, 2020), https://www.nbcnews.com/politics/justice-department/president-elect-biden-wary-trump-focused-investigations-sources-say-n1247959 ("Biden has raised concerns that investigations would further divide a country he is trying to unite and risk making every day of his presidency about Trump").

explain President Obama's refusal to indict those who caused the collapse of the financial markets leading to the Great Recession.

The existence of "civil lawsuits" provides yet another reason why the Attorney General might not proceed criminally. Even the former Republican Majority Leader Senator McConnell (R-KY), signaled the propriety of such remedies. Having voted *against conviction and disqualification*, he gave a speech the day after the trial, saying this:

> *There's no question, none, that President Trump is practically and morally responsible for provoking the events of the day, * * * *The people who stormed this building believed they were acting on the wishes and instructions of their president. And having that belief was a foreseeable consequence of the growing crescendo of false statements, conspiracy theories, and reckless hyperbole which the defeated president kept shouting into the largest megaphone on planet Earth.*
>
> *These criminals were carrying his banners. Hanging his flags and screaming their loyalty to him. It was obvious that only President Trump could end this * * * * Former aides publicly begged him to do so. Loyal allies frantically called the administration. The president did not act swiftly. He did not do his job* * * * Instead according to public reports he watched television happily as the chaos unfolded, kept pressing his scheme to overturn the election,"* * * * * 167 Cong. Rec. S735 (daily ed. Feb. 13, 2020).
>
> *President Trump is still liable for everything he did while in office * * * *He didn't get away with anything yet. We have a criminal justice system in this country. We have civil litigation. Id.* at S736.

Race and a Civil Rights Lawsuit Against Trump: Race permeated the Second Trump Impeachment trial. Two groups associated with the January 6th rally—the Proud Boys and the Oath Keepers—are white supremacist groups monitored by law enforcement.[14] Marchers wore "Camp Auschwitz shirts" and hurled anti-Black racist slurs at law enforcement officers defending the Capitol. Representative DeGette (D-CO) recounted the fact that one Capitol Police officer, after withstanding a day full of racial slurs, broke down in tears. 167 Cong. Rec. S654 (daily ed. Feb. 11, 2021). One civil lawsuit against former President Trump is based on the Enforcement Act of 1871, also called the Ku Klux Klan Act and the Civil Rights Act of 1871. That law bars anyone from:

> conspiring to prevent, by force, intimidation, or threat, any person * * * *holding any office, trust, or place of confidence under the United States * * * *from discharging any duties thereof; or to induce by like means any officer of the United States to leave any * * * * place[ ] where his duties as an officer are required to be

---

[14] Ryan Lucas, *Oath Keepers, Proud Boys Are Under Intense Scrutiny Following Capitol Riot*, NPR (Mar. 30, 2021), https://www.npr.org/2021/03/30/982599300/oath-keepers-proud-boys-are-under-intense-scrutiny-following-capitol-riot.

> performed, or * * * to molest, interrupt, hinder, or impede him in the discharge of his official duties. 42 U.S.C. § 1985(1).

Representative Bennie Thompson (D-MS), a Black Member of Congress, brought a civil action under this 19th-century act for civil damages and a declaratory judgment on the theory that the President, along with members of white supremacist groups—the Proud Boys and Oath Keepers—had violated his rights because they had interfered with his ability to perform his duties of office as a Member of Congress. *See Thompson v. Trump*, No. 21-cv-00400 (D.D.C. filed Feb. 16, 2021).

II. THE PRESIDENT'S DEFENSE

The House Managers presented a case extending 4 days. The President's lawyers used only part of a day on Friday to make their case. *See* 167 Cong. Rec. S667–S682 (daily ed. Feb. 12, 2021). The President made two legal arguments: first, that he could not be tried because his speech was protected by the First Amendment and second, that he was denied due process at the trial. We treat his claims and the House Managers' responses below. We begin with the President's factual response. We then turn to the First Amendment legal argument and the Due Process legal claims.

A. Factual Response

The President's lawyers insisted that the President was a man of "law and order" and *"to claim that the President, in any way, wished, desired, or encouraged lawless or violent behavior is a preposterous and monstrous lie."* 167 Cong. Rec. S668 (daily ed. Feb. 12, 2021) (statement of Mr. Van Der Veen).

The Speech Was Peaceful

> *The Article of Impeachment now before the Senate is an unjust and blatantly unconstitutional act of political vengeance.* * * *
>
> *No thinking person could seriously believe that the President's January 6 speech on the Ellipse was in any way an incitement to violence or insurrection. The suggestion is patently absurd on its face. Nothing in the text could ever be construed as encouraging, condoning, or enticing unlawful activity of any kind.*
>
> *Far from promoting "insurrection" against the United States, the President's remarks explicitly encouraged those in attendance to exercise their rights "peacefully and patriotically." Peaceful and patriotic protest is the very antithesis of a violent assault on the Nation's Capitol.*

The House Impeachment Article slanderously alleges that the President intended for the crowd at the Ellipse to "interfere with the Joint Session's solemn constitutional duty to certify the results of the 2020 Presidential election." This is manifestly disproven by the plain text of the remarks. 167 Cong. Rec. S668 (daily ed. Feb. 12, 2021) (statement of Mr. Van Der Veen).

When the President spoke, what did he call for? He called for rally attendees to peacefully and patriotically make their voices heard, for them to walk down Pennsylvania Avenue to cheer on Members of Congress.

President Trump went on for more than an hour, ending at 1:11. Now, why is this important? Because of all of the events that I am about to describe, they all occurred before—before—President Trump's remarks concluded.

At 12:49 p.m., the first barriers at the U.S. Capitol Grounds were pushed over, and the crowd entered the restricted area.

At 1:05 p.m., Acting Defense Secretary Christopher Miller received open source reports of demonstrator movements to the U.S. Capitol.

At 1:09 p.m., U.S. Capitol Police Chief Steven Sund called the House and Senate Sergeant at Arms, telling them he wanted an emergency declared, and he wanted the National Guard called.

The point: Given the timeline of events, the criminals at the Capitol were not there at the Ellipse to even hear the President's words. They were more than a mile away, engaged in their preplanned assault on this very building. This was a preplanned assault—make no mistake—and that is a critical fact. Id. at S680 (statement of Mr. Van Der Veen).

The President Was Pursuing Lawful Means of Contesting the Election

The President's lawyers claimed he lawfully challenged the presidential election, and argued that he was entitled to call election officials:

Not only President Trump's speech on January 6 but, indeed, his entire challenge to the election results was squarely focused on how the proper civic process could address any concerns through the established legal and constitutional system. The President brought his case before State and Federal courts, the U.S. Supreme Court, the State

> *legislatures, the electoral college, and, ultimately, the U.S. Congress.*
>
> *In the past, numerous other candidates for President have used many of the same processes to pursue their own election challenges. As recently as 2016, the Clinton campaign brought multiple postelection court cases, demanded recounts, and ridiculously declared the election stolen by Russia.* 167 Cong. Rec. S668 (daily ed. Feb. 12, 2021) (statement of Mr. Van Der Veen).
>
> *Moreover, there was nothing untoward with President Trump or any other candidate, for that matter, speaking with the lead elections officer of the State. That is why the Georgia secretary of state took a call, along with members of his team, one of whom decided to record it and release it to the press. Id.* at S680.

Challenging the Election Certification Was Not Unlawful

The President's lawyers urged that Democrats had challenged the certification of the 2016 election. They showed a tape of then-Vice President Biden gaveling down those objections.

> *In the past, numerous other candidates for President have used many of the same processes to pursue their own election challenges. As recently as 2016, the Clinton campaign brought multiple postelection court cases, demanded recounts, and ridiculously declared the election stolen by Russia.*
>
> *Many Democrats even attempted to persuade the electoral college delegates to overturn the 2016 results. House Manager* RASKIN *objected to the certification of President Trump's victory 4 years ago, along with many of his colleagues.* * * * * (caps in original).
>
>> Ms. JACKSON LEE. I object to the votes from the State of Wisconsin, which would not—should not—be legally certified.
>>
>> Vice President BIDEN. There is no debate—* * * *
>>
>> Mr. GRIJALVA. I object to the certification from the State of North Carolina.
>>
>> Ms. JACKSON LEE. I object to the 15 votes from the State of North Carolina.
>>
>> Mr. MCGOVERN. I object to the certificate from the State of Alabama. The electors were not lawfully certified.

Vice President BIDEN. Is it signed by a Senator?

Mr. RASKIN. Not as of yet, Mr. President.

Vice President BIDEN. In that case, the objection cannot be entertained. The objection cannot be entertained. Debate is not in order.[15] * * * *

167 Cong. Rec. S668 (daily ed. Feb. 12, 2021) (statement of Mr. Van Der Veen).

Violent Campaign Rhetoric Is Not Unlawful

The Presidents' lawyers played a set of tapes of statements made by Democratic politicians to purportedly show that President Trump supported law enforcement while Democrats supported violence. These tapes juxtaposed the President's pro-law enforcement rhetoric with statements by Members of Congress.

President TRUMP. *My administration will always stand against violence, mayhem, and disorder.*

Ms. PRESSLEY. *There needs to be unrest in the streets for as long as there is unrest in our lives.*

President TRUMP. *I stand with the heroes of law enforcement.*

Ms. WATERS. *And you push back on them, and you tell them they are not welcome anymore anywhere.* * * * *

167 Cong. Rec. S668 (daily ed. Feb. 12, 2021) (statement of Mr. Van Der Veen).

Moreover, many Democrat politicians endorsed and encouraged the riots that destroyed vast swaths of American cities last summer. When violent, leftwing anarchists conducted a sustained assault on a Federal courthouse in Portland, OR, Speaker PELOSI *did not call it insurrection; instead, she called the Federal law enforcement officers protecting the building "storm troopers." When violent mobs destroyed public property, she said: "People will do what they do."*

The attorney general of the State of Massachusetts stated:

Yes, America is burning, but that's how forests grow.

[15] As this indicates, the 2016 challenges were made by House Members who knew that these objections would fail since it takes a Senator and a House Member for a valid certification challenge.

> *Representative* AYANNA PRESSLEY (D-MA) *declared:*
>
> There needs to be unrest in the streets for as long as there's unrest in our lives.
>
> *The current Vice President of the United States,* KAMALA HARRIS, *urged supporters to donate to a fund that bailed violent rioters and arsonists out of jail. One of those was released and went out and committed another crime, assault. He beat the bejesus out of somebody. She said, of the violent demonstrations*:
>
> > Everyone beware * * * * Everyone beware * * * * they're not gonna stop before Election Day in November, and they're not gonna stop after Election Day. [T]hey're not going to let up—and they should not. * * * *
>
> *Id.* at S669 (statement of Mr. Van Der Veen) (quoting Vice President Harris).

The President Could Not Have Incited an Attack Pre-Planned by Others

The President's lawyers argued that violent criminals had planned the attack and this meant that the President could not have "incited it."

> *From the beginning, the President has been clear: The criminals who infiltrated the Capitol must be punished to the fullest extent of the law. They should be imprisoned for as long as the law allows.*
>
> *The fact that the attacks were apparently premeditated, as alleged by the House managers, demonstrates the ludicrousness of the incitement allegation against the President.*
>
> *You can't incite what was already going to happen.* 167 Cong. Rec. S668 (daily ed. Feb. 12, 2021) (statement of Mr. Van Der Veen).
>
> *President Trump's words couldn't have incited the riot at the Capitol. The day's events make this clear. Let's walk through the actual timeline. At 11:15 a.m. police security camera videos show crowds forming at First Street, near the Capitol Reflecting. Pool. This is a full 45 minutes before President Trump even took the stage on January 6. Let me repeat that. Violent criminals were assembling at the Capitol, over a mile away, almost an hour before the President uttered a*

single word on the Ellipse. You did not hear that fact during the hours and hours of the House managers' presentation, did you? 167 Cong. Rec. S673 (daily ed. Feb. 12, 2021) (statement of Mr. Schoen).

The President's Language—Particularly the Word "Fight"—Was Ordinary Political Rhetoric, Not Unlawful Incitement

The President's lawyers asked Senators to:

Consider the language that the House Impeachment Article alleges to constitute incitement:

> "If you don't fight like hell, you're not going to have a country anymore."

This is ordinary political rhetoric that is virtually indistinguishable from the language that has been used by people across the political spectrum for hundreds of years. Countless politicians have spoken of fighting for our principles. Joe Biden's campaign slogan was "Battle for the Soul" of America.

No human being seriously believes that the use of such metaphorical terminology is incitement to political violence. While the President did not engage in any language of incitement, there are numerous officials in Washington who have indeed used profoundly reckless, dangerous, and inflammatory rhetoric in recent years. 167 Cong. Rec. S668 (daily ed. Feb. 12, 2021) (statement of Mr. Van Der Veen).

The President's lawyers then played a long video. 167 Cong. Rec. S671–S673 (daily ed. Feb. 12, 2021). This video featured a variety of Senators and many, many Democratic politicians, including then-Vice President Biden using the word "fight." Prominently featured were women and women of color, as well as many of the Senators sitting in the impeachment trial (note that women and women of color represent a relatively small minority of Senators and Representatives). What follows is a sample.

Ms. DEAN. My fight.

Those fights.

And to fight.

To fight an administration.

Ms. HARRIS. Requiring us to fight and fight we will.

Their fight.

In their fight.

In their fight.

The fight is a fight. And so when we fight the fight that we are in.

When we are fighting this fight.

We fight this fight.

The strength of who we are is we will fight.

And we will fight.

We will fight the fight.

We are in a fight.

The fight.

Fight.

Fight.

It is a fight.

It is a fight.

And it is a fight born out of patriotism.

This is a fight.

Fighting.

I say fight on.

Fight on.

Fight on.

Fight on.

Ms. WARREN. I am here to say one more time in public, this is not a fight I wanted to take on, but this is the fight in front of us now.

Id. at S673.

III. HOUSE MANAGERS' REBUTTAL

In rebuttal, the House Managers emphasized that the impeachment offense was not about a single speech, but a plan of activity.

> *We know that he picked the date of that rally. In fact, there was another group that was going to have a rally at another date, and he got it moved to January 1. He synchronized exactly with the time that we would be in joint session, and as Representative CHENEY said: "He summoned that mob, he assembled that mob, he incited that mob, he lit the*

match." Come on, get real. We know that this is what happened. 167 Cong. Rec. S689 (daily ed. Feb. 12, 2021) (statement of Rep. Raskin).

We're talking about free speech? This was a pattern and practice of months of activity. That was the incitement. That is the incitement—the activity he was engaged in for months before January 6, not just the speech on January 6. All of it, in its totality, is a dereliction of duty of the President of the United States against the people who elected him—all of the people of this country. 167 Cong. Rec. S690–91 (daily ed. Feb. 12, 2021) (statement of Rep. Plaskett).

The House Managers explained why pre-planning of the January 6, 2021 march did not negate their case for incitement:

*We are not suggesting that Donald Trump's January 6 speech by itself incited the attack. We have shown that his course of conduct leading up to and including that speech incited the attack. The defense is correct that the insurrection was preplanned. That supports our point. We argue and the evidence overwhelmingly confirms that Donald Trump's conduct over many months incited his supporters to believe, one, his big lie, that the only way he could lose was if the election were rigged; two, that, to ensure the election would not be stolen to prevent the fraud, they had to stop the steal; and, three, they had to fight to stop the steal or they would not have a country anymore. This conduct took time, and it culminated in Donald Trump's sending a "save the date" on December 19, 18 days before the attack, telling his base exactly when, where, and who to fight * * * * Our point is this: This was not one speech. This was a deliberate, purposeful effort by Donald Trump, over many months, that resulted in the well-organized mob attack on January 6 * * * *. Donald Trump knew the people he was inciting leading up to January 6. He saw the violence they were capable of. He had a pattern and practice of praising and encouraging supporters of violence, never condemning it.* 167 Cong. Rec. S724–25 (daily ed. Feb. 13, 2021) (statement of Rep. Dean).

The Senate Majority Leader Schumer (D-NY), addressed the First Amendment claim forcefully. He contended that Presidents can be impeached for speech:

We heard the preposterous claim that the former President's incitement to violence was protected by the First Amendment. The First Amendment right to free speech protects Americans from jail, not Presidents from impeachment. If the President had said during World War II, "Germany should attack the United States on Long Island; we have left it undefended," I suspect Congress would have considered that an impeachable offense. Finally, defense counsel said that President Trump was not directly responsible for the violence at the Capitol: His words were merely a metaphor; his directions were merely suggestions; and the violent mob was just a spontaneous demonstration.

Yet wind the clock back, and ask yourself, if at any point Donald Trump did not do the things he did, would the attack on the Capitol have happened? There is only one answer to this question: Of course not. If President Trump hadn't told his supporters to march to the Capitol, if he hadn't implored them to come to Washington on January 6 in the first place, if he hadn't repeatedly lied to them that the election was stolen and their country was being taken from them, the attack would not have happened, could not have happened. January 6 would not have happened but for the actions of Donald Trump. 167 Cong. Rec. S734 (daily ed. Feb. 13, 2021) (statement of Sen. Schumer).

IV. THE PRESIDENT'S FIRST AMENDMENT DEFENSE

The President's lawyers' principal legal defense was the First Amendment. The House Managers had argued that the First Amendment claim was "frivolous," citing a letter signed by 140 law professors, including conservative law professors (included as Appendix C). The President's lawyers argued:

The House managers have made several references to this letter signed by 140 partisan "law professors" calling Mr. Trump's First Amendment defense "legally frivolous." This is really an outrageous attempt to intimidate Mr. Trump's lawyers.

Whenever a lawyer advances a truly "frivolous" argument, they may violate professional, ethical rules and could be subject to discipline.

This letter is a direct threat to my law license, my career, and my family's financial well-being. These "law professors" should be ashamed of themselves, and so should the House managers. 167 Cong. Rec. S674 (daily ed. Feb. 12, 2021) (statement of Mr. Van der Veen).

Text and Founders' Meaning

The House managers' position, as stated in their trial brief, is "The First Amendment does not apply at all to an impeachment proceeding." That is their position. This is plainly wrong. The text of the First Amendment expressly restricts Congress from regulating speech. It says:

> Congress shall make no law respecting an establishment of religion, or prohibiting the free exercise thereof; or abridging the freedom of speech, or of the press; or the right of the people peaceably to assemble, and to petition the Government for a redress of grievances. * * * *

This is distinctly not the intent of the Framers. The Framers were aware of the danger of any impeachment process that would make the President "the mere creature of the Legislature," a quote directly from the Framers while debating the impeachment process on the floor of the Constitutional Convention of 1787.

One Founding Father, James Wilson, wrote extensively on the impeachment process. Mr. Wilson was a renowned legal scholar at the time, a law professor at the University of Pennsylvania in Philadelphia. He was a major force in drafting and adopting the Constitution in 1787. * * * *

Wilson, in his law lectures, the first of their kind under the Constitution, plainly states that the Senate may not ignore the Constitution in impeachment proceedings. He states that lawful and constitutional conduct may not be used as an impeachable offense. Let me say that again. He states that lawful and constitutional conduct may not be used as an impeachable offense.

Read along with me:

> The doctrine of impeachments is of high import in the constitutions of free states. On one hand, the most powerful magistrates should be amenable to the law: on the other hand, elevated characters should not be sacrificed merely on account of their elevation. No one should be secure while he violates the constitution and the laws: everyone should be secure while he observes them.

To be clear, James Wilson is saying that the Constitution does indeed apply when judging whether to convict an official by impeachment. If the complained-of conduct is constitutional, it cannot be impeachable. Are we to ignore the words and teachings of James Wilson? 167 Cong. Rec. S675 (daily ed. Feb. 12, 2021) (statement of Mr. Van der Veen).

Precedent

The President's lawyers emphasized the Supreme Court precedent of *Brandenburg v. Ohio*:

> *The Brandenburg holding has been interpreted as having three basic prongs to determine if speech meets the definition of "incitement." The Brandenburg test precludes speech from being sanctioned as incitement to a riot unless—*
>
> *This is one—the speech explicitly or implicitly encouraged use of violence or lawless action,*
>
> *Two: the speaker intends that his speech will result in use of violence or lawless action, and—*
>
> *Three—the imminent use of violence or lawless action is the likely result of the speech.* 167 Cong. Rec. S677 (daily ed. Feb. 12, 2021) (statement of Mr. Van der Veen).
>
> *First, the speech in question must explicitly or implicitly encourage the use of violence or lawless action. But here the President's speech called for peaceful protests.*
>
> *Second, the speaker must intend that his speech will result in the use of violence or lawless action. And, again, as Mr. van der Veen pointed out, the President clearly deplores rioters and political violence and did so through-out his term as President and never hesitated to express his admiration for the men and women that protect this country.*
>
> *Finally, the third element under the Brandenburg test is the imminent use of violence—imminent use of violence—in other words, right then. The imminent use of violence or lawless action must be the likely result of the speech—the likely result of the speech. Well, that argument is completely eviscerated by the fact that the violence was preplanned, as confirmed by the FBI, Department of Justice, and even the House managers—not the result of the speech at all.* 167 Cong. Rec. S679 (daily ed. Feb. 12, 2021) (statement of Mr. Castor).

The President's lawyers argued that the House Managers had created a new legal standard, which was not consistent with the case law:

> *The Senate is presented with an extraordinary task of sitting in judgment of a former President's words in a speech that he gave at a political event. The House managers accused Mr. Trump of using his words to incite the horrific events at the Capitol on January 6, but yesterday, they gave you a new and novel standard of incitement, with an element of foreseeability, a negligence concept. They cite zero case law. They made it up. This task of applying a completely made-up legal standard of incitement to an impeachment proceeding is truly an unprecedented task for the Senate, and that is something the Senate must seriously consider when deciding the issue.* 167 Cong. Rec. S674 (daily ed. Feb. 12, 2021) (statement of Mr. Van Der Veen).

The President's lawyers also argued that two cases supported their claims that the President had special First Amendment rights as an elected official:

> *Mr. Trump was an elected official, and there is an entire body of law, Supreme Court landmark cases, supporting the conclusion that Mr. Trump actually has enhanced free speech rights because he is an elected official. These cases are ignored by the House managers and the law professors, and that, too, is total intellectual dishonesty.* * * * *
>
> *In* Wood v. Georgia, *the Supreme Court addressed the case involving a sitting sheriff whose reelection was being investigated by a grand jury impaneled by a judge based on allegations of irregular "Negro bloc voting." It was in the sixties. The sheriff spoke publicly in multiple press releases calling the grand jury investigations "racist," "illegitimate," and an attempt to "intimidate" voters. He even urged the grand jurors on how to decide the issues and "not let its high office be a party to any political attempt to intimidate" voters.* * * * *
>
> *The sheriff even sent a letter to the grand jurors with these allegations, which is an extraordinary step since laws in most States, including Georgia, prohibit attempts to influence or intimidate jurors. The sheriff was charged and convicted of contempt of court and obstruction of the grand jury. But the Supreme Court, in a decision written by Justice Brennan, reversed. The Court held that the First Amendment protected an elected public official's speech because the voting controversy directly affected the sheriff's political career:*

> The petitioner was an elected official and had the right to enter the field of political controversy, particularly where his political life was at stake. The role that elected officials play in our society makes it all the more imperative that they be allowed freely to express themselves on matters of current public importance.

Wood *thus stands for the proposition that a difference of political opinion, expressed in speech on an issue of voting irregularity, cannot be punishable where all that was done was to encourage investigation and peaceful political speech—just like Mr. Trump has done here. The legal scholars call that directly on point.*

A second case, Bond v. Floyd, *involved a State legislature punishing an elected official for protected political speech.* Bond *is particularly instructive here, too. In* Bond, *the Supreme Court squarely addressed a question of an elected official's punishment by a legislature for statements alleged to have incited public violation of law—the burning of draft cards. The Court unequivocally rejected the idea—advanced here by the House managers—that an elected official is entitled to no protection under the First Amendment. The Supreme Court held that the Georgia House of Representatives was in fact forbidden by the First Amendment from punishing Bond, by not seating him, for advocating against the policy of the United States.* 167 Cong. Rec. S676 (daily ed. Feb. 12, 2021) (statement of Mr. Van Der Veen).

Speech for political purposes is the kind of activity to which the First Amendment offers its strongest protection. These are bedrock principles recognized by our Supreme Court for decades. [In New York Times v. Sullivan, *the Court said:]*

> Our First Amendment decisions have created a rough hierarchy in the constitutional protection of speech. Core political speech occupies the highest, most protected position * * * *

Even political speech that may incite unlawful conduct is protected from the reach of government punishment. The Court has said:

> Every idea is an incitement, and if speech may be suppressed whenever it might inspire someone to act unlawfully, then there is no limit to the State's censorial power.

The government may not prohibit speech because it increases the chances of an unlawful act will be committed "at some indefinite time" in the future. The House managers showed you a series of tweets going all the way back to 2015 in an effort to prove "incitement." All of that evidence is totally irrelevant under the constitutional definition of incitement. * * * *

Mr. Trump did the opposite of advocating for lawless action—the opposite. He expressly advocated for peaceful action at the Save America rally. He explicitly stated—these are the words:

> I know that everyone here will soon be marching over to the Capitol building to peacefully and patriotically make your voices heard.

"To peacefully and patriotically make your voices heard"—that is how this President has spoken for years when he condemns violence, lawlessness, and rioters. Id.

What they don't tell you and didn't tell you * * * * *is at 2:38, President Trump urged protesters at the U.S. Capitol to stay peaceful:*

> Please support our Capitol Police and Law Enforcement. They are truly on the side of our Country. Stay peaceful!

Before we run the graphic, I just want to point out to you, President Trump's speech ended at 1:11 p.m. So at 2:38 p.m., by the time word reaches the President that there is a problem down here, he is out urging people to support the police, stay peaceful, support our Capitol Police and law enforcement. They are on the side of the country. Stay peaceful.

At 3:13 p.m., President Trump urged protesters at the U.S. Capitol to remain peaceful:

> No violence. Remember, WE are the Party of Law and Order. Respect the law and our great men and women in blue. * * * * 167 Cong. Rec. S680 (daily ed. Feb. 12, 2021) (statement of Mr. Castor) (caps in original).

Future Precedent

The President's lawyers also argued that a conviction would mean that any future President's words would be subject to impeachment by members of an opposing political party:

> *Do you want to create a precedent where the Senate will be tasked with sitting in judgment as to the meaning and implied intent of a President's words or words of any elected official?*
>
> *Will that allow and maybe encourage a majority party to weaponize the awesome power of impeachment against the minority to suppress a point of view?*
>
> *Will the Senate then have to deal with constant Articles of Impeachment by a majority party accusing minority Presidents or other elected officials of so-called inciteful or false speeches?* 167 Cong. Rec. S675 (daily ed. Feb. 12, 2021) (statement of Mr. Van Der Veen).
>
> *You must reject this invitation to ignore the First Amendment. It is anti-American and would set dangerous precedent forever.* * * * *
>
> *We are here under the Constitution. It is illogical what the House managers said. The Constitution does apply to this constitutional impeachment process. It is double talk. Nonsense. Illogical.* * * * * 167 Cong. Rec. S676 (daily ed. Feb. 12, 2021) (statement of Mr. Van Der Veen).

Shared Constitutional Norms

Finally, the President's lawyers argued that the impeachment was un-American:

> *You must reject this invitation to ignore the First Amendment. It is anti-American and would set dangerous precedent forever.* * * * *
>
> *Like every other politically motivated witch hunt the left has engaged in over the past 4 years, this impeachment is completely divorced from the facts, the evidence, and the interests of the American people.* 167 Cong. Rec. S676 (daily ed. Feb. 12, 2021) (statement of Mr. Van Der Veen).
>
> *History will record this shameful effort as a deliberate attempt by the Democratic Party to smear, censor, and cancel not just President Trump but the 75 million Americans who voted for him. Now is not the time for such a campaign of retribution; it is the time for unity and healing and focusing on the interests of the Nation as a whole. Id.* at S669.

PROBLEM 2-1

In the last Chapter, and above in the Section on "shared constitutional norms," we noted that the President's lawyers' arguments were tinged with rhetoric that emphasized the importance of America. Given what you have read above about the difference between **populism** and **democracy** (*see* Note, Part Two, Chapter 1), read President Trump's January 6, 2021 speech with this contrast in mind. It appears in Appendix B to this Chapter. Does it set up an "us versus them" contrast, characteristic of populism, or does it say that the President speaks for all voters, Democrat and Republican? Does it suggest that the President's supporters are engaged in an all-out struggle against elites that is a constant, dire struggle?

QUESTIONS ON THE PRESIDENT'S FIRST AMENDMENT DEFENSE

Were the First Amendment Arguments Frivolous?: No one denied that President Trump had First Amendment rights. Nor did anyone deny that political speech is the highest category of protected speech. This explains why the House Managers spent little time in their briefs on the cases cited by the President. This also explains why over one hundred law professors, some associated with the conservative *Federalist Society,* signed a letter stating that the First Amendment was not a defense. They explained:

> We, the undersigned constitutional law scholars, write to explain * * * * [that] [t]he First Amendment is no bar to the Senate convicting former President Trump and disqualifying him from holding future office. Although we differ from one another in our politics, disagree on many questions of constitutional law, and take different approaches to understanding the Constitution's text, history, and context, we all agree that any First Amendment defense raised by President Trump's attorneys would be legally frivolous. In other words, we all agree that the First Amendment does not prevent the Senate from convicting President Trump and disqualifying him from holding future office.
>
> No reasonable scholar or jurist could conclude that President Trump had a First Amendment right to [1] incite a violent attack on the seat of the legislative branch, or [2] then to sit back and watch on television as Congress was terrorized and the Capitol sacked. *Id.*

Letter from Law Professors on the First Amendment, Appendix C to this Chapter.

Impeachment Precedent and the First Amendment: As Professor Kate Shaw, a presidential scholar, explained in a law review article, technically, every President who has been impeached was impeached based in part on speech.

> Presidential speech actually played a significant role in every other major presidential impeachment effort in our history. Prior to President Trump, three presidents had faced serious impeachment threats: Andrew Johnson, in 1868; Richard Nixon, in 1974; and Bill Clinton, in 1998 and early 1999. In each of these episodes, the debate around impeachment encompassed, among other things, public presidential rhetoric—lies and

misrepresentations; statements that took aim at Congress or undermined the rule of law.

Katherine Shaw, *Impeachable Speech*, 70 Emory L. J. 1 (2020).

As Shaw explains, however, concerns about the "liberty of speech" did infect at least some of these proceedings. For example, in the Andrew Johnson impeachment, the Tenth Article of Impeachment relied upon the President's various "harangues." There was no vote on that article, and some Senators expressed concerns in light of free speech, one saying: "I doubt if we can at present make low and scurrilous speeches a ground of impeachment." *Id.* at 21 (quoting Cong. Globe, 40th Cong., 2d Sess. 509 (Supp. 1868)). Similarly, concerns were raised in the Bill Clinton impeachment that his lies to his Cabinet and to the public about his private marital affair could constitute a ground for impeachment, precisely because it would implicate a wide array of public speech. *Id.* at 36 (quoting Sen. Schumer).

Would President Trump Have a First Amendment Defense in a Criminal Prosecution?: Very definitely yes. Inciting a riot is a federal crime, and a crime in most states. However, incitement is hard to prove where the speaker's personal liberty is at stake—in a criminal case—for the reasons cited by the President's lawyers. *Brandenburg v. Ohio* holds that the First Amendment generally protects "advocacy of the use of force or of law violation." 395 U.S. 444, 447 (1969). In *Brandenburg*, a group of Ku Klux Klansmen were convicted of incitement under state law for burning a cross and saying, on live television, that they would be "marching on Congress" and "there might have to be some revengeance [sic] taken" against Congress, the Supreme Court, and the President for protecting civil rights. *Id.* at 446. The Klansmen alleged that their convictions violated their freedom of speech. *Id.* at 445. The Supreme Court agreed and held that incendiary speech only loses First Amendment protection, and thus becomes incitement, when (1) the speaker intends it to result in imminent violence, and (2) imminent violence is the result of the speech. *Id.* at 447–449.

These elements are difficult to satisfy, even when speech is followed by violence or unlawful conduct by those who heard it. *See, e.g., Hess v. Indiana*, 414 U.S. 105, 109 (1973) (holding that the First Amendment protects stating "we'll take the f * * * *ing street" while facing a crowd unlawfully blocking a street); *NAACP v. Claiborne Hardware Co.*, 458 U.S. 886, 928 (1982) (holding that the First Amendment protects stating "if we catch any of you going in any of them racist stores, we're gonna break your damn neck" urged in a civil rights speech by Black leader). But it is possible to pass the *Brandenburg* standard. *See, e.g., Rice v. Paladin Enterprises, Inc.*, 128 F.3d 233, 263–265 (4th Cir. 1997) (holding that the First Amendment does not protect written instructions on how to commit a murder subsequently used by a reader to carry out a triple-homicide); *U.S. v. Buttorff*, 572 F.2d 619, 624 (8th Cir. 1978) (holding that the First Amendment does not protect verbal instructions on how to conceal income from the IRS subsequently used by listeners to evade tax liability). Moreover, "fighting words" and "true threats" are outside the scope of the First Amendment. *See Chaplinsky v. New Hampshire*, 315 U.S. 568, 572 (1942) (finding that " 'fighting' words—those which by their very utterance inflict injury or tend to incite an immediate breach of the peace" are not protected by the First Amendment); *Watts v. United States*, 394 U.S. 705, 707 (1969) (noting that laws banning threats against public officials "must * * * * distinguish [a threat] from what is constitutionally protected speech"). It is a felony to threaten to kill the President or the Vice President, for example, and nothing in the First Amendment prevents such prosecutions.

Do you think that President Trump's speech on January 6th passes the *Brandenburg* test for incitement? What is the best argument put forth by the House Managers that President Trump intended his speech to result in a riot at the Capitol, or that the riot was the result of his speech? Do you think the riot would have happened without the speech? What about the transcript of rioters saying that they were going to "storm" the Capitol? Note that a federal court dismissed allegations of incitement against President Trump in a 2018 lawsuit. In *Nwanguma v. Trump*, a group of protestors brought a tortious incitement claim against then-candidate Trump after they had been beaten at one of his rallies. 903 F.3d 604, 606–607 (6th Cir. 2018). Trump instructed his supporters to "get 'em out of here" when the group began their peaceful protest. *Id.* at 606. "In response, members of the audience assaulted, pushed, and shoved" the protesters. *Id.* at 607. Audience members later admitted to assaulting the protesters because "Trump kept saying 'get them out, get them out'." *Nwanguma v. Trump*, 273 F.Supp.3d 719, 724 (W.D.Ky. 2017), *rev'd*, 903 F.3d 604 (6th Cir. 2018). Relying on *Brandenburg*, the Sixth Circuit dismissed the claim because "not a single word encouraged violence or lawlessness, explicitly or implicitly." *Nwanguma v. Trump*, 903 F.3d 604, 610 (6th Cir. 2018). The court explained that "the fact that audience members reacted by using force" was not enough to prove that the words were intended to, or were likely to, cause imminent violence. *Id.* Do you agree with the court that the President's instruction to "get 'em out of here" did not imply the use of force?

Was It Error to Emphasize the Speech as Opposed to the President's Conduct?: The First Amendment does not apply to conduct or failing to act when there is a duty to act. One might argue that the House Managers' focus on the speech took away from the President's obvious duty to protect the Capitol and the election certification process. As we explained earlier, the President has an express duty to protect the nation in the Constitution and in the constitutional oath. That includes a duty to protect proceedings concerning an election. In civil and criminal law, violation of an express legal duty can give rise to liability, even if based on an omission (*see* earlier note in Part Two, Chapter 1 on the failure to protect).

V. THE PRESIDENT'S DUE PROCESS DEFENSE

Due process is one of the most essential, but also one of the vaguest, of legal concepts. The Constitution provides, in the Bill of Rights, that no person shall be deprived of "due process of law." U.S. Const. amend. V, XIV. In other words, the government must abide by certain procedures, and they must be fair. What are the required procedures? What makes them fair? The Constitution provides only a few examples. A defendant cannot be charged with a capital crime except by a grand jury, for example. U.S. Const. amend. V. A property owner must be paid "just compensation" for anything of theirs that the government takes. *Id.* But, in most cases, it is up to lawyers to argue—and courts to decide—what exactly due process requires.

For that reason, due process requirements vary from case to case. Typically, courts say that individuals have a "right to be heard." In the case of a parking ticket, that may simply mean that you get notice of the offense and the opportunity to appear in court if you so choose, but you have no right to counsel or to a jury.[16] In a more serious case, the process due may include the right of cross-examination and counsel.[17] At a minimum, "[t]he [Supreme] Court has consistently held that some kind of hearing is required at some time" before a person is finally deprived of rights. *Wolff v. McDonnell*, 418 U.S. 539, 557–58 (1974); *see also Mathews v. Eldridge*, 424 U.S. 319, 333 (1976) ("the right to be heard before being condemned to suffer grievous loss of any kind * * * *is a principle basic to our society") (quoting *Joint Anti-Fascist Comm. v. McGrath*, 341 U.S. 123, 168 (1951) (Frankfurter, J. concurring)).

The President's lawyers accused the House of rushing their investigation of the Capitol Riot and withholding their findings from President Trump until shortly before trial—thereby inhibiting his ability to counter the evidence against him and prepare an argument.

> *The rush to judgment for a snap impeachment in this case was just one example of the denial of due process. Another, perhaps even more vitally significant, example was the denial of any opportunity ever to test the integrity of the evidence offered against Donald J. Trump* * * * * 167 Cong. Rec. S669 (daily ed. Feb. 12, 2021) (statement of Mr. Van Der Veen).
>
> *Mr. Trump was given no right to review the so-called evidence against him at trial. He was given no opportunity to question its propriety. He was given no chance to engage in factfinding. Id.* at S731.

[16] To comply with due process, not all hearings need be long, elaborate trials. They can be "brief," even "informal." *Londoner v. City and County of Denver*, 210 U.S. 373, 386 (1908). So long as whomever the government is trying to deprive of rights is afforded an "opportunity to be heard," generally by presenting arguments, countering the government's evidence, and cross-examining the government's witnesses. *Frank v. Mangum*, 237 U.S. 309, 347 (1915) (Holmes, J, dissenting).

[17] *See Mathews v. Eldridge*, 424 U.S. 319, 334 (1976) ("[d]ue process," unlike some legal rules, is not a technical conception with a fixed content unrelated to time, place and circumstances") (quoting *Cafeteria & Restaurant Workers v. McElroy*, 367 U.S. 886, 895 (1961)).

> *You get more due process than this when you fight a parking ticket. Id.* at S670.[18]

The House Managers replied that President Trump had been accorded all that due process required: a hearing, in the form of a Senate impeachment trial. They questioned the veracity of the President's due process claims because he ultimately refused to participate in his own defense.

> *During this trial, the President has counsel. They have argued very vigorously on his behalf. We had a full presentation of evidence, adversarial presentations, motions. The President was invited to testify. He declined. The President was invited to provide exculpatory evidence. He declined. You can't claim there is no due process when you won't participate in the process.* 167 Cong. Rec. S727 (daily ed. Feb. 13, 2021) (statement of Rep. Neguse).

> *Despite a full and fair opportunity to come forward, he has refused to come and tell his story. Id.* at S722 (daily ed. Feb. 13, 2021) (statement of Rep. Cicilline).

Rep. Neguse (D-CO) responded that the text of the Constitution's impeachment clauses mean that it is up to the Senate and the House, alone, to decide what procedures are "due" to an impeached President. *See* U.S. Const. art. I, § 2, cl. 5 ("The House of Representatives * * * * shall have the sole Power of Impeachment"); *id.* art. I, § 3, cl. 6 ("The Senate shall have the sole Power to try all Impeachments").

> *So just to be absolutely clear, the House, with the sole power of impeachment, determines what the process looks like in the House, and the Senate does the same for the trial.* 167 Cong. Rec. S727 (daily ed. Feb. 12, 2021)(statement of Rep. Neguse).

Rep. Neguse's arguments echoed the House Managers' reply brief. The Managers argued there that the House had exercised a power they alone possessed—impeachment—to solve a problem only they could solve—an imminently-dangerous President and an attack on the 2020 election. Since the Constitution confers the impeachment power on the House, they claimed, only the House can decide what procedures are required to exercise it.

> *The Constitution vests the House with the "sole Power of Impeachment" and the power to "determine the Rules of its*

---

[18] Implicit in these claims, which the House Managers viewed as highly exaggerated, is the idea that a Senate impeachment trial should look like a typical criminal trial.

> *Proceedings." Here, the House had to move quickly to address President Trump's dangerous misconduct, to discourage him from engaging in further abuse during the last days of his term, and to send an immediate signal that such an attack on our core democratic institutions will not be tolerated.*[19] House Managers Reply Brief at 23.

The President's lawyers responded with an argument that the Senate had no right to try a private citizen.

> *Nowhere in the Constitution is the power enumerated or implied. Congress has no authority, no right, and no business holding a trial of Citizen Trump, let alone a trial to deprive him of some fundamental civil rights*. 167 Cong. Rec. S731 (daily ed. Feb. 13, 2021) (statement of Mr. Van Der Veen).

> *The gravity of the deprivation at stake in an impeachment—especially a presidential impeachment—buttresses the conclusion that some due process limitations must apply. It would be incompatible with the Framers' understanding of the "delicacy and magnitude of a trust which so deeply concerns the political reputation and existence of every man engaged in the administration of public affairs."* President's Brief at 67.

QUESTIONS ON DUE PROCESS AND THE CONSTITUTION

Due Process in Impeachment Proceedings: On the one hand, most lawyers would say that due process applies to all citizens where a citizen's right—here, to run for office—is at stake. And many lawyers would say that the Bill of Rights applies to the rest of the Constitution: after all, it amends all of the Constitution—that is why the amendments were included at the end of the Constitution rather than inserted throughout the original document. *See* Jonathan Gienapp, The Second Creation: Fixing the Constitution in the Founding Era (2018). Certainly, if Congress decided to beat evidence out of a witness, or provided them no opportunity to reply to the charges, few would think that the proceedings satisfied due process. Nevertheless, most law professors make a strong distinction between an impeachment and a criminal trial. *See* Vikram D. Amar & Jason Mazzone, *The Power to "Try" "Cases of Impeachment": Some Reflections on the Finality, Transparency and Integrity of Senate Adjudications of Presidential Impeachments (Including that of Donald J. Trump)*, 95 Chi.-Kent L. Rev. 455 (2021). Professors Amar and Mazzone explain:

---

[19] We relied upon a copy of the brief as published by the New York Times. Future citations are to that version. *See Read the Brief From House Managers Asserting Trump Has 'No Good Defense'*, N.Y. Times (Feb. 9, 2021), https://www.nytimes.com/interactive/2021/02/09/us/politics/impeachment-managers-brief-on-trump-impeachment-defense-feb.html.

> It is clear (at least we think so) that impeachment proceedings are not criminal cases in which the Fifth and Sixth Amendments' criminal procedural protections themselves apply. Article I of the Constitution explicitly provides that "[j]udgment in cases of impeachment shall extend no further than to removal from Office [and disqualification from future office] but the Party * * * *shall * * * * be liable and subject to * * * *punishment according to law." *Id.* at 455.
>
> So, an impeachment defendant is never in danger of losing his liberty, or even his bank account. Instead, what is at stake is a public-sector job (not unlike a dismissal process for revoking tenure of a public law school professor). The impeachment-judgment clause makes clear the impeachment trial is not a mechanism for punishment the way the criminal law is; impeachment is primarily a device to enable removal from office of someone who is unfit to continue. For that reason, the protections of the Sixth Amendment's right of accused persons to confront witnesses against them (which applies only in "criminal prosecutions") have no direct application to impeachment proceedings. *Id.*

On the other hand, Amar and Mazzone argue that there may be some limits on Senate trials, even if the Supreme Court in the *Walter Nixon* case (*see* Part One, Chapter 2), refused to intervene in a Senate trial and left it up to the Senate whether to take testimony in a committee. Amar and Mazzone argue that the Court assumed that the "trial" in that judicial impeachment was basically constitutional, suggesting that a procedure that did not amount to a "trial" in that sense could violate the Constitution. *Id.* at 458 (reading the Supreme Court's *Walter Nixon* case as making a silent estimation that taking testimony in committee was not a constitutional violation).

Impeachment Rules: One of the most basic elements of due process is a set of rules, known to all parties in advance, and applied similarly across similar cases. Although impeachment is generally considered a "political trial" because elected representatives sit as jurors, impeachments are regulated by Senate Rules.[20] Most of those rules were created long before the First Trump Impeachment.[21] Additionally, the Senate typically passes a Resolution explaining the procedures specific to each impeachment trial before each trial begins. We have set out the Resolution for the Second Trump Impeachment Trial as Appendix D to this Chapter. One of the most powerful legal arguments for Congress's right to set appropriate procedures

---

[20] Elizabeth Rybicki & Michael Greene, Cong. Research Serv., R46185, The Impeachment Process in the Senate (2021) ("The Senate has a set of rules specific to the conduct of an impeachment trial, most of which originated in the early 19th century") https://crsreports.congress.gov/product/pdf/R/R46185.

[21] U.S. Congress, Senate, Procedure and Guidelines for Impeachment Trials in the United States Senate, prepared pursuant to Senate Resolution 439, 99th Congress, 2nd Sess., prepared by Floyd M. Riddick and Robert B. Dove, 99th Cong., 2nd Sess., August 15, 1986, S.Doc. 99-33 (Washington: GPO, 1986).

is that the Constitution provides Congress broad leeway in setting its own rules. U.S. Const. art. V, § 5, cl. 2. ("each House may determine the Rules of its Proceedings"). That raises a question about who should decide the "due process" question. As we saw at the beginning of this book, the Supreme Court has shown strong deference to Congress to create its own rules, and has refused to intervene in impeachment proceedings. Part One, Chapter 2. There are standing rules for impeachments that were applied as well as rules that the Senate agreed to for the Second Trump Impeachment in what is known as a "unanimous consent" agreement. A "unanimous consent" (called a "UC") agreement is typically negotiated by the party leaders in light of past precedent and governs the Senate's proceedings on the issues identified in the agreement. On the Second Trump Impeachment UC, *see* 167 Cong. Rec. S669 (daily ed. Feb. 12, 2021).

No Trial of Citizens: The Second Trump Impeachment Trial did see the return of an argument that the Congress had no power to try individuals, an argument based on the Constitution's "Bill of Attainder" clause (quoted in the next paragraph). In the First Trump Impeachment, arguments were made that the trial violated the Constitution because it constituted a "Bill of Attainder," meaning a punishment by legislative act without a trial. (*See* Part One, Chapter 3, Note on the Need for An Existing Law). In the Second Trump Impeachment, the President's lawyers reprised this argument by urging that Congress was punishing President Trump by preventing him from running for office again. Citizens, they argued, could not be punished in this fashion, because that would be a Bill of Attainder.

The problem with this argument is two-fold. First, the clause does not appear to apply to impeachments by its own terms. Article I, § 9, cl. 3 of the Constitution states: "No Bill of Attainder or ex post facto Law shall be passed." To read impeachment as an Attainder (meaning a trial of an individual) would read the impeachment clauses out of the Constitution since impeachment requires a trial of an individual official. Textual interpretations are best when they give meaning to all provisions of a Constitution, rather than privilege one over the other. Second, the Bill of Attainder clause certainly applies to citizens but President Trump was impeached by the House *when he was President*. Thus, the question has to be whether the Senate "trial" could be considered a "Bill of Attainder." The terms "Bill," "Law" and "passed" imply a piece of legislation, not a trial. Of course, had the Senate disqualified President Trump, that statement of disqualification might have been considered a "bill" which had "passed" both Houses. The only way this legal question could have been raised in a court would be if President Trump had been disqualified and then challenged that conviction. As we have seen in Part One, Chapter 2, however, it is unlikely that the Supreme Court would have heard an appeal from an impeachment because the Senate has broad powers to set the rules of its own proceedings and the Court would be hesitant to enter a highly politicized judgment constitutionally committed to the Congress.

APPENDIX A

IN THE HOUSE OF REPRESENTATIVES, U.S., January 13, 2021

Impeaching Donald John Trump, President of the United States, for high crimes and misdemeanors

Resolved, That Donald John Trump, President of the United States, is impeached for high crimes and misdemeanors and that the following article of impeachment be exhibited to the United States Senate:

Article of impeachment exhibited by the House of Representatives of the United States of America in the name of itself and of the people of the United States of America, against Donald John Trump, President of the United States of America, in maintenance and support of its impeachment against him for high crimes and misdemeanors.

ARTICLE I: INCITEMENT OF INSURRECTION

The Constitution provides that the House of Representatives "shall have the sole Power of Impeachment" and that the President "shall be removed from Office on Impeachment for, and Conviction of, Treason, Bribery, or other high Crimes and Misdemeanors". Further, section 3 of the 14th Amendment to the Constitution prohibits any person who has "engaged in insurrection or rebellion against" the United States from "hold[ing] any office * * * *under the United States". In his conduct while President of the United States— and in violation of his constitutional oath faithfully to execute the office of President of the United States and, to the best of his ability, preserve, protect, and defend the Constitution of the United States, and in violation of his constitutional duty to take care that the laws be faithfully executed—Donald John Trump engaged in high Crimes and Misdemeanors by inciting violence against the Government of the United States, in that:

On January 6, 2021, pursuant to the 12th Amendment to the Constitution of the United States, the Vice President of the United States, the House of Representatives, and the Senate met at the United States Capitol for a Joint Session of Congress to count the votes of the Electoral College. In the months preceding the Joint Session, President Trump repeatedly issued false statements asserting that the Presidential election results were the product of widespread fraud and should not be accepted by the American people or certified by State or Federal officials. Shortly before the Joint Session commenced, President Trump, addressed a crowd at the Ellipse in Washington, DC. There, he reiterated false claims that "we won this election, and we won it by a landslide". He also willfully made statements that, in context, encouraged—and foreseeably resulted in—lawless action at the Capitol, such as: "if you don't fight like hell you're not going to have a country anymore". Thus incited by President Trump, members of the crowd he had addressed, in an attempt to, among other objectives, interfere with the Joint Session's solemn constitutional duty to certify the results of the 2020 Presidential election, unlawfully breached and vandalized the Capitol, injured and killed law enforcement personnel, menaced Members of Congress, the Vice President, and Congressional personnel, and engaged in other violent, deadly, destructive, and seditious acts.

President Trump's conduct on January 6, 2021, followed his prior efforts to subvert and obstruct the certification of the results of the 2020 Presidential election. Those prior efforts included a phone call on January 2, 2021, during which President Trump urged the secretary of state of Georgia, Brad Raffensperger, to "find" enough votes to overturn the Georgia Presidential election results and threatened Secretary Raffensperger if he failed to do so.

In all this, President Trump gravely endangered the security of the United States and its institutions of Government. He threatened the integrity of the democratic system, interfered with the peaceful transition of power, and imperiled a coequal branch of Government. He thereby betrayed his trust as President, to the manifest injury of the people of the United States.

Wherefore, Donald John Trump, by such conduct, has demonstrated that he will remain a threat to national security, democracy, and the Constitution if allowed to remain in office, and has acted in a manner grossly incompatible with self-governance and the rule of law. Donald John Trump thus warrants impeachment and trial, removal from office, and disqualification to hold and enjoy any office of honor, trust, or profit under the United States.

APPENDIX B

President Donald J. Trump, Remarks at the March to Save America in Washington, D.C. (Jan. 6, 2021)[22]

Well, thank you very much. This is incredible.

---

[22] *Transcript of Trump's speech at rally before US Capitol riot*, Associated Press (January 13, 2021), https://apnews.com/article/election-2020-joe-biden-donald-trump-capitol-siege-media-e79eb5164613d6718e9f4502eb471f27. Note that this is the Associated Press's transcript of the speech. If the House Managers' accounts of the speech were correct, this reprint includes only some of the crowd's responses.

Media will not show the magnitude of this crowd. Even I, when I turned on today, I looked, and I saw thousands of people here. But you don't see hundreds of thousands of people behind you because they don't want to show that.

We have hundreds of thousands of people here and I just want them to be recognized by the fake news media. Turn your cameras please and show what's really happening out here because these people are not going to take it any longer. They're not going to take it any longer. Go ahead. Turn your cameras, please. Would you show? They came from all over the world, actually, but they came from all over our country.

I just really want to see what they do. I just want to see how they covered. I've never seen anything like it. But it would be really great if we could be covered fairly by the media. The media is the biggest problem we have as far as I'm concerned, single biggest problem. The fake news and the Big tech.

Big tech is now coming into their own. We beat them four years ago. We surprised them. We took them by surprise and this year they rigged an election. They rigged it like they've never rigged an election before. And by the way, last night they didn't do a bad job either if you notice.

I'm honest. And I just, again, I want to thank you. It's just a great honor to have this kind of crowd and to be before you and hundreds of thousands of American patriots who are committed to the honesty of our elections and the integrity of our glorious republic.

All of us here today do not want to see our election victory stolen by emboldened radical-left Democrats, which is what they're doing. And stolen by the fake news media. That's what they've done and what they're doing. We will never give up, we will never concede. It doesn't happen. You don't concede when there's theft involved.

Our country has had enough. We will not take it anymore and that's what this is all about. And to use a favorite term that all of you people really came up with: We will stop the steal. Today I will lay out just some of the evidence proving that we won this election and we won it by a landslide. This was not a close election.

You know, I say, sometimes jokingly, but there's no joke about it: I've been in two elections. I won them both and the second one, I won much bigger than the first. OK. Almost 75 million people voted for our campaign, the most of any incumbent president by far in the history of our country, 12 million more people than four years ago.

And I was told by the real pollsters—we do have real pollsters—they know that we were going to do well and we were going to win. What

I was told, if I went from 63 million, which we had four years ago, to 66 million, there was no chance of losing. Well, we didn't go to 66, we went to 75 million, and they say we lost. We didn't lose.

And by the way, does anybody believe that Joe had 80 million votes? Does anybody believe that? He had 80 million computer votes. It's a disgrace. There's never been anything like that. You could take third-world countries. Just take a look. Take third-world countries. Their elections are more honest than what we've been going through in this country. It's a disgrace. It's a disgrace.

Even when you look at last night. They're all running around like chickens with their heads cut off with boxes. Nobody knows what the hell is going on. There's never been anything like this.

We will not let them silence your voices. We're not going to let it happen, I'm not going to let it happen.

(Audience chants: "Fight for Trump.")

Thank you.

And I'd love to have if those tens of thousands of people would be allowed. The military, the secret service. And we want to thank you and the police law enforcement. Great. You're doing a great job. But I'd love it if they could be allowed to come up here with us. Is that possible? Can you just let him come up, please?

And Rudy, you did a great job. He's got guts. You know what? He's got guts, unlike a lot of people in the Republican Party. He's got guts. He fights, he fights.

And I'll tell you. Thank you very much, John. Fantastic job. I watched. That's a tough act to follow, those two. John is one of the most brilliant lawyers in the country, and he looked at this and he said, "What an absolute disgrace that this can be happening to our Constitution."

And he looked at Mike Pence, and I hope Mike is going to do the right thing. I hope so. I hope so.

Because if Mike Pence does the right thing, we win the election.

All he has to do, all this is, this is from the number one, or certainly one of the top, Constitutional lawyers in our country. He has the absolute right to do it. We're supposed to protect our country, support our country, support our Constitution, and protect our constitution.

States want to revote. The states got defrauded, They were given false information. They voted on it. Now they want to recertify. They want it back. All Vice President Pence has to do is send it back to the states to recertify and we become president and you are the happiest people.

And I actually, I just spoke to Mike. I said: "Mike, that doesn't take courage. What takes courage is to do nothing. That takes courage." And then we're stuck with a president who lost the election by a lot and we have to live with that for four more years. We're just not going to let that happen.

Many of you have traveled from all across the nation to be here, and I want to thank you for the extraordinary love. That's what it is. There's never been a movement like this, ever, ever. For the extraordinary love for this amazing country, and this amazing movement, thank you.

(Audience chants: "We love Trump.")

By the way, this goes all the way back past the Washington Monument. You believe this? Look at this. That is. Unfortunately gave, they gave the press the prime seats. I can't stand that.

No. But you look at that behind. I wish they'd flip those cameras and look behind you. That is the most amazing sight. When they make a mistake, you get to see it on television. Amazing. Amazing. All the way back.

And don't worry, we will not take the name off the Washington Monument. We will not cancel culture.

You know they wanted to get rid of the Jefferson Memorial. Either take it down or just put somebody else in there. I don't think that's going to happen. It damn well better not. Although, with this administration, if this happens, it could happen. You'll see some really bad things happen.

They'll knock out Lincoln too, by the way. They've been taking his statue down. But then we signed a little law. You hurt our monuments, you hurt our heroes, you go to jail for 10 years, and everything stopped. You notice that? It stopped. It all stopped.

And they could use Rudy back in New York City. Rudy. They could use you. Your city's going to hell. They want Rudy Giuliani back in New York. We'll get a little younger version of Rudy. Is that OK, Rudy?

We're gathered together in the heart of our nation's capital for one very, very basic and simple reason: To save our democracy.

You know most candidates on election evening and, of course, this thing goes on so long. They still don't have any idea what the votes are. We still have congressional seats under review. They have no idea. They've totally lost control. They've used the pandemic as a way of defrauding the people in a proper election.

But you know, you know, when you see this and when you see what's happening. Number one, they all say, "Sir, we'll never let it happen again." I said, "That's good. But what about eight weeks ago?" You know they try and get you to go.

They said, "Sir, in four years, you're guaranteed." I said: "I'm not interested right now. Do me a favor, go back eight weeks. I want to go back eight weeks. Let's go back eight weeks."

We want to go back and we want to get this right because we're going to have somebody in there that should not be in there and our country will be destroyed and we're not going to stand for that.

For years, Democrats have gotten away with election fraud and weak Republicans. And that's what they are. There's so many weak Republicans. And we have great ones. Jim Jordan and some of these guys, they're out there fighting. The House guys are fighting. But it's, it's incredible.

Many of the Republicans, I helped them get in, I helped them get elected. I helped Mitch get elected. I helped. I could name 24 of them, let's say, I won't bore you with it. And then all of a sudden you have something like this. It's like, "Oh gee, maybe I'll talk to the president sometime later." No, it's amazing.

They're weak Republicans, they're pathetic Republicans and that's what happens.

If this happened to the Democrats, there'd be hell all over the country going on. There'd be hell all over the country. But just remember this: You're stronger, you're smarter, you've got more going than anybody. And they try and demean everybody having to do with us. And you're the real people, you're the people that built this nation. You're not the people that tore down our nation.

The weak Republicans, and that's it. I really believe it. I think I'm going to use the term, the weak Republicans. You've got a lot of them. And you got a lot of great ones. But you got a lot of weak ones. They've turned a blind eye, even as Democrats enacted policies that chipped away our jobs, weakened our military, threw open our borders and put America last.

Did you see the other day where Joe Biden said, I want to get rid of the America First policy? What's that all about? Get rid of. How do you say I want to get rid of America First? Even if you're going to do it, don't talk about it, right? Unbelievable what we have to go through. What we have to go through.

And you have to get your people to fight. And if they don't fight, we have to primary the hell out of the ones that don't fight. You primary them. We're going to. We're going to let you know who they are. I can already tell you, frankly.

But this year, using the pretext of the China virus and the scam of mail-in ballots, Democrats attempted the most brazen and outrageous election theft and there's never been anything like this. So pure theft in American history. Everybody knows it.

That election, our election was over at 10 o'clock in the evening. We're leading Pennsylvania, Michigan, Georgia, by hundreds of thousands of votes.

And then late in the evening, or early in the morning, boom, these explosions of bullsh*t.

And all of a sudden. All of a sudden it started to happen.

(Audience chants: "Bullsh*t.")

Don't forget when Romney got beat. Romney, hey. Did you see his? I wonder if he enjoyed his flight in last night. But when Romney got beaten, you know, he stands up like you're more typical, "Well, I'd like to congratulate the victor." The victor? Who is the victor, Mitt? "I'd like to congratulate." They don't go and look at the facts. No, I don't know. He got, he got slaughtered. Probably, maybe it was OK, maybe it was. But that's what happened.

But we look at the facts and our election was so corrupt that in the history of this country we've never seen anything like it. You can go all the way back.

You know, America is blessed with elections. All over the world they talk about our elections. You know what the world says about us now? They said, we don't have free and fair elections.

And you know what else? We don't have a free and fair press. Our media is not free, it's not fair. It suppresses thought, it suppresses speech and it's become the enemy of the people. It's become the enemy of the people. It's the biggest problem we have in this country.

No third-world countries would even attempt to do what we caught them doing. And you'll hear about that in just a few minutes.

Republicans are, Republicans are constantly fighting like a boxer with his hands tied behind his back. It's like a boxer. And we want to be so nice. We want to be so respectful of everybody, including bad people. And we're going to have to fight much harder.

And Mike Pence is going to have to come through for us, and if he doesn't, that will be a, a sad day for our country because you're sworn to uphold our Constitution.

Now, it is up to Congress to confront this egregious assault on our democracy. And after this, we're going to walk down, and I'll be there with you, we're going to walk down, we're going to walk down.

Anyone you want, but I think right here, we're going to walk down to the Capitol, and we're going to cheer on our brave senators and congressmen and women, and we're probably not going to be cheering so much for some of them.

Because you'll never take back our country with weakness. You have to show strength and you have to be strong. We have come to demand that Congress do the right thing and only count the electors who have been lawfully slated, lawfully slated.

I know that everyone here will soon be marching over to the Capitol building to peacefully and patriotically make your voices heard.

Today we will see whether Republicans stand strong for integrity of our elections. But whether or not they stand strong for our country, our country. Our country has been under siege for a long time. Far longer than this four-year period. We've set it on a much greater course. So much, and we, I thought, you know, four more years. I thought it would be easy.

We've created the greatest economy in history. We rebuilt our military. We get you the biggest tax cuts in history. Right? We got you the biggest regulation cuts. There's no president, whether it's four years, eight years or in one case more, got anywhere near the regulation cuts.

Used to take 20 years to get a highway approved, now we're down to two. I want to get it down to one, but we're down to two. And it may get rejected for environmental or safety reasons, but we got it down to safety.

We created Space Force, We, we, we. Look at what we did. Our military has been totally rebuilt. So we create Space Force which, by and of itself, is a major achievement for an administration. And with us it's one of so many different things.

Right to Try. Everybody know about Right to Try. We did things that nobody ever thought possible. We took care of our vets, our vets. The VA now has the highest rating, 91%. The highest rating that it's had from the beginning, 91% approval rating.

Always, you watch the VA, it was on television every night, people living in a horrible, horrible manner. We got that done. We got accountability done. We got it so that now in the VA, you don't have to wait for four weeks, six weeks, eight weeks, four months to see a doctor. If you can't get a doctor, you go outside, you get the doctor. You have it taken care of and we pay the doctor.

And we've not only made life wonderful for so many people, we've saved tremendous amounts of money, far secondarily, but we've saved a lot of money. And now we have the right to fire bad people in the VA. We had 9,000 people that treated our veterans horribly. In primetime, they would not have treated our veterans badly. But they treated our veterans horribly.

And we have what's called the account, VA Accountability Act. And the accountability says if we see somebody in there that doesn't treat our vets well or they steal, they rob, they do things badly, we say: "Joe you're fired. Get out of here." Before you couldn't do that. You couldn't do that before.

So we've taken care of things, we've done things like nobody's ever thought possible. And that's part of the reason that many people don't like us, because we've done too much.

But we've done it quickly and we were going to sit home and watch a big victory and everybody had us down for a victory. It was going to be great and now we're out here fighting. I said to somebody, I was going to take a few days and relax after our big electoral victory. 10 o'clock it was over. But I was going to take a few days.

And I can say this. Since our election, I believe, which was such a catastrophe, when I watch. And even these guys knew what happened. They know what happened. They're saying: "Wow, Pennsylvania's insurmountable. Wow, Wisconsin." Look at the big leads we had, right. Even though the press said we would lose Wisconsin by 17 points. Even though the press said, Ohio's going to be close, we set a record; Florida's going to be close, we set a record; Texas is going to be close, Texas is going to be close, we set a record.

And we set a record with Hispanic, with the Black community, we set a record with everybody.

Today we see a very important event though. Because right over there, right there, we see the event going to take place. And I'm going to be watching. Because history is going to be made. We're going to see whether or not we have great and courageous leaders, or whether or not we have leaders that should be ashamed of themselves throughout history, throughout eternity they'll be ashamed.

And you know what? If they do the wrong thing, we should never, ever forget that they did. Never forget. We should never ever forget.

With only three of the seven states in question, we win the presidency of the United States. And by the way, it's much more important today than it was 24 hours ago, because I don't. I spoke to David Perdue, what a great person, and Kelly Loeffler, two great people, but it was a setup.

And you know, I said, "We have no backline anymore." The only backline, the only line of demarcation, the only line that we have is the veto of the president of the United States. So this is now, what we're doing, a far more important election than it was two days ago.

I want to thank the more than 140 members of the House. Those are warriors. They're over there working like you've never seen before. Studying, talking, actually going all the way back, studying the roots of the Constitution, because they know we have the right to send a bad vote that was illegally gotten.

They gave these people bad things to vote for and they voted because what did they know? And then when they found out a few weeks later, again, it took them four years to devise this screen.

And the only unhappy person in the United States, single most unhappy, is Hillary Clinton. Because she said: "Why didn't you do this for me four years ago? Why didn't you do this for me four years ago? Change the votes, 10,000 in Michigan. You could have changed the whole thing." But she's not too happy. You know, you don't see her anymore. What happened? Where's Hillary? Where is she?

But I want to thank all of those congressmen and women. I also want to thank our 13, most courageous members of the U.S. Senate. Senator Ted Cruz, Senator Ron Johnson, Senator Josh Hawley, Kelly Loeffler.

And Kelly Loeffler, I'll tell you, she has been, she's been so great. She worked so hard. So let's give her and David a little special hand because it was rigged against them. Let's give her and David.

Kelly Loeffler, David Purdue. They fought a good race. They never had a shot. That equipment should never have been allowed to be used, and I was telling these people don't let him use this stuff.

Marsha Blackburn, terrific person. Mike Braun, Indiana. Steve Daines, great guy. Bill Hagerty, John Kennedy, James Lankford, Cynthia Lummis, Tommy Tuberville, the coach, and Roger Marshall. We want to thank them. Senators that stepped up, We want to thank them.

I actually think though, it takes, again, more courage not to step up, and I think a lot of those people are going to find that out and you better start looking at your leadership, because your leadership has led you down the tubes.

You know, we don't want to give $2,000 to people. We want to give them $600. Oh, great. How does that play politically? Pretty good? And this has nothing to do with politics, but how does it play politically?

China destroyed these people. We didn't destroy. China destroy them, totally destroyed them. We want to give them $600 and they just wouldn't change.

I said give them $2,000, we'll pay it back. We'll pay it back fast. You already owe 26 trillion, give them a couple of bucks. Let them live. Give them a couple of bucks. And some of the people here disagree with me on that, but I just say, "Look, you've got to let people live."

And how does that play though? OK. Number one, it's the right thing to do. But how does that play politically? I think it's the primary reason, one of the primary reasons, the other was just pure cheating. That was the primary, super primary reason. But you can't do that, you got to use your head.

As you know, the media has constantly asserted the outrageous lie that there was no evidence of widespread fraud. Have you ever seen these people? While there is no evidence of fraud. Oh, really? Well, I'm going to read you pages. I hope you don't get bored listening to it. Promise? Don't get bored listening to it, all those hundreds of thousands of people back there. Move them up, please, yeah.

All they, all these people, don't get bored, don't get angry at me because you're going to get bored because it's so much.

The American people do not believe the corrupt, fake news anymore. They have ruined their reputation. But you know, it used to be that they'd argue with me. I'd fight. So I'd fight, they'd fight, I'd fight, they'd fight. Pop pop. You'd believe me, you'd believe them. Somebody comes out. You know, they had their point of view, I had my point of view, but you'd have an argument.

Now what they do is they go silent. It's called suppression and that's what happens in a communist country. That's what they do, they suppress. You don't fight with them anymore. Unless it's a bad story. They have a little bad story about me, they make it 10 times worse and it's a major headline.

But Hunter Biden, they don't talk about him. What happened to Hunter? Where's Hunter? Where's Hunter? They don't talk about him. They'll watch, all the sets will go off. Well, they can't do that because they get good ratings. Their ratings are too good. Now, where's Hunter? You know.

And how come Joe is allowed to give a billion dollars of money to get rid of the prosecutor in Ukraine? How does that happen? I'd ask you that question. How does that happen? Can you imagine if I said that? If I said that it would be a whole different ballgame.

And how come Hunter gets three and a half million dollars from the mayor of Moscow's wife, and gets hundreds of thousands of dollars to sit on an energy board, even though he admits he has no knowledge of energy? And millions of dollars up front.

And how come they go into China and they leave with billions of dollars to manage. "Have you managed money before?" "No, I haven't." "Oh, that's good. Here's about 3 billion." No, they don't talk about that.

No, we have a corrupt media. They've gone silent. They've gone dead. I now realize how good it was if you go back 10 years, I realized how good, even though I didn't necessarily love them, I realized how good. It was like a cleansing motion, right?

But we don't have that anymore. We don't have a fair media anymore. It's suppression. And you have to be very careful with that and they've lost all credibility in this country.

We will not be intimidated into accepting the hoaxes and the lies that we've been forced to believe.

Over the past several weeks, we've amassed overwhelming evidence about a fake election. This is the presidential election. Last night was a little bit better because of the fact that we had a lot of eyes watching one specific state, but they cheated like hell anyway.

You have one of the dumbest governors in the United States. And you know when I endorsed him, and I didn't know this guy, at the request of David Perdue, he said, "Friend of mine's running for governor." "What's his name?" And you know the rest. He was in fourth place, fifth place. I don't know, he was, he was doing poorly. I endorse him, he went like a rocket ship and he won.

And then I had to beat Stacey Abrams with this guy, Brian Kemp. I had to beat Stacey Abrams. And I had to beat Oprah, used to be a friend of mine. You know, I was on her last show, her last week, she picked the five outstanding people. I don't think she thinks that any more. Once I ran for president, I didn't notice there were too many calls coming in from Oprah. Believe it or not, she used to like me. But I was one of the five outstanding people.

And I had a campaign against Michelle Obama and Barack Hussein Obama, against Stacey.

And I had Brian Kemp, who weighs 130 pounds. He said he played offensive line in football. I'm trying to figure that out. I'm still trying to figure that out. He said that the other night, "I was an offensive lineman." I'm saying: "Really? That must have been a very small team." But I look at that and I look at what's happened and he turned out to be a disaster. This stuff happens.

You know, look, I'm not happy with the Supreme Court. They love to rule against me. I picked three people. I fought like hell for them. One in particular, I fought. They all said, "Sir, cut him loose." He's killing the senators. You know, very loyal senators, they're very loyal people, "Sir, cut him loose, he's killing us, sir, cut him loose." I must have gotten half of the senators.

I said: "No, I can't do that, it's unfair to him and it's unfair to the family. He didn't do anything wrong." They made up stories, they're all made-up stories. He didn't do anything wrong. "Cut him loose, sir." I said, "No, I won't do that. We got him through." And you know what, they couldn't give a damn. They couldn't give a damn. Let him rule the right way.

But it almost seems that they're all going out of their way to hurt all of us and to hurt our country. To hurt our country.

You know, I read a story in one of the newspapers recently how I control the three Supreme Court justices. I control them. They're puppets.

I read it about Bill Barr, that he's my personal attorney. That he'll do anything for me. And I said, "You know, it really is genius." Because what they do is that, and it makes it really impossible for them to ever give you a victory, because all of a sudden Bill Barr changed. If you hadn't noticed. I like Bill Barr, but he changed, because he didn't want to be considered my personal attorney.

And the Supreme Court, they rule against me so much. You know why? Because the story is—I haven't spoken to any of them, any of them, since virtually they got in—but the story is that they're my puppets. Right? That they're puppets.

And now the only way they can get out of that because they hate that it's not good in the social circuit. And the only way they get out is to rule against Trump. So let's rule against Trump. And they do that. So I want to congratulate them.

But it shows you the media's genius. In fact, probably if I was the media, I'd do it the same way. I hate to say it. But we got to get them straightened out.

Today, for the sake of our democracy, for the sake of our Constitution, and for the sake of our children, we lay out the case for the entire world to hear. You want to hear it?

(Audience responds: "Yeah")

In every single swing state, local officials, state officials, almost all Democrats, made illegal and unconstitutional changes to election procedures without the mandated approvals by the state legislatures.

That these changes paved a way for fraud on a scale never seen before. I think we go a long way outside of our country when I say that.

So, just in a nutshell, you can't make a change or voting for a federal election unless the state legislature approves it. No judge can do it. Nobody can do it. Only a legislature.

So as an example, in Pennsylvania, or whatever, you have a Republican legislature, you have a Democrat mayor, and you have a lot of Democrats all over the place. They go to the legislature. The legislature laughs at them, says we're not going to do that. They say, thank you very much and they go and make the changes themselves, they do it anyway. And that's totally illegal. That's totally illegal. You can't do that.

In Pennsylvania, the Democrat secretary of state and the Democrat state Supreme Court justices illegally abolished the signature verification requirements just 11 days prior to the election.

So think of what they did. No longer is there signature verification. Oh, that's OK. We want voter ID by the way. But no longer is there a signature verification. Eleven days before the election they say we don't want it. You know why they don't want to? Because they want to cheat. That's the only reason.

Who would even think of that? We don't want to verify a signature?

There were over 205,000 more ballots counted in Pennsylvania. Think of this, you had 205,000 more ballots than you had voters. That means you had two. Where did they come from? You know where they came from? Somebody's imagination, whatever they needed.

So in Pennsylvania, you had 205,000 more votes than you had voters. And the number is actually much greater than that now. That was as of a week ago. And this is a mathematical impossibility unless you want to say it's a total fraud.

So Pennsylvania was defrauded. Over 8,000 ballots in Pennsylvania were cast by people whose names and dates of birth match individuals who died in 2020 and prior to the election. Think of that. Dead people, lots of dead people, thousands. And some dead people actually requested an application. That bothers me even more.

Not only are they voting, they want an application to vote. One of them was 29 years ago, died. It's incredible. Over 14,000 ballots were cast by out-of-state voters, so these are voters that don't live in this state.

And by the way, these numbers are what they call outcome-determinative, meaning these numbers far surpass. I lost by a very little bit. These numbers are massive, massive.

More than 10,000 votes in Pennsylvania were illegally counted, even though they were received after Election Day. In other words, they were received after Election Day. Let's count them anyway.

And what they did in many cases is, they did fraud. They took the date and they moved it back so that it no longer is after Election Day. And more than 60,000 ballots in Pennsylvania were reported received back. They got back before they were ever supposedly mailed out. In other words, you got the ballot back before you mailed it, which is also logically and logistically impossible, right?

Think of that one. You got the ballot back. Let's send the ballots. Oh, they've already been sent. But we got the ballot back before they were sent. I don't think that's too good, right?

Twenty-five thousand ballots in Pennsylvania were requested by nursing home residents, all in a single giant batch, not legal, indicating an enormous, illegal ballot harvesting operation. You're not allowed to do it, it's against the law.

The day before the election, the state of Pennsylvania reported the number of absentee ballots that had been sent out. Yet this number was suddenly and drastically increased by 400,000 people. It was increased, nobody knows where it came from, by 400,000 ballots, one day after the election.

It remains totally unexplained. They said, "Well, ah, we can't figure that." Now, that's many, many times what it would take to overthrow the state. Just that one element. Four hundred thousand ballots appeared from nowhere right after the election.

By the way, Pennsylvania has now seen all of this. They didn't know because it was so quick. They had a vote. They voted. But now they see all this stuff, it's all come to light. Doesn't happen that fast. And they want to recertify their votes. They want to recertify. But the only way that can happen is if Mike Pence agrees to send it back. Mike Pence has to agree to send it back.

(Audience chants: "Send it back.")

And many people in Congress want it sent back.

And think of what you're doing. Let's say you don't do it. Somebody says, "Well, we have to obey the Constitution." And you are, because you're protecting our country and you're protecting the Constitution. So you are.

But think of what happens. Let's say they're stiffs and they're stupid people, and they say, well, we really have no choice. Even though Pennsylvania and other states want to redo their votes. They want to see the numbers. They already have the numbers. Go very quickly. And they want to redo their legislature because many of these votes were taken, as I said, because it wasn't approved by their legislature. You know, that, in itself, is legal. And then you have the scam, and that's all of the things that we're talking about.

But think of this. If you don't do that, that means you will have a president of the United States for four years, with his wonderful son. You will have a president who lost all of these states. Or you will have a president, to put it another way, who was voted on by a bunch of stupid people who lost all of these states.

You will have an illegitimate president. That's what you'll have. And we can't let that happen.

These are the facts that you won't hear from the fake news media. It's all part of the suppression effort. They don't want to talk about it. They don't want to talk about it. In fact, when I started talking about that, I guarantee you, a lot of the television sets and a lot of those cameras went off. And that's a lot of cameras back there. But a lot of them went off.

But these are the things you don't hear about. You don't hear what you just heard. I'm going to go over a few more states. But you don't hear it by the people who want to deceive you and demoralize you and control you. Big tech, media.

Just like the suppression polls that said we're going lose Wisconsin by 17 points. Well, we won Wisconsin. They don't have it that way because they lost just by a little sliver. But they had me down the day before, Washington Post/ABC poll, down 17 points.

I called up a real pollster. I said, "What is that?" "Sir, that's called a suppression poll. I think you're going to win Wisconsin, sir."

I said, "But why don't they make it four or five points?" Because then people vote. But when you're down 17, they say, "Hey, I'm not going to waste my time. I love the president, but there's no way."

Despite that, despite that, we won Wisconsin. It's going to see. I mean, you'll see. But that's called suppression because a lot of people when they see that. It's very interesting. This pollster said, "Sir, if you're down three, four, or five people vote. When you go down 17, they say, 'Let's save. Let's go and have dinner and let's watch the presidential defeat tonight on television, darling.' "

And just like the radical left tries to blacklist you on social media. Every time I put out a tweet, that's, even if it's totally correct, totally correct, I get a flag. I get a flag.

And they also don't let you get out. You know, on Twitter, it's very hard to come onto my account. It's very hard to get out a message. They don't let the message get out nearly like they should. But I've had many people say, "I can't get on your Twitter." I don't care about Twitter. Twitter's bad news. They're all bad news.

But you know what, if you want to, if you want to get out a message and if you want to go through Big tech, social media, they are really, if you're a conservative, if you're a Republican, if you have a big voice, I guess they call it shadow banned, right? Shadow banned. They shadow ban you, and it should be illegal.

I've been telling these Republicans, get rid of Section 230. And for some reason, Mitch and the group, they don't want to put it in there and they don't realize that that's going to be the end of the Republican Party as we know it, but it's never going to be the end of us. Never. Let them get out. Let, let the weak ones get out. This is a time for strength.

They also want to indoctrinate your children in school by teaching them things that aren't so. They want to indoctrinate your children. It's all part of the comprehensive assault on our democracy, and the American people are finally standing up and saying no. This crowd is, again, a testament to it.

I did no advertising, I did nothing. You do have some groups that are big supporters. I want to thank that, Amy, and everybody. We have some incredible supporters, incredible. But we didn't do anything. This just happened. Two months ago, we had a massive crowd come down to Washington. I said, "What are they there for?" "Sir, they're there for you."

We have nothing to do with it. These groups are for, they're forming all over the United States. And we got to remember, in a year from now, you're going to start working on Congress and we got to get rid of the weak Congress, people, the ones that aren't any good, the Liz Cheneys of the world. We got to get rid of them. We got to get rid.

You know, she never wants a soldier brought home, I brought a lot of our soldiers home. I don't know, somewhat like it. They're in countries that nobody even knows the name, nobody knows where they are. They're dying. They're great, but they're dying. They're losing their arms, their legs, their face. I brought them back home, largely back home. Afghanistan, Iraq.

Remember, I used to say in the old days: "Don't go in Iraq. But if you go in, keep the oil." We didn't keep the oil. So stupid. So stupid these people. And Iraq has billions and billions of dollars now in the bank. And what did we do? We got nothing. We never get. But we do actually, we kept the oil here or we get, we did good.

We got rid of the ISIS caliphate. We got rid of plenty of different things that everybody knows and the rebuilding of our military in three years. People said it couldn't be done. And it was all made in the USA, all made in the USA, best equipment in the world.

In Wisconsin, corrupt Democrat-run cities deployed more than 500 illegal, unmanned, unsecured drop boxes, which collected a minimum of 91,000 unlawful votes. It was razor-thin, the loss. This one thing alone is much more than we would need. But there are many things.

They have these lockboxes. And, you know, they'd pick them up and they disappear for two days. People would say where's that box? They disappeared. Nobody even knew where the hell it was.

In addition, over 170,000 absentee votes were counted in Wisconsin without a valid absentee ballot application. So they had a vote, but they had no application, and that's illegal in Wisconsin. Meaning those votes were blatantly done in opposition to state law and they came 100% from Democrat areas such as Milwaukee and Madison, 100%.

In Madison, 17,000 votes were deposited in so-called human drop boxes. You know what that is, right? Where operatives stuff thousands of unsecured ballots into duffle bags on park benches across the city, in complete defiance of cease-and-desist letters from state legislature.

Your state legislatures said don't do it. They're the only ones that can approve it. They gave tens of thousands of votes. They came in in duffle bags. Where the hell did they come from?

According to eyewitness testimony, Postal Service workers in Wisconsin were also instructed to illegally backdate approximately 100,000 ballots. The margin of difference in Wisconsin was less than 20,000 votes. Each one of these things alone wins us the state. Great state. We love the state. We won the state.

In Georgia, your secretary of state who, I can't believe this guy's a Republican. He loves recording telephone conversations. You know, that was? I thought it was a great conversation personally. So did a lot of other. People love that conversation because it says what's going on.

These people are crooked. They're 100%, in my opinion, one of the most corrupt, between your governor and your secretary of state. And now you have it again last night. Just take a look at what happened. What a mess.

And the Democrat Party operatives entered into an illegal and unconstitutional settlement agreement that drastically weakened signature verification and other election security procedures.

Stacey Abrams. She took them to lunch. And I beat her two years ago with a bad candidate, Brian Kemp. But they took, the Democrats took the Republicans to lunch because the secretary of state had no clue what the hell was happening. Unless he did have a clue. That's interesting. Maybe he was with the other side.

But we've been trying to get verifications of signatures in Fulton County, they won't let us do it. The only reason they won't is because we'll find things in the hundreds of thousands. Why wouldn't they let us verify signatures in Fulton County, which is known for being very corrupt. They won't do it. They go to some other county where you would live.

I said, "That's not the problem." The problem is Fulton County, home of Stacey Abrams. She did a good job, I congratulate her. But it was done in such a way that we can't let this stuff happen. We won't have a country if it happens.

As a result, Georgia's absentee ballot rejection rate was more than 10 times lower than previous levels because the criteria was so off.

Forty-eight counties in Georgia, with thousands and thousands of votes, rejected zero ballots. There wasn't one ballot. In other words, in a year in which more mail-in ballots were sent than ever before, and more people were voting by mail for the first time, the rejection rate was drastically lower than it had ever been before.

The only way this can be explained is if tens of thousands of illegitimate votes were added to the tally. That's the only way you could explain it.

By the way, you're talking about tens of thousands. If Georgia had merely rejected the same number of unlawful ballots as in other years, they should have been approximately 45,000 ballots rejected. Far more than what we needed to win, just over 11,000. They should find those votes. They should absolutely find that. Just over 11,000 votes, that's all we need. They defrauded us out of a win in Georgia, and we're not going to forget it.

There's only one reason the Democrats could possibly want to eliminate signature matching, opposed voter ID, and stop citizenship confirmation. "Are you a citizenship?" You're not allowed to ask that question, because they want to steal the election.

The radical left knows exactly what they're doing. They're ruthless and it's time that somebody did something about it. And Mike Pence, I hope you're going to stand up for the good of our Constitution and for the good of our country. And if you're not, I'm going to be very disappointed in you. I will tell you right now. I'm not hearing good stories.

In Fulton County, Republican poll watchers were ejected, in some cases, physically from the room under the false pretense of a pipe burst. Water main burst, everybody leave. Which we now know was a total lie.

Then election officials pull boxes, Democrats, and suitcases of ballots out from under a table. You all saw it on television, totally fraudulent. And illegally scanned them for nearly two hours, totally unsupervised. Tens of thousands of votes. This act coincided with a mysterious vote dump of up to 100,000 votes for Joe Biden, almost none for Trump. Oh, that sounds fair. That was at 1:34 a.m.

The Georgia secretary of state and pathetic governor of Georgia, have reached, although he says I'm a great president. You know, I sort of maybe have to change. He said the other day, "Yes, I do. I disagree with president, but he's been a great president." Good, thanks. Thank you very much.

Because of him and others, you have Brian Kemp. Vote him the hell out of office, please. Well, his rates are so low. You know, his approval rating now, I think it just reached a record low.

They've rejected five separate appeals for an independent and comprehensive audit of signatures in Fulton County. Even without an audit, the number of fraudulent ballots that we've identified across the state is staggering.

Over 10,300 ballots in Georgia were cast by individuals whose names and dates of birth match Georgia residents who died in 2020 and prior to the election.

More than 2,500 ballots were cast by individuals whose names and dates of birth match incarcerated felons in Georgia prison. People who are not allowed to vote.

More than 4,500 illegal ballots were cast by individuals who do not appear on the state's own voter rolls.

Over 18,000 illegal ballots were cast by individuals who registered to vote using an address listed as vacant, according to the Postal Service.

At least 88,000 ballots in Georgia were cast by people whose registrations were illegally backdated.

Sixty-six thousand votes, each one of these is far more than we need. Sixty-six thousand votes in Georgia were cast by individuals under the legal voting age.

And at least 15,000 ballots were cast by individuals who moved out of the state prior to November 3 election. They say they moved right back. They moved right back. Oh, they moved out, they moved right back. OK. They missed Georgia that much. I do. I love Georgia, but it's a corrupt system.

Despite all of this, the margin in Georgia is only 11,779 votes.

Each and every one of these issues is enough to give us a victory in Georgia, a big beautiful victory. Make no mistake, this election was stolen from you, from me and from the country.

And not a single swing state has conducted a comprehensive audit to remove the illegal ballots. This should absolutely occur in every single contested state before the election is certified.

In the state of Arizona, over 36,000 ballots were illegally cast by non-citizens. Two thousand ballots were returned with no address. More than 22,000 ballots were returned before they were ever supposedly mailed out. They returned, but we haven't mailed them yet.

Eleven thousand six hundred more ballots and votes were counted, more than there were actual voters. You see that? So you have more votes again than you have voters.

One hundred and fifty thousand people registered in Maricopa County after the registration deadline. One hundred and three thousand ballots in the county were sent for electronic adjudication with no Republican observers.

In Clark County, Nevada, the accuracy settings on signature verification machines were purposely lowered before they were used to count over 130,000 ballots.

If you signed your name as Santa Claus, it would go through.

There were also more than 42,000 double votes in Nevada. Over 150,000 people were hurt so badly by what took place. And 1,500 ballots were cast by individuals whose names and dates of birth match Nevada residents who died in 2020 prior to November 3 election. More than 8,000 votes were cast by individuals who had no address and probably didn't live there.

The margin in Nevada is down at a very low number, any of these things would have taken care of the situation. We would have won Nevada, also. Every one of these we're going over, we win.

In Michigan, quickly, the secretary of state, a real great one, flooded the state with unsolicited mail-in ballot applications sent to every person on the rolls in direct violation of state law.

More than 17,000 Michigan ballots were cast by individuals whose names and dates of birth match people who were deceased.

In Wayne County, that's a great one. That's Detroit. One hundred and seventy-four thousand ballots were counted without being tied to an actual registered voter. Nobody knows where they came from.

Also, in Wayne County, poll watchers observed canvassers rescanning batches of ballots over and over again, up to three or four or five times.

In Detroit, turnout was 139% of registered voters. Think of that. So you had 139% of the people in Detroit voting. This is in Michigan. Detroit, Michigan.

A career employee of the Detroit, City of Detroit, testified under penalty of perjury that she witnessed city workers coaching voters to vote straight Democrat while accompanying them to watch who they voted for. When a Republican came in, they wouldn't talk to him.

The same worker was instructed not to ask for any voter ID and not to attempt to validate any signatures if they were Democrats. She also told to illegally, and was told, backdate ballots received after the deadline and reports that thousands and thousands of ballots were improperly backdated. That's Michigan.

Four witnesses have testified under penalty of perjury that after officials in Detroit announced the last votes had been counted, tens of thousands of additional ballots arrived without required envelopes. Every single one was for a Democrat. I got no votes.

At 6:31 a.m. in the early morning hours after voting had ended, Michigan suddenly reported 147,000 votes. An astounding 94% went to Joe Biden, who campaigned brilliantly from his basement. Only a couple of percentage points went to Trump.

Such gigantic and one-sided vote dumps were only observed in a few swing states and they were observed in the states where it was necessary.

You know what's interesting? President Obama beat Biden in every state other than the swing states where Biden killed them, but the swing states were the ones that mattered.

They're always just enough to push Joe Biden barely into the lead. We were ahead by a lot and within a number of hours we were losing by a little.

In addition, there is the highly troubling matter of Dominion Voting Systems. In one Michigan county alone, 6,000 votes were switched from Trump to Biden and the same systems are used in the majority of states in our country.

Senator William Ligon, a great gentleman, chairman of Georgia's senate judiciary subcommittee. Senator Ligon, highly respected, on elections has written a letter describing his concerns with Dominion in Georgia.

He wrote, and I quote, The Dominion Voting Machines employed in Fulton County had an astronomical and astounding 93.67% error rate. It's only wrong 93% of the time in the scanning of ballots requiring a review panel to adjudicate or determine the voter's interest in over 106,000 ballots out of a total of 113,000.

Think of it. You go in and you vote and then they tell people who you supposed to be voting for. They make up whatever they want. Nobody's ever even heard.

They adjudicate your vote. They say, Well, we don't think Trump wants to vote for Trump. We think he wants to vote for Biden. Put it down for Biden.

The national average for such an error rate is far less than 1% and yet you're at 93%. The source of this astronomical error rate must be identified to determine if these machines were set up or destroyed to allow for a third party to disregard the actual ballot cast by the registered voter.

The letter continues. There is clear evidence that tens of thousands of votes were switched from President Trump to former Vice President Biden in several counties in Georgia.

For example, in Bibb County, President Trump was reported to have 29,391 votes at 9:11 p.m. Eastern time, while simultaneously Vice President Joe Biden was reported to have 17,213. Minutes later, just minutes, at the next update, these vote numbers switched with President Trump going way down to 17,000 and Biden going way up to 29,391. And that was very quick, a 12,000 vote switch all in Mr. Biden's favor.

So, I mean, I could go on and on about this fraud that took place in every state, and all of these legislatures want this back. I don't want to do it to you because I love you and it's freezing out here. But I could just go on forever. I can tell you this.

(Audience chants: "We love you.")

So when you hear, when you hear, while there is no evidence to prove any wrongdoing, this is the most fraudulent thing anybody has, this is a criminal enterprise. This is a criminal enterprise. And the press will say, and I'm sure they won't put any of that on there, because that's no good. And you ever see, while there is no evidence to back President Trump's assertion.

I could go on for another hour reading this stuff to you and telling you about it. There's never been anything like it.

Think about it. Detroit had more votes than it had voters. Pennsylvania had 205,000 more votes than it had more. But you don't have to go any. Between that, I think that's almost better than dead people if you think, right? More votes than they had voters. And many other states also.

It's a disgrace that the United States of America, tens of millions of people, are allowed to go vote without so much as even showing identification.

In no state is there any question or effort made to verify the identity, citizenship, residency or eligibility of the votes cast.

The Republicans have to get tougher. You're not going to have a Republican Party if you don't get tougher. They want to play so straight. They want to play so, sir, yes, the United States. The Constitution doesn't allow me to send them back to the States. Well, I say, yes it does, because the Constitution says you have to protect our country and you have to protect our Constitution, and you can't vote on fraud. And fraud breaks up everything, doesn't it? When you catch somebody in a fraud, you're allowed to go by very different rules.

So I hope Mike has the courage to do what he has to do. And I hope he doesn't listen to the RINOs and the stupid people that he's listening to.

It is also widely understood that the voter rolls are crammed full of non-citizens, felons and people who have moved out of state and individuals who are otherwise ineligible to vote. Yet Democrats oppose every effort to clean up their voter rolls. They don't want to clean them up. They're loaded.

And how many people here know other people, that when there are hundreds of thousands and then millions of ballots got sent out, got three, four, five, six, and I heard one, who got seven ballots. And then they say you didn't quite make it, sir.

We won in a landslide. This was a landslide. They said it's not American to challenge the election. This the most corrupt election in the history, maybe of the world.

You know, you could go third-world countries, but I don't think they had hundreds of thousands of votes and they don't have voters for them. I mean no matter where you go, nobody would think this.

In fact, it's so egregious, it's so bad that a lot of people don't even believe it. It's so crazy that people don't even believe it. It can't be true. So they don't believe it.

This is not just a matter of domestic politics, this is a matter of national security.

So today, in addition to challenging the certification of the election, I'm calling on Congress and the state legislatures to quickly pass sweeping election reforms, and you better do it before we have no country left.

Today is not the end, it's just the beginning.

With your help over the last four years, we built the greatest political movement in the history of our country and nobody even challenges that.

I say that over and over, and I never get challenged by the fakeness, and they challenge almost everything we say.

But our fight against the big donors, big media, big tech, and others is just getting started. This is the greatest in history. There's never been a movement like that.

You look back there all the way to the Washington Monument. It's hard to believe.

We must stop the steal and then we must ensure that such outrageous election fraud never happens again, can never be allowed to happen again.

But we're going forward. We'll take care of going forward. We've got to take care of going back. Don't let them talk. OK, well, we promised. I've had a lot of people. Sir, you're at 96% for four years. I said I'm not interested right now. I'm interested in right there.

With your help, we will finally pass powerful requirements for voter ID. You need an ID to cash a check. You need an ID to go to a bank, to buy alcohol, to drive a car. Every person should need to show an ID in order to cast your most important thing, a vote.

We will also require proof of American citizenship in order to vote in American elections. We just had a good victory in court on that one, actually.

We will ban ballot harvesting and prohibit the use of unsecured drop boxes to commit rampant fraud. These drop boxes are fraudulent.

Therefore, they get—they disappear, and then all of a sudden they show up. It's fraudulent.

We will stop the practice of universal unsolicited mail-in balloting.

We will clean up the voter rolls that ensure that every single person who casts a vote is a citizen of our country, a resident of the state in which they vote and their vote is cast in a lawful and honest manner.

We will restore the vital civic tradition of in-person voting on Election Day so that voters can be fully informed when they make their choice.

We will finally hold big tech accountable. And if these people had courage and guts, they would get rid of Section 230, something that no other company, no other person in America, in the world has.

All of these tech monopolies are going to abuse their power and interfere in our elections, and it has to be stopped. And the Republicans have to get a lot tougher, and so should the Democrats. They should be regulated, investigated, and brought to justice under the fullest extent of the law. They're totally breaking the law.

Together, we will drain the Washington swamp and we will clean up the corruption in our nation's capital. We have done a big job on it, but you think it's easy. It's a dirty business. It's a dirty business. You have a lot of bad people out there.

Despite everything we've been through, looking out all over this country and seeing fantastic crowds. Although this, I think, is our all-time record. I think you have 250,000 people. 250,000.

Looking out at all the amazing patriots here today, I have never been more confident in our nation's future. Well, I have to say, we have to be a little bit careful. That's a nice statement, but we have to be a little careful with that statement.

If we allow this group of people to illegally take over our country because it's illegal when the votes are illegal when the way they got there is illegal when the states that vote are given false and fraudulent information.

We are the greatest country on Earth and we are headed and were headed in the right direction.

You know, the wall is built. We're doing record numbers at the wall. Now, they want to take down the wall. Let's let everyone flow in. Let's let everybody flow in. We did a great job in the wall. Remember, the wall, they said it could never be done. One of the largest infrastructure projects we've ever had in this country, and it's had a tremendous impact, that we got rid of catch and release. We got rid of all of this stuff that we had to live with.

But now, the caravans, I think Biden's getting in, the caravans are forming again. They want to come in again and rip off our country. Can't let it happen.

As this enormous crowd shows, we have truth and justice on our side. We have a deep and enduring love for America in our hearts. We love our country.

We have overwhelming pride in this great country and we have it deep in our souls. Together, we are determined to defend and preserve government of the people, by the people and for the people.

Our brightest days are before us. Our greatest achievements, still away.

I think one of our great achievements will be election security. Because nobody until I came along had any idea how corrupt our elections were.

And again, most people would stand there at 9 o'clock in the evening and say I want to thank you very much, and they go off to some other life. But I said something's wrong here, something is really wrong, can have happened.

And we fight. We fight like hell. And if you don't fight like hell, you're not going to have a country anymore.

Our exciting adventures and boldest endeavors have not yet begun. My fellow Americans, for our movement, for our children, and for our beloved country.

And I say this despite all that's happened. The best is yet to come.

So we're going to, we're going to walk down Pennsylvania Avenue. I love Pennsylvania Avenue. And we're going to the Capitol, and we're going to try and give.

The Democrats are hopeless, they never vote for anything. Not even one vote. But we're going to try and give our Republicans, the weak ones because the strong ones don't need any of our help. We're going to try and give them the kind of pride and boldness that they need to take back our country.

So let's walk down Pennsylvania Avenue.

I want to thank you all. God bless you and God Bless America.

Thank you all for being here. This is incredible. Thank you very much. Thank you.

APPENDIX C

Constitutional Law Scholars on President Trump's First Amendment Defense[23]

February 5, 2021

Next week the Senate will conduct an impeachment trial to determine whether former President Trump should be disqualified from holding future office for inciting insurrection and subverting America's constitutional democratic process in multiple respects. At that trial, President Trump's lawyers plan to defend his actions on January 6 by arguing that the First Amendment shields him from conviction. We, the undersigned constitutional law scholars, write to explain why this is wrong.

The First Amendment is no bar to the Senate convicting former President Trump and disqualifying him from holding future office. Although we differ from one another in our politics, disagree on many questions of constitutional law, and take different approaches to understanding the Constitution's text, history, and context, we all agree that any First Amendment defense raised by President Trump's attorneys would be legally frivolous. In other words, we all agree that the First Amendment does not prevent the Senate from convicting President Trump and disqualifying him from holding future office.

I. <u>The First Amendment does not apply in impeachment proceedings, so it cannot provide a defense for President Trump.</u>

Many of us believe that the First Amendment simply does not apply here. The First Amendment limits the government's ability to make it unlawful to engage in speech, practice a religion, peaceably assemble, or petition the government. Thus, when lawyers say that a defendant established a First Amendment defense in a court case, what they mean is that the defendant demonstrated that the government could not make their conduct unlawful.

But Congress's power to impeach is not limited to unlawful acts. Instead, federal officers can be impeached for lawful conduct, and violations of an officer's oath of office can constitute impeachable "high Crimes or misdemeanors" under the Constitution even if no law has been violated. For example, federal judges can be—and have been—impeached for presiding over trials while intoxicated. That is

---

[23] Portions of this letter were inserted into the record. *See* 167 Cong. Rec. S649 (daily ed. Feb. 11, 2021) (statement of Rep. Neguse). For the full letter, *see Lawyers Call Trump's Defense 'Legally Frivolous'*, N.Y. Times (Feb. 5, 2021), https://www.nytimes.com/interactive/2021/02/05/us/first-amendment-lawyers-trump-impeachment-defense.html.

not a federal crime, but it is a violation of the judicial oath to faithfully and impartially execute a federal judge's duties. Likewise, a President or a Secretary of Defense could be impeached for not defending the United States against a foreign attack. Again, that is not necessarily a violation of any criminal law, but it is certainly a violation of an oath to defend the United States Constitution. And for the same reason, a President could be impeached for publicly renouncing their oath "to preserve, protect, and defend the Constitution of the United States." Imagine a President who publicly announces, "I no longer promise to preserve the Constitution." Such a declaration would not be illegal—indeed, the First Amendment would almost certainly bar Congress from making it illegal—but the President could still be impeached for betraying the oath of office.

As a result, asking whether President Trump was engaged in lawful First Amendment activity misses the point entirely. Regardless of whether President Trump's conduct on and around January 6 was lawful, he may be constitutionally convicted in an impeachment trial if the Senate determines that his behavior was a sufficiently egregious violation of his oath of office to constitute a "high Crime[ ] or misdemeanor[ ]" under the Constitution. If so, he can be convicted and disqualified from future office regardless of whether he would have a First Amendment defense in a subsequent criminal prosecution.

II. <u>Even if the First Amendment applies in impeachment proceedings, it does not prohibit conviction and disqualification for violating the President's Oath of Office.</u>

Many of us believe that, regardless of whether the First Amendment does or does not apply to impeachment, President Trump can be convicted and disqualified because he is accused of violating his oath through an "extraordinary, unprecedented repudiation of the President's duties to protect the government" through his "further acts and omissions after he incited the crowd to attack the Capitol"—namely, by allegedly watching the mob storm Congress on television and "not immediately taking action to protect Congress and the Capitol." While reasonable people can disagree as to the scope of free speech rights in specific contexts (such as the scope of the government's power to limit its own employees' public expression), no reasonable scholar or jurist could conclude that President Trump had a First Amendment right to incite a violent attack on the seat of the legislative branch, or then to sit back and watch on television as Congress was terrorized and the Capitol sacked.

On the contrary, the Constitution imposes an affirmative duty on the President to "take care that the laws be faithfully executed," and willful violations of that duty are an impeachable offense. Accordingly, if the Senate concludes that President Trump willfully failed to intervene to protect Congress from a mob—indeed, one he incited—in violation of the presidential duty to take care to faithfully execute the law, the First Amendment offers him no protection at all from impeachment. The First Amendment protects the freedoms of speech, press, religion, assembly, and petition; it does not grant the President the freedom to engage in a willful dereliction of duty.

III. <u>The President's speech and conduct around January 6 constitute unprotected incitement</u>

Even if the principles of First Amendment law are applicable in the impeachment context (and many of us believe they are not), many of us believe there is an extraordinarily strong argument that the Supreme Court's standards, articulated in *Brandenburg v. Ohio*, for when the Government may criminally punish an individual's deliberate incitement of others to engage in imminent lawless acts are satisfied in this case.

President Trump's speech, and the overall course of his conduct, advanced the factually baseless position that the election had been "stolen" and, further, that immediate action was necessary to prevent Vice President Pence and Congress from counting and confirming the votes of Electors that had been submitted (and certified) by the States. The evidence shows that President Trump deliberately assembled the crowd of supporters; that he steeled his supporters for action and knew that they were ready to take immediate action; that he directed them to take such immediate action; that President Trump said he would be with them in such action and supported such action; that he intended such action to accomplish the unlawful disruption of the constitutional processes of Congress in counting the votes of Electors and certifying the results; and that many persons in the mob that attacked Congress and the Capitol understood themselves to be doing exactly what President Trump had directed and intended for them to do.

In this context and under the circumstances, many of us believe there is a powerful case that even under the Supreme Court's narrow standards for when speech inciting violence is not constitutionally protected, President Trump's words and conduct were unprotected. His words and conduct were, in the words of the *Brandenburg* case, "directed to inciting or producing imminent lawless action and * * * * likely to * * * * produce such action." * * * *

As scholars of constitutional law, we know there are many difficult questions of First Amendment law. But the permissibility of President Trump's impeachment trial is not one of them. The First

Amendment is no defense to the article of impeachment leveled against the former President, because the First Amendment does not apply in impeachment proceedings; because the president does not have a First Amendment right to incite a mob and then sit back and do nothing as the hostile mob invades the Capitol and terrorizes Congress; or because, in context, President Trump engaged in unlawful incitement. Accordingly, while we express no view here on the ultimate question of whether the Senate should convict President Trump and disqualify him from future office, we urge the Senate not to base its decision on the erroneous understanding of the First Amendment urged by President Trump's lawyers. * * * * (Signatures omitted).

APPENDIX D

S. RES. 47

To provide for related procedures concerning the article of impeachment against Donald John Trump, former President of the United States.

IN THE SENATE OF THE UNITED STATES

FEBRUARY 9, 2021

Mr. SCHUMER (for himself and Mr. MCCONNELL) submitted the following resolution; which was considered and agreed to

---

RESOLUTION

To provide for related procedures concerning the article of impeachment against Donald John Trump, former President of the United States.

Resolved,

Section 1. The House of Representatives shall file its record with the Secretary of the Senate, which will consist of those publicly available materials that have been submitted to or produced by the House Judiciary Committee, including transcripts of public hearings or mark-ups and any materials printed by the House of Representatives or the House Judiciary Committee pursuant to House Resolution 24 or House Resolution 40. All materials filed pursuant to this section shall be printed and made available to all parties.

Sec. 2. When, pursuant to Senate Resolution 16, the Senate convenes as a Court of Impeachment on Tuesday, February 9, 2021, there shall immediately be 4 hours of argument by the parties, equally divided, on the question whether Donald John Trump is subject to the jurisdiction of a court of impeachment for acts committed while President of the United States, notwithstanding the expiration of his term in that office. Each side may determine the number of persons to present argument on the foregoing question. The Senate, without any intervening action, motion, or amendment, except for deliberation by the Senate, if so ordered under the Rules of Procedure and Practice in the Senate When Sitting on Impeachment Trials (referred to in this resolution as the "Rules of Impeachment"), shall then decide the foregoing question by the yeas and nays. If a majority of Senators voting, a quorum being present, shall vote in the negative, the Senate shall order that the article of impeachment be immediately dismissed and the Secretary shall notify the House of Representatives of the order of dismissal. If a majority of Senators voting, a quorum being present, shall vote in the affirmative, the Senate shall proceed as provided in this resolution.

Sec. 3. The former President and the House of Representatives shall have until 9:00 a.m. on Wednesday, February 10, 2021, to file any motions permitted under the Rules of Impeachment with the exception of motions to subpoena witnesses or documents or any other evidentiary motions. Responses to any such motions shall be filed no later than 11:00 a.m. on Wednesday, February 10, 2021. All materials filed pursuant to this section shall be filed with the Secretary and be printed and made available to all parties. Arguments on such motions shall begin at 12:00 p.m. on Wednesday, February 10, 2021, and each side may determine the number of persons to make its presentation, following which the Senate shall deliberate, if so ordered under the Rules of Impeachment, and vote on any such motions.

Sec. 4. Following the disposition of such motions, or if no motions are made, then the House of Representatives shall make its presentation in support of the article of impeachment for a period of time not to exceed 16 hours, over up to 2 session days. If no motions are made under section 3, the House of Representatives shall begin its presentation at 12:00 p.m. on Wednesday, February 10, 2021. Following the House of Representatives' presentation, the former President shall make his presentation for a period not to exceed 16 hours, over up to 2 session days. Each side may determine the number of persons to make its presentation. Each side shall have the right to decide for how many hours it shall make its presentation on each of the up to 2 session days allotted to it, except that neither side shall make its presentation for more than 8 hours on any single session day. The parties' presentations need not be limited to argument from the record described in section 1.

Sec. 5. Upon the conclusion of the period allotted for presentations by the parties as provided under section 4, Senators may question the parties for a period of time not to exceed 4 hours over not more than 1 session day.

Sec. 6. Upon conclusion of the period allotted for Senators' questions as provided under section 5, there shall be 2 hours of argument, equally divided between the parties, followed by deliberation by the Senate, if so ordered under the Rules of Impeachment, on the question of whether it shall be in order to consider and debate under the Rules of Impeachment any motion to subpoena witnesses or documents. The Senate, without any intervening action, motion, or amendment, shall then decide by the yeas and nays whether it shall be in order to consider and debate under the Rules of Impeachment any motion to subpoena witnesses or documents. Following the disposition of that question, other motions provided under the Rules of Impeachment shall be in order.

Sec. 7. (a) If the Senate agrees to allow either the House of Representatives or the former President to subpoena witnesses, the witnesses shall first be deposed and the parties shall be allowed other appropriate discovery. The Senate shall decide after deposition and other appropriate discovery which, if any, witnesses shall testify, pursuant to the Rules of Impeachment. No testimony shall be admissible in the Senate unless the parties have had the opportunity to depose such witnesses and to conduct other appropriate discovery.

(b) If the Senate agrees to allow either party to subpoena witnesses, provisions for the admission of evidence, issuance of subpoenas, arrangements for depositions, other appropriate discovery, testimony by witnesses in the Senate, if such testimony is ordered by the Senate, and any related matters are to be determined by subsequent resolution of the Senate.

Sec. 8. (a) If the Senate decides that no party shall be permitted to subpoena witnesses pursuant to section 6, the House of Representatives shall be recognized to make a motion to admit into evidence the materials relied upon by the House of Representatives during the trial. The House of Representatives shall be recognized to make such a motion, however, only if it has disclosed to the former President all materials it will move to admit into evidence at least 48 hours before making said motion. Arguments on the motion shall be limited to 1 hour equally divided. The Senate, without any intervening action, motion, or amendment, shall then decide by the yeas and nays whether to admit into evidence such materials. If a majority of Senators voting, a quorum being present, shall vote in the affirmative, the materials shall be admitted into evidence. If a majority of Senators voting, a quorum being present, shall vote in the negative, the materials shall not be admitted into evidence. The former President shall then be recognized to make a motion to admit into evidence the materials relied upon by the former President during the trial. The former President shall be recognized to make such a motion, however, only if he has disclosed to the House of Representatives all materials he will move to admit into evidence at least 48 hours before making said motion. Arguments on the motion shall be limited to 1 hour equally divided. The Senate, without any intervening action, motion, or amendment, shall then decide by the yeas and nays whether to admit into evidence such materials. If a majority of Senators voting, a quorum being present, shall vote in the affirmative, the materials shall be admitted into evidence. If a majority of Senators voting, a quorum being present, shall vote in the negative, the materials shall not be admitted into evidence.

(b) The disclosure requirements established under subsection (a) shall not apply to evidence discovered by the movant after the disclosure deadline, so long as the movant declares in writing that the movant was unaware of such evidence until after the disclosure deadline, and that such evidence could not reasonably have been discovered until after the disclosure deadline.

(c) The admission of any evidence pursuant to this section shall not be treated as a concession by any party as to the truth of the matter asserted by the parties, and the Senate as the trier of fact shall decide the weight to be given such evidence.

Sec. 9. Unless the Senate shall have already voted on the article of impeachment, the Senate shall convene as a Court of Impeachment at 2:00 p.m. on Sunday, February 14, 2021, notwithstanding rule III of the Rules of Impeachment.

Sec. 10. Immediately upon the conclusion of any action by the Senate under section 8, or immediately upon the next day on which the Senate reconvenes as a Court of Impeachment after the conclusion of such action, the Senate shall proceed to final arguments as provided in the Rules of Impeachment, waiving the 2-person rule contained in rule XXII of the Rules of Impeachment. Such arguments shall not exceed 4 hours, equally divided between the parties.

Sec. 11. At the conclusion of final arguments as provided under section 10, the Senate, without intervening action, except for deliberation if so ordered under the Rules of Impeachment, shall vote on the article of impeachment.

Appendix

THE CONSTITUTION OF THE UNITED STATES

We the People of the United States, in Order to form a more perfect Union, establish Justice, insure domestic Tranquility, provide for the common defence, promote the general Welfare, and secure the Blessings of Liberty to ourselves and our Posterity, do ordain and establish this Constitution for the United States of America.

ARTICLE I

Section 1. All legislative Powers herein granted shall be vested in a Congress of the United States, which shall consist of a Senate and House of Representatives.

Section 2. [1] The House of Representatives shall be composed of Members chosen every second Year by the People of the several States, and the Electors in each State shall have the Qualifications requisite for Electors of the most numerous Branch of the State Legislature.

[2] No Person shall be a Representative who shall not have attained to the Age of twenty five Years, and been seven Years a Citizen of the United States, and who shall not, when elected, be an Inhabitant of that State in which he shall be chosen.

[3] Representatives and direct Taxes shall be apportioned among the several States which may be included within this Union, according to their respective Numbers, which shall be determined by adding to the whole Number of free Persons, including those bound to Service for a Term of Years, and excluding Indians not taxed, three fifths of all other Persons. The actual Enumeration shall be made within three Years after the first Meeting of the Congress of the United States, and within every subsequent Term of ten Years, in such Manner as they shall by Law direct. The Number of Representatives shall not exceed one for every thirty Thousand, but each State shall have at Least one Representative; and until such enumeration shall be made, the State of New Hampshire shall be entitled to chuse three, Massachusetts eight, Rhode Island and Providence Plantations one, Connecticut five, New York six, New Jersey four, Pennsylvania eight, Delaware one, Maryland six,

Virginia ten, North Carolina five, South Carolina five, and Georgia three.

[4] When vacancies happen in the Representation from any State, the Executive Authority thereof shall issue Writs of Election to fill such Vacancies.

[5] The House of Representatives shall chuse their Speaker and other Officers; and shall have the sole Power of Impeachment.

Section 3. [1] The Senate of the United States shall be composed of two Senators from each State, chosen by the Legislature thereof, for six Years; and each Senator shall have one Vote.

[2] Immediately after they shall be assembled in Consequence of the first Election, they shall be divided as equally as may be into three Classes. The Seats of the Senators of the first Class shall be vacated at the Expiration of the second Year, of the second Class at the Expiration of the fourth Year, and of the third Class at the Expiration of the sixth Year, so that one third may be chosen every second Year; and if Vacancies happen by Resignation, or otherwise, during the Recess of the Legislature of any State, the Executive thereof may make temporary Appointments until the next Meeting of the Legislature, which shall then fill such Vacancies.

[3] No Person shall be a Senator who shall not have attained to the Age of Thirty Years, and been nine Years a Citizen of the United States, and who shall not, when elected, be an Inhabitant of that State for which he shall be chosen.

[4] The Vice President of the United States shall be President of the Senate, but shall have no Vote, unless they be equally divided.

[5] The Senate shall chuse their other Officers, and also a President pro tempore, in the absence of the Vice President, or when he shall exercise the Office of President of the United States.

[6] The Senate shall have the sole Power to try all Impeachments. When sitting for that purpose, they shall be on Oath or Affirmation. When the President of the United States is tried, the Chief Justice shall preside: And no Person shall be convicted without the Concurrence of two thirds of the Members present.

[7] Judgment in Cases of Impeachment shall not extend further than to removal from Office, and disqualification to hold and enjoy any Office of honor, Trust or Profit under the United States: but the Party convicted shall nevertheless be liable and subject to Indictment, Trial, Judgment and Punishment, according to Law.

Section 4. [1] The Times, Places and Manner of holding Elections for Senators and Representatives, shall be prescribed in each State by the Legislature thereof; but the Congress may at any time by Law make or alter such Regulations, except as to the Places of chusing Senators.

[2] The Congress shall assemble at least once in every Year, and such Meeting shall be on the first Monday in December, unless they shall by Law appoint a different Day.

Section 5. [1] Each House shall be the Judge of the Elections, Returns and Qualifications of its own Members, and a Majority of each shall constitute a Quorum to do Business; but a smaller Number may adjourn from day to day, and may be authorized to compel the Attendance of absent Members, in such Manner, and under such Penalties as each House may provide.

[2] Each House may determine the Rules of its Proceedings, punish its Members for disorderly Behavior, and, with the Concurrence of two thirds, expel a Member.

[3] Each House shall keep a Journal of its Proceedings, and from time to time publish the same, excepting such Parts as may in their Judgment require Secrecy; and the Yeas and Nays of the Members of either House on any question shall, at the Desire of one fifth of those Present, be entered on the Journal.

[4] Neither House, during the Session of Congress, shall, without the Consent of the other, adjourn for more than three days, nor to any other Place than that in which the two Houses shall be sitting.

Section 6. [1] The Senators and Representatives shall receive a Compensation for their Services, to be ascertained by Law, and paid out of the Treasury of the United States. They shall in all Cases, except Treason, Felony and Breach of the Peace, be privileged from Arrest during their Attendance at the Session of their respective Houses, and in going to and returning from the same; and for any Speech or Debate in either House, they shall not be questioned in any other Place.

[2] No Senator or Representative shall, during the Time for which he was elected, be appointed to any civil Office under the Authority of the United States, which shall have been created, or the Emoluments whereof shall have been encreased during such time; and no Person holding any Office under the United States, shall be a Member of either House during his Continuance in Office.

Section 7. [1] All Bills for raising Revenue shall originate in the House of Representatives; but the Senate may propose or concur with Amendments as on other Bills.

[2] Every Bill which shall have passed the House of Representatives and the Senate, shall, before it become a Law, be presented to the President of the United States; If he approve he shall sign it, but if not he shall return it, with his Objections to the House in which it shall have originated, who shall enter the Objections at large on their Journal, and proceed to reconsider it. If after such Reconsideration two thirds of that House shall agree to pass the Bill, it shall be sent, together with the Objections, to the other House, by which it shall likewise be reconsidered, and if approved by two thirds of that House, it shall become a Law. But in all such Cases the Votes of both Houses shall be determined by yeas and Nays, and the Names of the Persons voting for and against the Bill shall be entered on the Journal of each House respectively. If any Bill shall not be returned by the President within ten Days (Sundays excepted) after it shall have been presented to him, the Same shall be a Law, in like Manner as if he had signed it, unless the Congress by their Adjournment prevents its Return, in which Case it shall not be a Law.

[3] Every Order, Resolution, or Vote to Which the Concurrence of the Senate and House of Representatives may be necessary (except on a question of Adjournment) shall be presented to the President of the United States; and before the Same shall take Effect, shall be approved by him, or being disapproved by him, shall be repassed by two thirds of the Senate and House of Representatives, according to the Rules and Limitations prescribed in the Case of a Bill.

Section 8. [1] The Congress shall have Power To lay and collect Taxes, Duties, Imposts and Excises, to pay the Debts and provide for the common Defence and general Welfare of the United States; but all Duties, Imposts and Excises shall be uniform throughout the United States;

[2] To borrow money on the credit of the United States;

[3] To regulate Commerce with foreign Nations, and among the several States, and with the Indian Tribes;

[4] To establish an uniform Rule of Naturalization, and uniform Laws on the subject of bankruptcies throughout the United States;

[5] To coin Money, regulate the Value thereof, and of foreign Coin, and fix the Standard of Weights and Measures;

[6] To provide the Punishment of counterfeiting the Securities and current Coin of the United States;

[7] To establish Post Offices and post Roads;

[8] To promote the Progress of Science and useful Arts, by securing for limited Times to Authors and inventors the exclusive Right to their respective Writings and Discoveries;

[9] To constitute Tribunals inferior to the supreme Court;

[10] To define and punish Piracies and Felonies committed on the high Seas, and Offenses against the Law of Nations:

[11] To declare War, grant Letters of Marque and Reprisal, and make Rules concerning Captures on Land and Water;

[12] To raise and support Armies, but no Appropriation of Money to that Use shall be for a longer Term than two Years;

[13] To provide and maintain a Navy;

[14] To make Rules for the Government and Regulation of the land and naval Forces;

[15] To provide for calling forth the Militia to execute the Laws of the Union, suppress Insurrections and repel Invasions;

[16] To provide for organizing, arming, and disciplining, the Militia, and for governing such Part of them as may be employed in the Service of the United States, reserving to the States respectively, the Appointment of the Officers, and the Authority of training the Militia according to the discipline prescribed by Congress;

[17] To exercise exclusive Legislation in all Cases whatsoever, over such District (not exceeding ten Miles square) as may, by Cession of particular States, and the Acceptance of Congress, become the Seat of the Government of the United States, and to exercise like Authority over all Places purchased by the Consent of the Legislature of the State in which the Same shall be, for the Erection of Forts, Magazines, Arsenals, dock-Yards, and other needful Buildings;—And

[18] To make all Laws which shall be necessary and proper for carrying into Execution the foregoing Powers, and all other Powers vested by this Constitution in the Government of the United States, or in any Department or Officer thereof.

Section 9. [1] The Migration or Importation of such Persons as any of the States now existing shall think proper to admit, shall not be prohibited by the Congress prior to the Year one thousand eight hundred and eight, but a Tax or duty may be imposed on such Importation, not exceeding ten dollars for each Person.

[2] The privilege of the Writ of Habeas Corpus shall not be suspended, unless when in Cases of Rebellion or Invasion the public Safety may require it.

[3] No Bill of Attainder or ex post facto Law shall be passed.

[4] No Capitation, or other direct, Tax shall be laid, unless in Proportion to the Census or Enumeration herein before directed to be taken.

[5] No Tax or Duty shall be laid on Articles exported from any State.

[6] No Preference shall be given by any Regulation of Commerce or Revenue to the Ports of one State over those of another: nor shall Vessels bound to, or from, one State, be obliged to enter, clear, or pay Duties in another.

[7] No Money shall be drawn from the Treasury, but in Consequence of Appropriations made by Law; and a regular Statement and Account of the Receipts and Expenditures of all public Money shall be published from time to time.

[8] No Title of Nobility shall be granted by the United States: And no Person holding any Office of Profit or Trust under them, shall, without the Consent of the Congress, accept of any present, Emolument, Office, or Title, of any kind whatever, from any King, Prince, or foreign State.

Section 10. [1] No State shall enter into any Treaty, Alliance, or Confederation; grant Letters of Marque and Reprisal; coin Money; emit Bills of Credit; make any Thing but gold and silver Coin a Tender in Payment of Debts; pass any Bill of Attainder, ex post facto Law, or Law impairing the obligation of Contracts, or grant any Title of Nobility.

[2] No State shall, without the Consent of the Congress, lay any Imposts or Duties on Imports or Exports, except what may be absolutely necessary for executing its inspection Laws: and the net Produce of all Duties and Imposts, laid by any State on Imports or Exports, shall be for the Use of the Treasury of the United States; and all such Laws shall be subject to the Revision and Controul of the Congress.

[3] No State shall, without the Consent of Congress, lay any Duty of Tonnage, keep Troops, or Ships of War in time of Peace, enter into any Agreement or Compact with another State, or with a foreign Power, or engage in War, unless actually invaded, or in such imminent Danger as will not admit of delay.

ARTICLE II

Section 1. [1] The executive Power shall be vested in a President of the United States of America. He shall hold his Office during the Term of four Years, and, together with the Vice President, chosen for the same Term, be elected, as follows:

[2] Each State shall appoint, in such Manner as the Legislature thereof may direct, a Number of Electors, equal to the whole Number of Senators and Representatives to which the State may be entitled in the Congress: but no Senator or Representative, or Person holding an Office of Trust or Profit under the United States, shall be appointed an Elector.

[3] The Electors shall meet in their respective States, and vote by Ballot for two Persons, of whom one at least shall not be an Inhabitant of the same State with themselves. And they shall make a List of all the Persons voted for, and of the Number of Votes for each; which List they shall sign and certify, and transmit sealed to the Seat of the Government of the United States, directed to the President of the Senate. The President of the Senate shall, in the Presence of the Senate and House of Representatives, open all the Certificates, and the Votes shall then be counted. The Person having the greatest Number of Votes shall be the President, if such Number be a Majority of the whole Number of Electors appointed; and if there be more than one who have such Majority, and have an equal Number of Votes, then the House of Representatives shall immediately chuse by Ballot one of them for President; and if no Person have a Majority, then from the five highest on the List the said House shall in like Manner chuse the President. But in chusing the President, the Votes shall be taken by States, the Representation from each State having one Vote; a quorum for this Purpose shall consist of a Member or Members from two thirds of the States, and a Majority of all the States shall be necessary to a Choice. In every Case, after the choice of the President, the Person having the greatest Number of Votes of the electors shall be the Vice President. But if there should remain two or more who have equal Votes, the Senate shall chuse from them by Ballot the Vice President.

[4] The Congress may determine the Time of chusing the Electors, and the Day on which they shall give their Votes; which Day shall be the same throughout the United States.

[5] No person except a natural born Citizen, or a Citizen of the United States, at the time of the Adoption of this Constitution, shall be eligible to the Office of President; neither shall any Person be eligible to that Office who shall not have attained to the Age of thirty five Years, and been fourteen Years a Resident within the United States.

[6] In case of the removal of the President from Office, or of his Death, Resignation or Inability to discharge the Powers and Duties of the said Office, the Same shall devolve on the Vice President, and the Congress may by Law provide for the case of Removal, Death, Resignation or Inability, both of the President and Vice President,

declaring what Officer shall then act as President, and such Officer shall act accordingly, until the disability be removed, or a President shall be elected.

[7] The President shall, at stated Times, receive for his Services, a Compensation, which shall neither be increased nor diminished during the Period for which he shall have been elected, and he shall not receive within that Period any other Emolument from the United States, or any of them.

[8] Before he enter on the execution of his Office, he shall take the following Oath or Affirmation: "I do solemnly swear (or affirm) that I will faithfully execute the Office of President of the United States, and will to the best of my Ability, preserve, protect and defend the constitution of the United States."

Section 2. [1] The President shall be Commander in Chief of the Army and Navy of the United States, and of the Militia of the several States, when called into the actual Service of the United States; he may require the Opinion, in writing, of the principal Officer in each of the executive Departments, upon any subject relating to the Duties of their respective Offices, and he shall have Power to grant Reprieves and Pardons for Offenses against the United States, except in Cases of Impeachment.

[2] He shall have Power, by and with the Advice and Consent of the Senate, to make Treaties, provided two thirds of the Senators present concur; and he shall nominate, and by and with the Advice and Consent of the Senate, shall appoint Ambassadors, other public Ministers and Consuls, Judges of the supreme Court, and all other Officers of the United States, whose Appointments are not herein otherwise provided for, and which shall be established by Law: but the Congress may by Law vest the Appointment of such inferior Officers, as they think proper, in the President alone, in the Courts of Law, or in the Heads of Departments.

[3] The President shall have Power to fill up all Vacancies that may happen during the Recess of the Senate, by granting Commissions which shall expire at the End of their next Session.

Section 3. He shall from time to time give to the Congress Information of the State of the Union, and recommend to their Consideration such Measures as he shall judge necessary and expedient; he may, on extraordinary Occasions, convene both Houses, or either of them, and in Case of Disagreement between them, with Respect to the Time of Adjournment, he may adjourn them to such Time as he shall think proper; he shall receive Ambassadors and other public Ministers; he shall take Care that the Laws be faithfully executed, and shall Commission all the Officers of the United States.

Section 4. The President and all civil Officers of the United States, shall be removed from Office on Impeachment for, and Conviction of, Treason, Bribery, or other high Crimes and Misdemeanors.

ARTICLE III

Section 1. The judicial Power of the United States shall be vested in one supreme Court, and in such inferior Courts as the Congress may from time to time ordain and establish. The Judges, both of the supreme and inferior Courts, shall hold their Offices during good Behaviour, and shall, at stated Times, receive for their Services, a Compensation, which shall not be diminished during their Continuance in Office.

Section 2. [1] The Judicial Power shall extend to all Cases, in Law and Equity, arising under this Constitution, the Laws of the United States, and Treaties made, or which shall be made, under their Authority;—to all Cases affecting Ambassadors, other public Ministers and Consuls;—to all Cases of admiralty and maritime Jurisdiction;—to Controversies to which the United States shall be a Party;—to Controversies between two or more States;—between a State and Citizens of another State;—between Citizens of different States;—between Citizens of the same State claiming Lands under Grants of different States, and between a State, or the Citizens thereof, and foreign States, Citizens or Subjects.

[2] In all Cases affecting Ambassadors, other public Ministers and Consuls, and those in which a State shall be a Party, the supreme Court shall have original Jurisdiction. In all the other Cases before mentioned, the supreme Court shall have appellate Jurisdiction, both as to Law and Fact, with such Exceptions, and under such Regulations as the Congress shall make.

[3] The trial of all Crimes, except in Cases of Impeachment, shall be by Jury, and such Trial shall be held in the State where the said Crimes shall have been committed; but when not committed within any State, the Trial shall be at such Place or Places as the Congress may by Law have directed.

Section 3. [1] Treason against the United States, shall consist only in levying War against them, or in adhering to their Enemies, giving them Aid and Comfort. No person shall be convicted of Treason unless on the Testimony of two Witnesses to the same overt Act, or on Confession in open Court.

[2] The Congress shall have Power to declare the Punishment of Treason, but no Attainder of Treason shall work Corruption of Blood, or Forfeiture except during the life of the Person attainted.

ARTICLE IV

Section 1. Full Faith and Credit shall be given in each State to the public Acts, Records, and judicial Proceedings of every other State. And the Congress may by general Laws prescribe the Manner in which such Acts, Records and Proceedings shall be proved, and the Effect thereof.

Section 2. [1] The Citizens of each State shall be entitled to all Privileges and Immunities of Citizens in the several States.

[2] A Person charged in any State with Treason, Felony, or other Crime, who shall flee from Justice, and be found in another State, shall on demand of the executive Authority of the State from which he fled, be delivered up, to be removed to the State having Jurisdiction of the Crime.

[3] No Person held to Service or Labour in one State, under the Laws thereof, escaping into another, shall, in Consequence of any Law or Regulation therein, be discharged from such Service or Labour, but shall be delivered up on Claim of the Party to whom such Service or Labour may be due.

Section 3. [1] New States may be admitted by the Congress into this Union; but no new State shall be formed or erected within the Jurisdiction of any other State; nor any State be formed by the Junction of two or more States, or Parts of States, without the Consent of the Legislatures of the States concerned as well as of the Congress.

[2] The Congress shall have Power to dispose of and make all needful Rules and Regulations respecting the Territory or other Property belonging to the United States; and nothing in this Constitution shall be so construed as to Prejudice any Claims of the United States, or of any particular State.

Section 4. The United States shall guarantee to every State in this Union a Republican Form of Government, and shall protect each of them against Invasion; and on Application of the Legislature, or of the Executive (when the Legislature cannot be convened) against domestic Violence.

ARTICLE V

The Congress, whenever two thirds of both Houses shall deem it necessary, shall propose Amendments to this Constitution, or, on the Application of the Legislatures of two thirds of the several States, shall call a Convention for proposing Amendments, which, in either Case, shall be valid to all Intents and Purposes, as part of this Constitution, when ratified by the Legislatures of three fourths of the several States, or by Conventions in three fourths thereof, as the one or the other Mode of Ratification may be proposed by the Congress; Provided that no Amendment which may be made prior to the Year One thousand eight hundred and eight shall in any Manner affect the first and fourth Clauses in the Ninth Section of the first Article; and that no State, without its Consent, shall be deprived of its equal Suffrage in the Senate.

Article VI

[1] All Debts contracted and Engagements entered into, before the Adoption of this Constitution, shall be as valid against the United States under this Constitution, as under the Confederation.

[2] This Constitution, and the Laws of the United States which shall be made in Pursuance thereof; and all Treaties made, or which shall be made, under the Authority of the United States, shall be the supreme Law of the Land; and the Judges in every State shall be bound thereby, any Thing in the Constitution or Laws of any State to the Contrary notwithstanding.

[3] The Senators and Representatives before mentioned, and the Members of the several State Legislatures, and all executive and judicial Officers, both of the United States and of the several States, shall be bound by Oath or Affirmation, to support this Constitution; but no religious test shall ever be required as a Qualification to any Office or public Trust under the United States.

Article VII

The Ratification of the Conventions of nine States shall be sufficient for the Establishment of this Constitution between the States so ratifying the Same.

Done in Convention by the Unanimous Consent of the States present the Seventeenth Day of September in the Year of our Lord one thousand seven hundred and Eighty seven and of the Independence of the United States of America the Twelfth.

ARTICLES IN ADDITION TO, AND AMENDMENT OF, THE CONSTITUTION OF THE UNITED STATES OF AMERICA, PROPOSED BY CONGRESS, AND RATIFIED BY THE LEGISLATURES OF THE SEVERAL STATES, PURSUANT TO THE FIFTH ARTICLE OF THE ORIGINAL CONSTITUTION

Amendment I [1791]

Congress shall make no law respecting an establishment of religion, or prohibiting the free exercise thereof; or abridging the freedom of speech, or of the press; or the right of the people peaceably to assemble, and to petition the Government for a redress of grievances.

AMENDMENT II [1791]

A well regulated Militia, being necessary to the security of a free State, the right of the people to keep and bear Arms, shall not be infringed.

AMENDMENT III [1791]

No Soldier shall, in time of peace be quartered in any house, without the consent of the Owner, nor in time of war, but in a manner to be prescribed by law.

AMENDMENT IV [1791]

The right of the people to be secure in their persons, houses, papers, and effects, against unreasonable searches and seizures, shall not be violated, and no Warrants shall issue, but upon probable cause, supported by Oath or affirmation, and particularly describing the place to be searched, and the persons or things to be seized.

AMENDMENT V [1791]

No person shall be held to answer for a capital, or otherwise infamous crime, unless on a presentment of indictment of a Grand Jury, except in cases arising in the land or naval forces, or in the Militia, when in actual service in time of War or public danger; nor shall any person be subject for the same offence to be twice put in jeopardy of life or limb; nor shall be compelled in any criminal case to be a witness against himself, nor be deprived of life, liberty, or property, without due process of law; nor shall private property be taken for public use, without just compensation.

AMENDMENT VI [1791]

In all criminal prosecutions, the accused shall enjoy the right to a speedy and public trial, by an impartial jury of the State and district wherein the crime shall have been committed, which district shall have been previously ascertained by law, and to be informed of the nature and cause of the accusation; to be confronted with the witnesses against him; to have compulsory process for obtaining witnesses in his favor, and to have the Assistance of Counsel for his defence.

AMENDMENT VII [1791]

In Suits at common law, where the value in controversy shall exceed twenty dollars, the right of trial by jury shall be preserved, and no fact tried by a jury, shall be otherwise re-examined in any

Court of the United States, than according to the rules of the common law.

AMENDMENT VIII [1791]

Excessive bail shall not be required, nor excessive fines imposed, nor cruel and unusual punishments inflicted.

AMENDMENT IX [1791]

The enumeration in the Constitution, of certain rights, shall not be construed to deny or disparage others retained by the people.

AMENDMENT X [1791]

The powers not delegated to the United States by the Constitution, nor prohibited by it to the States, are reserved to the States respectively, or to the people.

AMENDMENT XI [1798]

The Judicial power of the United States shall not be construed to extend to any suit in law or equity, commenced or prosecuted against one of the United States by Citizens of another State, or by Citizens or Subjects of any Foreign State.

AMENDMENT XII [1804]

The Electors shall meet in their respective states and vote by ballot for President and Vice-President, one of whom, at least, shall not be an inhabitant of the same state with themselves; they shall name in their ballots the person voted for as President, and in distinct ballots the person voted for as Vice-President, and they shall make distinct lists of all persons voted for as President, and of all persons voted for as Vice-President, and of the number of votes for each, which lists they shall sign and certify, and transmit sealed to the seat of the government of the United States, directed to the President of the Senate;—The President of the Senate shall, in the presence of the Senate and House of Representatives, open all the certificates and the votes shall then be counted;—The person having the greatest number of votes for President, shall be the President, if such number be a majority of the whole number of Electors appointed; and if no person have such majority, then from the persons having the highest numbers not exceeding three on the list of those voted for as President, the House of Representatives shall choose immediately, by ballot, the President. But in choosing the President, the votes shall be taken by states, the representation from each state having one vote; a quorum for this purpose shall consist of a member or members from two-thirds of the states, and a majority of all the states shall be necessary to a choice. And if the House of Representatives shall not choose a President whenever the right of choice shall devolve upon them, before the fourth day of March next following, then the Vice-President shall act as President, as in the case of the death or other constitutional disability of the President.— The person having the greatest number of votes as Vice-President, shall be the Vice-President, if such number be a majority of the whole number of Electors appointed, and if no person have a majority, then from the two highest numbers on the list, the Senate shall choose the Vice-President; a quorum for the purpose shall consist of two-thirds of the whole number of Senators, and a majority of the whole number shall be necessary to a choice. But no person constitutionally ineligible to the office of President shall be eligible to that of Vice-President of the United States.

AMENDMENT XIII [1865]

Section 1. Neither slavery nor involuntary servitude, except as a punishment for crime whereof the party shall have been duly convicted, shall exist within the United States, or any place subject to their jurisdiction.

Section 2. Congress shall have power to enforce this article by appropriate legislation.

AMENDMENT XIV [1868]

Section 1. All persons born or naturalized in the United States, and subject to the jurisdiction thereof, are citizens of the United States and of the State wherein they reside. No State shall make or enforce any law which shall abridge the privileges or immunities of citizens of the United States; nor shall any State deprive any person of life, liberty, or property, without due process of law; nor deny to any person within its jurisdiction the equal protection of the laws.

Section 2. Representatives shall be apportioned among the several States according to their respective numbers, counting the whole number of persons in each State, excluding Indians not taxed. But when the right to vote at any election for the choice of electors for President and Vice President of the United States, Representatives in Congress, the Executive and Judicial officers of a state, or the members of the Legislature thereof, is denied to any of the male inhabitants of such State, being twenty-one years of age, and citizens of the United States, or in any way abridged, except for participation in rebellion, or other crime, the basis of representation therein shall be reduced in the proportion which the number of such male citizens shall bear to the whole number of male citizens twenty-one years of age in such State.

Section 3. No person shall be a Senator or Representative in Congress, or elector of President and Vice President, or hold any office, civil or military, under the United States, or under any State, who, having previously taken an oath, as a member of Congress, or as an officer of the United States, or as a member of any State legislature, or as an executive or judicial officer of any State, to support the Constitution of the United States, shall have engaged in insurrection or rebellion against the same, or given aid or comfort to the enemies thereof. But Congress may by a vote of two-thirds of each House, remove such disability.

Section 4. The validity of the public debt of the United States, authorized by law, including debts incurred for payment of pensions and bounties for services in suppressing insurrection or rebellion, shall not be questioned. But neither the United States nor any State shall assume or pay any debt or obligation incurred in aid of insurrection or rebellion against the United States, or any claim for the loss of emancipation of any slave, but all such debts, obligation and claims shall be held illegal and void.

Section 5. The Congress shall have power to enforce, by appropriate legislation, the provisions of this article.

AMENDMENT XV [1870]

Section 1. The right of citizens of the United States to vote shall not be denied or abridged by the United States or by any State on account of race, color, or previous condition of servitude.

Section 2. The Congress shall have power to enforce this article by appropriate legislation.

AMENDMENT XVI [1913]

The Congress shall have power to lay and collect taxes on incomes, from whatever source derived, without apportionment among the several States, and without regard to any census or enumeration.

AMENDMENT XVII [1913]

[1] The Senate of the United States shall be composed of two Senators from each State, elected by the people thereof, for six years; and each Senator shall have one vote. The electors in each State shall have the qualifications requisite for electors of the most numerous branch of the State legislatures.

[2] When vacancies happen in the representation of any State in the Senate, the executive authority of such State shall issue writs of election to fill such vacancies: Provided, That the legislature of any State may empower the executive thereof to make temporary

appointments until the people fill the vacancies by election as the legislature may direct.

[3] This amendment shall not be so construed as to affect the election or term of any Senator chosen before it becomes valid as part of the Constitution.

AMENDMENT XVIII [1919]

Section 1. After one year from the ratification of this article the manufacture, sale, or transportation of intoxicating liquors within, the importation thereof into, or the exportation thereof from the United States and all territory subject to the jurisdiction thereof for beverage purposes is hereby prohibited.

Section 2. The Congress and the several States shall have concurrent power to enforce this article by appropriate legislation.

Section 3. This article shall be inoperative unless it shall have been ratified as an amendment to the Constitution by the legislatures of the several States, as provided in the Constitution, within seven years from the date of submission hereof to the States by the Congress.

AMENDMENT XVIX [1920]

[1] The right of citizens of the United States to vote shall not be denied or abridged by the United States or by any State on account of sex.

[2] Congress shall have power to enforce this article by appropriate legislation.

AMENDMENT XX [1933]

Section 1. The terms of the President and Vice President shall end at noon on the 20th day of January, and the terms of Senators and Representatives at noon on the 3d day of January, of the years in which such terms would have ended if this article had not been ratified; and the terms of their successors shall then begin.

Section 2. The Congress shall assemble at least once in every year, and such meeting shall begin at noon on the 3d day of January, unless they shall by law appoint a different day.

Section 3. If, at the time fixed for the beginning of the term of the President, the President elect shall have died, the Vice President elect shall become President. If a President shall not have been chosen before the time fixed for the beginning of his term, or if the President elect shall have failed to qualify, then the Vice President elect shall act as President until a President shall have qualified; and the Congress may by law provide for the case wherein neither a President elect nor a Vice President elect shall have qualified, declaring who shall then act as President, or the manner in which one who is to act shall be selected, and such person shall act accordingly until a President or Vice President shall have qualified.

Section 4. The Congress may by law provide for the case of the death of any of the persons from whom the House of Representatives may choose a President whenever the right of choice shall have devolved upon them and for the case of the death of any of the persons from whom the Senate may choose a Vice President whenever the right of choice shall have devolved upon them.

Section 5. Sections 1 and 2 shall take effect on the 15th day of October following the ratification of this article.

Section 6. This article shall be inoperative unless it shall have been ratified as an amendment to the Constitution by the legislatures of three-fourths of the several States within seven years from the date of its submission.

AMENDMENT XXI [1933]

Section 1. The eighteenth article of amendment to the Constitution of the United States is hereby repealed.

Section 2. The transportation or importation into any State, Territory, or possession of the United States for delivery or use therein of intoxicating liquors, in violation of the laws thereof, is hereby prohibited.

Section 3. This article shall be inoperative unless it shall have been ratified as an amendment to the Constitution by conventions in the several States, as provided in the Constitution, within seven years from the date of the submission hereof to the States by the Congress.

AMENDMENT XXII [1951]

Section 1. No person shall be elected to the office of the President more than twice, and no person who has held the office of President, or acted as President, for more than two years of a term to which some other person was elected President shall be elected to the office of the President more than once. But this Article shall not apply to any person holding the office of President when this Article was proposed by the Congress, and shall not prevent any person who may be holding the office of President, or acting as President, during the term within which the Article becomes operative from holding the office of president or acting as President during the remainder of such term.

Section 2. This article shall be inoperative unless it shall have been ratified as an amendment to the Constitution by the legislatures of three-fourths of the several States within seven years from the date of its submission to the States by the Congress.

AMENDMENT XXIII [1961]

Section 1. The District constituting the seat of Government of the United States shall appoint in such manner as the Congress may direct: A number of electors of President and Vice President equal to the whole number of Senators and Representatives in Congress to which the District would be entitled if it were a State, but in no event more than the least populous State; they shall be in addition to those appointed by the States, but they shall be considered, for the purposes of the election of President and Vice President, to be electors appointed by a State; and they shall meet in the District and perform such duties as provided by the twelfth article of amendment.

Section 2. The Congress shall have power to enforce this article by appropriate legislation.

AMENDMENT XXIV [1964]

Section 1. The right of citizens of the United States to vote in any primary or other election for President or Vice President, for electors for President or Vice President, or for Senator or Representative in Congress, shall not be denied or abridged by the United States or any State by reason of failure to pay any poll tax or other tax.

Section 2. The Congress shall have power to enforce this article by appropriate legislation.

AMENDMENT XXV [1967]

Section 1. In case of the removal of the President from office or of his death or resignation, the Vice President shall become President.

Section 2. Whenever there is a vacancy in the office of the Vice President, the President shall nominate a Vice President who shall take office upon confirmation by a majority vote of both Houses of Congress.

Section 3. Whenever the President transmits to the President pro tempore of the Senate and the Speaker of the House of Representatives his written declaration that he is unable to discharge the powers and duties of his office, and until he transmits to them a written declaration to the contrary, such powers and duties shall be discharged by the Vice President as Acting President.

Section 4. Whenever the Vice President and a majority of either the principal officers of the executive departments or of such other body as Congress may by law provide, transmit to the President pro tempore of the Senate and the Speaker of the House of Representatives their written declaration that the President is unable to discharge the powers and duties of his office, the Vice President shall immediately assume the powers and duties of the office as Acting President. Thereafter, when the President transmits to the President pro tempore of the Senate and the Speaker of the House of Representatives his written declaration that no inability exists, he shall resume the powers and duties of his office unless the Vice President and a majority of either the principal officers of the executive department or of such other body as Congress may by law provide, transmit within four days to the President pro tempore of the Senate and the Speaker of the House of Representatives their written declaration that the President is unable to discharge the powers and duties of his office. Thereupon Congress shall decide the issue, assembling within forty-eight hours for that purpose if not in session. If the Congress, within twenty-one days after receipt of the latter written declaration, or, if Congress is not in session, within twenty-one days after Congress is required to assemble, determines by two-thirds vote of both Houses that the President is unable to discharge the powers and duties of his office, the Vice President shall continue to discharge the same as Acting President; otherwise, the President shall resume the powers and duties of his office.

AMENDMENT XXVI [1971]

Section 1. The right of citizens of the United States, who are eighteen years of age or older, to vote shall not be denied or abridged by the United States or by any State on account of age.

Section 2. The Congress shall have power to enforce this article by appropriate legislation.

AMENDMENT XXVII [1992]

No law, varying the compensation for the services of the Senators and Representatives, shall take effect, until an election of Representatives shall have intervened.

Table of Cases

Index

References are to Pages